INTRODUCING **Web Design**

INTRODUCING

Web Design

Everything you need to know about designing
and maintaining your website

ROB YOUNG

An imprint of Pearson Education
London ■ New York ■ Toronto ■ Sydney ■ Tokyo ■ Singapore
Madrid ■ Mexico City ■ Munich ■ Paris

PEARSON EDUCATION LIMITED

Head Office:
Edinburgh Gate
Harlow CM20 2JE
Tel: +44 (0)1279 623623
Fax: +44 (0)1279 431059

London Office:
128 Long Acre
London WC2E 9AN
Tel: +44 (0)20 7447 2000
Fax: +44 (0)20 7240 5771
website: www.it-minds.com

First published in Great Britain in 2001

ISBN 0 130 28565 X

British Library Cataloguing-in-Publication Data
A catalogue record for this book is available from the British Library.

10 9 8 7 6 5 4 3 2 1

Typeset by Pantek Arts Ltd, Maidstone, Kent.
Printed and bound in Great Britain by Biddles Ltd.

The publisher's policy is to use paper manufactured from sustainable forests.

CONTENTS

ACKNOWLEDGEMENTS

We are grateful to the following for permission to reproduce screenshots:

Alien Skin Software; CNET Networks, Inc.; Digital Workshop; FortuneCity.com, Inc.; Guestbook4free.com; HTML Validator; The Information Commissioner; Net Benefit plc; NetObjects, Inc.; Netscape Communications Corporation. Netscape Communicator browser window © 1999 Netscape Communications Corporation. Used with permission. Netscape Communications has not authorized, sponsored, endorsed, or approved this publication and is not responsible for its content; New Jersey Online; Opera Software AS; The Patent Office; WebSTAT.com; World Pay Ltd.; Yahoo! Reproduced with permission of Yahoo! Inc. © 2000 by Yahoo! Inc. YAHOO! and the YAHOO! logo are trademarks of Yahoo! Inc.

While every effort has been made to trace the owners of copyright material, in a few cases this has proved impossible and we take this opportunity to offer our apologies to any copyright holders whose rights we have unwittingly infringed.

INTRODUCTION

I t's settled: the Internet is here to stay. All the arguments that it's just a flash-in-the-pan or an over-hyped pastime for computer nerds have fallen apart, and several hundred million of us worldwide are actually making daily use of the Net. Or, more accurately for some of us perhaps, we're *trying* to make use of the Net, and cursing in all sorts of imaginative ways when we can't get a connection. That's a pretty good indication of just how important the Internet has become: 'no Net connection' is right up there with 'car won't start' and 'turkey won't defrost'.

If you have something to offer to all these people, a website presents a unique and powerful opportunity to get it noticed. What 'it' is doesn't really matter – a website is a tool with any number of uses. What *does* matter is the 'get it noticed' part. If you're going to put time, effort, and perhaps money, into building a site, you want people to visit it and to keep coming back. And that's what this book is all about.

A few years ago, web design was all about HTML, the simple text-based language used to write web pages. You'd put together some decent looking pages fairly quickly and hope that people would visit them. The chances were pretty good – you had a lot less competition than you do now, and sites were geared more to their content than to visual appeal and interactivity.

These days, things are a lot different. Although HTML is still the basis of web design and the content of a website is the number one issue, there's much more involved:

▶ You definitely have competition out there! Whether your site is better than the rest or not, you need to promote it if you want people to find it.

▶ Style matters. Regardless of the content of your site, visitors enjoy smart effects and interactive elements created using the Web's 'other languages' – JavaScript, Dynamic HTML and Java.

▶ Used effectively, graphics, sound and animation can add impact to a site, making it more enjoyable and intuitive to use.

▶ The optional extras: add counters to your pages to see which are most popular; sell products and services with online payment facilities; add chat rooms and discussion forums; and much more.

The aim of this book, then, isn't just to help you learn HTML, it's to help you learn how to design, publish and promote a whole website effectively. After all, if the car won't start, a book about spark plugs isn't much help, is it?

How Is This Book Organized?

This book is split into five parts to help you find the answers you want quickly and easily.

Part 1, *Site Design With HTML*, introduces the building blocks of website design – a pair of easy-to-use text languages called HTML and CSS. We'll start off simply, with one basic web page, and gradually introduce new items and features. Along the way you'll find plenty of copy-and-use examples, both in the book and on the accompanying CD-ROM.

Part 2, *Graphics & Multimedia*, shows you how to create images, animations, sounds and other multimedia content to include in your pages (and where to find off-the-peg content if art isn't your thing!).

Part 3, *Web Scripting & Programming*, introduces the Web's most useful scripting language, JavaScript, and shows how you can use it to make your pages interactive and dynamic. Of course, if you don't fancy actually *learning* the language, you'll find plenty of useful tricks and ready-made gadgets to copy into your own pages.

Part 4, *Website Publishing & Promotion*, explains how to get your site onto the World Wide Web, and how to let the rest of the world know it's there. We'll also look at ways you might expand your website in future (selling products or services online, for example) and some of the aspects of running a businesslike site.

The *Appendices* section includes a number of handy web design references to turn to while you're designing your site, along with a list of useful websites offering information, free services and content.

How Should I Use It?

Although you could read the book from cover to cover, it's not a 'whodunnit' so there's no harm in skipping back and forth a bit. There's a lot of information packed into this book, and you certainly don't have to learn it all – or even read it all – if you don't want to. I do have a few suggestions to help you decide where to start:

▶ If you're new to all aspects of web design, Part 1 will get you on the road to building your first site. If you want to, you can then skip to Part 4 to find out how to go about publishing and promoting the site before dabbling in graphics creation, scripting and programming.

▶ If you have a site built with one of the visual site design programs (Microsoft FrontPage or NetObjects Fusion, for instance), I'm still going to treat you as a beginner and point you towards Part 1. I'll explain why in Chapter 2.

▶ If you have some web design experience, Part 1 may still be worth a look if you want to brush up your HTML or style sheet skills. But perhaps you're itching to liven up the site with scripting, animation, Java, graphics? Or maybe you need some help in attracting visitors to your site or adding extra features? Choose your poison and head for Parts 2, 3 or 4.

Icons & Conventions

I've used a few special features and conventions throughout the book that make it easier to find your way around. In particular, you'll see that chapters are split into bite-sized chunks with sub-headings. If something looks too dull or too complicated, just skip to the next heading.

You'll also find some icons and text in boxes containing extra information that you may find useful:

 A question-and-answer format highlighting questions or problems that may arise while you're reading something or trying it out for yourself.

 A selection of hints, tips and incidental notes that may save you some time, point you in a new direction, or help you avoid common pitfalls.

 Explains any technical terms I couldn't avoid using, or any related jargon you may come across when dealing with a particular aspect of web design, programming or promotion.

 Indicates that the software program being mentioned is included on the free CD-ROM attached to the inside back cover of this book.

I've also used different type styles and keyboard conventions to make particular meanings clear, as shown below:

Convention	Description
Bold type	Indicates a new term being encountered, or an Internet address.
SCRIPT/CODE	Indicates HTML, scripting or programming code.
ITALIC CODE	In some cases, you'll have to type a particular filename into your HTML or scripting code, enter your own email address, or something similar. Italic code text indicates that you need to replace what I've typed with your choice of text.
Ctrl+C	A key combination, saving frequent mouse excursions to pull-down menus. The keys to press will be separated by '+' signs. This example means to press and hold the Ctrl key while pressing 'C' once.
Enter	Although I've referred to the 'Enter' key throughout, on your keyboard this might be labelled 'Return' instead.
Directories	To Mac owners and users of Windows 95 and later, these are better known as 'folders'. On the Internet, as in MS-DOS and Windows 3x, they're known as 'directories', but they're all the same thing.

A Few Assumptions...

Although I'm assuming you're new to web design and its related skills (graphics, scripting, programming and so on), I'm going to take a few other things for granted. First, I'll assume that you can find your way around Windows (or Mac OS, or Linux, or whatever operating system you're using). That essentially means that you know how to install software, and create, open, edit and save files. Although I've concentrated on Windows computers throughout this book, you can create a website using any computer and operating system – only your choice of software will differ.

Second, I'm assuming that you know your way around the Internet, to the extent that you know what web pages, URLs, email addresses and links are. Although I'll explain a few Internet basics along the way, I don't have space for a complete guided tour. (If a guided tour is what you want, take a look at another of my books, *Exploring the Internet*, also published by Prentice Hall.) I'm also assuming that your computer has a modem, or some equivalent device, and an Internet connection.

Finally, I'm assuming that you *care* about the finished result. You want people to visit, to enjoy it or find it useful, and to keep coming back. You want to take a considered and businesslike approach. (It's worth remembering that a website can actually *become* a business with a little luck and a lot of work!) But if you just 'want a website', that's fine too – once you've claimed your cyberspace allotment and dug it over for a while, I think you'll soon want to grow a bigger marrow on it.

SITE DESIGN WITH HTML

▶ **IN THIS PART**

FIRST THINGS FIRST

▶ **IN THIS CHAPTER**

The Web – you use it, you like it, but what is it?

Learn how URLs work, and how the Web is linked together

Meet HTML, the 'language' used to write web pages

Find out what's involved in getting a website up and running

Are you the curious type? Have you ever wondered how web pages are written, how entire sites are constructed, or how the whole lot gets onto the World Wide Web for the rest of us to use? If you have, and you've found the answers, it's time to get that smug look ready. If you haven't, it's because up to now you've never really needed to know – one of the great things about the Web is that you can use it without understanding how it works. You need to know a bit more before you can *write* for the Web, of course, and in this chapter we're going to race through the basics. But first, a more pressing question...

What is The World Wide Web?

If I were to give you a snappy one-line definition of the Web, it would be something like 'It's a dynamic, distributed, graphical, hypertext-based information publishing system'. Although that does describe it pretty accurately it probably doesn't tell you anything at all, so let's break it up into something a lot *less* snappy.

First and foremost, the Web is an *information publishing system*. That's easy enough – you can write a page containing some sort of information, and publish it on the Web where it can be seen by others. It's *graphical* in the sense that the information on the page doesn't have to be text: you can include images, animation, small programs, and more. The *dynamic* part means that pages you've published can be changed: you can edit them as often as you need to; rename them; or remove them entirely.

The word *distributed* means 'spread around'. Let's take a small example of this first: back in 1995, the first edition of Microsoft's *Encarta* encyclopaedia was small enough to fit on a single CD-ROM; three years later it had grown to the point that two CDs were needed – in other words, the information had to be *distributed* across two CDs. The Web works in a similar way, except that the CDs are replaced with computers called **web servers**. When you sign up for an account with almost any Internet service provider (ISP) nowadays, they allocate some space for you on the hard disk of their web server which is where your finished site will be stored. ISPs all over the world have their own web servers, so the pages that make up the World Wide Web are *distributed* amongst all these computers. The benefits of this are twofold: first, the Web can never get to the point that it's full; and second, the millions of Web users around the world aren't all connecting to the same computer every time they surf.

web server

JARGON BUSTER A server is a computer whose main task in life is to send information to another computer connected to it. On the Internet, those connections are made by telephone lines and modems, but a server could sit in the corner of a small office and be connected to other computers in that office by a mass of cables. Internet servers usually do one particular job: a web server stores and sends web pages, an email server holds your email messages until you're ready to retrieve them, and so on.

Lastly, the Web is *hypertext based*. Hypertext is a system of clickable text-links often used in Windows Help files and multimedia encyclopaedias that lets you view information in a non-linear way: rather than working in a 'straight line' from page 1 to page 2 to page 3, you may be able to jump from page 1 to a related note on page 57. The Web takes this system a few stages further:

▶ These links don't have to take you to another point in the same document, or even to another document on the same computer: you can jump to a page on a computer on the other side of the world.

▶ A hypertext link in a web page doesn't have to be a word or phrase: it could be a picture that you click on, or a small part of a larger picture, with different parts linking to different pages (known as an **image map**), or even a small program such as a **Java applet**, as you'll learn in Part 3.

▶ The link doesn't necessarily open a new web page: it could play a video or a sound, display a picture, download an application, run a program... The list goes on, and gets longer all the time!

The address bar shows the URL of the page you're viewing

A hypertext link, and the hand pointer that appears when you move the mouse over it

▶ **Hypertext links in a typical web page**

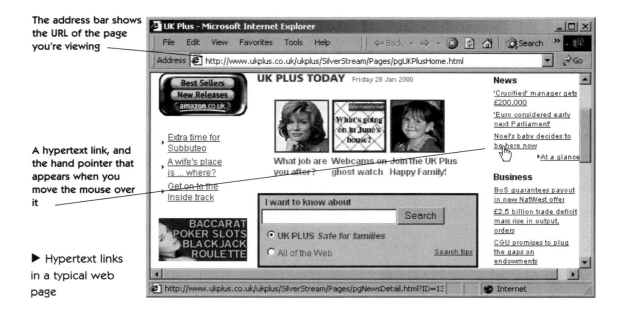

How Does Hypertext Work?

Every file on the World Wide Web has its own unique address, in much the same way as every house in the world. This is known as its **URL** (short for Uniform Resource Locator). You've probably come across a lot of these already on your Web wanderings: every time you arrive at a new page, its URL is shown in your browser's address bar. As an example, let's take the URL of the Radio 1 website at the BBC and break it up into its component parts. The URL is **http://www.bbc.co.uk/radio1/index.html**.

http://   This is one of the Internet's many protocols, and it stands for HyperText Transfer Protocol. It's the method web servers use to transfer web pages around the Net, so almost all web page URLs have the http:// prefix.

www.bbc.co.uk/   This is the name of the computer on which the file is stored, identifying one single computer among all the web servers of the world. Most web servers' names (though not all) begin with www.

radio1/

This is the directory path to the page we want to open. Just as on your own computer, the path may consist of several directory names separated by slashes. Most web designers structure their sites so that different areas are in different directories with intuitive names: the BBC site also has directories called **radio2** and **radio3**, among many others. Notice that URLs always use forward slashes rather than the backward slashes used for paths in Windows.

index.html

This is the name of the file we're opening. The .html (or .htm) extension indicates that it's a web page, but browsers can handle many different types of file.

GOOD QUESTION!

Why do some URLs contain no filename?

Sometimes you'll come across a URL that ends with a directory name, such as **http://www.bbc.co.uk/radio1/** or **http://www.bbc.co.uk/radio1** (the final slash is optional). When a browser sends this URL to a web server, the server looks in that directory for a **default file**, often called **index.htm** or **index.html**. If a file with this name is found, it's sent back to the browser. If not, the server may send back a rather dull-looking list of the files in that directory, or (more often these days) it may send an even duller-looking 'file not found' message.

Once you know how URLs work, hypertext links are easy to understand. When you write a web page and want to include a link to another file, you type two things into the page: the first is the URL of the file to link to, and the second is the text that visitors to the page will be able to see and click on. There's a little more to it than that, but not much.

When your browser displays this page, it recognizes that what you typed is a link and treats it differently from ordinary text. Initially it displays the text in a different colour and underlines it. If the mouse moves over the text, the usual mouse pointer turns into a hand shape and the URL of the linked page is shown in the status bar at the bottom of the browser window. If you click this text, the browser sends a request for the appropriate page to your service provider's computer which is then passed along a chain of computers until it reaches the web server holding the required file. If all goes well, that web server finds the file and sends it back along the chain for your browser to display.

GOOD QUESTION!

What's all that 'chain of computers' business about?

The Internet was constructed in such a way that if one computer can't talk directly to another, it can send a request to a different computer, which passes it to a third, and so on until the request reaches a computer that can talk to the intended recipient. The result is that the request should always be able to find a path from A to B, even if a computer somewhere between the two is out of action.

HTML: The Language Of The Web

A moment ago I explained very briefly how a hypertext link was added to a web page, and said there was a little more to it. Here we are at the 'little more' – a language called **HTML** (HyperText Markup Language) which is the subject of Part 1 of this book and the basis of the later parts.

So what's HTML all about? Well, we've met hypertext already – the clickable links that are used to navigate from one web page to another. A markup language is a set of codes or symbols added to plain text to indicate how it should be presented to the reader, noting bold or italic text, typefaces to be used, paragraph breaks, and so on. When you type text into your word processor, it adds those codes for you but tactfully hides them from view: if you wanted bold text, for example, it shows you bold text instead of those codes. In HTML, however, you have to type those codes along with the text, and your browser puts the whole lot together before displaying it.

These codes are known as **tags**, and they consist of ordinary text placed between less-than and greater-than signs (also known as angle brackets). Let's take an example:

`<B>Welcome to my home page!</B> Thank you for visiting.`

The first tag, <B>, means 'turn on bold type'. Halfway through the line the same tag is used again, but with a forward slash inserted straight after the less-than sign: this means 'turn off bold type'. If you displayed a page containing this line in your browser it would look like this:

Welcome to my home page! Thank you for visiting.

Of course, there's more to a web page than bold text, so clearly there must be many more of these tags. Don't let that put you off – over the coming chapters I'll introduce a few at a time, and you don't have to learn them all! There's a little bundle that you'll use a lot, and you'll get to know those very quickly. Others will begin to sink in once you've looked them up and used them a few times. You'll find an alphabetical list of HTML tags in Appendix A.

Web Design In A Nutshell

You might think of web design as deciding upon a 'look and feel' for a website, or the actual writing of the pages. I prefer to use the term in a much wider context, covering everything from the initial concept through to publishing and maintaining the site. Here, in a slightly-expanded nutshell, are the six steps involved in getting a website off the ground.

1   **Think.** Right now, you probably want to write some experimental pages, get to grips with HTML, and try out a few things. But before you start work on your 'big idea' for a website, you need to take some thinking time. To start with, what is the big idea? How will it beat or complement any similar sites? Who is the site aimed at? How will it be structured (for instance, can you split it into distinct areas or topics)? What sort of style or feel should it have? A little planning at the start can save a lot of wasted time along the way.

2   **Write.** Sit down and write all the web pages that make up your site. (Okay, this probably looks like several dozen steps in one at the moment, but it should at least be one of the most enjoyable parts!)

3 **Test.** Before you publish your site (and, particularly, before you start promoting it) you need to be sure it all works. While the site is still on your own computer's hard disk, you can look at all the pages, check spelling, make sure the links between your pages work, and ask a few friends or colleagues for their opinions.

4 **Publish.** Publishing a site means uploading it from your own hard disk to a web server. Your ISP probably gave you some free web space when you subscribed to their service, but you may choose to purchase space from a specialized hosting company. Either way, this is an easy step using a process called **FTP** (File Transfer Protocol) which we'll meet in Part 4. Once the site is on the Web, you'll test it again by typing its URL into your browser's address bar to make sure all the necessary files were uploaded, all the links still work, and the pages load at a reasonable speed.

JARGON BUSTER

uploading

If you've surfed the Web, you already know about **downloading** – the act of copying a file from the Web to your own computer. This is what every page has to do before your browser can display it. Uploading is the exact opposite – copying a file from your own computer to some remote computer.

5 **Promote.** Promoting a site simply means telling the world (or as much of it as you can reach) what your site's URL is and how much their lives will be enriched by visiting it. There are many ways to promote a site, and we'll delve into those in Part 4.

6 **Maintain.** There may be some types of site that can be published and left unchanged forever, but they're few and far between. Your site probably contains links to other sites, so you'll need to check that those sites still exist and update the links if necessary. A good site should always be evolving as you think of new ideas and features, react to relevant events, or make improvements based on user-feedback. If your site is regularly updated, it should attract regular visitors rather than being a 'one hit wonder'.

GOOD QUESTION!

Is any of this going to cost money?

To a large extent, creating a website is something you can do for free. There are certainly options available that could part you from some cash (effective forms of promotion are one example; buying your own domain name is another), but you won't necessarily need to buy software or pay for web space, so that gets your wallet through the first four steps unopened.

Ten Rules Of Web Design

Of course, there are really no 'rules' at all – would the Internet be as popular if there were? Nevertheless, the world of web design has millions of flags planted on it, and everyone exploring it has learnt something useful along the way. Here (in no particular order) are ten of the most important tips to keep in mind as you get started:

1   **Make it easy to navigate.** If people can't work out what your cute linking icons mean, or can't find their way to what they want, they'll go away and won't come back. Whatever style your site navigation takes, be it text links, images, or something more exotic, it should always be immediately obvious what leads where.

2   **Give what you promised.** If your promotion promises free software, unique information, or something equally tasty, make sure it's on your site and easy to find from the home page. From there you can tempt visitors to other parts of your site.

3   **Include contact information.** Invite feedback from visitors by including an email address at the very least. A company website should provide complete contact information for different departments, preferably with people's names and email addresses, company name and address, and phone/fax numbers.

4   **Keep each page short.** With the wonders of hypertext at your disposal, don't force visitors to scroll further and further down a long page. Instead, split it up into separate short pages and add links back and forth between them.

5   **Give something away free.** Maybe the whole point of your site is to give away free stuff, in which case this is academic. Similarly, the content of your site may be unique enough to attract visitors without using any other forms of temptation. Otherwise, giving away something people want is a tried and trusted means of attracting visitors, whether it's software, information, entertainment, services or products.

6   **Don't be clever for the sake of it.** Throughout this book and on the accompanying CD-ROM you'll find neat tricks, controls, effects and add-ons. Some serve no useful purpose at all – they're just fun, or 'cool' – but most do. Remember they're not compulsory, though! The content of your site is what matters most, and gratuitous trickery can spoil an otherwise great site.

7   **Make it visual.** Reading text on screen is never pleasant: visitors will often skip text presented in large chunks or long paragraphs. Use graphics to break up a page that has to contain a lot of text; keep paragraphs short; use bulleted lists where possible; and make sure each page looks attractive.

8   **Make it interactive.** Web users like interactivity: if a link changes colour when they move the mouse over it, or a button depresses when they click it, it provides comforting feedback that something has happened. You don't want the entire page to dance before their eyes, but sensible use of scripting or Java (covered in later parts of the book) can add a huge amount to the experience of visiting your site.

9   **Use a spellchecker.** Poor spelling leaves a more telling impression than great knowledge or talent.

10 **Keep it up to date.** Check that links to other sites still work, and update your pages regularly to keep visitors returning. It's a good idea to note when the site was last updated (perhaps in an easy-to-find *What's New?* page) along with notes of what you changed or added and links to the relevant pages – your regular visitors will appreciate it.

2

CHOOSE YOUR WEAPONS

IN THIS CHAPTER

Battle of the browsers – get equipped for site testing

What you need to write a web page

Helpful software you can use (if you really want to)

Deciding what your website is actually *about*

I've already said that I'm assuming you have a computer with an Internet connection and you've done some web-surfing. That means you probably have what you need to get started in web design: a web browser and a text editor. Another handy thing to have is some idea of what your website is actually for! In this chapter we'll work through that short checklist to make sure everything's present and correct, and I'll point out some options and alternatives as we go along.

Expand Your Browser Collection

It would be nice to think that one web browser is all you need, but it isn't. The most popular browsers are Microsoft Internet Explorer, Netscape and Opera. These are all free (although Opera will display banner advertisements in a small section of its window in the free edition), and between them they account for around 99% of the browser market. At the time of writing, Internet Explorer leads Netscape by 84% to 13%, with Opera at around 2%, but even the lowest percentages add up to significant numbers of users, so you need to be sure your site looks right in all three browsers.

GOOD QUESTION!

Won't my site look the same in all browsers then?

Not necessarily. The HTML language has evolved through several versions, currently standing at version 4. At the same time, the popular browsers have advanced through a few versions too (a huge number of versions in Netscape's case), fixing bugs and adding support for the latest features of HTML plus a few extras of their own, so older browsers won't know anything about these new features. In addition, of course, the popular browsers are designed by three different software companies, so there's bound to be some difference in the way they interpret some elements of HTML.

As with any other type of software, there have been different versions of the popular browsers over the years, and computer users don't all rush to grab the latest version when it's released, whether it's free or not. While the vast majority of your visitors will be using the current versions of Internet Explorer, Opera or Netscape, around 10% could be using significantly older versions. The bottom line is that you should test your site in the current versions of the popular browsers (which, at the time of writing, are Internet Explorer 5.5, Opera 5.0 and Netscape 6.01). Depending on your target audience and the style of your site, you might also want to test in older browsers such as Netscape 3.0, and Internet Explorer 3.0.

In the cases of Netscape and Opera, this is quite easy to deal with: you can install as many versions of Netscape on a single computer as you want to, provided you install each into a different directory. With Internet Explorer it's tricky: only one version can be installed at a time, so if you want to test in IE4 as well as IE5 you'll either need a second computer or a second operating system installed on your main computer with a 'dual-boot' option to choose which operating system to load at startup.

BY THE WAY

Netscape – Trials & Tribulations

Without getting too involved in Netscape's somewhat tortured recent history, many long-time Netscape users loyally stuck with the company's long series of version 4.x browsers, waiting for the promised Netscape 5 to bring the quality and reliability that version 4 lacked. For many, this was a stand against Microsoft's perceived dominance of the Internet. During the writing of this book, the new edition (renamed Netscape 6) was released, and has been widely regarded as a disappointing step backwards. The result may be that a few Netscape users continue to use the best of the 4.x series, a few show solidarity by using Netscape 6 regardless, and others switch to Opera (a move made easier by Opera's well-timed introduction of a free edition).

You'll find the current Windows versions of Internet Explorer, Opera and Netscape on the free CD-ROM inside the back cover of this book. You can keep up to date with the latest releases or grab older Netscape versions by visiting these websites:

IT'S ON THE CD

▶ Microsoft Internet Explorer
http://www.microsoft.com/windows/ie or
http://www.microsoft.com/mac/ie

▶ Netscape
http://home.netscape.com/download
http://home.netscape.com/download/archive (past
versions)

▶ Opera
http://www.operasoftware.com

Pick Your Web Design Software

I mentioned earlier that building a website needn't cost you a penny, and
here's my first chance to demonstrate that. Because HTML is a completely
text-based language, all you need to write a web page is a text editor.
Whichever operating system you use, you'll have a text editor – Windows
includes a text editor called Notepad, for example, which is good enough for
the job. Better text editors will let you keep several documents open at once,
which can be useful as your site expands; I've included a few of the best on
the accompanying CD-ROM.

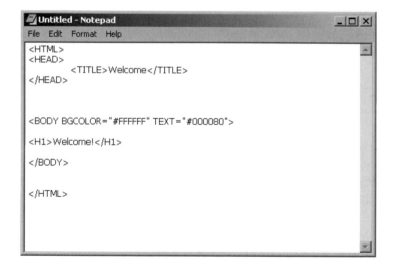

▶ A web page in
Notepad – no
expensive
software needed!

If you prefer, you can use any word processor that will let you save a file in
plain text (ASCII) format. Almost any word processor should do that, including
Windows WordPad, Microsoft Word, Lotus WordPro and Corel WordPerfect.

Throughout this book I'm going to assume that you're using a text editor of some description – it doesn't matter which you choose. There are other options available too, though, and you may prefer to plump for one of those instead, so let's quickly run through them.

JARGON BUSTER

WYSIWYG

A delightful acronym (pronounced 'wizzywig') for 'What you see is what you get'. This is used to describe many different types of software that can show you on the screen exactly what something will look like when you print it on paper or view it in your web browser.

WYSIWYG Editors

In theory, WYSIWYG editors are the perfect tools for designing web pages and entire sites: instead of looking at plain text with HTML tags dotted around it, you see your web page itself gradually taking shape, with images, colours and formatting all displayed. It's a lot like working with desktop publishing (DTP) software, and most DTP applications now offer the option of saving your results as a web page. Another benefit is that WYSIWYG editors come with a set of preset templates and predefined styles or themes: you can sort through the templates to find the right look and feel for your site, and then simply 'fill in the blanks' to add your own content and change the captions on buttons and banner headings.

Maybe now you're thinking: *Yippee! I don't have to learn all that HTML stuff!* Unfortunately that's not quite the case. Once in a while, for instance, the editor won't do what you want it to do, so you'll have to switch to its text-editing mode and juggle the HTML tags yourself. You'll certainly have to delve into the text of the page if you want to add scripts and some of the other items we'll come to later in the book. And what if you see something clever on someone else's page and want to find out how it was done? If you don't know the language, you might remain envious forever!

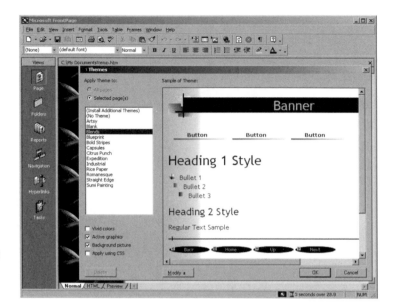

▶ Setting a site theme in the popular WYSIWYG editor, **Microsoft FrontPage**

GOOD QUESTION!

How do I see how someone else's page was put together?

In Internet Explorer, right-click on the page and choose **View Source** to see the HTML code in Notepad. In Netscape, right-click and choose **View Frame Source**. You can also choose a similar option from either browser's **View** menu.

What I particularly dislike about WYSIWYG applications is that, unless you have the time and patience to really master them, they take away your creative control. My early experience with HTML is that it's far easier to learn the language than it is to puzzle out how the WYSIWYG software works, but if you'd like to give this method a shot, here are three of the most popular applications:

Microsoft FrontPage   Along with WYSIWYG page design, FrontPage also includes complete site-management features: it can help you work out a structure for the site and how pages should be linked together, keep track of the images and other files you've used, and upload anything new to your website. You can find out more about FrontPage by visiting **http://www.microsoft.com/frontpage**. It's also included in Microsoft Office 2000 Premium Edition and the snappily-titled Office XP Professional Special Edition.

Microsoft FrontPage Express As you'd expect, Express is a free, cut-down version of FrontPage. There are no templates or styles included, and Express doesn't try to manage your entire site or structure. Instead, it provides an uncomplicated set of tools for visually creating pages one at a time (although you can have multiple pages open at once). You can decide for yourself where you save the pages, how you link them together, and when and how you upload them to your site, so the simplicity of Express gives a good balance between designing pages visually and keeping some control over what's happening. FrontPage Express was included with Windows 98 and Internet Explorer 5.0 (although not with any later versions of these), and will still be available on your system if you've since upgraded to Windows 98 Second Edition. For users of Internet Explorer 5.5 or a later Windows version, unfortunately, FrontPage Express is history.

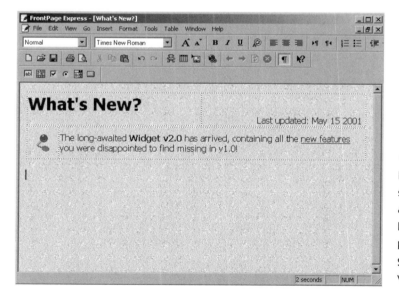

◀ **FrontPage Express** has a simple set of tools and features that help you design a page without getting in your way.

NetObjects Fusion   Fusion is a somewhat simpler program to get to grips with than FrontPage, although it offers a similar set of site management and structuring tools and likes to take control of a project in a similar way. It's a stylish program that offers a vast range of high-quality templates and page styles, and has a benefit over FrontPage that you can start designing a page without first deciding how your site will be structured. An evaluation copy of Fusion can be downloaded from **http://www.netobjects.com**.

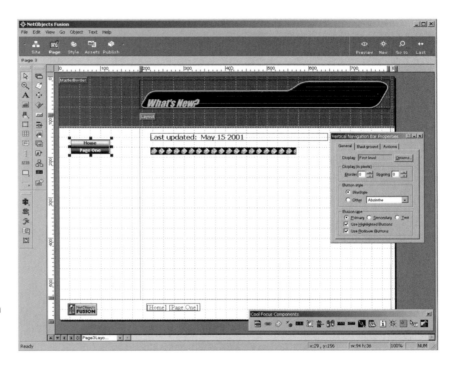

▶ Building a page from a template in **NetObjects Fusion**.

If you like the sound of the WYSIWYG method, two other very popular applications worth looking at are:

▶ **Macromedia Dreamweaver** from **http://www.macromedia.com**

▶ **Adobe GoLive** from **http://www.adobe.com**

HTML Markup Editors

Using a markup editor is rather like using Notepad – you see all the HTML code on the page in front of you. But instead of having to type all the tags yourself, a markup editor will insert them for you at the click of a button or the press of a hotkey, in the same way that you use your word processor. For example, if a piece of text should be in bold type, you click the Bold button on the toolbar (or press Ctrl+B) and then type the text in the usual way. This makes for a speedier way of working, and helps you avoid typing mistakes in the tags that might prevent them from doing anything.

Markup editors are also ideal for newcomers to HTML. If you don't know one tag from another, just click the appropriate buttons on the toolbar to insert them: once you've seen them appear on the page a few times, you'll soon start to remember what's what!

Here are three of the most popular and feature-packed markup editors. These are all shareware applications that you'll need to register if you decide to use them beyond their trial periods, but I wholeheartedly recommend picking one of these to start you off:

▶ **HomeSite** from **http://www.allaire.com**

▶ **HTMLed** from **http://www.ist.ca**

▶ **HoTMetaL Pro** from **http://www.sq.com**

Text Converters

I mentioned earlier that modern desktop publishing software has started to add web design options, with applications such as Serif PagePlus and Microsoft Publisher all joining the party. Not to be outdone, word processors like Lotus WordPro and Microsoft Word have also added features to turn your documents into web pages. At their simplest, they'll let you create an ordinary word-processed document and then choose a **Save as Web Page** option from the File menu to convert it into a web page. The result won't look as effective as other pages on the Web, but it's an ideal way to convert a long document when the only other option is to add all the tags yourself!

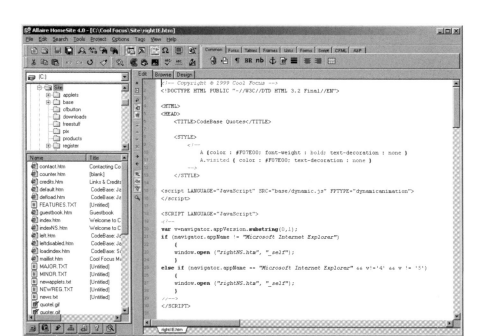

▶ Handy colour coding and one-click tag insertion in **HomeSite**.

BY THE WAY

Using Office on the Web

If you use Microsoft Office 97 or later, the web authoring features don't stop at Word. Excel allows you to save a worksheet in HTML format, and PowerPoint helps you create multimedia pages by converting slides to web format. You'll also find a media library of pictures, sounds and animations that you can include in your web pages, however you choose to create them.

You can also create web pages from scratch in these programs. For example, Microsoft Word has its own Web Page Wizard that can set you up with a ready-to-edit template like the one shown in the next screenshot. To start it up, go to **File, New...**, then click the **Web Pages** tab and double-click **Web Page Wizard**. You can add and delete elements on the page, and use the standard drawing and editing toolbars to slot in anything else you need.

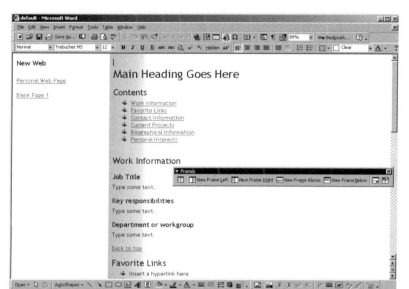

◀ Creating a web
page from a
Microsoft Word
template.

Do I Need Any Other Software?

Right now, you just need one or more browsers for viewing and checking
your pages, and a text editor (or something similar) to write them. As you
work your way through the book, you'll certainly need some other bits and
pieces – an FTP program to upload your finished site to the Web, for
instance, and a graphics application to create and edit images. Beyond that, a
lot will depend on how involved in each aspect of web design you become.

Most of the software you need is either free or very cheap (and I've
included everything you need on the accompanying CD-ROM to save you
finding and downloading it), but there are always more expensive
applications with more features if you decide you want them or need them.
Every time we come to a new area of web design, I'll let you know what's
available, what you need and what you can get away with.

What's The Big Idea?

The last thing you need, of course, is the 'big idea' – what your site is actually about. Hopefully you have that already, but if you're at the '*I just want a website*' stage, here are a few examples of big ideas:

▶ If you have artistic or musical talents, why not share your creations with the world?

▶ Provide a central point of information for a club or organization, giving details of news and planned events, and encouraging new members to join online.

▶ Promote your business or product range, with the ability to sell (and perhaps deliver) your products or services over the Internet.

▶ Share factual information about a specialized interest, hobby or skill.

▶ Run a 'matchmaking' service for pen-pals, dating or employment.

▶ Create a regularly updated directory of the best sites available covering a particular topic or aimed at a particular audience, and what each has to offer.

▶ Design a 'travelogue' site of pictures, videos and information about a part of the world you've visited, making a useful reference for anyone else planning to go there.

▶ Provide entertainment – collections of jokes, stories and anecdotes; an activity site for children; movie and music reviews; online games.

You've probably seen hordes of sites like those above – none of the ideas is going to win awards for originality – but that doesn't matter at all. A brand new idea can be hugely popular, but only for as long as it remains the best or only example out there. What *does* matter is whether the site itself is original, enjoyable and functional. Adding a new twist to an old idea or taking it a stage further than other sites can pay dividends, as can finding a 'gap in the market' to complement existing sites. Packaging sells too, of course: I'm not suggesting you should simply steal ideas and repackage them (and never steal actual content!), but you may be able to liven up an unoriginal idea with a site that's easier to use, more comprehensive or more stylish than the competition.

Ugh, that's horrible!

While you're planning your site, consider what you like (and especially what you dislike) about other sites you've visited and avoid committing the same crimes yourself. It's easy to start adding things **because you can** and forget how irritating they are. Background music that can't be turned off, garish background images that make the text hard to read, links that don't give any clue about what they're linking to – a quick critical look at a few websites from a user's point of view will teach you a lot as a designer.

If you're designing a site for your company or business, things are a little easier. After all, your company and its products or services are unique (well, whether they are or not, that's your approach). Your website is your big chance to explain who you are and what you do, and combine a marketing opportunity with another point of contact for customer support and feedback.

Hand-in-hand with the big idea go the structure and style of the site. The *style* of a site covers an immense number of things, from the choice of colours and fonts to the use of graphics, animation and Java, and whether each page should have a similar layout. A website is a balanced mixture of style and content, so we'll obviously revisit the style question pretty frequently. You could think of *structure* loosely as the main sections of your site, like chapters in a book or articles in a magazine. Since each section will probably cover a number of pages, you'd create a new directory for each section to keep it organized.

If you prefer to plan as you go along and fine-tune towards the end of the job, that's fine (I do that too). Nevertheless, there are two fundamental questions you need to ask yourself at an early stage:

▶ *Why would anyone visit this site?*

▶ *Why would they come back a second, third or fourth time?*

If you've got good answers for those, you're ready to roll!

3

A SIMPLE WEB PAGE

Every great website starts with a single page, and in this chapter we'll get that first page under way. To keep things simple, we're just going to deal with the text elements of a page to begin with, using headings and paragraphs, alignment, and useful text effects such as bold and italic. In later chapters we'll look at ways of making everything more attractive with images, colours and layout options, and we'll link pages together to create a mini website.

You'll find chapter-by-chapter example pages and files on the accompanying CD-ROM to let you see the results in your own browser or 'recycle' lumps of code for your own site. As you work through these chapters, try creating the same example pages yourself and experimenting with some of the tags to see what happens. Remember, you can't break anything by doing it wrong, so it pays to be adventurous!

Get Organized!

First, we need to sort out where all the files that will eventually make up your website are going to be kept: if they're scattered around your hard disk in different places you'll have to remember the names and locations of all those files later on, and that won't be much fun! Make a new folder somewhere on your hard disk, and call it **Site** (or something more imaginative but equally recognizable). Open this new folder, and create another inside it called **images**. (I do recommend using that name for it: this is where all the image files used on your site will be kept, so the name will be easy to remember and understand in future. We'll return to this in Chapters 5 and 6.)

This leads to two important points about the naming of files and folders (or **directories**, as folders are known on the Internet):

1 Names are case sensitive, so if your site includes a link to **MyPicture.jpg**, but you actually called the file **mypicture.jpg**, the image won't be displayed. For this reason, it's simplest to name all files and directories using *entirely lowercase names*, removing that potential hazard.

2 The names of files and directories mustn't include spaces. This is a basic rule that applies to any Internet address, including email addresses. The

names can be as long as you like, and you can use hyphens, underscores or dots to separate individual words in the names if you really can't bear the idea of having files named **whatsnew.htm** or **productsandservices.htm**.

Throughout the book, I'll refer to your 'Site directory' and your 'images directory', meaning the two directories you've just created, whatever you've chosen to call them.

Make A Template File

There are a few bits and pieces that will appear in almost every web page you write, so let's begin by making a template file you can use every time you start work on a new page. Start Notepad, or whichever text editor you're using, and type the text below. Don't worry about the exact number of spaces, tabs or carriage returns you type.

```
<!DOCTYPE HTML PUBLIC "-//W3C//DTD HTML 4.0//EN">
<HTML>
<HEAD>
        <TITLE>Untitled</TITLE>
</HEAD>
<BODY>


</BODY>
</HTML>
```

Save this file in your Site directory, giving it the name **template.htm** or **template.html**. When saving from Notepad, make sure you type the .htm or .html extension after the name as well: if you just type **template** as the filename, Notepad will save the file as **template.txt**.

As I mentioned in Chapter 1, the pieces of text between the < and > signs are known as **tags** and they tell the browser how to display the page. None of the tags in this template page does anything exciting by itself, but it's worth knowing what they're for. The first line is known as the Document Type Descriptor (a phrase you can now forget forever), and it tells the browser that the document is written in the latest version of the HTML

29

Does it matter whether I use .htm or .html as the extension when I save a page?

No, all browsers recognize either of those file extensions as being web pages. However, you'll find life a lot easier if you make a decision now and stick to the same extension for every page you save!

language. You can actually leave this out of your documents, as many web authors do, since web browsers take it for granted. I'm going to ignore it in all future examples too.

The rest of the page is placed between the <HTML> and </HTML> tags, and it's divided into two separate chunks: the **head** (the section between the <HEAD> and </HEAD> tags) and the **body** (between <BODY> and </BODY>). You'll notice that these tags are used in pairs. The first instance is the *opening* tag, and the second (which is the same, but has a forward slash after the < symbol) is the *closing* tag. Tags that work in pairs like this are known generally as **containers**: they *contain* anything placed between them, and could be thought of as on/off switches marking the beginning and end of a section, or the start and finish of an ongoing effect to be applied to their contents. (A good example of this is the tag for bold text I mentioned on page 9.)

The **head** section is pretty dull: all it contains is the title of the page, inserted between the <TITLE> and </TITLE> tags. There are other bits and pieces that can be slotted in here, and you'll meet some of those later in the book, but the title is the only element that *must* be there.

The **body** section is the one that matters. Between these two tags you'll type all the text that should appear on the page, and put in the tags needed to display images, set colours, insert hyperlinks to other pages and sites, and anything else you want your page to contain.

Do I have to type tags in capitals?

GOOD QUESTION!

No, browsers don't care about the case of the tags. If you prefer <title>, or <Title>, or even <tItLe>, it's all the same to your browser. But typing tags in capitals makes them stand out from the ordinary text on the page, which can be useful when editing a page, and it tends to be simpler to do when you've got to use the Shift key to type the < and > symbols anyway.

Now that you've created and saved a basic template file, let's start adding to it to build up a respectable looking page. In your Site directory, make a copy of the file (so that you keep this template file unchanged for creating more pages from later). Rename the copy to **index.htm** or **index.html**, and open it in Notepad.

Add A Title, Heading & Text

The first thing to do is to replace the word **Untitled** with a sensible title for the page, such as **A1 Graphic Design Company** or **My EastEnders HomePage**. Pick something that describes what the page will be about, but keep it fairly short: the text between the <TITLE> and </TITLE> tags will appear in the title bar at the very top of most browsers, and if your entry is too long to fit, it'll just get chopped off!

Choose your title carefully!

BY THE WAY

For a couple of reasons, the title of the page is more important than it might seem. First, most search engines will list the title of your page in their search results, so it needs to be appetizing enough that people will want to visit it (more on that in Chapter 24). Second, if someone likes your page enough to add it to their Favorites or Bookmarks list, this is the title they'll see in the list when they open it.

Now we'll add some text to the page. To keep things simple, type the same as I've entered below. When you've done that, save the file, but don't close Notepad yet.

```
<HTML>
<HEAD>
        <TITLE>The Computing Site Directory</TITLE>
</HEAD>
<BODY>
<H1>The Computing Site Directory</H1>
Here's an example first paragraph.

<P>And here's a second paragraph.
</BODY>
</HTML>
```

Now take a look at your masterpiece in a browser. There are several ways you can do that: one is to go to your Site directory and double-click the **index.htm** file so that your default browser starts and displays it; another is to start your browser and use the **Open** option on its File menu to browse for the file. Simpler still, just drag the file's icon from your Site directory and drop it onto the browser window. When your browser opens the page, it should look like the next screenshot.

▶ That first page
when displayed in
Internet Explorer

So what are those new tags all about? Let's take the **<P>** tag first. This tells your browser to present the text that follows as a new paragraph, which automatically inserts a blank line before it. And this raises an important point about HTML: you can't insert blank lines just by pressing Enter or Return on the keyboard. Although you can see blank lines in Notepad when you do that, a browser will just ignore them, which is why you have to start a new paragraph by entering <P>. So why did I leave a blank line between the two 'paragraphs' in the HTML code above? Simply because it makes the code easier to read: if blank lines in the code are going to be ignored by the browser, you can sprinkle them around liberally to make the code easier to understand at a glance. I could have written the code this way and the result would have been the same in the browser:

Here's an example first paragraph.<P>And here's a second paragraph.

Notice that unlike the few other tags we've come across so far, there's no </P> tag needed: the act of starting a new paragraph isn't an ongoing effect that has to be switched off again later.

GOOD QUESTION!

How do I start a new line without starting a new paragraph?

Another tag, <BR>, will give you a 'line break'. In other words, the text that follows the <BR> tag will start at the beginning of the next line with no empty line inserted before it. As an example, you could type a list of items, with a <BR> tag after each to place it on a separate line (more on that in Chapter 4).

The other pair of tags that cropped up was **<H1>** and **</H1>**, which formats a line of text as a heading. You can choose from six sizes: H1 is the largest, followed by <H2> and </H2>, and so on down to the smallest, <H6> and </H6>. In one nifty little manoeuvre these tags change the size of the text placed between them and make it bold. They also start a new paragraph for the heading automatically (so you don't need a <P> tag at the start of the line) and start a new paragraph for whatever follows the heading.

Try experimenting with the different heading sizes by altering the <H1> and </H1> tags. After each change, resave the file and click your browser's **Refresh** button to make it load and display the new copy of the page.

▶ The same text displayed in each of the six heading sizes

Be Bold (Or Be Italic...)

If you've got the idea of the heading tags, you can see that HTML certainly isn't rocket science. Heading tags are easy to use, but not unusually so: there's a large bundle of formatting tags that work in exactly the same way – you type the opening tag, some text, and the closing tag. Let's run through some of those now as a quick and painless way to expand your HTML vocabulary.

The tags for bold and italic text are especially easy to remember: **<B>** for bold, and **<I>** for italic, with the appropriate closing tag (</B> or </I>) when you want the effect to stop. And, just as in your word processor, you can combine these tags to produce combined effects, so if your document contained this:

This is <I>italic</I>. This is <B>bold</B>. This is <B><I>bold and italic</I></B>.

the result would look like this in a browser:

This is *italic*. This is **bold**. This is ***bold and italic***.

You could also use those tags like this:

<B>This is <I>bold and italic</I>. This is bold but no longer italic.</B>

which a browser would display like this:

This is *bold and italic*. This is bold but no longer italic.

Does the order of the tags matter?

Not really – provided you 'switch off' any ongoing effects before the next piece of text, you'll get the result you wanted. However, it's good coding practice to work on a 'last on, first off' basis, as in <B><I>Some Text Here</I></B>.

If you really feel the urge, you can underline text using another memorable pair of tags, **<U>** and **</U>**, but be careful how you use underlining: most people surfing the Web expect underlined text to be a hyperlink, so they might find your gratuitous use of these tags confusing.

A Few More Text-Formatting Tags

Here's a quickfire list of similar text-formatting tags. Experiment with these by typing their opening and closing tags into your index.htm page, with a word or two between them, resaving the file and clicking the Refresh or Reload button in your browser. The next screenshot shows the result of using each tag.

Tag	Meaning
<SUP>	Formats text as superscript
<SUB>	Formats text as subscript
<STRIKE>	Strikes through (crosses out) the text. An alternative tag that does the same thing is <S>.
<TT>	Displays the text in a typewriter-style font
<EM>	Emphasizes the text (usually by making it italic)
<STRONG>	Applies a strong emphasis to the text (usually by making it bold)
<KBD>	Often used to indicate text that should be typed by a user. Browsers usually display this in a mono-spaced font.
<CODE>	Often used to indicate examples of mathematical or programming code. Browsers usually display this using a mono-spaced font.

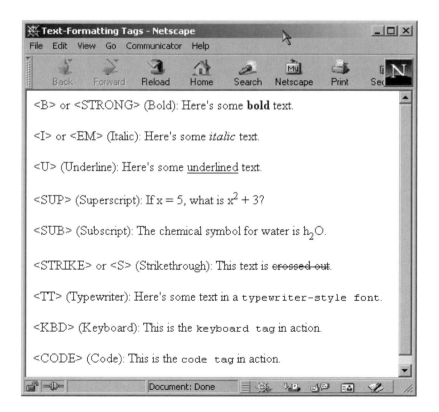

▶ The common text-formatting tags displayed by Netscape.

You can see from the screenshot that there are several tags that apparently do the same thing, such as <KBD> and <CODE> or <I> and <EM>. In practice, you can use these interchangeably if your pages are primarily aimed at users of Internet Explorer, Opera and Netscape – the tags really will gave the same result whichever you choose. In other browsers there may be subtle differences between <KBD> and <CODE>: in common with any markup language, HTML provides a fairly broad definition for each tag, and it's left to the various software companies to decide precisely how their browser should handle it.

BY THE WAY

What's that blinking thing?

One of the most derided tags in existence is <BLINK>, which makes any text placed between its opening and closing tags flash on and off. It serves no purpose other than to irritate, so it's fortunately never been accepted into the HTML specification, but Netscape browsers continue to support it. In other browsers, the tag is ignored and the text it contains is displayed normally.

Adding Information With Attributes

All the tags we've seen so far are easy to understand and use: they're either self-contained tags like <P> and <BR> that you slot in to create paragraph or line breaks, or pairs of tags that work as on/off switches like <B> and </B>. However, there are other tags that need to contain a little more information about what you want to do. A good example is the <FONT> tag, which we'll look at more closely in Chapter 5. By itself it isn't saying anything useful: which font? what size? what colour? You provide this extra information by adding **attributes** to the tag such as SIZE=3, FACE=Arial, and so on, so a complete font tag might look like this:

`<FONT SIZE=3 FACE=Arial>`

Attributes are additional pieces of information slotted into a tag. The name of the tag always comes first (the word FONT in the font tag, for example), and the attributes follow the name. Each attribute is separated by a space, and needs an equals sign between the attribute itself and the value you want to set for it. It doesn't matter what order the attributes appear in, and you don't need to include a particular attribute if you don't want to change its value from whatever it was previously set to.

We've already met one tag that has an optional attribute – the heading tag <H1> to <H6>. This can take an **ALIGN** attribute to specify whether the heading is aligned to the left, middle or right of the page, using the values **LEFT**, **CENTER** or **RIGHT**. In our example page we didn't include this attribute for the heading tag, so we got the default result: a left-aligned heading. We'd have got exactly the same result if we'd used this instead:

```
<H1 ALIGN=LEFT>The Computing Site Directory</H1>
```

Clearly there's no point in bloating our web page with extra code that won't do anything useful, but try replacing that line with either:

```
<H1 ALIGN=CENTER>The Computing Site Directory</H1>
```

or

```
<H1 ALIGN=RIGHT>The Computing Site Directory</H1>
```

As usual, save the edited page and refresh your browser to see the result. In the next screenshot I've aligned the heading to the centre of the page. Because the window is a little smaller, the browser has wrapped the heading onto a second line: this is handled automatically for all headings and paragraphs. (Of course, if I wanted the heading always to be split over two lines, I could insert a <BR> tag before the word 'Directory'.)

BY THE WAY

Watch the spelling!

HTML is an American language, so watch out for those little differences in spelling such as **color** instead of colour, and **center** instead of centre. If you spell the name of a tag or attribute wrongly, the browser won't try to make sense of it, it'll just ignore it.

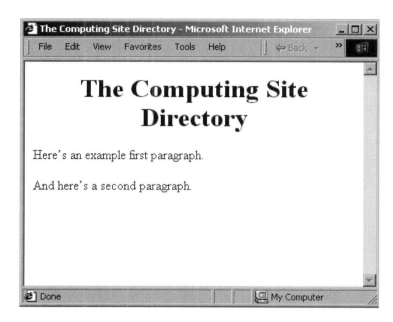

◀ Our original page with its heading aligned to the centre (or, er, the 'center').

Aligning Whole Paragraphs

If you can choose how a heading should be aligned on the page, surely you can do the same thing with a paragraph of ordinary text? Yes you can, and the <P> tag comes to the rescue here in much the same way that the heading tag did earlier: by offering an ALIGN attribute with one of the following values after its = sign:

Value	Meaning
LEFT	Aligns the paragraph to the left of the page.
CENTER	Centres the paragraph on the page.
RIGHT	Aligns the paragraph to the right of the page.
JUSTIFY	Justifies the paragraph (a straight edge to the left and right of the page, achieved by adding extra space between words). This is a recent addition to HTML that only the latest browsers understand: older browsers will ignore it and use the default value, LEFT.

At the moment our example page just contains a couple of short dummy paragraphs – not enough to do any serious paragraph formatting with – so let's replace those with something more meaningful so that the page looks like this:

```
<HTML>
<HEAD>
        <TITLE>The Computing Site Directory</TITLE>
</HEAD>
<BODY>
<H1 ALIGN=CENTER>The Computing Site Directory</H1>
<P>Welcome to the Computing Site Directory, the number one resource for all
your computing needs: industry news and comment, freeware and shareware
software, magazines and journals, hardware driver updates, and much more.

<P>Select a category below to choose from a frequently-updated list of the
best sites available. If any link is broken, please contact the Webmaster.
</BODY>
</HTML>
```

If you were to look at the page in your browser now, you'd see that both paragraphs are aligned to the left: the <P> tags don't include the ALIGN attribute, so we're getting the default alignment. In fact, apart from replacing the text to be displayed, the only change I've made is to add a <P> tag before the first paragraph as well as the second. At the moment that first <P> tag is being ignored: the heading automatically created a paragraph break for us, so we've got the equivalent of two <P> tags in a row before the first paragraph. HTML doesn't allow paragraphs to be blank, so one of these is disregarded. (We could type <P><P><P><P><P> and all but one of those would be ignored!)

GOOD QUESTION!

So how can I create extra white space between paragraphs?

After a <P> tag (or **instead** of one) you can type as many <BR> tags as you like. Unlike the <P> tag these **are** cumulative.

Now alter those paragraphs again to look like the following (the changes are shown in bold type) and view the result in your browser.

<P ALIGN=CENTER>Welcome to the Computing Site Directory, the number one resource for all your computing needs: industry news and comment, freeware and shareware software, magazines and journals, hardware driver updates, and much more.**</P>**
<P ALIGN=CENTER>Select a category below to choose from a frequently-updated list of the best sites available. If any link is broken, please contact the Webmaster.**</P>**

We've made the same two changes to both paragraphs. First, we've centred the paragraphs by adding the ALIGN=CENTER attribute. Second, we've added a closing </P> tag to mark the end of the paragraph. Yes, I know I said earlier that the <P> tag was self-contained. I lied. But although it *does* have a closing tag, that closing tag is only needed when you use the ALIGN attribute: it tells the browser where to stop applying the alignment. If you didn't include the closing </P> tag, you could find that text further down the page was still being centred or right-aligned.

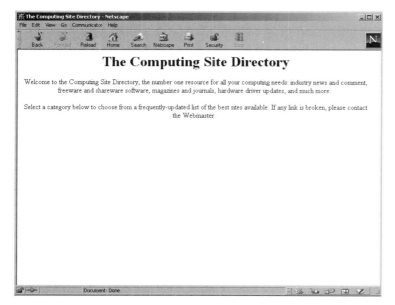

◀ Adding
<P ALIGN=CENTER>
to both
paragraphs.

BY THE WAY

Widen paragraph margins

If it bugs you that the paragraph text stretches from the extreme left to the extreme right of the browser window, you can use another tag pair, **<BLOCKQUOTE>...</BLOCKQUOTE>**, to indent the left and right margins. These tags create a new paragraph for whatever follows, and they have a cumulative effect: you can use the opening tag two or three times in a row to create wider margins. Remember to use the same number of closing tags later in the page!

The Easy Way to Centre

Part of the reason I've used the <P> tag to align the paragraphs was to introduce the concept of adding attributes to tags. Most of the time you'll want your paragraphs to be left-aligned, which needs no ALIGN attribute and no closing </P> tag, and you probably won't want to right-align or justify text very often. That just leaves centred text, and there's a better and more memorable way to do that: the **<CENTER>...</CENTER>** tag pair.

The handy thing about the <CENTER> tag is that it can be applied to anything on a page: a heading, a paragraph, an image, you name it. Just put the opening tag before the first of the content to be centred and the closing tag where the centring should end. So a less fussy way to centre the heading and the two paragraphs would be this:

```
<HTML>
<HEAD>
        <TITLE>The Computing Site Directory</TITLE>
</HEAD>
<BODY>
<CENTER>
<H1>The Computing Site Directory</H1>
Welcome to the Computing Site Directory, the number one resource for all your
computing needs: industry news and comment, freeware and shareware
software, magazines and journals, hardware driver updates, and much more.
```

```
<P>Select a category below to choose from a frequently-updated list of the
best sites available. If any link is broken, please contact the Webmaster.
</CENTER>
</BODY>
</HTML>
```

We're back to one <P> tag, no closing </P> tags, and no ALIGN attributes! It's a lot easier to understand, and it gives the same result as the more complicated version of the page.

Webmaster

JARGON BUSTER

The Webmaster is the person who maintains a website, and is responsible for checking, updating and troubleshooting it. This isn't necessarily the person who designed and developed the site, although the majority of Webmasters were involved in those stages too. The female equivalent is Webmistress, but it's okay to be a female 'Webmaster' if you prefer that. Internet job descriptions are very free and easy: there are people with the words 'Web Wizard' on their office doors and business cards!

DIV: The Easy Way To Align

Apart from the heading and paragraph tags there are other tags that can take an optional ALIGN attribute, such as images and tables (covered later in the book). If your page contains a number of headings, paragraphs, images and/or tables that have to be aligned the same way, that could add up to a lot of ALIGN attributes. A better option is to use a single tag, **<DIV>** (short for *division*). This also takes an ALIGN attribute, but it works just like the <CENTER> tag: everything between the <DIV> and </DIV> tags will be aligned the same way. In fact, the <CENTER> tag is actually just an abbreviated form of <DIV ALIGN=CENTER>. If an element somewhere between the opening and closing <DIV> tags needs to be aligned differently, just add the ALIGN attribute to its tag: individual tags' own ALIGN attributes override the <DIV> alignment.

▶ *The <DIV> tag really comes into its own when used with style sheets. Skip ahead to Chapter 9 to find out more.*

LISTS, LINKS & SPECIAL CHARACTERS

▶ **IN THIS CHAPTER**

Make simple lists using <BR> tags

Smarter looking lists with bullets and numbering

Create hypertext links to other web pages or email addresses

Learn how to link your own site's pages together

Use foreign characters & symbols, and add invisible comments

In Chapter 3 we put together a basic web page incorporating a heading and a couple of paragraphs of text, and got to grips with a bundle of HTML formatting tags and their attributes. In this chapter we'll get down to the nitty-gritty – how one page links to another to create a website of multiple pages. Along the way we'll look at some more aspects of text formatting such as lists, word breaks and spacing, and how you can display symbols and foreign-language characters in a web page. We'll also cover something that's vital in any programming or markup language: how to add comments and notes to the page for your own reference without mucking up its appearance.

He's Making A List...

If you've followed Chapter 3 and created the same example web page I did, your second paragraph refers to a list of categories on the page from which the visitor can choose a section of the site to visit. We'll start by making that list of categories, and later in this chapter we'll convert them to links.

The simplest way to make a list in a web page is to separate each item by either a <BR> or a <P> tag (depending on how much space you want between each item). For example, we could insert the following just before the closing </CENTER> tag in our web page, which would give the result shown in the next screenshot.

```
<P>Computing News and Reviews
<BR>Free Software
<BR>Shareware Software
<BR>Software Companies
<BR>Hardware Companies
<BR>Magazines and Journals
<BR>Hardware Drivers
```

(Because we've placed this list before the closing </CENTER> tag, every item is centred on the page. For a left-aligned list, place the added code *after* the </CENTER> tag instead.)

◀ A simple list of items separated by
 (line break) tags

The <P> tag is used to place a paragraph break between our second paragraph and the beginning of the list. The <BR> tags then create a line break before the next item of text. Although this is a perfectly valid way to make a list, and I'm going to stick with it for our example page, HTML includes some easy-to-use tags for creating numbered, bulleted and 'definition' lists, so let's run through those.

Bulleted Lists

HTML refers to a bulleted list as an *unordered list*, and uses the tags **<UL>** and **</UL>** to mark the beginning and end of the list. Each item in the list is prefixed with an **<LI>** tag (short for List Item). The **<LI>** tag automatically places each item onto a new line, so there's no need to insert line or paragraph breaks. We could make an unordered list of the same items like this:

```
<UL>
<LI>Computing News and Reviews
<LI>Free Software
<LI>Shareware Software
<LI>Software Companies
<LI>Hardware Companies
<LI>Magazines and Journals
```

```
<LI>Hardware Drivers
</UL>
```

▶ A bulleted (or unordered) list

In Internet Explorer, the type of bullet used is decided for you – you have no control over that. Netscape and Opera add a **TYPE** attribute to the <UL> tag which lets you choose the shape of the bullet:

Attribute	Result
TYPE=DISC	The default bullet, a solid circle
TYPE=CIRCLE	A hollow circular bullet
TYPE=SQUARE	A solid square bullet

GOOD QUESTION!

What will Internet Explorer do if I use TYPE=SQUARE?

Internet Explorer (and any other browser) will always ignore any attributes they don't understand, so your list will still be displayed properly but with the default bullet style.

Numbered Lists

The numbered list is known as an *ordered list*, using the tags **<OL>** and **</OL>**, but it's constructed in the same way as the unordered list above, still using the <LI> tag for each list item:

```
<OL>
<LI>Computing News and Reviews
<LI>Free Software
<LI>Shareware Software
<LI>Software Companies
<LI>Hardware Companies
<LI>Magazines and Journals
<LI>Hardware Drivers
</OL>
```

The code above would create a list that looked like this:

1. Computing News and Reviews
2. Free Software
3. Shareware Software
4. Software Companies
5. Hardware Companies
6. Magazines and Journals
7. Hardware Drivers

In an ordered list, there are two possible attributes, **TYPE** and **START**, that can be added to the <OL> tag, and this time they're supported by all three popular browsers. (In some other browsers, though, you may find that one or both are ignored.) The TYPE attribute sets the numbering system to be used:

Attribute	Result
TYPE=1	The default numbering system: 1, 2, 3…
TYPE=i	Small roman numerals: i, ii, iii…
TYPE=I	Large roman numerals: I, II, III…
TYPE=A	Uppercase letters: A, B, C…
TYPE=a	Lowercase letters: a, b, c…

If the list should start at a number other than 1, you can use the **START** attribute to specify the starting point. For example, the following code:

```
<OL TYPE=a START=4>
<LI>Computing News and Reviews
<LI>Free Software
<LI>Shareware Software
<LI>Software Companies
</OL>
```

would be displayed as:

    d. Computing News and Reviews
    e. Free Software
    f. Shareware Software
    g. Software Companies

Notice that even though the list is set to use lowercase letters in the TYPE attribute, you always use numbers to set the starting position in the START attribute.

In Internet Explorer and Netscape only, you can add one or both of the TYPE and START attributes to the <LI> tag in an ordered list. These reset the numbering system and/or the current number for that item and all the items following it.

BY THE WAY

Making a list more compact

The <UL> and <OL> tags (along with <DL>, mentioned below) have another optional attribute, **COMPACT**. Unlike other attributes we've come across, this has no equals sign and no value to choose: just add the word COMPACT to the tag, making sure there's a space before it. Its effect is to make the browser lay out a list in the most compact way possible. This has little effect with unordered and ordered lists, but in a definition list the two lines used for each item will usually be combined into one.

Definition Lists

A definition list is intended to create a list of terms and definitions, with the term aligned to the left, and its definition placed on the following line and indented. The whole list is enclosed between **<DL>...</DL>** tags (short for *definition list*, as you probably guessed), but this time we don't use the <LI> tag for the individual list items. Instead, each item needs two tags: **<DT>** for *definition term*, and **<DD>** for, well I'm not sure, but *definition definition* springs to mind.

Here's an example of a definition list. When displayed in your browser, it would look like the following screenshot.

```
<DL>
<DT>www.microsoft.com<DD>The place to download Internet Explorer.
<DT>home.netscape.com<DD>The place to download Netscape Navigator.
<DT>www.operasoftware.com<DD>The place to download Opera.
</DL>
```

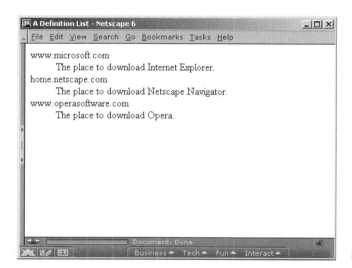

◀ A definition list
in Netscape 6

Linking To Other Sites

Before we start adding more pages to our example site and linking them together, let's take a quick detour and find out how to create links to *other* websites first. In HTML, links are known as **anchors**, and they use the **<A>...</A>** tag pair. This is a tag that does nothing at all without attributes, and the attribute we need is **HREF** (short for Hypertext REFerence) to specify the URL of the site we're linking to. Between the opening and closing anchor tags goes the text that visitors can click on to visit that site. Here's an example that links to Microsoft's website:

```
<A HREF="http://www.microsoft.com">Click here to visit Microsoft's site.</A>
```

GOOD QUESTION!

Why is the URL in double-quotes in the HREF attribute?

To do things by the book, the value of **any** attribute should really be enclosed between double-quotes: ALIGN="LEFT", TYPE="DISC", and so on. In practice, though, the only time quotes are actually needed is when the value contains a space or any punctuation that may make it unclear where the value ends. The simple rule is: if in doubt, use quotes – it certainly won't do any harm.

If you added that line of code to the body of a web page, the result would look like the next screenshot. As you can see, the text is automatically underlined, a hand-cursor appears when the mouse moves over it, and the URL it links to is shown in the browser's status bar. What's more, it works! If you click it, you'll arrive at the URL you typed into the HREF attribute.

Although we just placed one short line of text between the <A> and </A> tags, we could have used something much longer – several paragraphs, for example. You can use other tags within the linking text as well, perhaps to make the link bold or italic, or format it as a heading, so the code below is perfectly valid (although perhaps not altogether practical!) and gives the result shown in the following screenshot.

◀ A hypertext
link to
www.microsoft.com

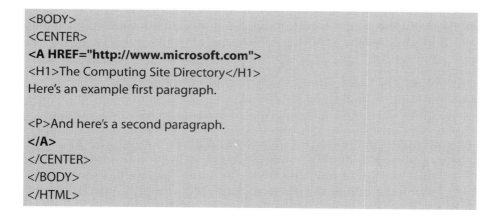

```
<BODY>
<CENTER>
<A HREF="http://www.microsoft.com">
<H1>The Computing Site Directory</H1>
Here's an example first paragraph.

<P>And here's a second paragraph.
</A>
</CENTER>
</BODY>
</HTML>
```

◀ An entire web
page contained
inside an anchor
tag. A bit
impractical, but it
works!

Linking To Particular Pages Or Files

The link we used in the examples above was to the URL
http://www.microsoft.com. We haven't specified a filename, so if this link
were clicked Microsoft's server would send back the default web page from
the root directory of this site – in other words, the first page of the Microsoft
website. If we'd wanted to link to a particular page on that site, we could
have entered the complete URL of that page – perhaps something like
http://www.microsoft.com/uk/preview/default.htm.

Links don't necessarily have to point to web pages, though. You can create a
link to an image file, a sound or movie file, a zip archive, or any other type
of file at all – the anchor tag is constructed in exactly the same way and only
the URL has to change. If the user's browser is capable of displaying the
file, it will. Otherwise, the user will be offered the choice of downloading
and saving the file on their hard disk or choosing a program on the hard
disk that is able to display or play the file.

JARGON BUSTER

protocol

When two computers need to communicate but don't speak the same
language, they follow a set of rules called a **protocol,** just as a Czech and a
Frenchman who don't speak each other's language may still be able to
communicate in Spanish. Internet protocols are all known by bunches of initials, such as:

HTTP (HyperText Transfer Protocol) used for World Wide Web resources.
SMTP (Simple Mail Transfer Protocol) used for sending email messages.
NNTP (Network News Transfer Protocol) used for transferring Usenet newsgroups.
FTP (File Transfer Protocol) used for transferring files from one computer to another.

▶ *You can also place named 'markers' at various points in a web page, and create
links that scroll that part of the page into view after loading. Skip ahead to
Chapter 10 to find out how.*

Linking to Non-Web Resources

Links to web pages and other files stored on web servers will nearly always use URLs starting with **http://**, the protocol computers use to transfer resources around the World Wide Web. Links don't have to point to files on web servers, however. Here are some of the other prefixes you can use to link to other types of resource:

Prefix	Meaning
ftp://	A link to a file on an FTP server – usually a computer that stores an indexed archive of files. An FTP link would look like this: **ftp://sunsite.doc.ic.ac.uk/index.txt**.
gopher://	A link to a file on a Gopher server. Gopher was the forerunner of the Web and it's now largely ignored, but there are still a few Gopher servers around. Here's an example Gopher link: **gopher://info.mcc.ac.uk/11/miscellany/sitcom**.
news:	A link to a particular Usenet newsgroup, such as **news:alt.fan.jen-aniston**. Notice that this prefix has no double-slash after the colon.
mailto:	A link to an email address, which also has no double-slash after the colon, allowing someone to send you email. We'll look at this in more detail in **Creating Email Links**, below.
file:///	A link to a file on your own computer, such as **file:///c:\mydirectory\myfile.htm**. You'd never use this in normal web design (since files on your own computer aren't accessible to the world at large, so the link wouldn't work), but you might use it to create an HTML index of your own files and keep that index page on your hard disk.

Creating Email Links

An email link looks like any other link on the page, but when a visitor clicks it their email program will start and they can send a message to the email address included in the anchor tag. That email address is added to the To field of the message automatically, so all they need to do is type the message and click the Send button.

Email links use the same <A>...</A> tag as other links, with the URL replaced by an email address. The only other difference is that the email address is prefixed with **mailto:**. Here's an example – just replace my email address with your own:

> <A HREF="mailto:*rob@codebase.co.uk*">Click here to send me mail.</A>

All three popular browsers let you take this one step further by specifying the subject line of the message too. Immediately after the email address, type **?subject=** followed by the subject line. (Remember that users can easily change this in their mail window before clicking the Send button, so don't rely on it!)

We can make use of this in our example web page. At the moment, our second paragraph ends with the words *If any link is broken, please contact the Webmaster*. Let's encourage user feedback by making the last few words an email link: just replace that sentence with the following, once again replacing my email address with your own:

> If any link is broken, please <A HREF="mailto:*rob@codebase.co.uk*?subject= Broken link">contact the Webmaster</A>.

If you've followed the changes we've made to our example page, it should look something like the next screenshot.

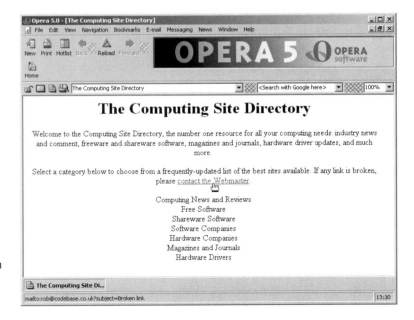

▶ Our example web page with an added email link, shown in Opera.

Linking To Pages On Your Own Site

The links we created to Microsoft's website a few pages back used something called an **absolute URL**. In fact, that's probably the only type of URL you've come across so far: an absolute URL gives the whole path to the page or file you want to link to, including the http:// prefix and the name of the computer (such as www.microsoft.com). When you want to create links to pages on your own site, you can use a different, simpler method.

To demonstrate this, of course, we're going to need a second page to link to! Make a copy of the template file you created in Chapter 3 and call it **news.htm**. (Apart from the template file, your Site directory should now contain index.htm and news.htm.)

Open news.htm in your editor and alter it to look like this:

```
<HTML>
<HEAD>
        <TITLE>Computing News and Reviews</TITLE>
</HEAD>
<BODY>
<CENTER>
<H1>Computing News and Reviews</H1>
</CENTER>
</BODY>
</HTML>
```

Save the changes and reopen index.htm in the editor. At the beginning of our list of categories we've got a *Computing News and Reviews* item, so let's make it into a link to the news.htm page by enclosing it in an anchor tag:

```
<P><A HREF="news.htm">Computing News and Reviews</A>
```

Yes, it's just a filename. This is called a **relative URL** – it tells the browser to look for a file called news.htm and display it. Since the browser doesn't know where else to look, it searches the directory containing the document it's displaying at the moment. As long as news.htm really is in that same directory, the browser will find and open it when the link is clicked. You can test this by saving the index.htm file and refreshing the browser in the usual way, then clicking this new link. (If a file with that name *isn't* in that directory, the browser will display the all-too-familiar 'not found' message instead.)

▶ It's a website! Well almost – the first item in our list of categories is now a working link.

GOOD QUESTION!

What's so great about relative URLs?

First, less typing, which also minimizes the opportunities to make mistakes. More importantly, though, you can test these links in your browser while you're designing your site to check that they work. If you used an absolute URL such as **http://www.mysite.com/mypage.htm**, your browser would have to connect to the Internet, find www.mysite.com and retrieve mypage.htm from it. That's time-consuming, and it would only work if you'd actually uploaded mypage.htm to the server.

You can also make a browser look somewhere different for a file in a similar way. Go to your Site directory and create a new directory inside it called **pages**. Move the news.htm file into this new directory. If you click the link we just created, it will now fail because the browser can't find the file: we need to change the link to the following:

```
<P><A HREF="pages/news.htm">Computing News and Reviews</A>
```

This tells the browser to look in the current directory for another directory named **pages**, and search inside that for a file named news.htm. If you test this in your browser, the news.htm page should once again be found and opened. (For another example, you could create a new directory inside 'pages' called 'morepages' and move news.htm into that. The link would then need to be: <A HREF="pages/morepages/news.htm">. For the purposes of our example site, we'll leave news.htm in the 'pages' directory.)

What we're lacking now is a link back to our index.htm page from news.htm. If news.htm were still in the Site directory, we'd use <A HREF="index.htm"> but it's now in a subdirectory called 'pages', so we need to tell the browser to look in the *parent* directory of 'pages' to find the file. If you're familiar with MS-DOS, you'll recognize this straightaway: to move up one level in the directory tree, you just type two dots followed by the usual forward slash. So we can add the following line to the news.htm page, after the heading:

```
<A HREF="../index.htm">Home</A>
```

◀ The news.htm page with a link back to the homepage, index.htm.

And if news.htm were in that 'morepages' directory, the anchor tag to get back to the index page would be <A HREF="../../index.htm">Home</A>.

What Next?

If you're treating this as a tutorial and building the same site, follow the same steps for the remaining six items in the category list on the index page. Make six copies of news.htm inside the 'pages' directory, give the files appropriate names, and edit their <TITLE> and <H1> tags to correspond to the six categories. You can then add the appropriate anchor tags to those six list items so that the list looks something like this:

```
<P><A HREF="pages/news.htm">Computing News and Reviews</A>
<BR><A HREF="pages/free.htm">Free Software</A>
<BR><A HREF="pages/shareware.htm">Shareware Software</A>
<BR><A HREF="pages/softcomp.htm">Software Companies</A>
<BR><A HREF="pages/hardcomp.htm">Hardware Companies</A>
<BR><A HREF="pages/mags.htm">Magazines and Journals</A>
<BR><A HREF="pages/drivers.htm">Hardware Drivers</A>
```

Voilà! You now have a fully linked together (if rather dull!) website consisting of eight pages.

Spaces & Word Breaks

Now that you've worked with HTML for a while, you may have come across this phenomenon: you type two or three spaces into the code, but the browser insists on using just one. Hopefully you didn't spend too much time thumping the keyboard in frustration – that's supposed to happen! Just as browsers ignore your use of the Enter or Return key in your code, they also ignore the Tab key and cut multiple spaces down to one.

You can get around this by using one of a set of special character codes, ** ** (short for *non-breaking space*). This code must be in lowercase letters, and placed between an ampersand and a semi-colon. To insert three spaces in a row, then, you'd enter **   **.

An important point to remember when using   is that it really is a non-breaking space. HTML regards an ordinary space between two words as a place it can wrap the text onto a new line if necessary. If you were to replace all the spaces between words with one or more   codes, browsers would be forced to display a paragraph as a single line stretching past the right edge of the window!

BY THE WAY

Prevent breaks between words

Where the line breaks in your paragraphs occur depend upon the font being used, the size of the user's browser window, and many other variables that you have no control over. If you have a few words in a paragraph that **must** appear together on the same line, don't use the   code between each word: enclose the words between **<NOBR>...</NOBR>** (no break) tags instead. If the enclosed words are longer than you could reasonably expect to fit on a single line in an average-sized browser window, it's advisable to choose a place where the line could be broken if necessary and put a single **<WBR>** (word break) tag there. As an example: <NOBR>These words should be on one line <WBR>but might be split here.</NOBR>

Special Characters

There are several other characters that browsers can't display when typed into a page in the usual way. These are known as *reserved* characters: they form a part of the HTML language so they have a special meaning to a browser. Like the non-breaking space, there are codes you can use if you need to display these characters in a web page:

Character	HTML Code
< (less than)	<
> (greater than)	>
" (quote)	"
& (ampersand)	&

Along with the standard English character set (A–Z, a–z, 0–9, and a few symbols such as ,.?#+=[]) the HTML language supports the full ISO-8859-1 character set, usually known by its friendlier name, Latin-1. This character set includes many foreign language characters and other symbols that don't appear on our keyboards, so similar codes are used to insert them into a web page, using either of two methods:

▶ By typing the number of the character in the ISO-8859-1 character set prefixed with **&#** and followed by a semi-colon.

▶ By typing the HTML name of the character, such as ** ** or **"** mentioned earlier. Although these are easier to remember, not all characters have names.

As an example, to display the line *"She played an unusual rôle."* in a web page, you'd type either of the following:

"She played an unusual rôle."

"She played an unusual rôle."

Yes, it looks a mess, but browsers understand it. You can combine the numbers and names, of course, so in the first example above we could replace " with ". You don't need to learn all these by heart, either: turn to Appendix C and you'll find a complete list to refer to.

Commenting HTML Code

Whatever language you're programming or coding in, it's useful to be able to add your own notes or **comments** to the code that will be ignored when the code is compiled, run, or (in the case of web pages) displayed in a browser. You may want to mark particular sections of code to make them easier to find during editing, add reminders about what a section of code does, or make a note of items you want to add later. HTML has its own comment tag pair, **<!--** and **-->** just for this purpose. Anything enclosed between these tags will be ignored by the browser when the page is displayed.

Another handy use for these tags is to *comment out* sections of HTML code: you can effectively remove chunks of text or HTML code from the page by enclosing them between comment tags rather than actually deleting them. In the code below, for example, only the first two items in the list would be displayed on the page. The remaining five are enclosed between comment tags, making them invisible to the browser.

```
<P><A HREF="pages/news.htm">Computing News and Reviews</A>
<BR><A HREF="pages/free.htm">Free Software</A>
<!--<BR><A HREF="pages/shareware.htm">Shareware Software</A>
<BR><A HREF="pages/softcomp.htm">Software Companies</A>
<BR><A HREF="pages/hardcomp.htm">Hardware Companies</A>
<BR><A HREF="pages/mags.htm">Magazines and Journals</A>
<BR><A HREF="pages/drivers.htm">Hardware Drivers</A>-->
```

COLOURS, FONTS & RULES

At this stage you're the proud owner of a basic website consisting of several pages (although only the index page contains anything useful so far). As it stands, it won't win any awards, but what matters most is that you've worked with a bundle of HTML tags and their attributes and seen the effect they have on plain text when the result is viewed in a browser. Armed with this experience, let's improve the look of the site by adding colours, choosing fonts, and applying a few more design touches.

You Too Can Have A <BODY> Like Mine!

Even in our most impressive page, **index.htm**, everything still looks a bit dull. The background is white, the text is black, the hyperlinks are either blue or purple (depending upon whether you've clicked them or not) – these are the default colours set up by most browsers, and they use those colours because we haven't told them to use anything different. All this is easily changed, though, by adding attributes to the <BODY> tag.

I mentioned at the beginning of Chapter 3 that the <BODY> tag and its closing </BODY> tag must be included in every page, and that's certainly true: they tell the browser where the displayable part of the page begins and ends. The <BODY> tag's attributes are all optional, but for any attribute that's missing a browser will use its own default setting, and different browsers may have different defaults. Since most web authors like to keep as much control as possible over how their pages will be displayed, they add these attributes. There's quite a number of possible attributes (some more of which we'll look at in Chapter 10), but for the moment we're concerned with colour, which brings the total down to five:

This attribute...	...has this effect
BGCOLOR	sets the background colour of the page
TEXT	sets the colour of ordinary text on the page
LINK	sets the colour of a hyperlink
VLINK	sets the colour of a link to a previously-visited page
ALINK	sets the colour of an 'active' link (the time between the link being clicked and the new page opening)

Without further ado, open index.htm in your editor and change its <BODY> tag so that it looks like this:

```
<BODY BGCOLOR=MAROON TEXT=WHITE LINK=YELLOW VLINK=OLIVE
ALINK=LIME>
```

Save the page and view the result in your browser. Okay the colour scheme may not be to your taste (in fact, I hope it isn't!), but you can clearly see the difference made by adding colour attributes to the <BODY> tag. Try swapping colours around to find a scheme you prefer. There are 140 **named colours** to choose from like those above, so skip ahead to Appendix B and pick a few from the list, or take a look at the Colour Chart on the CD-ROM that accompanies this book. If you'd like each page of your site to use a similar scheme, copy-and-paste the new <BODY> tag into your other pages to replace their empty <BODY> tags.

▶ *Rather than copying and pasting identical <BODY> tags into all your pages to change their colours, you could create a single style sheet to be applied to every page, so that a simple change to the sheet would be reflected throughout your site. Skip ahead to Chapter 9 to learn about style sheets.*

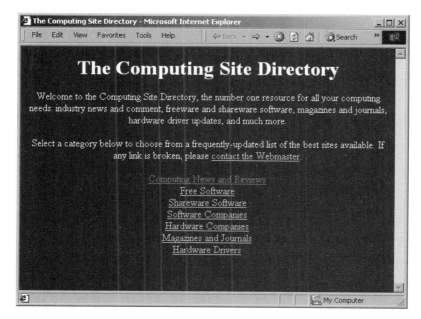

◀ A little added colour (perhaps it looks better in black and white!)

Named Colours Or Hexadecimal Colours?

Convenient as they seem, the 140 *named colours* aren't the best way to specify colour settings in your pages. For a start, these names are not supported by all browsers. More importantly, being limited to just 140 colours from a possible 16.7 million is pretty limiting. For these reasons, colours in web pages are usually given using **hexadecimal** (usually just called hex) values.

If you've never worked with graphic design, that probably sounds frighteningly obscure, so let's start with something simpler and work our way up to it. If you plan to create your own graphics for your pages (something we'll be covering in Part 2) you'll need to know how the **RGB colour model** works, and RGB and hexadecimal work in exactly the same way: the only difference is in the way the values are written.

The RGB Colour Model

Every colour a computer monitor can display consists of a mixture of the three primary colours, red, green and blue (which is where we get the name RGB). Each of these three colours can have a value of anything from 0 to 255 inclusive, so **0, 0, 0** gives black (each colour set to zero), and **255, 255, 255** gives white (each colour set to full intensity). In the same way, **255, 0, 0** gives bright red; **0, 255, 0** gives bright green; and **0, 0, 255** gives bright blue.

Using this method, you can notate any of over 16.7 million colours ($256 \times 256 \times 256$) by combining various amounts of the three primary colours. At this point, of course, it helps to have some idea of which primary colours you need to combine to produce a particular shade, and in what proportions, but simple experimentation in any graphics program will give you a feel for it fairly fast. Here are a few examples to point you in the right direction:

255, 255, 0	Yellow
128, 0, 255	Purple
255, 128, 0	Orange
0, 255, 255	Turquoise (usually known as Aqua)
192, 192, 192	Silver-grey
255, 0, 255	Shocking pink
0, 0, 160	Navy blue

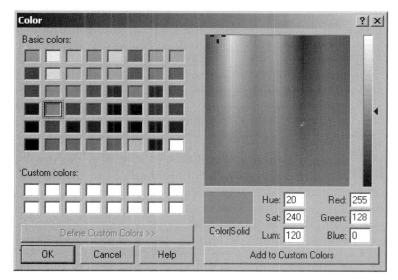

◀ A standard Windows colour dialog shows the RGB value of the selected colour in the lower-right corner.

Converting RGB Colours To Hex

Finding the colours you want to use in RGB format is the first step: graphics applications use the RGB colour model, so you'll get used to finding the colours you need when you start designing graphics for the Web. To use matching colours for the text or background of a web page, however, you'll need to convert the RGB value to something a browser can understand: a **hexadecimal** value.

Now brace yourself: it's mathematics time (yurgh). At the moment our RGB values are *decimal* values (counting in ones, tens and hundreds using the figures 0–9, the way we naturally count anything). Hexadecimal counts in sixteens, which leads to an obvious drawback: it runs out of figures at 9! To get around this the letters A to F are added, so you count like this in hex:

0, 1, 2, 3, 4, 5, 6, 7, 8, 9, A, B, C, D, E, F

At **F** you've reached the equivalent of 15. To take the next step, you count **10** (one lot of 16 and zero units) and continue: 11, 12, 13, 14, 15, 16, 17, 18, 19, 1A, 1B, 1C, 1D, 1E, 1F, 20, and so on. And when you reach 9F? A0, A1, etc. The highest number available is FF which (as I'm sure you've just totted up!) equals 255.

And relax: that's pretty much the end of the maths. The bottom line is that the three decimal numbers that make up your RGB colour have to be converted into three hex numbers. Each hex number must be two characters long (so you'd write 1 as 01, 5 as 05, and so on). Finally, remove the commas so you have a six-character result that looks something like: **80FFCC**.

As far as handling the conversion goes, the masochistic method is to divide each decimal number by 16, giving the first character of the two-figure number, and the remainder will form the second character (remembering to use the letters A–F for numbers higher than 9). A less painful method is to use a scientific calculator. Windows' own Calculator accessory has a Scientific mode available on its View menu. In that mode, type the decimal number then click the **Hex** radio-button to convert it, as shown in the next screenshot. Finally, and more simply still, you can use a little program called RGB2Hex I wrote for the job, which is included on the accompanying CD-ROM.

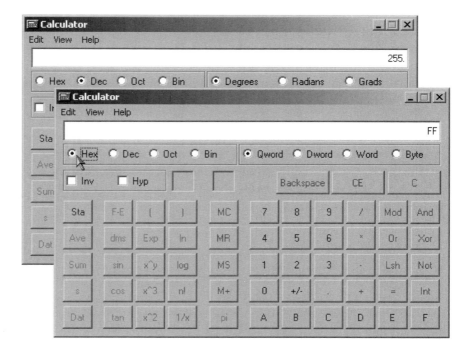

▶ Using the Windows Calculator to convert between decimal and hex. Type the number (top) then click the Hex button (bottom).

Choosing colours

BY THE WAY

Picking your colours needs a balance of practicality and style. The **practicality** aspect really comes down to logic: text, link and visited-link colours must make your text easy to read over the background colour, and the background colour shouldn't usually be too garish. Bright backgrounds make the page feel as though it's glowing after reading for a short while. The **style** comes down to your corporate colours (if you have them) or a suitable colour scheme for the subject matter. Dark blue background and white text gives a very different impression from maroon background and yellow text, for example, and this impression is made before your logo has appeared or your text has been read.

Once you've got the hex representation of the colour you want to use, you can type it into a web page in the same way as the named colours mentioned at the beginning of this chapter. The only change you need to make is to insert a # symbol before the hex number so that browsers recognize this as a number rather than a name. The colours we specified in the <BODY> tag earlier using names would now look like this:

```
<BODY BGCOLOR=#800000 TEXT=#FFFFFF LINK=#FFFF00 VLINK=#808000
ALINK=#00FF00>
```

▶ *Although you have over 16 million colours available, it pays to consider whether your choice of colours can be displayed correctly on visitors' monitors – in other words, what colour palette visitors are likely to use. Skip ahead to Chapter 11 for more on colour palettes, including the 'web-safe' palette.*

Adding A Background Image

If you feel the urge, another attribute you can add to the <BODY> tag is **BACKGROUND**. This specifies a GIF or JPEG image file to be used as a background to the web page, and the image is automatically **tiled** to fill the user's browser window. Because this is a file that the browser has to find, it's entered as a URL just like the HREF attribute of the anchor tag (see Chapter 4). And, as with the anchor tag, although you could enter an *absolute* URL you'd have to go online to see the result, so a *relative* URL is preferable.

JARGON BUSTER

tiled image

When an image is **tiled**, multiple copies of the image are placed side-by-side in rows and columns to fill a specified area. You'd usually want to choose or create an image that can be tiled seamlessly so that the joins between each individual tile are invisible.

At the beginning of Chapter 3 you created a directory named **images** in your Site directory, and here's your big chance to use it. Find any GIF or JPEG image on your hard disk, or download one from the Web, and copy it into your 'images' directory. You can then add the following attribute to the <BODY> tag of index.htm, changing 'space.jpg' to your own image file's name:

BACKGROUND="images/*space.jpg*"

The first of the two following screenshots shows the result of using the background image I chose. If I published a page that looked like this, I'd deserve to have my computer taken away: the size of the image is distracting, its repetition is too obvious, and it involves so many colours that the text of the page would be hard to read whatever text colour was used. In the second screenshot I've used something far more subtle: it has a much smaller pattern involving several shades of one colour, and it isn't as eye-catchingly repetitive. A smaller pattern (although it wouldn't reproduce well on the page of this book) would be a better choice still.

One final point about background images. When someone visits your site, the image itself can't begin to download until the browser has received the page itself and read its <BODY> tag. This means that the browser will already be displaying the correct background colour (BGCOLOR) and probably some of the text as well. To ensure that visitors can read your page while the image downloads, always set the BGCOLOR to something that matches the background image as closely as possible.

◀ **Bad:** an appalling choice of background image. Just shoot me.

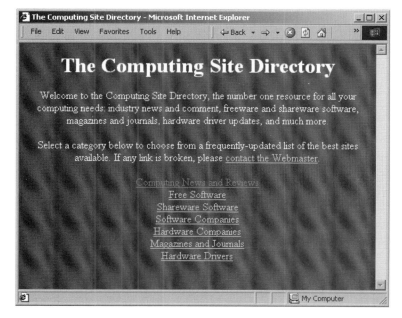

◀ **Good:** the less aware you are of the image, the better.

Caching & The Images Directory

An obvious question at this point would be: *Why not just put the background image file in the same directory as the index.htm file?* Then we'd just use the attribute BACKGROUND="space.jpg" and the browser would still find the image and display it. Follow that logic a bit further, though: if you insist upon keeping every image in the same directory as the first page you use it on, you'll have images scattered throughout your site's directories. You'll either have to remember where each image is when you want to include it in another page or, worse still, you might end up making copies of the same image file in different directories! Although the picture itself is the same, these are different files with different URLs, so they all have to be downloaded by the user.

An important aspect of keeping your site fast and responsive is to *reuse* files whenever possible – not only image files, but sound files, scripts, and other content we'll meet later in the book. The first time an image is downloaded by the user's browser, it's **cached** on his hard disk in case it's needed again. The browser handles the caching, storing a copy of the file along with the file's URL. If another page on your site includes the same image (i.e. links to the image file that has the *same* URL) the browser can load it directly from the user's hard disk this time – there's no downloading involved, so the user sees the image almost immediately. By keeping all your image files in one directory, you can easily find out whether you've already used a particular image on your site and link to the same file in other pages.

Set Up Your Font Options

At the moment you're stuck with a single font throughout your site (probably Times New Roman in Windows, and Geneva on a Mac). Like the colour options mentioned at the beginning of this chapter, your browser sets a default font, and different browsers may use different defaults. Fortunately the **<FONT>...</FONT>** tag pair leaps to your rescue, allowing you to choose and change the font face, size and colour whenever you need to. Here's an example of a <FONT> tag using all three possible attributes:

```
<FONT FACE="Tahoma,Verdana,Arial"  SIZE=4 COLOR=#FF0000>
```

Let's take these attributes one at a time. The **FACE** attribute sets the name of the font you want to use, and to prevent errors it's best always to enclose its value in double-quotes. Obviously you'd want to choose a font face that's available on your own system so that you can see what it looks like, but the same font needs to be on the system of anyone visiting your site too; if it isn't, their browser will revert to its default font. You can't control what fonts your users have available, of course, and adding suggestions on your site that visitors should install a particular font will be treated with deserved indifference. You can keep a bit of extra control by listing more than one font name (separated by commas) as in the example above. If the first font isn't available, the browser will try for the second, and so on. This way, you can start by specifying the font you'd want used in a perfect world, and work through to something that's at least bearable and likely to be available.

BY THE WAY

Beware faceless browsers!

Not all browsers support the FACE attribute. The 'big three', Internet Explorer, Opera and Netscape, all do, but the majority of others don't. With this in mind, and the fact that some browsers allow users to override font face and size settings in web pages anyway, your font choices are best thought of as something to hope for, rather than something to rely on.

Font sizes in HTML work differently from in your word processor. There are seven sizes numbered (unsurprisingly) from 1 to 7, where 1 is smallest. The default size for text is 3, so if you wanted to make your text slightly larger, you'd use SIZE=4. The SIZE attribute doesn't affect the headings we covered in Chapter 3, so if there's a heading tag somewhere between your <FONT> and </FONT> tags it will still be formatted in its usual way.

The colour of the text has already been set in the TEXT attribute of the <BODY> tag, covered at the start of this chapter, but you might want to slip in an occasional <FONT COLOR=#FFFF00>...</FONT> to change the colour of a certain word, paragraph or heading. After the closing </FONT> tag, the text colour will revert to the one set in the <BODY> tag.

Big text, small text

If you find it hard to keep track of the font size you're currently using, don't bother trying! Instead you can use <BIG> and </BIG> to make the text one step larger than its current setting, or <SMALL> and </SMALL> to make it one step smaller. You can also use plus and minus signs with the <FONT SIZE=?> value to make the size larger or smaller than the BASEFONT size (see below). For example, if the BASEFONT were set at its default size of 3, you could switch temporarily to size 5 text using <FONT SIZE="+2">...</FONT> or to size 2 text using <FONT SIZE="-1">...</FONT>.

Choosing Font Faces

The ability to specify several fonts gives you a lot of flexibility, but you want to include at least one font that the majority of users are likely to have available. The increased use of Internet Explorer has been useful in that department: recent versions have included a 'font pack' known as Web Core Fonts which contains Arial, Times New Roman, Georgia, Verdana, Comic Sans MS, Trebuchet MS and Impact, so these fonts will be available on the majority of users' systems (including Macs). The same font pack is included with recent Windows versions, and can be downloaded from **http://www.microsoft.com/truetype**.

Good design dictates that you don't use too many different fonts on a page: more than two or three will be distracting. If you create images for the site, try to use the same fonts for any text in the images too. As a general rule, you might settle on one font for headings and banners, another for body text, and use the SIZE attribute or bold and italic tags to create differences. Finally, consider what your choice of font says about your site: in the following screenshot, the first heading says that we don't expect to be taken seriously; the second is very formal but rather severe; the third does expect to be taken seriously but has a friendlier air about it.

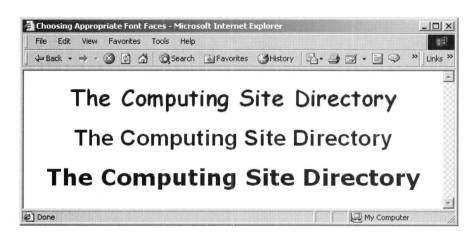

◀ Your choice of font face can say a lot about your site.

The <BASEFONT> Tag – If You Want It!

Unless you're happy for browsers to use their default font to display your pages, you'll probably want to specify the font names to be used for the whole page and the default size of the text. There are two ways you can do that. One is to use the tag that's built for the job, **<BASEFONT>**, which has no closing tag. <BASEFONT> should be placed in the head of the page (between the <HEAD> and </HEAD> tags) and can take the same three attributes as <FONT>. The problem is that some browsers support only the SIZE attribute of this tag, so you can't use it reliably to specify a font face. The default SIZE value is 3, so if you don't include a <BASEFONT SIZE=?> tag the default font size for your page will remain at 3.

The other method is to enclose the entire body of the page between <FONT>...</FONT> tags to specify face and size. Although slightly messier, this does at least work! You may want to add these tags to your web page template file to save adding them manually to every page you create (specifying your own preferred font faces in place of mine, of course):

```
<HTML>
<HEAD>
      <TITLE>Untitled</TITLE>
</HEAD>
<BODY>
<FONT FACE="Tahoma,Verdana,Sans-serif" SIZE=3>
```

```
</FONT>
</BODY>
</HTML>
```

Adding Fonts To The Index Page

Having discovered the <FONT> tag, let's improve the look of our index.htm page by setting a few fonts for it. Alter the code of the page to match the code below (I've marked the changes in bold type), and the result should look similar to the following screenshot when viewed in your browser:

```
<HTML>
<HEAD>
        <TITLE>The Computing Site Directory</TITLE>
</HEAD>
<BODY BGCOLOR=#FFFFF0 TEXT=#000000 LINK=#0000FF VLINK=#000080
ALINK=#FF0000>
<CENTER>
<FONT FACE="Georgia,Times New Roman" SIZE=3>
<FONT FACE="Verdana,Arial"><H1>The Computing Site
Directory</H1></FONT>
Welcome to the <FONT COLOR=#800000>Computing Site Directory</FONT>,
the number one resource for all your computing needs: industry news and
comment, freeware and shareware software, magazines and journals, hardware
driver updates, and much more.

<P>Select a category below to choose from a frequently-updated list of the
best sites available. If any link is broken, please <A
HREF="mailto:rob@codebase.co.uk?subject=Broken link">contact the
Webmaster</A>.

<P>
<FONT FACE="Verdana,Arial" SIZE=4>
<A HREF="news.htm">Computing News and Reviews</A>
<BR><A HREF="free.htm">Free Software</A>
<BR><A HREF="shareware.htm">Shareware Software</A>
<BR><A HREF="softcomp.htm">Software Companies</A>
<BR><A HREF="hardcomp.htm">Hardware Companies</A>
```

```
<BR><A HREF="mags.htm">Magazines and Journals</A>
<BR><A HREF="drivers.htm">Hardware Drivers</A>
</FONT>
</CENTER>

</FONT>
</BODY>
</HTML>
```

◀ The index.htm page, with improved colours and the addition of a few <FONT> tags.

The first <FONT> tag sets the default font to use for the page; its corresponding </FONT> tag is just above the closing </BODY> tag. This means that everything on the page will be displayed in that font face and size unless we specify something different for particular sections. And we've done just that in three places:

▶ The heading has <FONT> tags enclosing it that specify a different font face. Its size is set by the <H1> tags (we could make it smaller using <H2> or <H3>) and its colour is set in the body tag's TEXT attribute.

▶ The words 'Computing Site Directory' in the first paragraph have been set to a different colour. Because we haven't included FACE or SIZE attributes, these remain the same as the other text in that paragraph, set in the very first <FONT> tag.

▶ The list of links has been set to a different face and size in a similar way. Adding a COLOR attribute here would be ignored: the link colours are set by the LINK/ALINK/VLINK attributes of the body tag and can only be changed through the use of style sheets (see Chapter 9).

In choosing the font faces to use, I've stuck to a tried and tested formula: serif fonts for body text, and sans-serif fonts for headings or large text. That's certainly not a 'must do', but it's worth keeping in mind as a 'might want to do'.

JARGON BUSTER

serif and sans-serif fonts

In a serif font the characters have small hooks or ornaments (known as **serifs**) which add an informal air to the text. Serif fonts are commonly used for blocks of text and can make reading easier if chosen carefully. Sans-serif fonts don't have these ornamental flourishes and are used mostly for headings. When specifying the FACE attribute of the <FONT> tag, you can add **Serif** or **Sans-serif** to the end of the list of font names to ensure that if none of the suggested fonts is available you'll at least have the **type** of font you want. Reading on-screen text is rather different from reading text on paper, so your choice of font for the body text is more important. Curiously, many users find sans-serif fonts easier to read on screen, and Microsoft's **Verdana** font (a sans-serif font) was specifically designed for web-based body text.

Horizontal Rules (OK)

Horizontal rules are straight lines with an engraved 3D look that divide a page into sections. For the simplest type of rule, the only tag you need is **<HR>**. This automatically puts a horizontal rule across the full width of the page, placing a paragraph break before and after it. Because the rule isn't an effect that needs to be 'switched off' there's no closing tag.

If you want to, you can get clever with the <HR> tag by adding some (or all!) of its available attributes:

Use this attribute...	...for this result
ALIGN=	Use **LEFT** or **RIGHT** to place the rule on one side of the page. Without this attribute the rule will be centred.
SIZE=	Enter any number to set the height (thickness) of the rule in pixels. The default size is 2 pixels high.
WIDTH=	You could enter a number to specify the width of the rule (in pixels), but as you don't know how wide the user's browser window is, this is usually to be avoided. Instead, specify a percentage of the window's width, such as **WIDTH="70%"**.
COLOR=	Enter a colour name or hex number to set the colour of the rule. Only Internet Explorer supports this; other browsers will ignore it. The default colour varies according to the page's background colour (<**BODY** **BGCOLOR**>).
NOSHADE	This removes the 3D shading from the rule leaving a solid line. There's no equals sign and no value to add.

It's worth playing with the <HR> tag to find out what you can do with it. For example, the following piece of code places a square bullet in the centre of the page which makes a smart, 'minimalist' divider:

```
<HR WIDTH=10 SIZE=10 NOSHADE COLOR=#0000FF>
```

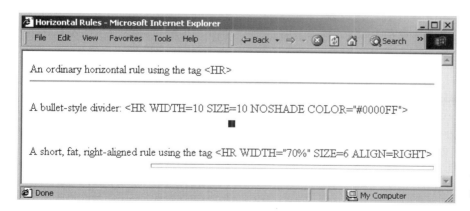

◀ The <HR> tag in action.

Animated Text With <MARQUEE>

Marquee is Microsoft's name for a piece of text that scrolls across the screen (a Windows screensaver of the same name does this too). In other circles, this kind of device is more usually referred to as a 'ticker', short for ticker-tape. The **<MARQUEE>** tag gives you a way to do this with HTML, but for reasons we'll come to in a moment it's best avoided, so we'll zip through its workings quickly. Begin by placing this code on a page:

```
<MARQUEE ALIGN=MIDDLE HEIGHT=10 WIDTH=80% BGCOLOR=#800000
SCROLLAMOUNT=3 SCROLLDELAY=3 BEHAVIOR=SCROLL DIRECTION=LEFT
LOOP=INFINITE VSPACE=0 HSPACE=0>This text is scrolling</MARQUEE>
```

All the possible attributes are included in the code above, and you'll recognize some straightaway such as BGCOLOR (used in the <BODY> tag), WIDTH (from the <HR> tag mentioned above), and ALIGN (which in this tag has the possible values of LEFT, RIGHT, TOP, MIDDLE, BOTTOM). HEIGHT can be specified as a percentage of the page height or (much more usefully) in pixels. DIRECTION can be either LEFT or RIGHT, and you can experiment with the SCROLLAMOUNT and SCROLLDELAY values to achieve a comfortable speed. LOOP can be a number to specify how many times the text should be scrolled, or INFINITE for continuous looping. BEHAVIOR can be SCROLL (move into the display area from one side of the marquee and out of the other side), SLIDE (slide from one side to the other and then stop before repeating) or ALTERNATE (slide back and forth from one side to the other without disappearing).

The two final attributes are ones we'll meet again in the next chapter. VSPACE sets the number of pixels of extra space to be placed above and below the marquee (*vertical space*); HSPACE sets the space to its left and right (*horizontal space*). The text placed between the opening and closing tags is the text to be scrolled; the font size, face and colour will be taken from the current <FONT> tag settings, just as if this were ordinary paragraph text.

It's a neat enough effect, so why not use it? First, it's a Microsoft invention that only Internet Explorer supports. Worse still, some other browsers don't even display static text in its place, so it's only good for non-essential text. But the biggest problem is that Internet Explorer apparently has to put a lot of energy into scrolling the marquee, at the expense of other animated or interactive content on the page which immediately becomes extremely sluggish. There are far better ways to put 'tickers' on a web page by adding a JavaScript or a Java applet (a search for 'ticker script' or 'ticker applet' at any search engine will turn up links to plenty of either). These can be viewed in all browsers and they won't lock up Internet Explorer's resources in the process.

GETTING GRAPHIC: IMAGES & BUTTONS

So far the example site we're building is 'text only' – not a single image in sight. From the point of view of speed, that's not a bad thing: we could work through the seven empty 'category' pages we created, adding links and descriptions for hundreds of great computing sites, and our entire site would probably still weigh in at less than 30 Kb! There won't be much that's attractive or fun about the site, but maybe the content is good enough to make up for that?

The odds are that you want a more stylish site, though, and a well-chosen image or two can make a lot of difference to visual impact and layout. In this chapter, we'll stick to the basics – how to get images onto the page and use them as links – and leave a more detailed look at graphics and multimedia until Part 2. (If you don't fancy creating your own graphics just yet, you can use the same images I have: just copy them to your 'images' directory from the CD-ROM accompanying this book.)

Add Spice With An Image

In Chapter 5 we found out how to add a tiled background image to a web page by adding the BACKGROUND attribute to the page's <BODY> tag. To do that, we used a relative URL giving the location of the image file relative to the location of the current web page. Adding an **inline image** to the page works in just the same way, but there's a particular tag we use to do the job: the **<IMG>** tag.

JARGON BUSTER

inline image

This really just means 'an image on a web page'. The word **inline** is often used to differentiate between an image displayed amongst the text of the page itself and an image used as a background or shown only if a link to the image is clicked.

Returning to our index.htm page, I've created an image to replace the heading at the top of the page and called it **banner.gif**. At the moment we're using the code below to put the heading on the page and set a font for it:

```
<FONT FACE="Verdana,Arial"><H1>The Computing Site
Directory</H1></FONT>
```

To replace that heading with the image, we can just replace that lump of code with this:

```
<IMG SRC="images/banner.gif"><P>
```

Once again, I've put the image file in the 'images' directory so that we'll know where to find it if we want to reuse it on future pages. I've also added a <P> tag: the <H1> tag we were using before gave us a paragraph break after the heading which the <IMG> tag doesn't, so we need to add it ourselves. If you're using the banner.gif image from the CD-ROM, the result should look like the following screenshot.

◀ The index.htm page with an image replacing the text heading.

The code above shows the <IMG> tag at its most basic. The **SRC** attribute (short for 'source') tells the browser where to find the image file you want to display, following the same rules as those for relative URLs covered in

Chapter 4. You can use *absolute* URLs in the SRC attribute if you're linking to images on another website, but remember that your computer will have to go online to retrieve those images whenever you view the page. The only thing the <IMG> tag does is to put an image on the page, so of all the possible attributes that could be added to this tag, the SRC attribute is the only one that *must* be included.

GOOD QUESTION!

What types of image file can I use on the Web?

Images that appear in a web page must be in either GIF (.gif) or JPEG (.jpg) format. Browsers can display both types of file, and images saved in these formats are automatically compressed, making them download faster than they would if saved in some other formats. There are differences between GIF and JPEG which make one format better than another for particular images, but that's another topic we'll put off until Part 2!

Aligning Images

Like most of the HTML tags that add something new to the page (a paragraph, a heading, a horizontal rule, etc.), the <IMG> tag can have an ALIGN attribute to give you some control over where the image should be placed in relation to the items around it. In fact, you have a *lot* of control! The <IMG> tag's ALIGN attribute has more values available than any we've seen so far.

This attribute...	...does this
ALIGN=TOP	Aligns the top of the image with the top of the tallest item on the same line.
ALIGN=TEXTTOP	Aligns the top of the image with the top of the tallest text on the same line. This is similar to **ALIGN=TOP**, but ignores anything on the line that isn't text.
ALIGN=MIDDLE	Aligns the baseline of the text on the same line with the middle of the image.
ALIGN=ABSMIDDLE	Aligns the middle of the line of text with the middle of the image.

ALIGN=BOTTOM	Aligns the baseline of the text on the same line with the bottom of the image. (**ALIGN=BASELINE** does the same thing.)
ALIGN=ABSBOTTOM	Aligns the bottom of the text with the bottom of the image. This is subtly different from **ALIGN=BOTTOM**: the **baseline** of the text is the line that characters like 'm', 'b' and 'r' sit on; characters like 'g' and 'y' drop below that line, and **bottom** is the lowest point that those characters reach.
ALIGN=LEFT	Places the image on a new line against the left margin, with any text that follows the image wrapped to its right.
ALIGN=RIGHT	Places the image against the right margin, with text wrapped to its left.

The next screenshot shows the result of using those ALIGN values in an image tag and placing a short line of text immediately after the image, such as <IMG SRC="images/box.gif" ALIGN=TOP>Align=TOP. I've put a <P> tag after the text in each case to create a reasonable gap between each image for clarity. If no gap were needed, a <BR> tag could have been used instead, which leads us neatly to the issue of wrapping text around images.

For the last image in the screenshot I've used ALIGN=LEFT and displayed the text 'Align=LEFT' after it. If I'd then put in a <BR> tag and added some more text, it would appear immediately below the words 'Align=LEFT', but still alongside the image. If I wanted to make sure that added line of text would appear *below* the image, against the left margin, I'd use **<BR CLEAR=LEFT>**. The CLEAR attribute of the <BR> tag forces anything that follows to be placed below any image on the current line. The possible values for CLEAR are:

▶ **LEFT.** Put the following text at the next point where the left margin is clear.

▶ **RIGHT.** Put the text at the next point where the right margin is clear.

▶ **ALL.** Put the text at the next point where both margins are clear.

Creating Space Around Images

Using the ALIGN attribute, then, you can place the image roughly where you want it in relation to text or other images around it. What's needed is a bit more fine-tuning: after all, if you use ALIGN=ABSMIDDLE, the image will be

▶ Fine-tuning the alignment of an image with a line of text.

butted right up against any text on the same line, and any text on the line preceding or following it.

The answer comes in the form of two more attributes which add some blank space around the image: **HSPACE** inserts space either side of the image (*horizontally*), and **VSPACE** adds space above and below it (*vertically*). Just enter a number in pixels after the equals sign. As usual with attributes, if you only need to use one of these, there's no need to enter the other. In the next screenshot, the first image is inserted using <IMG SRC="images/box.gif" ALIGN=LEFT>; the second uses <IMG SRC="images/box.gif" ALIGN=LEFT VSPACE=10 HSPACE=15>.

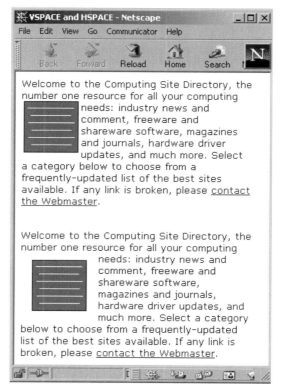

◀ Adding HSPACE and VSPACE attributes to the image tag in the second example adds blank space around the image.

Get The Size Right!

Two of the most important <IMG> attributes are **WIDTH** and **HEIGHT**, with which you specify the dimensions of the image. If you've experimented with the image tag, you'll have noticed that your browser displays the image properly without these attributes, so you're probably wondering why you'd go to the bother of finding and entering the image's dimensions.

At the moment you're looking at pages and images that are already on your computer – there's no downloading involved yet, so your browser loads the page and shows the images in the blink of an eye. When your page is on the Web and someone visits it, things work a bit differently. When the browser arrives at an <IMG> tag with no WIDTH or HEIGHT attributes, it has to download the image, work out its dimensions and display it before it can decide how to lay out anything below the image. However, if the browser already knows how much space to reserve for the image, it can display an empty box until the image has downloaded, with the text correctly positioned around it.

Size matters!

BY THE WAY

If you need another good reason to add **WIDTH** and **HEIGHT** attributes, here it is: most browsers have an option to surf the Web without displaying images, and some people use it – pages load faster that way. Where images should appear on the page, the browser draws a 'placeholder' box containing a small icon. If you don't enter the dimensions of your images, those users will see a tiny box just large enough to contain the icon, which might upset your carefully planned page layout. With the image dimensions entered, the placeholder box will be the size you wanted it to be.

You can find an image's dimensions easily by loading it into almost any good graphics program. I've also included a little Windows program called Image Size on the CD-ROM that will tell you the dimensions of a GIF or JPEG image when you drop the file into its window. Make a mental note of the figures and then add them to your tag like this:

```
<IMG SRC="images/banner.gif" WIDTH=503 HEIGHT=58>
```

Bear in mind that when you enter the dimensions of an image, the browser will take your word for it! In other words, the browser will resize the image to these dimensions regardless of what the original image was supposed to look like. This can be useful to increase or decrease the size of an image without creating a new version of it (or to create weird effects), but it's also a prime opportunity to screw things up!

◀ It's a good idea to specify the image dimensions (top), and an even better one to get them right (bottom)!

Use Alternative Text

Another useful attribute of the image tag is **ALT**, which specifies alternative text to display in place of the image. This is shown in the placeholder box on the page while the image is downloading, and in Internet Explorer and Netscape (though not necessarily in other browsers) it's also displayed in a tooltip when the mouse moves over the image. For any visitors surfing without images displayed, this alternative text is the only clue to what that image would be if they could see it.

So let's change the <IMG> tag in the index.htm page to add the correct dimensions and some alternative text. For visitors who've turned off image display, the page will look something like the following screenshot.

```
<IMG SRC="images/banner.gif" WIDTH=503 HEIGHT=58 ALT="The Computing Site Directory">
```

▶ *If you like the idea of the tooltip text provided by the ALT attribute for images, you can do the same for almost anything else on the page (in Internet Explorer at least). Find out how in Chapter 10.*

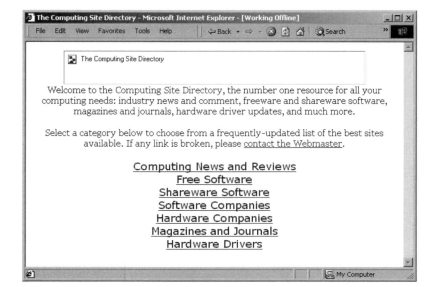

▶ With dimensions and alternative text added, the result is still meaningful when images are switched off.

Button It! Images As Links

In Chapter 4 you learnt how to create hypertext links to a web page or file using the tag <A HREF="*URL*">*clickable text*</A>. But the clickable section that appears on the page doesn't have to be text: you can use an image instead. (In fact, you can use an image *and* text if you want to – just place it all between the opening and closing anchor tags as you want it to appear on the page.)

Let's replace the seven category links on the index.htm page with button images to demonstrate this. I've created seven images, all with the same dimensions but with different text on each, and you can grab those from the CD-ROM. In the section of the page containing the seven links, remove the <FONT> tags surrounding this block of code (we won't be displaying text there any longer so they're redundant), and replace the text between each anchor tag with the appropriate image tag like this:

```
<P><A HREF="pages/news.htm"><IMG SRC="images/news.jpg" WIDTH=185
HEIGHT=27></A>
<BR><A HREF="pages/free.htm"><IMG SRC="images/free.jpg" WIDTH=185
HEIGHT=27></A>
```

```
<BR><A HREF="pages/shareware.htm"><IMG SRC="images/shareware.jpg"
WIDTH=185 HEIGHT=27></A>
<BR><A HREF="pages/softcomp.htm"><IMG SRC="images/softcomp.jpg"
WIDTH=185 HEIGHT=27></A>
<BR><A HREF="pages/hardcomp.htm"><IMG SRC="images/hardcomp.jpg"
WIDTH=185 HEIGHT=27></A>
<BR><A HREF="pages/mags.htm"><IMG SRC="images/mags.jpg" WIDTH=185
HEIGHT=27></A>
<BR><A HREF="pages/drivers.htm"><IMG SRC="images/drivers.jpg"
WIDTH=185 HEIGHT=27></A>
```

GOOD QUESTION!

If an image is used as a link, what happens if images aren't displayed?

For users who've switched off image-display, the placeholder box they see instead will still act as a link. The hand cursor that appears when the mouse enters the box will make that clear, but adding an **ALT** attribute to the image tag is one way to let them know what it links **to**.

If you look at the page in your browser, you'll see that there's a problem: because we're using these images as links, the browser puts a border around each one in the same colour as hyperlinked text. The intention, of course, is to make it clear that these *are* links, but on this page that should be pretty obvious to anyone visiting; those borders just make the page look messy. Fortunately the <IMG> tag has another attribute, **BORDER**, that can help us out. We can add any number after the equals sign to set the thickness of the border, and zero is as valid as any other figure, so add a BORDER=0 attribute to each of the <IMG> tags. The result should look like the following screenshot.

▶ The index.htm page, after replacing the text links with images.

GOOD QUESTION!

Why are there gaps between each button?

We still have a <BR> tag between the links to place each on a separate line, and you may find that a few pixels of background colour are visible between each button. This is because the <BR> tags are **starting** lines rather than **finishing** them. Although it shouldn't make any difference, it does. Remove the <BR> tags from the beginning of each line and place them after each </A> tag instead.

Border Or No Border?

The BORDER attribute can be added to any <IMG> tag, whether the image is a link or not. Non-linking images don't have a border by default, but you can create one by adding BORDER=1 to the tag (changing the number according to the thickness you want).

Looking around the Web, you'll notice that most site designers remove the border from linking images. What matters most is that visitors can tell that an image is a link by looking at it, and the design of the image itself can usually get that across. Images containing text, for example, are generally expected to be links, as are any similarly-styled collections of images placed close together. If a page doesn't contain much in the way of hyperlinked text, most visitors will wave the mouse over images to see if they're links. In these situations, hypertext-coloured borders are unnecessary and probably spoil the appearance of the page.

One of the few situations in which you might want to consider leaving the border intact is if you have a single image on the page some way away from other images. For example, you may have an envelope icon at the bottom of the page acting as an email link (see Chapter 4). A border will help to draw attention to it as well as making it clear that it's a link.

Alternative Text Or No Alternative Text?

The ALT attribute is a worthwhile addition to *ordinary* pictures on the page (the kind that paint a thousand words, but don't link anywhere), but for *linking* images it may be annoying. As visitors move the mouse over the images to navigate your site, tooltips keep popping up to show the alternative text. That's certainly not a huge problem, but you may not want it to happen.

A popular option is to leave out the ALT attribute and add plain hypertext links elsewhere on the page for users who can't see the images. Since these would rarely be needed, they can use a small font and be tucked away near the bottom of the page. Most designers place these all on one line, with each link in square brackets. We can do this by adding the following code below the images:

```
<P>
<FONT FACE="Verdana,Arial,Sans-serif" SIZE="1">
[<A HREF="pages/news.htm">News &amp; Reviews</A>]
[<A HREF="pages/free.htm">Freeware</A>] [<A HREF="
pages/shareware.htm">Shareware</A>] [<A
HREF="pages/softcomp.htm">Software Companies</A>]
```

```
[<A HREF="pages/hardcomp.htm">Hardware Companies</A>]
[<A HREF="pages/mags.htm">Magazines &amp; Journals</A>]
[<A HREF="pages/drivers.htm">Hardware Drivers</A>]
</FONT>
```

This code is very similar to what we were using before we added button images: I've reduced the font size to 1, and removed the <BR> tags between each link. Then it's a simple case of enclosing each anchor tag between square brackets, with a space separating the closing square bracket and the next opening bracket. For compactness, I've also replaced the word 'and' with **&**, the character code for an ampersand that we met in Chapter 4. The final result should look like the screenshot below.

▶ Adding
hypertext
alternatives for
users who won't
see the linking
buttons.

7

TABLES, THE NUMBER ONE LAYOUT TOOL

If the word *tables* has got you thinking of rows and columns of dull-looking data, you're on the right lines: that's what HTML tables were originally planned for. What makes them especially valuable to web designers is that a cell in a table can contain anything at all – text, images, another table, you name it – and its contents can be aligned separately from anything else on the page. This gives a similar kind of design freedom to that found in desktop publishing. Even without getting to grips with style sheets (as we will in Chapter 9) tables can be used to put things almost exactly where you want them on the page.

The Obvious Table

The easiest way to get started with tables is to create an 'obvious' table – a structured list of items grouped into rows and columns. This introduces the three tags that matter most in table creation: **<TABLE>**, **<TR>** and **<TD>**. Here's what each of those does:

<TABLE>   Used as a <TABLE>...</TABLE> pair to mark the beginning and end of a table.

<TR>   Used by itself to mark the start of a new row of cells. The closing </TR> is optional – browsers know that an opening <TR> tag indicates the end of any previous row.

<TD>   Used by itself to mark the start of a new cell in a row. Once again, the closing </TD> should be optional.

GOOD QUESTION!

Should I use closing </TD> and </TR> tags or not?

It's best to use them. In the examples on the first few pages of this chapter I've left them out for clarity, and because these are fairly simple examples all browsers will display them properly. The problem comes when you have tables with lots of cells or complicated layouts: whole chunks of table might go missing in some browsers if they don't have the closing tags to show where cells and rows finish.

```
You can contact some imaginary people at the email addresses below:
<TABLE BORDER=1>
<TR><TD>Anthony Turnip<TD>anthony@turnipfamily.com
<TR><TD>Duane Pipe<TD>dp@gutter.org
<TR><TD>Bill Stickers<TD>1045878@parkhurst.co.uk
</TABLE>
```

The code above creates the simple table shown in the next screenshot. The entire table is contained between <TABLE> and </TABLE> tags, and consists of three rows and two columns – in other words, each of the three rows contains two cells. I've placed the code for each row on a separate line for clarity.

◀ A simple 3-row 2-column table with visible borders.

You'll notice that I've added an attribute to the <TABLE> tag, **BORDER=1**. By default, an empty <TABLE> tag won't show a border around the table or any of its cells, and I wanted to make it obvious in the screenshot what effect those <TR> and <TD> tags were having. But it's the option of having those borders hidden that makes table such a great page layout tool: to hide the table borders, either remove the BORDER=1 attribute or set its value to 0 instead.

There are two other points to notice in this example. First, the table is aligned to the left of the page if we don't specify anything different. Second, it appears on a new line even though there's no <BR> tag after the sentence preceding it. In fact, if you add a single <BR> tag after the previous line you won't see any difference. To create some space above the table, you'd either use a <P> tag or *several*
 tags.

Edging your bets

I usually add a BORDER=0 attribute to table tags anyway. Once in a while you get a bit lost about which row or column you're working in, or the table doesn't display as expected, so you can just change the 0 to a 1, refresh the browser to see where all the cells are, then fix the problem and switch back to 0 again. (Incidentally, adding the word BORDER to the tag with no equals sign or value will also give a single-pixel border.)

Customizing The Table Tag

The BORDER attribute mentioned above is just one of the <TABLE> tag's attributes, and it's simple enough to work with: set it to zero to hide the borders or to any positive number to create tables with thicker visible borders. It's worth noting that if you remove the BORDER attribute, although no borders will be shown, the table will be laid out as if the border were still there: setting it to 0 regains the space that would have been used for the border.

There are several other attributes you can add to the <TABLE> tag that affect the appearance of the whole table:

This attribute...	..does this
ALIGN	Sets the alignment of the table on the page, using LEFT, CENTER or RIGHT. The default alignment is LEFT. (You can also do this by enclosing the table in <CENTER> or <DIV ALIGN=?> tags.)
BGCOLOR	Sets the background colour for the entire table (although individual rows and cells can override this using their own BGCOLOR attributes, as we'll see later).
WIDTH	Sets the width of the table either using an exact number of pixels (not usually a good idea) or as a percentage of the browser's width, such as WIDTH="80%".
HEIGHT	Sets the height of the table. You wouldn't usually use this, since the browser will automatically create a table tall enough to display whatever data it contains.

CELLPADDING	Sets the amount of space between a cell's four edges and its contents. The default is 1, so you can create extra space around a cell's contents using something like CELLPADDING=5.
CELLSPACING	Sets the amount of space between each cell in the table. The default spacing is 2 pixels.

Here are two modified examples of the table used in the earlier example. The first adds space around the table contents using cellpadding and cellspacing along with a thicker border; the second goes all out for compactness:

```
<TABLE BORDER=5 CELLPADDING=5 CELLSPACING=10 ALIGN=CENTER
BGCOLOR=#FFFFF0>
<TR><TD>Anthony Turnip<TD>anthony@turnipfamily.com
<TR><TD>Duane Pipe<TD>dp@gutter.org
<TR><TD>Bill Stickers<TD>1045878@parkhurst.co.uk
</TABLE>
<P>
<TABLE BORDER=0 CELLPADDING=0 CELLSPACING=0 BGCOLOR=#FFFFF0>
<TR><TD>Anthony Turnip<TD>anthony@turnipfamily.com
<TR><TD>Duane Pipe<TD>dp@gutter.org
<TR><TD>Bill Stickers<TD>1045878@parkhurst.co.uk
</TABLE>
```

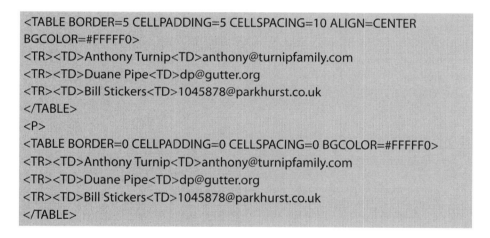

◀ Two very different ways of displaying the same information in a table.

Table Design With Internet Explorer

Internet Explorer versions 2 and upwards offer a few extra tricks with the <TABLE> tag. Most other browsers won't know what to do with these, so (as with all unsupported attributes) they'll ignore them gracefully.

BACKGROUND works like the same attribute in the <BODY> tag (see Chapter 5), letting you add a tiled image behind the content of all the table's cells.

BORDERCOLOR lets you set a colour to be used to draw the borders of the table and its cells. This will give a 2-dimensional (flat) look to the table.

With **BORDERCOLORLIGHT** and **BORDERCOLORDARK** you can choose two separate colours to achieve your own style of 3D table design: the first attribute sets the colour of the two lighter edges of the table or cell, the second sets the colour of the two darker edges.

▶ A 2D result using BORDERCOLOR in the first example, compared to a 3D result using BORDERCOLORLIGHT and BORDERCOLORDARK below.

And Back To Borders...

The <TABLE> tag has two more attributes that determine where and how borders are displayed: **FRAME** and **RULES**. FRAME determines how the outside edges of a table are displayed, and RULES sets the internal borders. The BORDER attribute must be included for either of these to have any effect. Unlike the Internet Explorer additions mentioned above, these are included in the HTML specification. Unfortunately, Netscape 4 and Opera don't support them, and Netscape 6 just leaves out a few borders that have little bearing on what your code specifies, so the end result is still that they're Internet Explorer-only effects.

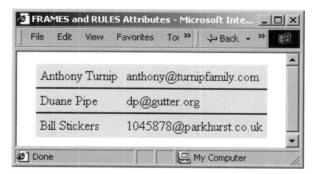

◀ A simple table with cellpadding set to 0 and the addition of FRAME=VOID RULES=ROWS.

The values for FRAME can be ABOVE, BELOW, RHS or LHS (borders at the top, bottom, right or left sides respectively), HSIDES (top and bottom borders), VSIDES (left and right borders), VOID (no borders), or BOX (all four borders).

RULES can be ROWS (horizontal borders between each row), COLS (vertical borders between each column), NONE (no internal borders) or ALL (all internal borders).

Rows: Just Containers For Cells

Compared to the <TABLE> tag, the **<TR>** tag that starts a new row in a table is pretty dull, so we can skip through its possible attributes quickly. Because a row is just a container for cells, the attributes for a row can provide a quick way of making settings that apply to every cell in that row. As we'll see later in the chapter, individual cells can still override these settings.

This attribute...	...does this
ALIGN	Sets how contents of cells in the row should be aligned, using **LEFT**, **CENTER**, **RIGHT** or **JUSTIFY**, which are all self-explanatory, or **CHAR**, explained below.
CHAR	If you use **ALIGN=CHAR**, the contents of each cell will be aligned to the first instance of a particular character in a cell's contents. Use CHAR="*character*" to specify the character used, such as CHAR="." to align numbers to a decimal point.
VALIGN	Sets the vertical alignment of the content in all this row's cells, which can be **TOP**, **MIDDLE**, **BOTTOM** or **BASELINE**.
BGCOLOR	Sets the background colour of all the cells in this row. This overrides any **BGCOLOR** attribute used in the <TABLE> tag.

Along with the four attributes above, you can also use Internet Explorer's BORDERCOLOR, BORDERCOLORLIGHT and BORDERCOLORDARK attributes mentioned on page 104, which will override the colours set in the <TABLE> tag.

BY THE WAY

Fonts in tables

If you display tables in Internet Explorer, you'll find that the contents of the cells use whatever font was set at that point in the page, as if you'd added another paragraph of text. Netscape and Opera, on the other hand, don't pick up the current font settings: every table cell uses the browser's default font unless specifically told otherwise. If you particularly want a certain font face, colour or size in your table cells, you have to include a <FONT> tag in each cell. (You can get around this much more neatly by using style sheets, which we'll come to in Chapter 9.)

Cells: What Tables Are All About

As you've seen in the examples earlier in this chapter, all the displayable content of a table appears in a cell – in other words, it comes after a **<TD>** tag. The <TD> tag has a range of attributes to set the appearance of the cell and its content: WIDTH, HEIGHT, ALIGN, BGCOLOR, CHAR and VALIGN, all of which we've come across already, and the Internet Explorer-specific

BACKGROUND, BORDERCOLOR, BORDERCOLORLIGHT and BORDERCOLORDARK. If any of these attributes is included in a <TD> tag, its value will take precedence over the same attribute used in the <TABLE> or <TR> tag.

The <TD> tag has two extra attributes of its own:

▶ **COLSPAN** lets you join several cells together horizontally to create a single wide cell that spans several columns. For example, COLSPAN=3 creates a single cell of three columns.

▶ **ROWSPAN** joins cells vertically to create a single cell spanning two or more rows, such as ROWSPAN=2.

Here's some code that shows how the COLSPAN and ROWSPAN attributes work, with the result shown in the next screenshot. The table contains four rows. The first row uses four <TD> tags to create four perfectly ordinary cells. In the second row there's a single <TD> tag with a COLSPAN=4 attribute making this cell span four columns (the entire width of this table). The third row contains four cells again, but the first <TD> tag includes a ROWSPAN=2 attribute: as long as there's another row below this one, this first cell will take the height of that row as well. Finally, the fourth row contains just three cells because the ROWSPAN attribute in the previous row has used one cell's worth of space.

```
<TABLE BORDER CELLPADDING=4 CELLSPACING=7 ALIGN=CENTER>
<TR><TD>ROW1 CELL1<TD>ROW1 CELL2<TD>ROW1 CELL3<TD>ROW1 CELL4
<TR><TD COLSPAN=4>ROW2 CELL1
<TR><TD ROWSPAN=2>ROW3 CELL1<TD>ROW3 CELL2<TD>ROW3
CELL3<TD>ROW3 CELL4
<TR><TD>ROW4 CELL1<TD>ROW4 CELL2<TD>ROW4 CELL3
</TABLE>
```

Tables In The Real World

As I mentioned earlier, for the purpose of making the examples in this chapter easier to read, and because HTML technically allows it, I've been leaving out the closing </TR> and </TD> tags. From here on in, I'm going to include them, and I recommend that you get into the habit too: although most browsers can render simple tables with these tags missing, once a table starts to get complicated you might find all kinds of odd things

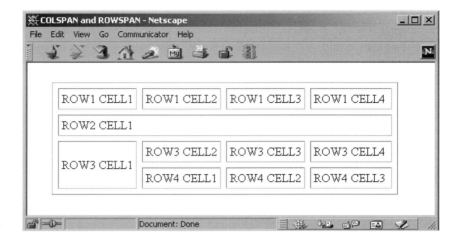

▶ A table using ROWSPAN and COLSPAN to create cells that span multiple columns or rows.

happening such as missing cells, missing rows, or missing content that should have been below the table.

A Typical Data Table

The code opposite creates a table displaying a typical kind of tabular data, pictured in the next screenshot. The data itself is pretty dull, but there are a few points of interest about the table:

▶ In the first two rows I've used empty cells (<TD></TD>). There was nothing to be displayed in these cells and by leaving them blank no borders are shown around them. To show the borders, just include a non-breaking space ( ) between the opening and closing tags.

▶ The <CAPTION> tag makes an appearance. If used, this must immediately follow the <TABLE> tag (although there are any number of other ways to place a text caption above a table of course). The caption will be aligned to the top centre by default, but you can choose from TOP, BOTTOM, LEFT and RIGHT for its ALIGN attribute.

▶ For effect in Internet Explorer, I've used the BORDERCOLORLIGHT and BORDERCOLORDARK attributes to swap the usual highlight and shadow colours, giving a raised-3D appearance. (If you look at the complete page on the CD-ROM, you'll notice I've also used a style sheet to set a few extra options. More about styles and style sheets in Chapter 9.)

```
<TABLE BORDER=1 BGCOLOR=#C0C0C0 BORDERCOLORLIGHT=#000000
BORDERCOLORDARK=#FFFFFF CELLSPACING=3 CELLPADDING=6
ALIGN=CENTER>

<CAPTION ALIGN=LEFT><B>Company Computers</B></CAPTION>

<TR>
        <TD></TD><TD COLSPAN=2 ALIGN=CENTER>PC</TD><TD
COLSPAN=2 ALIGN=CENTER>Mac</TD>
</TR>

<TR>

<TD></TD><TD>Desktop</TD><TD>Notebook</TD><TD>Desktop</TD><TD
>Notebook</TD>
</TR>

<TR ALIGN=CENTER>
        <TD>Office1</TD><TD>3</TD><TD>1</TD><TD>1</TD><TD>0
</TD> </TR>

<TR ALIGN=CENTER>
        <TD>Office2</TD><TD>0</TD><TD>0</TD><TD>2</TD><TD>0
</TD></TR>

<TR ALIGN=CENTER>
        <TD>Office 3</TD><TD>1</TD><TD>2</TD><TD>1</TD><TD>1
</TD></TR>

<TR ALIGN=CENTER>
        <TD>Office4</TD><TD>1</TD><TD>1</TD><TD>1</TD><TD>0
</TD></TR>

</TABLE>
```

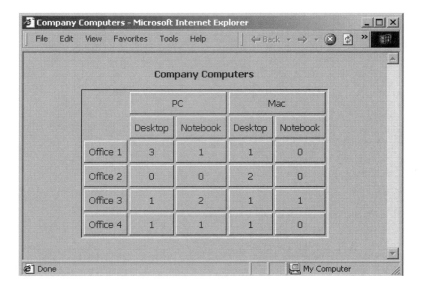

▶ A typical table that uses column spanning, empty cells, and a <CAPTION> tag.

Page Layout Using Tables

The next example uses a table for layout only. It consists of two rows, each with three cells. In the first row the middle cell is empty, and in the second row the two outer cells are empty. The three cells that do contain something useful are all identical: their content is aligned to the centre and vertically aligned to the top.

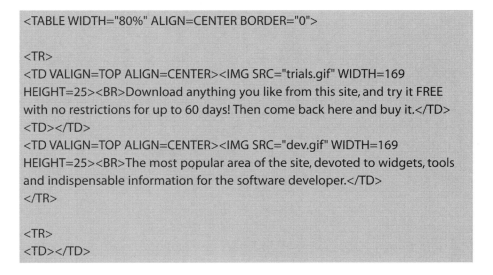

```
<TABLE WIDTH="80%" ALIGN=CENTER BORDER="0">

<TR>
<TD VALIGN=TOP ALIGN=CENTER><IMG SRC="trials.gif" WIDTH=169
HEIGHT=25><BR>Download anything you like from this site, and try it FREE
with no restrictions for up to 60 days! Then come back here and buy it.</TD>
<TD></TD>
<TD VALIGN=TOP ALIGN=CENTER><IMG SRC="dev.gif" WIDTH=169
HEIGHT=25><BR>The most popular area of the site, devoted to widgets, tools
and indispensable information for the software developer.</TD>
</TR>

<TR>
<TD></TD>
```

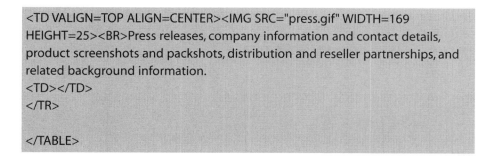

```
<TD VALIGN=TOP ALIGN=CENTER><IMG SRC="press.gif" WIDTH=169
HEIGHT=25><BR>Press releases, company information and contact details,
product screenshots and packshots, distribution and reseller partnerships, and
related background information.
<TD></TD>
</TR>

</TABLE>
```

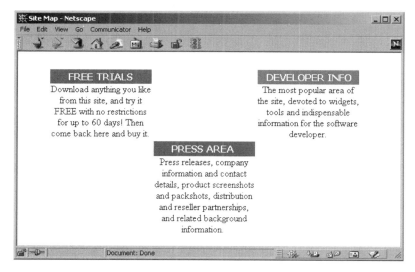

◀ Without tables, it wouldn't be possible to create even simple-looking layouts like this.

The table itself is centred and limited to 80% of the window width. This means that each column could be about a quarter as wide as the browser, making the paragraphs of text wider and with fewer lines. If you wanted to keep each column to the same width as the image, just remove the WIDTH=80% attribute from the <TABLE> tag, and add a WIDTH=169 attribute to the three <TD> tags containing text. The result will be a table of about 507 pixels wide containing three columns of unchanging widths.

Setting *fixed* widths for tables or cells (widths in pixels rather than as percentages) is something to avoid, other than in cases where you know the number of pixels you're specifying is small enough to fit into a reasonably-sized window. If you set particular widths for cells, remember that the width of a cell also sets the width for the whole column of cells it's contained in! If you try to give the top-left cell a width of 50 and the cell below it a width of 75, one or both will have to be ignored by the browser.

JARGON BUSTER

nested tables

A 'nested' table simply means one table created inside the cell of another. You'll come across 'nested framesets' in the next chapter which means a new set of frames created inside another frame.

A More Advanced Page Layout

In the next example, the table has been used partly for effect as well as for layout: I've used the BGCOLOR attribute of the <TD> tag to create a stripe of colour, and the WIDTH and HEIGHT attributes to make sure the stripe is always 20 pixels wide. I've also made use of the <TD> tag's WIDTH attribute in the first row: every cell but one has a fixed width, so when the browser's size is changed, the downward-pointing stripe at the right remains the same distance from the edge of the window.

▶ Three rows, six columns, and a little judicious use of the BGCOLOR attribute.

```
<TABLE WIDTH="100%" BORDER=0 CELLPADDING=0 CELLSPACING=0>
<TR>
<TD WIDTH=70> </TD>
```

```
<TD WIDTH=20 BGCOLOR=#3A6EA5 HEIGHT=20> </TD>
<TD WIDTH=20> </TD>
<TD HEIGHT=75 VALIGN=MIDDLE><IMG SRC="cfisoftware.jpg" WIDTH=366
HEIGHT=59></TD>
<TD WIDTH=20> </TD>
<TD WIDTH=120> </TD>
</TR>

<TR>
<TD WIDTH=70> </TD>
<TD BGCOLOR=#3A6EA5 HEIGHT=20> </TD>
<TD COLSPAN=3 BGCOLOR=#3A6EA5 HEIGHT=20 ALIGN=CENTER>
<!-- ... LINKS INSERTED HERE... -->
</TD>
</TR>

<TR>
<TD COLSPAN=4 HEIGHT=7 ALIGN=RIGHT VALIGN=BOTTOM>
<FONT FACE="Tahoma,Arial,Sans-Serif" SIZE=2 COLOR=#3A6EA5>
COOL FOCUS INTERNATIONAL LTD </FONT></TD>
<TD BGCOLOR=#3A6EA5 HEIGHT=20> </TD>
<TD> </TD>
</TR>
</TABLE>
```

GOOD QUESTION!

How do you go about planning a table like this?

The golden rule is to work out the maximum number of cells you're going to need in a row before you start writing. In this example, the maximum was six cells (used in the first row). You can then make sure that every row contains that number of cells, remembering to include **COLSPAN** figures too. The third row, for instance, has one cell that spans four columns, plus two single cells.

▶ The same page with a visible table border to show how the rows and columns are arranged.

8

FRAMES & WINDOWS

▶ **IN THIS CHAPTER**

Make links open new browser windows

Pick sensible names for your windows and frames

Meet the <BASE>, <FRAMESET> and <FRAME> tags

How to remove the borders between frames

Internet Explorer's 'floating' frames

Frames give you a different way of structuring your site (or perhaps just a part of it) by splitting the browser window into two or more 'panes', with each pane displaying a different document. In some ways these frames function like separate windows – for example, a frame can be scrolled if it contains a long document, or resized by dragging its border, and opening a document in one frame doesn't affect the documents displayed in any others.

Whether you use frames or not is one of those 'big decisions' you'll have to make about your site. Either way, you're not restricted to using a single browser window – any time it makes sense to do so, you can force a link to open in a new window. In this chapter we'll look at how frames are created, what you can do to change their appearance and behaviour, and, most importantly, how you can make documents open into particular frames or windows.

Working With Multiple Windows

Before we delve into the (slightly more complicated) world of frames, let's deal with windows. This gives us an easy way to get to grips with a new attribute of the <A> tag introduced in Chapter 4: the **TARGET** attribute. So far the only attribute we've used in the <A> tag is HREF, which gives the URL of the page to open. Because we haven't specified anything different, the new page replaces the old one in the browser when the link is clicked. The TARGET attribute lets you choose a different window (or, as you'll learn later, a particular frame) where the page should be opened, like this:

```
<A HREF="mypage.htm" TARGET=MyNewWindow>
```

When you click a link that includes the TARGET attribute in its anchor tag, the browser checks to see if a frame or window with the given name exists. If it does, the page is retrieved and opened into it; if it *doesn't* exist, the browser opens a new window and assigns the given name to it. The name isn't actually displayed anywhere in the window itself, so the name you choose can be as simple or as silly as you want it to be.

Let's take a simple example: make a new web page containing the code below and call it 001.htm. Next create three pages named 001a.htm,

001b.htm and 001c.htm, each containing some dummy text so that you can tell which page has opened where.

```
<HTML>
<HEAD>
        <TITLE>Main Window</TITLE>
</HEAD>

<BODY>
<H1>Main Window</H1>

<A HREF="001a.htm" TARGET=WindowOne>Open a window called
&quot;WindowOne&quot;</A><P>

<A HREF="001b.htm" TARGET=WindowTwo>Open a window called
&quot;WindowTwo&quot;</A><P>

<A HREF="001c.htm" TARGET=WindowOne>Load a different page into
&quot;WindowOne&quot;</A><P>

</BODY>
</HTML>
```

Open 001.htm into your browser (it should look like the top window in the next screenshot) then follow these steps:

1   Click the first link. A new window will open containing the page you called 001a.htm. This is because the browser couldn't find an existing window called WindowOne, so it had to create one.

2   Click the second link. As in step 1, you should have another new window containing 001b.htm, for exactly the same reason.

3   Click the last link. Because you *do* now have a window called WindowOne the browser doesn't need to open a new one. The page named 001c.htm opens into the window called WindowOne that was created in step 1.

▶ You can make a link open into a different window using the TARGET attribute in the anchor tag.

GOOD QUESTION!

How do you adjust the size and position of the new windows?

Using plain HTML, as we are in the example above, you can't: the new window will usually be the same size as the main window and placed slightly below it. If you fancy playing with JavaScript, you can set the size and location of the new window, choose whether it should have toolbars, menus and status bar, prevent it from scrolling, and more. Turn to Chapter 16 to find out how.

While we're on the subject, opening new windows is a great way to annoy people! Most users know that they can shift-click a link to open it in a new window and prefer to choose for themselves. You might want to open links to other websites in a new window, especially if your site uses frames – it's not good manners to load someone else's site into one frame of your own site. Otherwise, good reasons for new windows are few and far between.

Naming Frames & Windows

Choosing names for frames and windows isn't complicated – the rules are minimal, and basically just say that names mustn't start with an underscore (the underscore character is used by internal HTML names which we'll meet in a moment). Frame names are also case sensitive, so **windowone** isn't the same thing as **WindowOne**. (This is well worth remembering: if you're working with frames and your pages persist in opening new windows rather than loading into your carefully constructed set of frames, it's almost always a simple mistake like a missing capital letter in the name that's causing the problem!) To those 'rules', I'd add a few more:

▶ **Keep the names short.** Using *left* rather than *leftframe* means less typing, smaller pages and fewer chances to make mistakes. As with filenames, I'd also recommend sticking to lowercase so that you never need to remember where the capital letters are.

▶ **Make names simple.** *top* for a top frame, *left* for a left frame, and *main* for the frame containing the changing content, are all far easier to remember and understand later than *MyFrame* and *MyOtherFrame*.

▶ **Avoid hyphens and underscores.** Although names mustn't start with an underscore, at least one recent browser doesn't like underscores *anywhere* in a frame name. Why take chances? Keep 'em alphabetical!

You can also refer to frames or windows using the five names supplied by HTML explained in the table below. Notice that these all start with an underscore and they're always lowercase.

This name...	...refers to
_self	The same frame or window as the one containing the link being clicked. If you don't use a **TARGET** attribute in the anchor tag, this is the frame or window used by default.
_top	The window containing the link being clicked. If the window is split into frames, the frames will all be closed and the new document will replace them. (If the current window isn't split into frames, this means the same as _self.)
_parent	The frame or window containing the **parent document** of the current frame; in other words, the document that created the frame being clicked. If the current frame doesn't have a parent, this defaults to _self. Rather than using _parent, it's simpler to refer to the required frame by whatever name you assigned it.
_blank	A new window without a name. This will always result in a new window being opened: if you have three links with **TARGET="blank"**, the result will be three extra windows open after all have been clicked.
_new	A new window, but one that's reused by the browser. If you have three links with **TARGET="_new"**, a new window will open when the first is clicked, and the second and third will open into that same window.

GOOD QUESTION!

Surely I'd never need to use the '_self' name?

The _self name probably seems a bit redundant when you could simply leave out the **TARGET** attribute to achieve the same result. In fact, the only time you need to use _self is when you've used a <BASE> tag (see below) to set a particular frame or window as the default for all links but need to open a link into the current frame.

Setting A Default Target With <BASE>

Imagine you've got one frame or window containing a long list of links, and another frame or window you've called 'main' where those linked pages should open. Your page of links might look something like this:

```
<HTML>
<HEAD>
        <TITLE>Links</TITLE>
</HEAD>
<BODY>
<A HREF="page1.htm" TARGET="main">Page 1</A><BR>
<A HREF="page2.htm" TARGET="main">Page 2</A><BR>
<A HREF="page3.htm" TARGET="main">Page 3</A><BR>
<A HREF="page4.htm" TARGET="main">Page 4</A><BR>
</BODY>
</HTML>
```

Every link has to open into the 'main' frame, so every link needs an identical TARGET attribute. Surely there's a better way?

Yes there is, and it comes in the form of the **<BASE>** tag. This takes exactly the same TARGET attribute and sets the frame or window name to be used by default for any link that doesn't have its own TARGET attribute. The <BASE> tag goes into the head of the page rather than its body, so that link page can be changed to this:

```
<HTML>
<HEAD>
        <TITLE>Links</TITLE>
        <BASE TARGET="main">
</HEAD>
<BODY>
<A HREF="page1.htm">Page 1</A><BR>
<A HREF="page2.htm">Page 2</A><BR>
<A HREF="page3.htm">Page 3</A><BR>
<A HREF="page4.htm">Page 4</A><BR>
</BODY>
</HTML>
```

Does it matter where in the head of the page the <BASE> tag is put?

The section between <HEAD> and </HEAD> is very free and easy: the entire section is read and acted upon before the body of the page is dealt with, so wherever you place a particular tag the result will be the same.

Why Use Frames At All?

A common use of frames is to split the window into two: the smaller frame contains the site navigation, and the larger frame displays the pages opened when the links are clicked. Perhaps you can find a good reason to use a third frame – a fixed copyright notice, advertising banner display, company logo or secondary navigation – but you probably won't find *good* reasons to use any more than that. Remember that for each frame you create there's a document to be downloaded when someone visits your site! With this in mind, there are two main reasons for using frames:

▶ **To keep the size of individual pages to a minimum.** Navigating your site should be easy and obvious, so every page should preferably have links to all the main pages or areas of your site. This could amount to a hefty chunk of identical code in every page, so moving it into a single permanent navigation frame will make all your other pages smaller. (It also gives you just a single page to update if you add or remove a page!)

▶ **To keep a consistent style and feel to the site.** Most frame-based sites work on the basis that one frame updates when a link is clicked and the others remain the same, so the 'look' of the site hardly changes regardless of which page the main frame is displaying.

Frames don't suit every site, of course. If the content of more than one frame needs to change when links are clicked, the result might be more confusing for the user than sticking to a 'single-page view'. Instead of using frames, you could create a template file containing your logos, links and

Do all browsers support frames?

GOOD QUESTION!

Although frames are a recent addition to the HTML specification (they didn't become part of the standard until HTML 4.0), the popular browsers have supported them for some time – Netscape from v2.0 and Internet Explorer from v3.0. The result is that all but a tiny percentage of web users have frame support, but it's a good idea to include the <NOFRAMES> tag, covered later in the chapter, to catch the stragglers.

anything else that should appear on every page, then create each page from that template, ensuring that the whole site will have a reassuringly consistent style and feel. Alternatively, you may be able to use Server Side Includes (SSI), covered in Chapter 10, to create a single navigation page that's magically inserted into all your other pages at the correct point just before the pages leave the server.

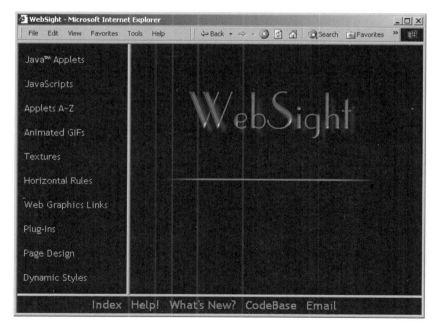

◀ A typical framed site: two permanent navigation frames and a 'main' frame for the changing content.

Getting Started With Frames

In the previous screenshot you can see a fairly typical use of frames, with the borders between the three frames clearly visible. The left and bottom frames contain links to other pages on the site, and the larger 'main' frame is where those pages will be displayed.

To build a site like this takes four web pages. Three of those you can see in the three frames, and they're no different from any other web page. The fourth page is the one that defines the **frameset** – it creates the frames and opens the required pages into them when the site is first shown. Appropriately enough, this is done using the **<FRAMESET>** tag.

Dividing The Window: The <FRAMESET> Tag

With the exception of the <NOFRAMES> tag (which we'll come to later in the chapter), the framesetting page contains no displayable content at all. As a result, it has no <BODY>...</BODY> section either: the body of the page is replaced by the framesetting code, so a template for a framesetting page would look like this:

```
<HTML>
<HEAD>
        <TITLE>Untitled</TITLE>
</HEAD>
<FRAMESET>

</FRAMESET>
</HTML>
```

The **<FRAMESET>** tag tells the browser that the window is to be split into frames, but currently it isn't doing any more than that. To define how many frames we want and what size they should be, we have to add either of two attributes to the <FRAMESET> tag: **COLS** or **ROWS**. Which of these attributes you use depends on whether you want to split the window into columns or rows, but both are used in exactly the same way:

```
<FRAMESET COLS="width1, width2, width3">
```

or

```
<FRAMESET ROWS="height1, height2, height3">
```

In both the code samples above, the window is split into three frames. In the first it's split into three columns of the specified widths; in the second it's split into three rows of the specified heights.

There are three different ways of specifying the width or height for a frame: as a fixed value in pixels, as a percentage of the entire width or height of the browser, or with an asterisk (*). The asterisk tells the browser to devote whatever space is left to this frame after creating the others. Each value is separated by a comma (and a space if you like to keep things tidy!). Here's an example <FRAMESET> tag that creates a window split like the one in the next screenshot. (Don't try typing this into your own page to test it just yet: you won't get the result I'm showing here, for reasons we'll come to in a moment.)

```
<FRAMESET COLS="25%, 80, *">
```

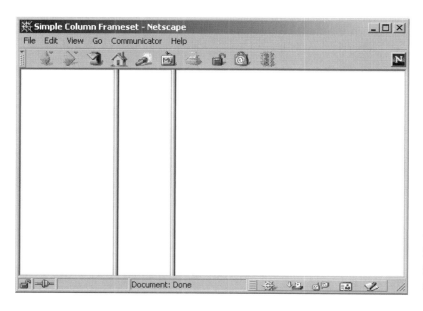

◀ A simple 3-column frameset using COLS="25%,80,*"

That line of code has split the window into three columns. The leftmost column occupies 25% of the size of the window; the middle column is fixed at 80 pixels wide; and the column on the right takes whatever space is left. If you resize the window, the width of the leftmost frame will change slightly, the rightmost frame will change more, and the middle frame will remain at 80 pixels wide.

BY THE WAY

Avoid fixed frame sizes!

There's only one instance when you might consider specifying a frame's width or height in pixels: when you know the maximum size of the content it will display (for example, an image of a particular size) **and** if the size is a lot smaller than the user's browser window would ever reasonably be. Otherwise stick to percentage values and use at least one asterisk in each <FRAMESET> tag.

Let's take another example, this time using the ROWS attribute: the complete tag is <FRAMESET ROWS="25%,*,25%">, giving the result shown in the next screenshot. The first thing you'll notice is that the asterisk doesn't have to be the last value defined: the browser has quite happily split the window into three frames where the outer frames occupy 25% of the window's size and the centre frame takes the rest. That leads to another point: why not just put 50% where the asterisk is? In the example above we could certainly do that and the result would be the same. However, it's good practice to get into the habit of always including an asterisk: that way there's never any risk of creating a frameset adding up to more or less than 100%.

GOOD QUESTION!

What happens if I use more than one asterisk?

Using multiple asterisks is quite valid. After the percentage values and pixel values have been determined, the remaining space is split equally between the asterisk values. For instance, the code <FRAMESET ROWS="25%,*,25%,*"> would split the browser into four identically sized rows. The code <FRAMESET ROWS="*,*,*,*"> would do exactly the same: as there are no numbers to work with, the browser splits its remaining 100% into four equal portions.

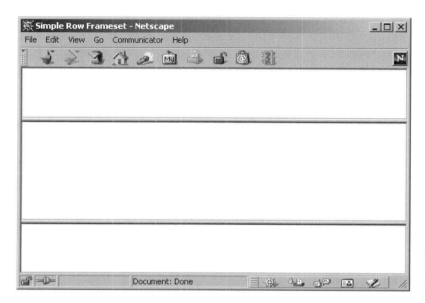

◀ A 3-row frameset using ROWS="25%,*, 25%".

Filling & Naming: The <FRAME> Tag

I've been cheating a bit in the examples from the previous section: although the <FRAMESET> tag and its ROWS or COLS attribute is required, alone it won't produce the examples in the screenshots. A frame can't be empty – it has to contain a document – and there's nothing in the code we've seen so far to load any documents. For this step we need to add a **<FRAME>** tag for each frame we created in the <FRAMESET> tag, like this:

```
<HTML>
<HEAD>
        <TITLE>My Frameset</TITLE>
</HEAD>
<FRAMESET COLS="25%,*">
        <FRAME SRC="leftframepage.htm">
        <FRAME SRC="mainframepage.htm">
</FRAMESET>
</HTML>
```

Two frames are defined in the <FRAMESET> tag, so two <FRAME> tags are needed to load documents into each. The first <FRAME> tag corresponds to the first value in the COLS or ROWS attribute ('25%' in this example), the second <FRAME> tag to the second value, and so on. The **SRC** attribute of the <FRAME> tag is short for 'source': it works in the same way as the SRC attribute of the <IMG> tag, covered in Chapter 6, specifying the URL of the page to be loaded into the frame.

The page in the example code above is complete: you can load this page into a browser and the two frames will be shown. Provided the pages specified in the <FRAME> tags really do exist, they'll be loaded into the frames, otherwise the frames will contain 'page not found' messages.

We're off to a good start, then, but we're missing out on something important: the frames don't have names, so if one of our pages contains links, we can't target the links to a different frame. That's easily fixed using another attribute of the <FRAME> tag, **NAME**, like this:

```
<HTML>
<HEAD>
        <TITLE>My Frameset</TITLE>
</HEAD>
<FRAMESET COLS="25%,*">
        <FRAME SRC="leftframepage.htm" NAME="left">
        <FRAME SRC="mainframepage.htm" NAME="main">
</FRAMESET>
</HTML>
```

If you want to try a working example, create a blank page called **mainframepage.htm** (a copy of your original HTML template will do for that), and a page called **leftframepage.htm** that contains links to a few dummy pages (if you followed the first example in this chapter you can reuse the same dummy files). In the head section of leftframepage.htm, add a <BASE TARGET="main"> tag. Then create a new page containing the code above and open that page into your browser. When you click the links in the left frame, the resulting pages should open into the main frame. (If you have problems, compare your code with the example in the screenshot below which, as usual, you'll find on the accompanying CD-ROM.)

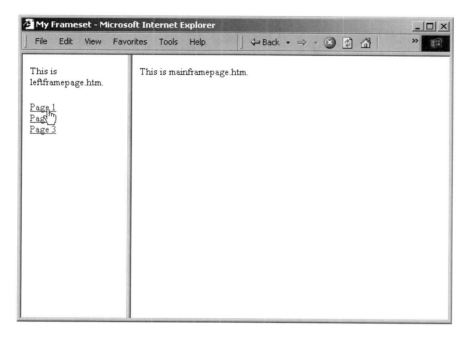

◀ A working frameset: links in the left frame target the main frame.

Title fight

BY THE WAY

With a bundle of web pages open, each of which has its own title, you might expect things to get a bit hit-or-miss in the <TITLE> tag department. In fact, when pages are displayed in a framed environment, their <TITLE> tag is ignored completely and the title of the framesetting page is used exclusively. This makes your choice of title for that page all the more important since it remains permanently on show.

Customizing Your Frames

The SRC attribute of the <FRAME> tag is *required* and must specify the URL of the document to load into the frame when it's created. The NAME attribute is optional, but you'll need to include it for any frame that you need to target from a link. Apart from those, there are a few extra attributes that you can add to the <FRAME> tag to customize its behaviour or appearance.

This attribute...	...does this
BORDERCOLOR	In Netscape only, this attribute can be used to set a particular colour for the frame's border. (You can also use this in the <FRAMESET> tag to set the colour of all the borders in the frameset.)
MARGINWIDTH	Takes a value in pixels to set the width of the left and right margins of a frame.
MARGINHEIGHT	Takes a value in pixels to set the height of the top and bottom margins of a frame.
SCROLLING	Takes a setting of **auto**, **yes** or **no** to whether the user should be able to scroll the frame. The default setting is **auto**, meaning that scrollbars will be added to the frame if the content is too wide or long to fit the frame; **yes** means that scrollbars will always be visible; **no** means that the frame can never be scrolled. Avoid using **no** unless you're absolutely sure that the content of a frame will always be fully visible without the need to scroll though it.
NORESIZE	By default all frames can be resized by dragging them. To prevent a frame from being resized by the user, include this empty attribute in its <FRAME> tag.
FRAMESPACING	In Internet Explorer only, this attribute can be used to create blank space around a frame by entering a value in pixels.

Making Borderless Frames

If there's one thing you're probably itching to change already, it's those borders. Perhaps you've even tried adding a BORDER=0 attribute somewhere (well it works with tables, doesn't it?). With frames the solution isn't quite as neat: Netscape and Internet Explorer each have their own ways of 'turning off' the frame borders, and both have to be addressed to cover all bases: BORDER=0 for Netscape, and FRAMEBORDER=0 for Internet Explorer. Internet Explorer also needs FRAMESPACING to be set to zero. Put it all together and add it to the <FRAMESET> tag to give something like this:

```
<FRAMESET COLS="25%, *" BORDER=0 FRAMEBORDER=0
FRAMESPACING=0>
        <FRAME SRC="leftframepage.htm" NAME="left">
        <FRAME SRC="mainframepage.htm" NAME="main">
</FRAMESET>
```

Adding those attributes to the example from a couple of pages back gives the result shown in the next screenshot. You'll notice that once the borders are removed it doesn't matter whether you've included the NORESIZE attribute or not – borderless frames can't be resized by the user.

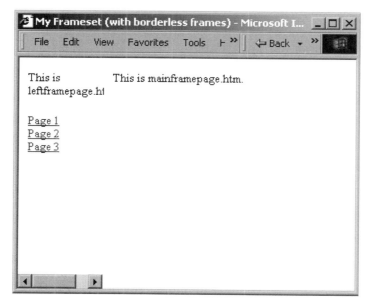

◀ The same working frameset example, this time with borderless frames.

You can also see a scrollbar in the left frame of the screenshot: forcing users to scroll too far on the Web is never a good thing, but in a frame-based site the appearance of scrollbars in a frame is ugly, fiddly to deal with, and should be avoided as much as possible. You could add the SCROLLING=NO attribute to the <FRAME> tag, but that's avoiding the issue rather than dealing with it: some users may *never* be able to see your last two paragraphs! Instead, try to ensure that your frame-based site splits its content into a larger number of smaller documents so that the likelihood of a page having to be scrolled is decreased. And (as I've failed to do in the screenshot) make sure each frame is wide enough to display its widest or tallest content: unbroken text, images, and so on.

<NOFRAMES>: No Site?

These days you'd have to walk a long way to find a web user who doesn't have a frames-capable browser. All the same, you don't necessarily want to ignore those people: at the moment their browsers don't understand anything at all on our framesetting page, so if they visit the site they'll just see a blank page!

We can put that right by adding a 'safety net' to our framesetting code. Somewhere between the opening and closing <FRAMESET> tags, add a **<NOFRAMES>...</NOFRAMES>** tag pair. Between these two tags you can insert ordinary HTML – as much or as little as you want to. For instance, you may want to simply add a note that your site requires a frames-capable browser, along with links to the Microsoft/Opera/Netscape websites, or you might want to create an entire front page containing links to your remaining pages. Browsers that don't understand the <FRAMESET> and <FRAME> tags will see this ordinary HTML and display it; more recent browsers will ignore the content within the <NOFRAMES> tags in favour of the framesetting tags.

A Complex Frameset

So far all our frameset examples have been simple ones: we've split the browser into columns or rows, but we haven't tried to combine the two. A good candidate for a more complex frameset is our long-running 'Computing Site Directory' site, last seen at the end of Chapter 6. The figure below shows the result we want to achieve; for complex framesets, as with complex tables, it's a good idea to scribble a rough diagram of what you're trying to create before you start.

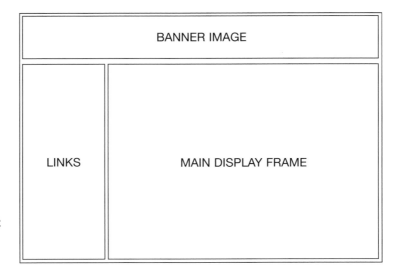

▶ A rough mock-up of the frameset we want to create.

Now we hit the first complication: do we use the ROWS or COLS attribute in the <FRAMESET> tag? The window is quite clearly split into two rows, the lower row containing the two larger frames, but there's also a column split between the two large frames. The answer is to see whether any frames stretch from the extreme left to the extreme right of the window: if they do, use ROWS; if they don't, use COLS. In this case, the top frame fills the entire width of the browser, so we'll use ROWS.

The top frame is just going to contain the banner image: it's a fixed size (58 pixels high), so we can set a pixel value for the height of that frame, allowing a few extra pixels for frame and page margins (and testing carefully in all browsers to make sure the frame really is tall enough for the image!). The remainder of the window is left for the frames below. So far, then, we can enter the following code into the page:

```
<FRAMESET ROWS="80, *">
        <FRAME NAME="top" SRC="banner.htm" SCROLLING=NO NORESIZE>
        <!-- more code here -->
</FRAMESET>
```

Now we've got a line missing from the code. Normally we'd put a second <FRAME> tag there to create the frame that forms the second row, but in our mock-up we've got *two* frames in that row. That means we need another <FRAMESET> tag instead. Putting one frameset inside another in this way is known as a **nested frameset**. We don't have to do anything any differently though: we just treat the remaining space as if it were the entire browser window. We want to split the space into two columns, so we'll use the COLS attribute in this frameset tag:

```
<FRAMESET ROWS="80, *">
        <FRAME NAME="top" SRC="banner.htm" SCROLLING=NO NORESIZE>
        <FRAMESET COLS="220, *">
                <FRAME NAME="left" SRC="links.htm">
                <FRAME NAME="main" SRC="home.htm">
        </FRAMESET>
</FRAMESET>
```

The left frame is going to contain our linking images which, like the banner, are a fixed size. That means we can set a fixed width of 220 pixels for the left frame, with the remainder of the window devoted to the main display frame. The resulting code goes in our **index.htm** page, straight after the closing </HEAD> tag. We add a <NOFRAMES> tag before <BODY> and a closing <NOFRAMES> tag after </BODY> so that visitors without frames-capable browsers will see the page as we originally built it. Finally, we delete the last </FRAMESET> from the code above and put it after the closing </NOFRAMES> tag instead.

Having created the frameset in index.htm, we need to create the three pages to be loaded into the frames. We're basically pulling lumps out of the original index page and dropping them almost unaltered into new pages, so this is fairly straightforward (and once again you'll find all the pages on the CD-ROM). In quickfire mode, here are the steps to be taken:

1   Make a page called **banner.htm** which contains just the <IMG> tag for the banner image between <CENTER> tags. You can also copy the <BODY> tag from the original index page to this one.

2   Make a page called **links.htm**. Into that, copy the block of code that put the linking button-images on the page, once again between <CENTER> tags and using the same <BODY> tag. In the head of the page, add <BASE TARGET="main"> so that all the links open into the frame called *main*.

3   Make a page called **home.htm** that uses the same <BODY> and <FONT> tags as the original index and copies the two introductory paragraphs.

All that's missing now are the text-only links that we used to have at the bottom of the page for visitors who couldn't see our buttons. As you can see in the screenshot, I've added a link to a text-only page with the code: <A HREF="linktext.htm" TARGET="_self">Text Menu</A>.

Internet Explorer's Floating Frames

Before we leave frames behind, here's a variation on the frames theme introduced by Internet Explorer in v3.0: the *floating frame*, otherwise known as the *inline* frame, which introduces the **<IFRAME>...</IFRAME>** tag pair. The word 'inline' gives a clue to its use: in just the same way that an 'inline image' is an image placed on an ordinary web page, an 'inline frame'

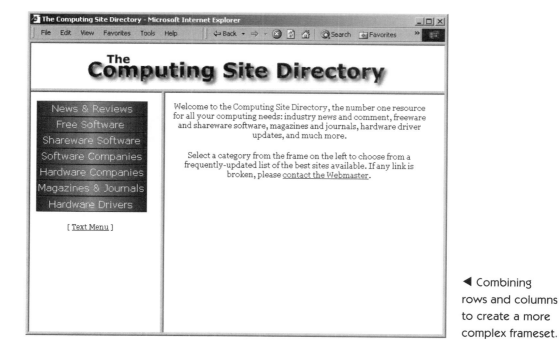

◀ Combining rows and columns to create a more complex frameset.

GOOD QUESTION!

What happens if I try to load another framesetting page into an existing frame or in a <FRAME> tag's SRC attribute?

Quite simply, it will work as planned. The frame's area will be split into the two (or more) frames in the new frameset, and you can refer to any of the new frames by name as usual. You can also still refer to the original frame by name and load another document into it. Bear in mind that you must choose different names for the new frames: you can't create a frame called 'right' inside an existing frame called 'right', for instance.

creates a frame on the page. The <IFRAME> tag takes the same **SRC** attribute as the <FRAME> tag to specify the URL of the document to be loaded into it, and the optional **NAME** attribute. Also derived from the <FRAME> tag are the SCROLLING, MARGINHEIGHT and MARGINWIDTH attributes, and the ubiquitous WIDTH, HEIGHT and ALIGN attributes lifted straight from the <IMG> tag. The remaining attribute is FRAMEBORDER=0, which turns off the 3D border around the frame.

Although HTML 4.0 includes support for the floating frame, Netscape 4.x and Opera don't, so its usefulness is limited. (It is supported by Netscape 6, however.) Fortunately you can add some alternative HTML to the page before the closing </IFRAME> tag and non-IE browsers will display that instead.

The code sample below shows the body of the page in the next screenshot. A floating frame on the page is displaying a page called 'home.htm'. If the same page were opened in Netscape 4 or Opera, the ordinary HTML between the opening and closing <IFRAME> tags would be shown. (Note that these tags *always* work as a pair, even if you don't plan to include alternative text: without the closing tag, the rest of your page will appear to have gone missing!)

```
<BODY>

<IFRAME SRC="home.htm" ALIGN=RIGHT HEIGHT=230>
<B>This is the text you'll see if your browser doesn't support floating
frames.</B><BR>
</IFRAME>

Here's some ordinary text inside an ordinary HTML page that just happens to
contains an &lt;IFRAME&gt; tag. <P>To the right is the result of that tag: a
floating frame containing a page called <B>home.htm</B>.

</BODY>
```

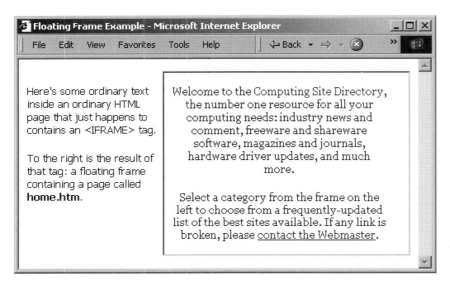

Here's some ordinary text inside an ordinary HTML page that just happens to contains an <IFRAME> tag.

To the right is the result of that tag: a floating frame containing a page called **home.htm**.

Welcome to the Computing Site Directory, the number one resource for all your computing needs: industry news and comment, freeware and shareware software, magazines and journals, hardware driver updates, and much more.

Select a category from the frame on the left to choose from a frequently-updated list of the best sites available. If any link is broken, please contact the Webmaster.

◀ A 'floating frame' in Internet Explorer.

9

STYLE SHEETS: EASY DESIGN & REDESIGN

▶ **IN THIS CHAPTER**

What are style sheets, and are they worth bothering with?

Create simple but useful style sheets

CSS property names and measurements

How to customize and create your own style classes

Move styles into separate files for complete flexibility

Tasty effects that only style sheets can produce

By now you've probably realized that HTML isn't much like desktop publishing in Serif PagePlus or presentation graphics in Microsoft PowerPoint: you can't determine precisely where items will be placed on the page, and if you can get everything the way you want it in one browser, there's little chance of it looking exactly the same in another.

That's not a limitation of HTML though: the whole point of a *markup language* like HTML is that content is king and stylistic options are only needed to make the meaning of the content clearer. A heading doesn't need to be 30-point extra-bold Arial in green and indented by 26 pixels to be recognized as a heading, it just needs to be bigger.

The trouble is, you want your heading to be 30-point extra-bold Arial in green, and you don't care a jot how a markup language is meant to be used! If that means wrapping every heading on your site in <FONT> tags, you'll do it. And if redesigning your site means editing 500 identical font tags, you'll do that too. But wouldn't it be nice if there were a quicker, easier and more reliable way to exert some control over appearance? Looks like you've come to the right chapter...

What Are Style Sheets?

The 'quicker, easier and more reliable way' comes in the form of **Cascading Style Sheets** or CSS (often just referred to as *style sheets*). Style sheets let you specify just once that a heading should be 30-point Arial in green, and apply that style to a whole page or, better still, an entire site. The result is a faster and more economical way to get a consistent appearance to a set of web pages, and gives you as little as one line of code to edit if you decide that all the headings on your site would actually look better in blue. Not only that, style sheets give vastly more control over the positioning and styling of any element on the page than HTML alone can offer, as you can see from the next screenshot.

A 'style sheet' itself is pretty much what it sounds like: a list of named styles known as rules that you define yourself and can then apply by name to elements on the page. Styles can be created in three different ways:

◀ Style sheets at work: try doing this with ordinary HTML!

▶ An **external style sheet** is a separate document containing the defined style rules. This document can be used by any web page that should share those styles by **linking** the style sheet to the document.

▶ An **embedded style sheet** is a list of style rules included in the head section of the web page itself. Those styles are accessible to that page only.

▶ **Inline styles** are styles added as attributes to ordinary HTML tags using a <P STYLE="*style info*"> or <H1 STYLE="*style info*"> tag.

BY THE WAY

The age-old compatibility question

By now you'll probably be expecting this: style sheets don't have universal support among browsers. The most reliable support comes from versions 4 and higher of Internet Explorer and Netscape, and Opera 3 or higher. Internet Explorer 3 had some support, but not enough to be relied on. Even now, some style properties are supported by one browser and not by another. The answer, as always, is to test in the browsers that matter before publishing, and (if you choose to) to include the minimum amount of stylistic HTML to make your pages look okay in older browsers such as Netscape 3.

141

Why Should I Use Them?

First and foremost, you should use style sheets because they give you the kind of control over the design of your site that you want. Second (and equally important) they help to reduce the size of your site, making it faster and more responsive: instead of bloating every page of your site with repetitive style-related HTML tags, you can shift all that information into one external document. Third, as you'll learn in Chapter 18, Dynamic HTML lets you combine styles and scripting to create pages that respond to user input or build themselves automatically according to what browser the visitor is using.

Finally, a large chunk of HTML has already been deprecated in favour of CSS: although browsers will probably continue to support them for some time to come, tags like <FONT> are on their way out, along with general attributes like ALIGN and BORDER.

JARGON BUSTER

deprecated

This means that the element has been marked for removal from the language in a future version and users are being given warning that this will happen. When something has been 'deprecated', users are encouraged to switch to an alternative method of achieving the same result.

Creating A Simple Style Sheet

To start with we'll stick with *embedded styles*, style sheets included in a web page rather than in a separate document. To define style rules in a web page we use the **<STYLE>...</STYLE>** tag pair somewhere in the head of the page like this:

```
<HTML>
<HEAD>
        <TITLE>Untitled</TITLE>
```

```
<STYLE TYPE="text/css">
<!--
style rules here
-->
</STYLE>
</HEAD>
```

One of the first things you'll notice about the added code is that everything between the opening and closing <STYLE> tags is commented out by being enclosed between <!-- and --> tags (see the *Commenting HTML Code* section of Chapter 4). This prevents errors in older browsers that don't recognize the <STYLE> tags. You'll come across the same thing when we look at the <SCRIPT> tag in Part 3.

GOOD QUESTION!

If the style rules are commented out, how can compatible browsers read them?

Code within the <STYLE> tags is written in the 'language' of CSS which is different from HTML. Browsers that understand CSS switch into that mode when they see the <STYLE> tag, and the <!-- tag is meaningless in CSS so the browser ignores it. Older browsers that don't understand the <STYLE> tag ignore that, and the next thing they see is a bunch of commented-out text which, of course, they won't display. If you want to comment-out lines of CSS, type /* as the beginning of the comment and */ as the end marker. The same comment marks are used in other languages including JavaScript and Java, which we'll meet in Part 3.

Now let's define a style rule for headings. If you wanted every heading in your page to use the Verdana font, the HTML way of doing that would be:

```
<FONT NAME="Verdana,Arial,sans-serif"><H1>My First Heading</H1></FONT>
etc...
<FONT NAME="Verdana,Arial,sans-serif"><H1>My Second
Heading</H1></FONT>
etc...
```

143

Let's create a style rule for that instead:

```
<HTML>
<HEAD>
        <TITLE>Untitled</TITLE>
        <STYLE TYPE="text/css">
        <!--
        H1 {font-family: Verdana,Arial,sans-serif}
        -->
        </STYLE>
</HEAD>
<BODY>
<H1>My First Heading</H1>
etc...
<H1>My Second Heading</H1>
etc...
</BODY>
</HTML>
```

The added line (shown in bold type) creates a style rule for the <H1> tag. The rule specifies that the <H1> tag should use the Verdana font if possible, so all <H1> tags on the page will do so without the need for font tags or repetition.

The format of a style rule always follows the same simple format:

tag-name { property1: value1; property2: value2; property3: value3 }

The tag name (minus its < and > signs) starts the rule, and is followed by property names and their values all enclosed in curly brackets. There's a colon between the property name and its value, and there's a semi-colon between each name-and-value pair (the semi-colon is optional after the last value). The use of spaces and carriage returns is ignored, as in HTML, and the property names aren't case sensitive.

If you copy the code above into a new page and open it in your browser, you'll see that everything else about the headings remains unchanged: they have the same colour, alignment and size as they would if we'd specified the font face using a <FONT> tag. When you specify a value for a particular property, you're effectively overriding its default value; any properties you leave out will remain at their defaults.

Let's test that by adding another property to our H1 rule. At the moment the headings in your browser are probably black, so change the style rule to this (not forgetting the semi-colon after the font-family property):

```
H1 {font-family: Verdana,Arial,sans-serif; color: #000080}
```

Look at the result in your browser now, and you'll find that the headings are navy blue.

BY THE WAY

Use the style type

Make sure you include the <STYLE> tag's **TYPE** attribute, with the value **TYPE="text/css"**, as I have in this chapter's examples. Although CSS is the default type of style sheet, Netscape browsers also support a second type, the JavaScript style sheet (**JSS**, specified as **TYPE="text/javascript"**), and get a bit confused if the type attribute isn't explicitly given in the tag. Property names in JavaScript style sheets are similar to CSS property names, but instead of a hyphen between two words of a name they capitalize the first letter of the second word (**fontSize** instead of **font-size**, for example).

A Few CSS Property Names

You can probably see that creating a style rule for a tag isn't rocket science: all you're lacking at this stage are the property names to use. Without further ado, then, here's a list of some of the most useful ones:

This property...	...does this
font-family	Specifies the names of the font faces to be used, in order of preference, such as **font-family: Arial,Helvetica,sans-serif**.
font-style	Sets the style of the font, with a choice of **normal** or **italic**.
font-weight	Sets the weight of the font, with a choice of **normal** or **bold**, or a fixed weight of 100, 200, 300, 400, 500, 600, 700, 800 or 900. (Normal is 400, Bold is 700. Others may actually be ignored in some browsers.)
font-size	Sets the size of font. There are named sizes (**large**, **medium**, **small**, **x-large**, **x-small**, **xx-large** and **xx-small**) or sizes can be given using one of the CSS units of measurement covered below.

This property...	...does this
font-variant	A choice of **normal** or **small-caps**.
text-decoration	A choice of **none**, **underline**, **overline** or **line-through**.
text-align	Aligns text with a choice of **left**, **center**, **right**, or **justify**.
text-indent	Sets how far text is indented from the left margin.
letter-spacing	Sets the amount of space between each letter.
color	Sets the foreground colour of text contained in the element. A hex colour (**color: #00FF00**), a colour name (**color: green**) or an RGB colour (**color: RGB(0,255,0)**).
background-color	Sets the background colour of an element using the same syntax as the colour property. (You can also use the shorter property name, **background**.)
background-image	Places an image behind the element using the syntax **background-image: url(*myimage.jpg*)**.
left	Sets the position of the left edge of the element.
top	Sets the position of the top edge of the element.
width	Sets the width of the element.
height	Sets the height of the element.
padding	Sets the amount of white space to be placed around the element.
z-index	Sets the front-to-back position of the element where 0 is the default value and higher numbers mean that the element is closer to the front (and, therefore, in front of elements with a lower z-index), such as **z-index: 5**.
border-style	Sets the style of border shown, with a choice of **solid**, **double**, **groove**, **ridge**, **inset**, **outset**, **dotted** and **dashed.**
border-width	Sets the width of borders, with a choice of **thin**, **medium**, **thick**, a percentage value, or a CSS unit of measurement.

That's not an exhaustive list of properties by any means, but it should give you plenty to go on with – you'll find a more complete list in Appendix D. Not every property can be used with every HTML tag (or *element*), of course: the font-style and text-align properties clearly have no place in an image tag, for instance, because an image doesn't have associated text, but they could be used in a style rule for a paragraph or a table.

What happens if I use a property that isn't supported?

GOOD QUESTION!

As with HTML tag attributes, if a browser doesn't recognize a property name you enter it will just ignore it. That may be because you've experimented with an inappropriate property in an element (such as **text-decoration** for **IMG** elements), or because you've made a spelling mistake. It may also be because you've missed the hyphen out of a property name: in this case, Netscape browsers may still recognize the property but Internet Explorer won't.

CSS Measurement Units: Even *More* Flexibility!

Quite a number of properties cover widths, positions, indents and sizes – properties that need a numerical value – and style sheets let you specify these as precisely as you want to by giving you a choice of units of measurement that you can use interchangeably. The two you'll probably want to use most are pixels (notated as **px**) and points (**pt**), but any unit can be used in any numerical property.

Unit name	Unit notation	Meaning
Pixels	px	A pixel is a single dot on the screen.
Points	pt	A point is 1/72 inch, the unit used to measure the height of fonts.
Picas	pc	12 points.
Ems	em	The width of the current font's letter m.
Exes	ex	The height of the current font's letter x.
Millimetres	mm	A figure in millimetres.
Centimetres	cm	A figure in centimetres (10 mm).
Inches	in	A figure in inches (2.54 cm).

Margins, Borders & Padding

These are collectively known as 'box properties', since they apply to content that exists in a block such as paragraphs of text (<P>..</P> tags), page divisions (<DIV>...</DIV> tags), images (<IMG> tags) or the page body itself (<BODY>...</BODY> tags). Separate margin, border and padding widths can be set for the top, right, bottom and left sides of the block using these fairly obvious property names:

▶ **Margins.** margin-top, margin-right, margin-bottom, margin-left

▶ **Borders.** border-top, border-right, border-bottom, border-left

▶ **Padding.** padding-top, padding-right, padding-bottom, padding-left

Margins can be negative values if needed. The border properties can set the style and width of the border (from the border-style and border-width properties in the table above) and set a colour for a particular border. Here's an example using the paragraph tag. Using this style rule and enclosing a couple of ordinary paragraphs of text between ordinary <P> and </P> tags gives the result shown in the next screenshot.

P { font-family: Arial; font-size: 11pt; margin-left: 15px; margin-top: 25px; border-top: solid 2px #0000FF; border-left: 6px #008000 double; padding-left: 1pc; padding-top: 3mm}

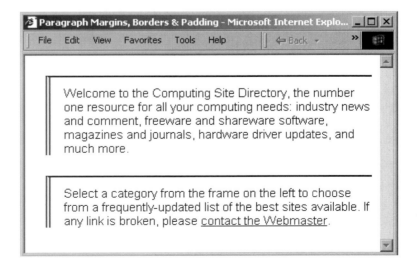

▶ The result of applying border, margin and padding styles to a page's paragraphs.

Building A Complete Style Sheet

A complete style sheet is simply a list of the rules you want to apply to particular HTML elements. As is usual for anything appearing in the head of a page, the order in which you define them doesn't matter. The code below shows an example of a style sheet containing five style rules. Let's look at each rule individually to see what it's doing, then see the result in a web page:

```
<STYLE TYPE="text/css">
<!--
BODY {font-family: Georgia, serif; font-size: 11pt; background-color: #FFFFE0;
color: #000080; margin: 2pc}
A {font-weight: 900; text-decoration: none}
I {background-color: #000080; color: #FFFFE0}
TD {font-family: Georgia, serif; font-size: 11pt; text-align: center}
H1, H2 {font-family: Tahoma, sans-serif; color: #800000}
-->
</STYLE>
```

▶ The **BODY** rule is setting a default font face and size for the whole page (the equivalent of enclosing the body of the page between <FONT>...</FONT> tags in HTML). It also sets the page's background colour to pale yellow (equivalent to <BODY BGCOLOR="#FFFFE0">) and the text colour to navy blue (equivalent to <BODY TEXT="#000080">). Finally we've used **margin: 2pc**: we can use this instead of using the separate margin-left/right/top/bottom properties to set the same 2-pica margin around all four edges at once.

▶ The **A** rule specifies that any links should have a font weight of 900 (the 'heaviest' available weight of bold text). It also sets text decoration to 'none', which, for ordinary text, would be redundant. For links, which are automatically underlined, it removes the underlining.

▶ The **I** rule specifies that any italic text in the page (text enclosed between <I>...</I> tags) should have a navy background and pale yellow text – the inverse of other text on the page.

▶ The **TD** (table data) rule doesn't appear to do anything very useful: apart from setting the text alignment it just repeats the same font family and size properties we've already set in the BODY rule. However, you may remember from Chapter 7 that table cells in Netscape and Opera don't inherit the font set for the rest of the page, so you had to include an identical <FONT> tag in every cell. Netscape 4 has the same problem even when the font is set in a CSS BODY style, but this time we can get around it far more economically: we just add a rule specifying the font to use in any TD tag.

▶ Finally there's a rule marked for **H1, H2**. This is a perfectly valid way of creating a rule that will be applied to two different tags. In this case, any H1 heading or H2 heading we use in the page will be shown using the specified font type and colour.

To see the result of using this style sheet, grab your template file to make a new web page, and copy the code above into its head section. Then copy this code into its body section and look at the result in your browser.

```
<BODY>
<H1>The Computing Site Directory</H1>
<TABLE BORDER=0><TR><TD>
Welcome to the <I>Computing Site Directory</I>, the number one resource
for all your computing needs: industry news and comment, freeware and
shareware software, magazines and journals, hardware driver updates, <I>and
much more</I>.

<P>Select a category from the frame on the left to choose from a frequently-
updated list of the best sites available. If any link is broken, please <A
HREF="mailto:rob@codebase.co.uk">contact the Webmaster</A>.
</TD></TR></TABLE>
</BODY>
```

Contextual Styles

By this point the power and flexibility of style sheets should be becoming clear. And it gets better: not only can you define exactly what italic text should look like, for instance, you can define what italic text should look like *when used in a heading*!

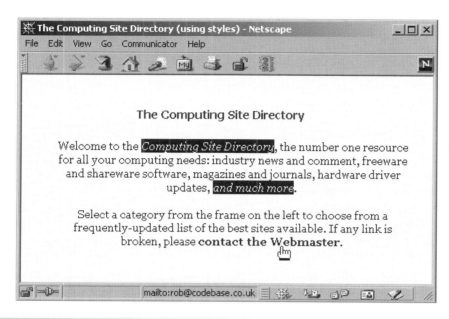

◀ Combining a complete style sheet with a complete web page.

```
I {color: #FF0000}
H2 I {color: #0000FF}
```

The first rule above simply states that italic text should be bright red. The second is the interesting one: it states that any italic text used between <H2>...</H2> tags should be bright blue. Clearly there's a clash between these two style rules: for italic text within heading tags both rules should apply but they're obviously mutually exclusive. However, browsers use established ways of deciding which style rule should take precedence, and rules for more specific situations win over generalized rules.

BY THE WAY

Comma or no comma?

Notice that in contextual style rules there's no comma between the tag names. If you were to change **H2 I {color: #0000FF}** to **H2, I {color: #0000FF}** this rule would now state that H2 heading text **and** italic text should be blue, rather than just italics used **within** a heading.

This type of rule is known as a **contextual** style rule: it defines how an element should be shown when used in a particular context. You can use it to great effect:

- ▶ **TD A {text-decoration: none}**. Links inside table cells shouldn't be underlined.

- ▶ **OL OL LI {font-variant: small-caps}**. List items appearing in an ordered list that's nested inside another ordered list should be displayed using small capitals. (See Chapter 4 for more on lists.)

- ▶ **B B {font-weight: 900}**. Bold text used inside a listing that's already bold should have a font weight of 900. As an example: <B>Bold text and <B>very bold text</B></B>. (Without this contextual style rule, of course, the inner pair of <B> and </B> tags is ignored, since the text is already bold.)

The screenshot below shows an example of a page using three different style rules for italic text: the two in the code sample above, plus **I I {color: #00FF00}** setting a different colour for italic text nested inside more italic text. The body of the page looks like this:

```
<H2>The <I>Computing Site</I> Directory</H2>
Welcome to the <I>Computing <I>Site</I> Directory</I>.
```

▶ Contextual styles let you set rules that will be applied only when a tag is used inside another tag.

Creating Your Own Style Classes

The examples we've used so far allow a fair bit of flexibility, particularly with the aid of contextual rules, but we're still a bit restricted. We can set a style rule for P tags that determine what a paragraph of text should look like, but what if we want an occasional paragraph of text to look a bit different?

The solution is actually very easy: we can *extend* the existing tags by creating our own named variations on them. Imagine we'd already defined a fairly plain-looking paragraph style like this:

P {font-family: Arial; font-size: 11pt; color: #000080}

We'd also like our document to contain a couple of paragraphs that have a border around them. We can do it like this:

P.boxed {border: 1px solid; padding: 5px}

We've created a new **style class** based on P and named 'boxed'. All we had to do was put a dot after the basic tag name, followed by the name we wanted to use for the new style.

To use the class we've defined, we add a **CLASS** attribute to the basic tag in the form **CLASS="*classname*"**. The CLASS attribute is a generic attribute that can be added to any tag that places something on the page or marks out a page section – <A>, <IMG>, <P>, <TD> and so on.

In the screenshot below, the text is split into three paragraphs, each enclosed between <P> and </P> tags. The second paragraph differs from the other two in just one respect: its opening <P> tag is **<P CLASS="boxed">**. As a result, this paragraph inherits all the properties of an ordinary HTML

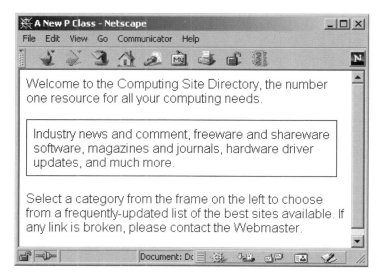

◀ You can define any number of classes based on existing tags and refer to them by name in the CLASS attribute when you want to use them.

153

paragraph, and the font family, size and colour set in the first rule for the P tag. It also has the border and padding we've defined for any paragraph using the 'boxed' class.

In a similar way we could define a class of bold text that's always green by creating a new bold-text class called 'green' (or something much less appropriate if you prefer – the choice of name is up to you!).

```
B.green {color: #00FF00}
...
Here is some <B CLASS="green">green bold text</B>.
```

So far so good, but what if you also wanted a green italic class, a green paragraph class and a green list-item class at various points in your document? One solution would be to create I.green, P.green and LI.green classes in the same way as the code above, but there's a much better way: create a class that doesn't extend any particular tag! Here's how:

```
<HEAD>
<TITLE>Untitled</TITLE>
<STYLE TYPE="text/css">
<!--
.green {color: #00FF00}
-->
</STYLE>
</HEAD>
<BODY>

Some <I CLASS="green">green italic text</I>, followed by some <B
CLASS="green">green bold text</B>.

<P CLASS="green">Now here's an entire paragraph of green text.</P>
</BODY>
```

Class names always begin with a dot (in fact that's the rule we've been using over the last couple of pages, but before the dot there was a recognizable tag name). Otherwise you don't have to do anything different. So instead of the P.boxed class we created on page 153 we could have created a **.boxed** class. That way we could still have used the <P CLASS="boxed"> tag wherever we needed a bordered paragraph, but we could also have used <DIV CLASS="boxed"> to put a border around a section of the page containing any content at all, or <MARQUEE CLASS="boxed"> to make a marquee with a box around it (see Chapter 5). Because the .boxed class doesn't extend a specific tag, it can be applied to any HTML tag you choose.

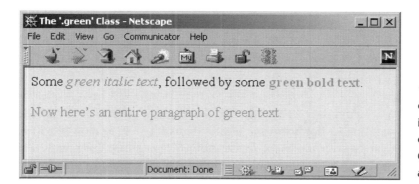

◀ Define a class of green text, call it .green, and you can add CLASS="green" to any tag you like.

Using & Reusing External Style Sheets

So far we've only worked with one way of getting style information into a web page, the **embedded** style sheet. The problem with putting style information in the head of a web page like this is that the style rules you create are only accessible to that page – if the rest of your pages should look the same, you'll need the same set of style rules in those pages too. And, needless to say, if you want to restyle your entire site, you've got to edit the style rules in every page.

A far more efficient way of working is to create **external** style sheets which can be used by any web page on your site. And it's easier than falling off a log: just move all the rules into a separate text file, leaving out the <STYLE> and </STYLE> tags and the comment tags, and give the resulting file a .css extension. You now have an external style sheet!

The second step is to *link* that style sheet to a web page. That just takes a single line of code in the head of the page:

```
<HTML>
<HEAD>
      <TITLE>Untitled</TITLE>
      <LINK REL=STYLESHEET TYPE="text/css" HREF="mystyle.css">
</HEAD>
```

The **<LINK>** tag tells the browser that an external file is to be read in conjunction with this page; the REL attribute specifies the relationship of the web page to the external file; and the TYPE attribute specifies its MIME type as "text/css" (just as in the <STYLE> tag). The only part of the tag you need to change is the **HREF** attribute which gives the absolute or relative URL of the style sheet to be read.

Apart from the fact that the style rules only need to be downloaded once when the visitor arrives at your site, using an external file will greatly improve your life as a web designer. You can link this style sheet to every web page on your site, refer to style classes named in the file, and at the drop of a hat you can restyle the entire site just by making a few changes to this one file (or, perhaps, several files if you prefer to split the rules into several files and use multiple <LINK> tags to link them).

I certainly recommend using external style sheets – it's easy, it's free, it's legal, so why wouldn't you? In much the same way that you created a directory called 'images', I'd suggest creating a directory called **styles** and keeping your style sheet files there. That way you can be sure that you've edited all the style sheets you actually use, and that you're not forcing visitors to download two identical style sheet files stored in different locations.

Using Inline Styles

Once in a while you'll want to do something special in just one web page, something that needs CSS to accomplish, such as making text overlap an image. You could create a named class (something like **.overlap**) in your external style sheet, or add it as an embedded style in the head of the page, but if you really do need it only once, it would be simplest just to type it into the tag it applies to.

This is known as an **inline style:** it applies CSS properties and values to the current tag using a **STYLE** attribute. As with the CLASS attribute, mentioned earlier, the STYLE attribute can be used with any tag that places content on the page or marks out a section. So to move some text upwards so that it overlaps an image placed above, you might place it between <DIV> tags containing an inline style, like this:

```
<IMG SRC="fan.jpg" WIDTH=248 HEIGHT=338>
<DIV STYLE="margin-left: 165px; margin-top: -210px; font-size:
24pt"><B><I>Everybody needs fans!</I></B></DIV>
```

The STYLE attribute is followed by an equals sign and the list of **property: value** pairs you want to apply, separated by semi-colons in the usual way with the whole lot enclosed in quotes. Because you're itching to know whether such a tasty effect really can be done that easily, the screenshot below shows the proof. Better still, it looks identical in each of the major browsers (you can check for yourself by opening the same page on the accompanying CD-ROM).

◀ Using an inline style to force text to overlap an image.

The 'cascading' effect

What is it about Cascading Style Sheets that **cascades** anyway? In fact, although it's a rather odd word to use for it, **cascading** refers to the different priority levels of the various types of style rule. External style sheets have the lowest priority, followed by embedded style sheets, followed by inline styles. So if an external style sheet contains a rule setting all **H1** heading text to green, but an embedded style rule sets **H1** text to red, headings would be red in that document. And if a particular **<H1>** tag includes an inline style setting the text colour to blue, that particular heading would be blue.

Fun With <DIV> & <SPAN>

Two tags that are more or less purpose-built to use inline styles are the **<DIV>** and **<SPAN>** tags. The <SPAN> tag is used to apply a style to some ordinary text within a paragraph, like this:

```
Here's some normal text. <SPAN STYLE="background: #0000FF">Here some
text with a blue background.</SPAN> And more normal text.
```

Using the <SPAN> tag here simply applies a blue background to the text it encloses. It doesn't alter the layout of the paragraph at all. (You can use <SPAN CLASS="..."> to apply a named style class instead if you need to.) There's really only one situation in which <SPAN> is useful: when you want to apply an effect that isn't available in HTML, as in the example above.

The <DIV> tag is a lot more useful. If you wanted to apply an inline style that indented a large chunk of content by 50 pixels, and that 'chunk' included images, paragraphs and headings, you'd have to apply the same inline STYLE attribute to all of them, or define a style class and apply it to each tag using CLASS attributes. In other words, you're repeating yourself, and in any form of programming you should avoid doing that if possible: it makes the code larger and increases the risk of mistakes.

<DIV> works a lot like the <BODY> tag, in that any amount of content and other tags can be placed between its opening and closing tags. So you can use this tag, with a STYLE attribute to define an inline style, to enclose that

chunk of content. The <DIV> tag automatically starts a new line for the chunk of content and whatever follows the closing </DIV> tag – in other words, it makes a *division* between this block and its surroundings. (It also supports an optional ALIGN attribute, as I mentioned at the end of Chapter 3.) So a simple solution to our 'chunk indentation' problem would be something like this:

```
<DIV STYLE="margin-left: 50px; color: #0000FF">
<IMG SRC="blah.gif">
<P>Blah blah blah...
<H1 STYLE="color: #FF0000">Big Blah</H1>
<P>More blah
</DIV>
```

There are two extra points of interest to the code above. First, although I've included a color property in the style, the <IMG> tag clearly doesn't support it. No problem – it's gracefully ignored for that tag and applied only to the textual content. Second, I've added a color property to the heading tag. This has greater priority than the same property in the division tag, so the heading will indeed be red.

Two Cool Tricks With Styles

To round off our look at styles, here are a couple of tricks you've probably seen used on other people's sites. The first is to place a background image in the centre of the browser (or a table) rather than having it tiled to fill the entire window. Here's the code to do it, and the next screenshot shows the result. Just replace the text squares.gif with the URL of the image you want to use. The background-position property takes two values setting the horizontal and vertical position respectively. You can set either or both values to exact pixel values or percentages of window width/height rather than using center if you prefer.

```
BODY {background-repeat: no-repeat; background-position: center center;
background-attachment: fixed; background-image: url(squares.gif)}
```

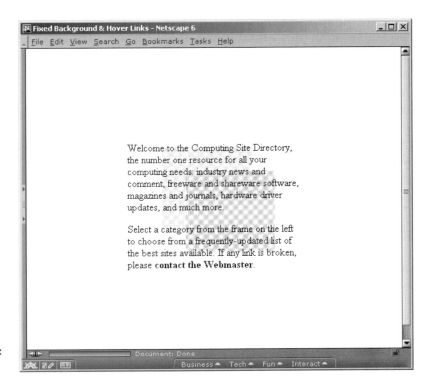

Welcome to the Computing Site Directory, the number one resource for all your computing needs: industry news and comment, freeware and shareware software, magazines and journals, hardware driver updates, and much more.

Select a category from the frame on the left to choose from a frequently-updated list of the best sites available. If any link is broken, please contact the Webmaster.

▶ A centred, non-repeating background image in Netscape 6.

There's a catch with this, unfortunately. Netscape 4 will happily display only one copy of the image, but places it in the top-left corner of the page.

The second effect is one ignored by Netscape 4 as well, but without any such irritating side-effects. This effect lets you create links that react to the mouse passing over them. How they react is up to you: they can change colour, become bold or italic, gain an underline, you name it. Here's the code that makes it happen:

```
A:link {color: #000000; font-weight: bold; text-decoration: none}
A:active {color: #800000}
A:visited {color: #808080}
A:hover {color: #CC0000; text-decoration: underline}
```

The :link, :active, :visited and :hover items are known as **pseudo classes**; these can currently be used only for anchors (there are a few other pseudo class names, but no browser yet supports them for any tag at all). The first three rules set the basic style of an unfollowed link, its style when clicked, and its style when you return to the page after following the link. We've specified that all links should be bold and not underlined. The **:hover** class specifies what happens when the mouse moves over a link: it changes to a brightish red and gains an underline. Experiment with these as much as you like. For instance, you could make the 'hovered' link italic, increase its font size, or give it a background colour.

▶ *Dynamic HTML combines CSS with JavaScript to add stylish effects and interactivity to your web pages. Skip ahead to Chapter 18 to find out more. Or turn to Appendix D for a list of CSS property names and available values.*

10

SHORT TAKES

Over the last few chapters we've delved into all the important areas of HTML, from the basics of putting text on the page and laying it out to more advanced topics like tables and style sheets. Just add a good idea and stir well. But before we turn our attentions to other aspects of web design, here's a quick look at some of the HTML-related options, tags and suggestions that didn't quite fit anywhere else.

Trim That <BODY>!

You may have noticed that the amount of white space around the inside edges of the window varies from one browser to another. If you haven't noticed, create a table in an otherwise blank page, set its width and height to 100% and its border to 1, create a single row containing a single cell, and put some dummy text in the cell. The borders of the table will be clearly indented from the edges of the window.

Once in a while you'll want to get rid of that white space, or at least limit it. The <BODY> tag leaps to your rescue with a set of six margin-setting attributes:

This attribute...	...does this
TOPMARGIN	Sets the size of the margin at the top of the page.
LEFTMARGIN	Sets the size of the left margin.
BOTTOMMARGIN	Sets the size of the bottom margin.
RIGHTMARGIN	Sets the size of the right margin.
MARGINWIDTH	Sets the size of left and right margins in Netscape.
MARGINHEIGHT	Sets the size of the top and bottom margins in Netscape.

Apart from setting all margins to zero, which is the way these attributes are most often used, you can set particular margin sizes to any value you like (measured in pixels). Note the last two attributes, used by Netscape: to achieve a matching result across the range of popular browsers, you need to combine the appropriate top/bottom/right/left attributes with a MARGINWIDTH and/or MARGINHEIGHT attribute.

More Body Attributes

Here are two extra attributes that can be used in the <BODY> tag, both of which apply only to Internet Explorer browsers.

The first can be used in conjunction with the BACKGROUND attribute (see page 71), which places a tiled background image on the page. Adding **BGPROPERTIES=FIXED** to the <BODY> tag forces the background to behave like a watermark: when the page is scrolled, the image stays still and the content scrolls over it. This is a hard trick for the browser to pull off, and it can cause some quite noticeable flickering during scrolling. If you decide to use it, try to pick a very simple background image rather than a strongly patterned or highly coloured one.

The second attribute allows you to switch off scrolling for the page, preventing the appearance of scrollbars: just add **SCROLL=NO**. This is similar to the SCROLLING attribute of the <FRAME> tag (see page 130) – it's there if you need it, but it has the potential for making the bottom of your page unreadable, so use it with caution!

Tooltip Titles

In Chapter 6 I recommended the use of the ALT attribute in <IMG> tags to provide a text alternative for users who won't see the images. The same option is available for any tag at all, using the recently-added **TITLE** attribute: you can add this to <DIV> or <P> tags to provide a tooltip message when the mouse pauses over a particular area or paragraph, <H?> and <A> tags to provide hints for headings and links, or even <B> tags to provide a tooltip for a piece of bold text. If you need to provide a hint for text that doesn't have a handy tag enclosing it already, you can use the <SPAN> tag (mentioned on page 158) like this:

```
I used to have a <SPAN TITLE="Its name was Colin">hamster</SPAN>,
but it died.
```

This attribute applies to Internet Explorer 4, Netscape 6, Opera 5, and later versions. As you can see from the 'Bold text' tooltip in the next screenshot, the most specific uses of TITLE have priority. Although the first paragraph

165

has been titled in its opening <P> tag, you still see the tooltip for the <B> tag when you move over its text. (Remember that users won't know there's a tooltip without hovering over the text, though!)

▶ A composite shot showing the results of using the TITLE attribute in heading, paragraph, bold and anchor tags.

GOOD QUESTION!

Why would I use the TITLE attribute?

Marking whole blocks of content with a tooltip title makes little sense and may well just irritate your users. A use of TITLE I like best is for links: you could use a title to tell the user that a link is to a page on an external site, downloads a file of a certain size, or opens in a new window. However, these are all things that could (and perhaps should) be explained in a more reliable way.

Link Anchors Within Pages

We covered all the important aspects of links and the <A> (anchor) tag in Chapter 4 – linking to sites, linking to specific pages on your own site and external sites, and email links. Here's one more way you can use the anchor tag: rather than linking to a particular page, you can link to a particular *part* of a page. When the link is clicked, the new page loads and immediately scrolls to the targeted section.

There are two steps to making this happen. First you need to put a 'marker' at the desired point in the target page, which is done using the **NAME** attribute of the <A> tag:

```
<A NAME="recipe4"><H1>Pickled Kangaroo</H1></A>
```

Here we've got a heading enclosed by an <A NAME="..."> tag which assigns this part of the page the name **recipe4**. The name you choose must be unique within the page, it mustn't contain spaces, and it's case sensitive (so it makes sense to use lowercase characters only).

Let's assume this code was in a page called recipes.htm. In a different page, you could add a link to open recipes.htm *and* jump to this particular recipe like this:

```
Grab a jumper and look at my <A HREF="recipes.htm#recipe4">pickled kangaroo recipe</A>.
```

The link doesn't look much different from others we've used. To link to a named marker in a page, just add a hash sign straight after the URL, followed by the name of the marker.

If you want to jump to a marker in the *current* page, simply leave out the URL. If our recipes.htm page had a list of the recipes it contained at the top of the page, you could provide a quick link that jumped down to this one using:

```
<A HREF="#recipe4">Pickled Kangaroo</A>
```

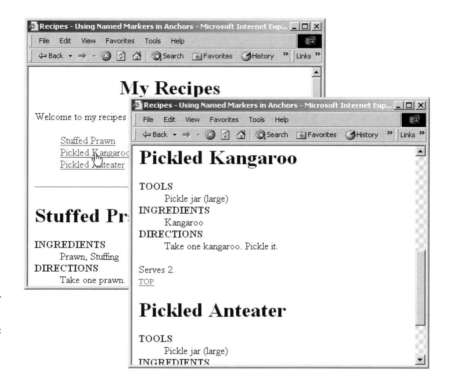

▶ Use <A NAME> to link to named parts of the same (or a different) web page.

There are two final points to note on this topic: if the marker you try to link to doesn't exist, it'll be ignored and the page will open as if no #name marker were added to the URL. This leads to the second point: you can use this behaviour to provide links back to the top of a long page at various points. Just include <A HREF="#top">Back To Top</A> and, as you haven't defined a marker with this name, the page will be scrolled back to the top.

GOOD QUESTION!

Why do links to markers in the same page show in 'visited' colour?

When you provide links to markers in the same page, the browser knows that these are effectively links to the current page. Because you're reading that page now, any links to it (including those within it) must have been visited. You can force a different colour by adding a STYLE="color:#0000FF" attribute to the link.

Embedding Pages With SSI

One of the most important considerations in designing a website is making it easy to navigate. Ideally a visitor should be able to jump straight from one page to another without endless clicks on the Back and Forward buttons to search out your list of links. One way to do this is to place the menu of links in a permanent frame (see Chapter 8). If you prefer not to use frames but want to achieve the same result, SSI (or Server Side Includes) may provide an alternative. I say 'may' because not all web servers support SSI: if you like the idea, either give it a try with a test page, or have a chat with your web host.

If you can use it, SSI solves the problem of including an identical menu in every page, and updating all those pages whenever you need to add or alter a link. Create one page with the menu in place, and check it to make sure it looks just as you want it. Then remove the entire menu section and paste it into a new web page (we'll assume you call it menu.htm). Where the menu appeared in the first page, place this code instead:

```
<!--#include virtual="menu.htm"-->
```

Finally, change the extension of the page containing this SSI tag to .shtml. When someone views your page, the web server will replace the SSI tag with the code in the page referred to by the URL. By including a similar tag in all your pages, you can include the same menu in each while still having just one copy of the menu itself to maintain.

Breadcrumbs: The Hansel & Gretel Concept

Still on the subject of navigation, here's a popular idea that does two jobs in one: it shows your visitors whereabouts they are in your site, *and* lets them jump to a different section. This tends to be used in large sites with a directory structure, such as Yahoo! (shown in the next screenshot).

The name 'breadcrumbs' is taken from the Hansel & Gretel fairytale in which two children venture into the woods, leaving a trail of breadcrumbs behind them to help them find their way home again. In web design the concept is just the same, although it doesn't involve sacrificing your lunch. Using the sketched-out structure of your site, you work out the path a user would take from the home page to any other, and place a list of links to each step along the path at the top of each page.

▶ Yahoo!'s use of breadcrumbs helps you see where you are and (perhaps) how you got here.

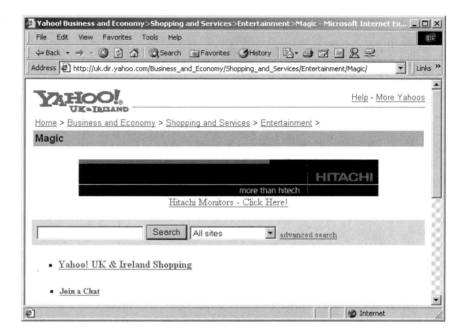

As you can see in the screenshot, the path we're expected to have taken through Yahoo!'s categories is shown at the top of the page, with a link to each category. The catch is that we may have actually arrived at this page by a quite different route, but the breadcrumbs still give a context to the page, as well as offering links to related or more generalized topics.

Timed Reloads & Gateway Pages

Inviting the user to click links isn't the only way to move from page to page in your site. There are several ways involving scripting (which we'll come to in Part 3), and another somewhat simpler way: **meta refresh**. This involves placing a **<META>** tag like this somewhere in the head of the page:

```
<META HTTP-EQUIV="REFRESH" CONTENT="1; URL=flags2.htm">
```

When the page begins to load, an invisible timer counts down the seconds from the first value in the CONTENT attribute (just one second in this example). When the required number of seconds has passed, the browser automatically links to the URL in the CONTENT attribute's second value. On first sight this probably looks like a great way to irritate your users, and it certainly could be. (In fact, I've included a tricksy example in this chapter's folder on the CD-ROM.)

There's another use for meta refresh which is less irritating and does have a stylistic value: the **gateway page**. This is usually a simple page used as the front page of your site (generally the index.htm or default.htm page in the root directory of the site), and it contains just your logo, neatly centred. To this you add a similar <META> tag, with a delay of three or four seconds, linking to the main page of your site. For a belt-and-braces approach, make your logo act as a link and add a text link as well, so that regular visitors don't have to wait at the door every time they come.

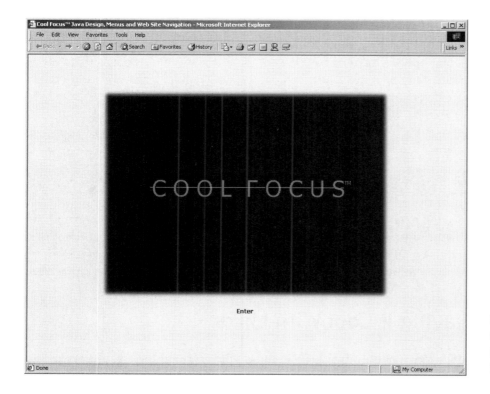

◀ A gateway page offers an easy way to make a stylish first impression.

A gateway page is a bit like the cover of a book: it doesn't do anything useful by itself, but it gives a hint at what's inside. If you like the idea, go ahead and use it; in Chapter 17 we'll look at a way to add some practicality to the style by swapping the <META> tag for some script that can identify different browsers and direct each to a custom-written page.

BY THE WAY

So why the blank page...?

Make sure you keep the size of the gateway page's image very small (20 Kb is an absolute maximum). Otherwise users will see a blank page and be whisked to the next before the image has even downloaded!

More With Meta: Page Expiry

When someone visits your site, their browser stores a copy of each page they visit in their cache, and usually reloads the same page from the cache on their next visit (although the exact browser behaviour depends on which caching options the user has chosen). If your site contains pages that you update daily or weekly, how can you be sure visitors really are seeing their newest versions?

The secret is to *pre-expire* the pages using another handy <META> tag option, like this:

```
<META HTTP-EQUIV="Expires" CONTENT="Fri, 01 Jan 1999 00:00:01 GMT">
```

Since the page has expired as soon as it's loaded, it won't be cached and the browser will be forced to fetch the page from your site again next time the user visits. Of course, you can change the date to anything you like, perhaps to specify a future date when you know the current page will be replaced.

Playing It Cool With Links

Here's a rule of thumb to keep in mind while writing the text of your pages: if you ever find yourself thinking the words *Click here*, think again! A book doesn't include the words *Turn the page here*; the instructions are implicit in the design. The same should be true of your website. If the user can see that particular text is a link, the context should make clear what information the link will lead to, and the user can either click or continue reading without picking his or her way through a minefield of instructions.

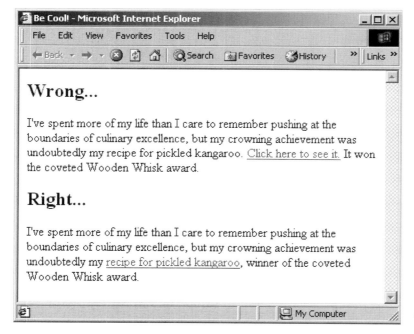

◀ The right way (on two counts) to be cool with your inline links.

Notice that in the screenshot's second example I didn't just link the words 'pickled kangaroo'. By including the words 'recipe for', I'm making it clear that this is a link to a recipe, not to information about pickled kangaroos.

Ins & Outs Of Punctuation

On a similar subject, remember that punctuation should usually be placed *outside* the anchor tags. Punctuation that precedes or follows a link refers to the sentence rather than the link itself, and it shouldn't receive the same formatting. Even if a link forms a complete sentence (as in the first example in the screenshot above), its full-stop belongs to the paragraph. Only when an entire paragraph acts as a link would you keep its final full-stop inside the anchor tags.

PART

2

GRAPHICS & MULTIMEDIA

▶ **IN THIS PART**

11

WEB GRAPHICS: THE BASICS

▶ **IN THIS CHAPTER**

Page weight or page *wait*? How to judge the size of your pages

Find free graphics instead of creating your own

Choose your software, filters & effects

Meet GIF & JPEG, the Web's two graphics formats

Get to grips with colour palettes and dithering

The goal of web design is to make someone visit *twice*. As always, content is king, and if you offer something worth having (and update it regularly) return visits are on the cards. You can gain brownie points by making the site attractive, easy to navigate, fast and stylish. Conversely, you can give visitors a good reason *not* to come back by not doing these things, or by overdoing some of them.

Over the next few chapters, we'll look at some of the graphical and multimedia elements you can use – images, animations, sounds and Java applets, among others – and how to work with them. I'll also tell you what software you need, and we'll fire it up and find out how it works. In short, we'll aim for some of those 'attractive and stylish' brownie points. We'll try to do it without irritating anyone, of course, so I'll issue the odd warning along the way. In fact, here's one now.

What's The Page Wait?

Before you get too carried away with the possibilities of adding graphics and multimedia elements to your pages, let me introduce a new term: **page weight**. The 'weight' of a page is the combined size of the page itself and any style sheets, script files, Java applets, sounds and (most significantly) images that have to be downloaded to display the page. It's a good term to say out loud every once in a while: it sounds like 'page wait', which is what it really means.

GOOD QUESTION!

How can I find out the page weight?

You can find the size of any file in Windows by right-clicking it and choosing Properties, or by selecting one or more files and looking at their combined size in the status bar of the folder window. On a Mac, Control+click a file and choose Get Info. For weight purposes, always assume that nothing on the page has been cached.

The mathematics of page loading time are not an exact science. Some of the files used by the page may have been downloaded before and can be loaded from the cache (see page 74); for others, the visitor's computer has to connect to the web server to fetch them, and the time taken to connect is variable. In addition, of course, some users may be surfing with an old, slow modem while others are using a fast ADSL connection.

As a general rule, unless you know different, assume that the average user has a 56 Kbps modem, and aim for a maximum page weight of about 50 Kb (kilobytes). The maximum speed of this modem is about 50,000 bits per second, meaning that your content downloads at around 6 Kb per second on a good day with the wind behind it.

Help! I'm Artistically Challenged!

We can't all be good artists (I'm pretty awful, in fact), but modern graphics programs offer a lot of features to help the graphically inept produce amazing results. All it takes is the ability to recognize what's effective when you see it, and to spend some time getting to know your chosen software.

If you really can't be tempted into experimenting, though, there are plenty of ways to get your hands on free artwork for the Web. One of those is the Web itself, of course, and I've included a list of sites offering free graphics in Appendix F. If you have one of the WYSIWYG site creation programs I mentioned in Chapter 2, you may be able to use the graphics provided with the software's templates. If you have an Office suite such as Microsoft Office, Microsoft Works or Lotus SmartSuite, you may be able to use images from their clip-art galleries. You can also buy CD-ROMs containing thousands of examples of free-use graphics, although the quality of these can vary enormously.

BY THE WAY

Check the format!

If you use graphics or photographs that haven't been specifically designed for web use, they probably won't be in the correct format. Check the file extension, and if it isn't .gif, .jpg or .jpeg you'll need to convert them (see page 182).

If you have a scanner, you can scan photographs or graphics you've created on paper. Most good graphics programs have an **Acquire** option among their menus: clicking that will start the scanning process and load the finished result into the graphics software for touching up and saving in the correct format for the Web.

What Do I Need?

To create and edit images for use on the Web, you'll need a graphics program capable of working with GIF and JPEG formats (which I'll explain in a moment). These are very common formats, so you may find that the software bundled with your operating system (such as Windows Paint) or your scanner or printer (Adobe PhotoDeluxe, perhaps) will do the job.

Graphics is one area where the quality of the tool can make a lot of difference to the quality of the result, so here are three of the tools used by most professional designers:

▶ **Adobe PhotoShop** from **http://www.adobe.com**, a heavyweight program for all types of graphics work, including desktop publishing (although a 'light' edition is available).

▶ **Macromedia Fireworks** from **http://www.macromedia.com**, a simpler and cheaper program aimed at web graphics creation, with many useful features.

▶ **Paint Shop Pro** from **http://www.digitalworkshop.co.uk**, one of the most popular graphics tools among web designers, with an animation program included.

Both Fireworks and Paint Shop Pro can be downloaded on 30-day trials, so I'd recommend starting with one of these. For our dealings with graphics, I'm going to plump for Paint Shop Pro, which you'll find on the accompanying CD-ROM.

◀ Create text shadows and other effects easily with filters like Eye Candy's Shadowlab tool.

Plug-ins & Filters

Filters are processing tools that create particular special effects such as shadows, textures, cutouts and mosaics, and most good graphics programs (including the three mentioned above) come with a range of built-in filters. You can never have too much of a good thing, though, so an industry has sprung up to provide extra filters that can 'plug in' to your graphics application.

Adobe PhotoShop pioneered the use of plug-ins, and the majority of the filters available are aimed at PhotoShop users, but PhotoShop's plug-ins can be used with Paint Shop Pro and Fireworks too. A search on the Web for 'photoshop plugins' will lead you to a number of sites offering free or shareware filters, but here are three to start you off:

▶ **Eye Candy** and **Xenofex** are two of the best sets of filters you'll find, available from **http://www.alienskin.com**

▶ **Kai's Power Tools** (KTP) is a strange-looking but powerful beast from **http://www.corel.com**

▶ **Filter Factory** offers a huge range of free PhotoShop plug-ins at **http://showcase.netins.net/web/wolf359/plugins.htm**

GIF & JPEG: What & Why?

If you start Paint Shop Pro, open an image file or create a new image, and then choose **Save As** from its File menu, you'll see a long list of available file formats in the **Save As Type** drop-down list. These include BMP (Windows bitmap), Tagged Image File Format (TIFF), Windows Meta File (WMF) and dozens of others. Most importantly, they include **CompuServe GIF** and **JPEG**, and these are the two formats we can use in web pages.

▶ **JPEG** (pronounced *jay-peg*) stands for Joint Photographic Experts Group and, as the name suggests, it was designed for working with photographs (or more generally, images containing lifelike colouring and shading).

▶ **GIF** (pronounced with a hard or a soft 'g' according to taste) is an acronym for Graphics Interchange Format, and again the clue is in the name: GIF was designed as a format for computer-created images – pictures that typically contain blocks of a single colour.

These two formats have a lot in common, but most importantly they're both **compressed** formats. The information that forms the image is squeezed into a smaller file via some software wizardry, making the result small enough to include on a web page. This compression can achieve spectacular results: I've just converted an uncompressed 360 Kb image to JPEG format, resulting in a 12 Kb file with no noticeable difference in picture quality. (I've included the result in this chapter's folder on the CD-ROM.)

In many cases, converting an image from one format to another is simplicity itself: you just open the original image, choose **Save As** from the File menu, and select the new type from the **Save As Type** list. (The new file will have a different extension from the original, so you can compare the quality and file size before deciding which to discard.) The only spanner in the works comes when you need to convert an image to a format that uses a lower **colour depth** than the original.

Pixels & Colour Depths

In case you're new to 'pixels', they're the tiny dots that make up what you see on your computer screen. Every pixel is set to a particular colour, and the computer uses numbers to represent those colours. When you create an image in your graphics program, you're setting lots of pixels to particular colours and then saving the result as a long list of numbers.

You're probably aware that computers don't count like we do. We can use a single digit to denote the number 5, and six digits for the number 121,355. A computer needs to know in advance the highest number one of our image's pixels can have, and uses the same length of number for every pixel. If we decide an image can only contain two different colours, a very short number (just a single digit) can be used to hold the information about each pixel. When I explained the workings of colour in Chapter 5, I mentioned that you have 16.7 million different colours to choose from, and if we plump for photo-realistic results, where the image can contain any of those 16.7 million colours, the computer has to use a 24-digit number to store every pixel. That's the case even if the number is zero: to the computer it's 00000000 00000000 00000000.

From this it should be clear that you can make a saving in file size by creating an image that uses as few different colours as possible. Rather than using the word 'digits' as I have been, we use the word 'bits', and the maximum number of colours that can be used in an image is called the image's **colour depth**. So our photo-quality image has a 24-bit colour depth, and our 2-colour image has a 1-bit colour depth.

Colour Palettes

When you start work on a new image in Paint Shop Pro (or almost any graphics program) you'll be able to choose the colour depth right at the start. If you know you want to create a simple image using no more than 16 colours, you choose a colour depth of 4 bits and start work. Like an artist, you work from a **palette** of colours, and each time you use a new colour in the image, it's added to your palette. When you've used 16 different colours, you've reached your limit. You can change one of these colours to something different, which will change the colour of any pixels using the replaced colour, or you can increase the colour depth to expand the size of your palette.

BY THE WAY

Activate your filters

To apply a filter to an image, the image must be set to a colour depth of 24 bits. If you've previously reduced the colour depth, you can increase it to 24-bit colour without altering the appearance of the image. Differences only appear on changes downward.

In fact, it's easiest to start with a 24-bit image, giving you a palette of 16.7 million different colours to choose from. When the time comes to save the finished image, Paint Shop Pro can tell you how many colours you've actually used in the image (as in the screenshot below), and you can then change the colour depth to find the best balance between file size and image quality.

▶ After creating a 24-bit image, choose **Count Colors Used** from Paint Shop Pro's Color menu to see how many colours you've actually used.

184

Pick A Palette

The image shown in the screenshot above is one of the sample images provided with Paint Shop Pro. It has a colour depth of 24 bits, and PSP reports that it uses 17,069 of the 16.7 million colours available. If we want to use this image on the Web, we now have to choose whether to save it as GIF or JPEG.

▶ **JPEG images** are always 24-bit, so to save as JPEG we would keep our current palette and head for the Save option. JPEG's built-in compression works very well for lifelike, shaded images like this one, but tends to produce **artefacts** (see below) when dealing with areas of solid colour.

▶ **GIF images** can be 1, 4 or 8 bits (palettes of 2, 16 or 256 colours), so we would have to reduce the colour depth of the image before saving it.

This image is obviously a candidate for JPEG format: the high number of colours and the non-blocky style give JPEG's compression plenty to get its teeth into, giving us a small file and a result indistinguishable from the original. We could still try saving the image in GIF format by reducing the size of its palette to 256 colours or fewer. This leads us to a set of options about how the colours are chosen for the smaller palette, and introduces another term, **dithering**.

JARGON BUSTER

artefacts

These are small dots or blobs of a different colour which can appear on an image containing blocks of solid colour when converted to JPEG format. This isn't a flaw in the JPEG format at all, it's simply the wrong format to use for this type of image. And if the artefacts weren't bad enough, the size of the JPEG file will usually be much larger than the GIF, since JPEG's compression has no shading or contrast to work with.

▶ The original image (**left**) and a close-up of the artefacts that appear when saved as JPEG.

Dithering (Or Faking It)

In our example image, we have over 17,000 different colours. If we now tell Paint Shop Pro to switch from the 24-bit palette to an 8-bit (256-colour) palette, most of the image's pixels will change colour. With so few colours available, you might expect the wooden table to look like a brown plastic block, or the light reflections in the bottle to become a solid green, but fortunately we can prevent some loss of detail by using **dithering** or **error diffusion**.

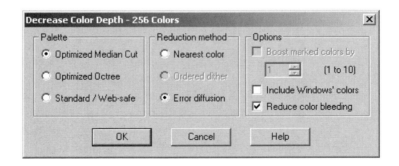

▶ The bewildering array of options that faces you when decreasing an image's colour depth.

When you choose **Decrease Color Depth** from Paint Shop Pro's Color menu, you'll see the dialog shown in the screenshot above. If you choose the **Nearest Color** option and click OK, you'll get something close to the result you were expecting: a new palette is built according to the dominant colours in the image, and less important colours will be changed to the closest match in the new palette. The image on the left in the next screenshot shows the loss of detail, particularly in the shaded background.

Choosing either **Ordered dither** or **Error diffusion** instead (and checking the **Reduce color bleeding** option) produces a much better result. These options simulate a colour that isn't actually in the palette by placing pixels of colours that *are* in the palette side-by-side. Because the human eye can't determine the colour of something as small as a single pixel, it sees the combined effect of these different colours. The second image in the screenshot is dithered, and looks almost identical to the original – certainly good enough to use on a web page.

◀ Dithering (**right**) fools the eye into seeing colours that aren't there, giving a more faithful and usable version of the image.

Decisions, Decisions...

At this point, then, we've found that even in photo-quality images we can find ways to save in 256-colour GIF format that give a similar quality to a 16.7-million-colour JPEG version of the same image. What next?

From the differences, strengths and weaknesses I've mentioned in the two formats available, you'll soon start to recognize which is better for a particular image. To start with, though, I recommend saving every image in JPEG format, then decreasing the colour depth to 256 colours and saving in GIF format. Open each image to compare the quality, and look at the size of each file. You obviously want to use the smallest good quality file.

BY THE WAY

Start at the top...

If you plan to save images as both JPEG and GIF to compare results, start with the highest colour depth first. Save as JPEG (24-bit colour), then reduce the colour depth to 256 colours and save as GIF, which will remove some colour information from the image. If you want to try a 16-colour GIF too, do that last. (You'll have to pick a slightly different filename to avoid overwriting the previously saved 256-colour GIF.) Most programs will let you 'undo' a switch of palette if the result is too ghastly to bother saving.

▶ *The GIF format offers some extra features that you won't get with JPEG: transparency (which we'll look at in Chapter 13) and animation (Chapter 14).*

The Web-Safe Colour Palette

Having introduced you to the notion of having 16.7 million colours to play with, I'm going to put a spanner in the works. Or it *could* be a spanner if you choose to take notice of it: these days many web designers ignore it, but here goes.

To be able to view accurately any 16.7-million-colour images you create, your system must be able to *display* 16.7 million different colours. If your graphics card is set to display a maximum of 256 colours, for instance, your colours will be forced to fit this much smaller palette for display purposes. (That doesn't affect the image you create, of course, but it does affect the way you see it.) The same goes for anyone visiting your site with a lower colour depth system, and a surprising number of people still have 256-colour displays. When one of your 256-colour visitors views your page colours and images, his system will convert the colour to the nearest match in its own palette, and the system palettes of Windows and Mac operating systems are different.

Enough bad news. Fortunately the Windows and Mac palettes are only a *little* different: they have 216 colours in common, and those are the basis of the web-safe palette. By sticking to these 216 colours, you can be sure that users on 256-colour systems will still see your pages and images exactly as you intended.

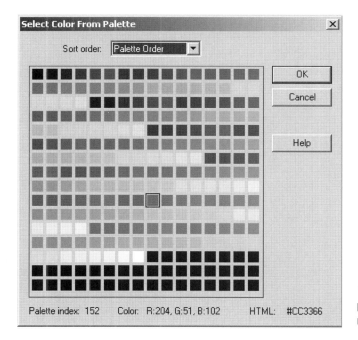

◀ The web-safe palette provided by Paint Shop Pro.

Most graphics programs aimed at the creation of web images will let you apply the web-safe palette, and Paint Shop Pro is no exception: you may have noticed a **Standard/Web-safe** palette option in the dialog on page 186, and you can use that combined with error diffusion to produce a web friendly image.

When choosing colours for text and backgrounds in your page, you probably won't have the same handy list of safe colours to pick from, but they're easy to remember. Working in hex (as we do for web pages) you can use any combination

of 00, 33, 66, 99, CC and FF, producing colours such as
CCFF00, 999933 and 6600FF. The little RGB2Hex program I've
included on the CD-ROM makes it easy to convert a chosen
24-bit-palette colour to its nearest web-safe colour.

12

WORKING WITH GRAPHICS SOFTWARE

IN THIS CHAPTER

How to use the basic drawing, painting and filling tools

Select areas for copying or applying effects

The Number One web effect: drop-shadowed text!

Resize, crop and save the finished image

The benefits of building images in layers

If you're about to take your first steps in graphics creation, Paint Shop Pro, Fireworks and PhotoShop are all going to look a bit daunting on first sight. In this chapter we'll look at the tools, options and basic moves you'll use most often. I'm going to use Paint Shop Pro for this tutorial (you can install PSP from the accompanying CD-ROM), but you'll find all the same options and tools in the other two programs; only their names and locations will differ, and their Help files should point you in the right direction.

Creating A New Image

Let's get cracking by creating the banner-style image shown in the screenshot below. As a quick overview of what's involved, we're going to build a 200-pixel-square block of four colours, apply a texture to it and fade its edges, then add the text with a subtle drop-shadow effect.

▶ The end result, with a bit of luck! A colourful banner using some popular web-style effects.

The first step in creating a new image is the **New Image** dialog, shown in the next screenshot. Choose **New** from the File menu or click the button on the extreme left of the toolbar. We want to begin with a 100-pixel-square image, so set both the **Width** and **Height** fields to 100. Make sure the **Image**

type is set to 16.7 million colours so that any colour or effect we want to use later will be available. Ignore the other options and click **OK**.

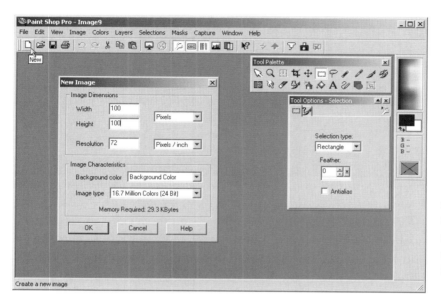

◀ To get started, click the New button, set the dimensions and choose the image type.

This gives us a new, small image that PSP refers to as Image1 until we save it. The image is filled with a single colour which you could have chosen from the **Background color** field of the **New** dialog, but it's easy to change, and that's our first job.

Choosing Colours

In Paint Shop Pro's colour palette at the right of the program, you'll see two interlocking coloured squares. The upper square shows your current foreground colour, and the lower square is the background colour. Clicking either of these will open a dialog box to let you pick a different colour. We want a bright red, so click either square and choose the brightest red from the Basic Colors section of the dialog (255, 0, 0; hex code #FF0000).

When you click **OK** to close the dialog, you'll see the square you clicked change to the same colour.

I can only draw with one colour at a time, so why have foreground and background colours?

If you select the **Paint Brush** tool from the Tool Palette and draw on the image by dragging the left or right mouse buttons, you'll find that the left button draws with foreground colour, the right with background colour. Most of the time this just means that you can quickly switch between two colours without mucking around with dialog boxes. But with some options you choose, as you'll find out later, graphics programs use your current background colour to fill an area or create an effect.

Now we need to paint the entire image red, and the quickest way to do that is by using the **Flood Fill** tool, a little paint tin icon in the Tool Palette window. Click that icon to select it, then move the mouse onto the image. If you set bright red as your foreground colour, click the image with the left mouse button; if red is your background colour, use the right mouse button. Voilà – your image becomes a red square.

Next we need to make two more identical images. We could repeat the same procedure a couple more times, but there's a quicker way. Press Ctrl+C to copy the image to the clipboard, then Ctrl+V (this is PSP's shortcut to Edit, Paste, As New Image) to make an exact copy. Press Ctrl+V again to make the second copy.

The two new images are both red, so follow the steps we used earlier to change one image to bright blue (0, 0, 255; hex code #0000FF) and the other to bright green (0, 255, 0; hex code #00FF00).

Avoid accidental clicks!

If you want to select an image to work on, get into the habit of clicking on its title bar, not inside the picture itself. If you click the picture while a painting tool such as the Paint Brush or Flood Fill is selected, you'll paint the image! Fortunately, all good graphics programs have Undo options to restore your masterpiece to its former glory.

Copying & Pasting Selections

The next step is to combine these three images to make a 200 × 200 grid of colours. Click the **New** button again to create a new image, and set its width and height to 200. In the **Background color** field, choose White.

Choose the **Selection** tool from the Tool Palette, then click the title bar of the red image to select it and press Ctrl+C to copy it to the clipboard, then switch to your new large image. Instead of pasting as a new image as we did before, we need to paste *as a new selection*, by pressing Ctrl+E. When you do that, you'll see the red square appear in the new image, below the mouse cursor. When you move the mouse the square will follow. Position the square in the top-left corner of the image, as in the screenshot below, then click once to make it 'stick' in that position. When you do that, you'll see an animated dotted border called a **marquee** (sometimes referred to as 'marching ants'): while the marquee is visible, you can click and drag the selected square to fine-tune its position. (You may find it useful to choose **Zoom In By 5** from the View menu to see a close-up view of that top corner. Click the **Normal Viewing** button on the toolbar to return to the original view.)

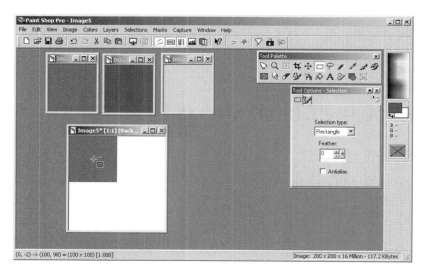

◀ Paste and position the separate images using the Selection tool.

With the red square in position, copy and position the blue and green squares in exactly the same way, blue to the top-right corner, green to the bottom-left. Now you're left with a single white square in the bottom-right corner, and we really wanted this to be yellow. Of course, we could have created a small yellow square and pasted that in, or we could have chosen yellow as the background colour when we created the new image. But this gives us an opportunity to see how the Flood Fill tool really works.

Set your foreground or background colour to yellow (255, 255, 0; hex code #FFFF00) and choose the Flood Fill tool again, then click inside the white square in the large image. Lo and behold, the white square turns yellow, but the other squares are unchanged. This is because, despite earlier appearances, the Flood Fill tool doesn't colour the entire image: instead it looks at the colour of the pixel you clicked, and works outwards in all directions until it reaches a boundary of different coloured pixels.

▶ Use the Flood Fill tool to recolour an area containing a single colour.

Applying Global Effects

At this point we can discard the three small images we created. When you close these images, Paint Shop Pro will ask if you want to save them, so say No.

The next step in our master plan is to apply a textured effect. Paint Shop Pro includes a wide range of effects, distortions and filters on its Image menu, so choose **Effects**, **Texture**. In the dialog that appears, you can choose from a wide range of preset textures, or create your own using the Texture, Image and Light sections, and you'll see a preview of the result as you choose different settings. Pick anything you like (I've chosen the Gravel preset) and click **OK**.

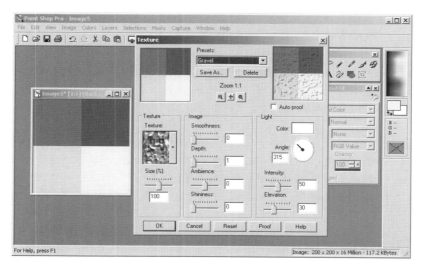

◀ Choose a preset texture, or create and save your own concoctions.

Selecting Areas

Because we didn't select any particular area of the image in advance, PSP has applied the texture to the whole image, which is exactly what we wanted. We could have applied different textures to each square by selecting it in advance using the Selection tool. Making precise selections can be a fiddly job, so it's worth zooming in to get a closer look at what you're doing. You can use the options on the View menu to do that, but the **Zoom** tool gives you more control.

GOOD QUESTION!

How does the Zoom tool work?

With the Zoom tool selected, click repeatedly with the left mouse button to zoom in, or the right mouse button to zoom out. Try to click over the area of the image you want to zoom in on, which saves the need to use the scrollbars to find it afterwards. For very detailed work, you can switch on the grid (View, Grid). Neither the Zoom tool nor the Grid changes your image, they just give you a different view of it.

197

To select an area of the image, click in the top-left corner of the required area, then drag the mouse diagonally down to the bottom-right corner. The dotted marquee will expand as you drag. When it borders the area you want to work on, release the mouse button. You can select multiple areas by holding the Shift key, or click in an unselected area of the image to remove the selection marquees and start again.

Once you've selected an area, you can click inside it and drag that portion of the image somewhere else (leaving behind a hole filled with your current background colour), use the Flood Fill tool to fill it with a different colour, Copy or Cut it to the clipboard, or apply an effect or filter to it.

Drawing Lines

The next task with the image we're working on is to divide it into four separate squares again by drawing two lines. We want these lines to match the background colour of the web page which will eventually contain this image – for now, we'll keep it simple, so set the foreground colour to white.

For freehand drawing you'd use the **Paint Brush** tool, but the Curse Of The Wobbly Hand makes that hopeless for straight lines. Instead, pick the **Draw** tool. When you change tools, you'll see the Tool Options window change to let you choose how the tool should behave. (If you can't see this window, right-click on any toolbar and choose **Tool Options**.) Choose Single Line, Filled, with a width of 3 pixels, and leave the checkboxes empty.

Zoom in on the top of the image, at the join between the two upper squares, and position the mouse at the very top of the join. Before you click and drag, though, hold down the Shift key. This ensures that you get a perfectly straight vertical or horizontal line with no effort. Now, draw a line all the way to the bottom of the image. Do the same to draw a horizontal line across the middle of the image, as in the screenshot below. Finally, click the **Normal View** button on the toolbar to see the image at its usual size again.

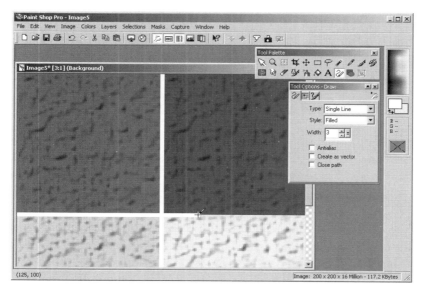

◀ Using the Shift key with the Draw tool results in a perfectly straight line.

Creating A Feathered Selection

Next we want to 'fade out' the borders of the image. This is known as **feathering**, and it's an option built into the Selection tool. This time we need to make sure our background colour matches the background of the web page. A moment ago we set white as the *foreground* colour, and there's a quick way to swap the two colours over: click the double-headed arrow beside the two colours.

Pick the Selection tool, and you'll see the Tool Options window change again. In this window, set the selection type to Circle, and set Feather to 40.

Now we want to select a circular area in the middle of the image. Click in the centre of the picture where the two lines cross, and drag downwards until the selection marquee stretches about halfway along each line, as in the first screenshot below. As soon as you release the mouse button, the selection will spring outward to include our 40-pixel feathered area, as shown in the second screenshot. Press Ctrl+C to copy the selected area of the image to the clipboard, then Ctrl+V to paste it as a new image.

▶ After creating the selection in the normal way (**left**) the marquee will expand to include the 40-pixel feathering (**right**).

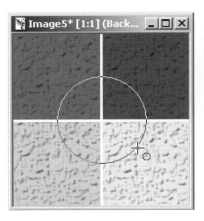 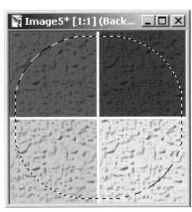

The newly created image looks a bit weird: you can see a blob of colour in the centre, but the background is a grid of white and grey squares. This is Paint Shop Pro's **layering** at work, and the grid indicates that the background is transparent. We'll look at layers later in this chapter, but for now we just want a normal non-layered image, so choose **Merge, Merge All (Flatten)** from the Layers menu.

▶ Pasting the selection forms a new transparent layer (**left**) so we 'flatten' the layers to form a normal non-layered image (**right**).

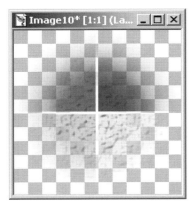 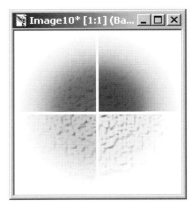

Resizing The Image Canvas

That's the first part of the image done and dusted. All that's left to do is to add the text and create its drop-shadow effect. At the moment, though, there's no space for the text, so we need to increase the size of the image.

With the image selected, you can see its width, height and colour depth in Paint Shop Pro's status bar. Mine is 190 pixels wide by 190 high, but yours may be a little different. We don't need to change its height, but we want to add enough extra width to let us slot the text in. It's sensible to make it larger than we need and cut it down when we've finished, so we'll set the width to 500.

Make sure the background colour is still set to white, and choose **Canvas Size** from the View menu to see the dialog shown in the next screenshot. Set the **New Width** to 500, and the **New Height** to your image's current height. In the lower section, make sure neither box is checked (we want to make the existing image wider without changing its position at the left edge) and click **OK**.

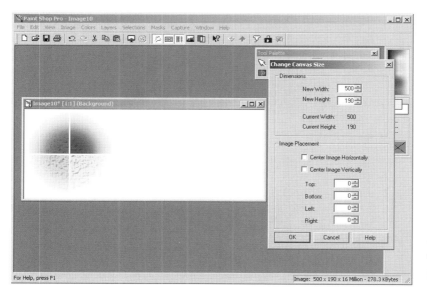

◀ Use the Canvas Size option to change the width without altering its height or position.

Adding Text

Adding text to an image is a doddle, though positioning it afterwards takes a little more care. Choose the **Text** tool from the Tool Palette and click the image at the approximate position you want the text to be placed. The Text Entry dialog (shown in the next screenshot) will appear. This dialog works like a mini word processor, letting you choose different fonts, colours and styles, so type any text you like and format it in any way you want to. To give us control over the position of the text and apply effects to it, choose **Floating** in the Create As section, and choose **Antialias**.

▶ The Text Entry dialog lets you type whole paragraphs of formatted text.

JARGON BUSTER

antialias

Because all characters are created from pixels (which are square), circular characters like 'e' and characters with diagonals such as 'y' will have slightly jagged edges. Antialiasing is similar to dithering, mentioned in the previous chapter: it adds different coloured pixels to the edges of the characters to blend them into the background. Antialiasing works well with large fonts, but can result in very blurred text when the font size is below about 14 points.

When you've got the text formatted as you want it, click **OK**. The text will appear as a floating selection on the image, as in the screenshot below. The next task is to switch to the Selection tool and drag the text to the location you want it (zooming in first, if necessary). When you start to drag, make sure you click on a character rather than in a space *between* two characters or the selection will be removed (although you can replace it using the Undo shortcut, Ctrl+Z).

◀ Click on a selected character and drag the text to its final resting place.

Adding A Drop-Shadow

The final creative step isn't going to be rocket science: we've already applied a textured effect, and this isn't much different. The text you added should still be selected; if it isn't, press Ctrl+Z one or more times until the selection marquee reappears. From the Image menu, choose **Effects, Drop Shadow**.

As with all the available effects, you can play with the drop-shadow dialog, click **OK** to apply it, then choose Undo and start again until you get a result you like. I'm going to use an opacity of 38, a blur setting of 3, and offset the shadow by 3 pixels horizontally and vertically. After clicking outside the selected text to remove the marquee, you'll be left with something like the following screenshot.

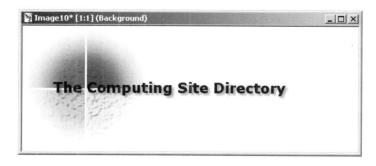

◀ The (almost) finished image, replete with drop-shadowed text.

Cropping An Image

To keep our options open, we made the image larger than we really needed, and we don't want to leave it that way – it just makes the file's size unnecessarily large. So the final task before saving is to **crop** the image to the minimum size. For this we use the **Crop** tool in the Tool Palette to mark out the area we want to keep. We want to keep the same height, but reduce the width, and this involves dragging from the extreme top-left corner which is easier to hit if you zoom in by a few steps. When you see **0, 0** in Paint Shop Pro's status bar, you know you're over that first pixel and you can click and start dragging to mark out the selection.

Keep dragging until you reach just beyond the end of the text and its drop-shadow, then release the mouse button. Finally, click the **Crop Image** button on the Tool Options panel to remove the unselected area.

Saving The Finished Result

The last step is to save the image ready for use on the Web, of course, which means saving in either JPEG or GIF format. If you've worked through Chapter 11 you already know the differences between those two formats, and you may have done a sneaky check on the number of colours used in the image by choosing **Count Colors Used** from the Colors menu. Mine uses 8752 colours, and yours won't be a lot different. That's much more than the GIF format's 256-colour maximum, and there's a fair amount of shading in the image as a result of the feathering, antialiased text and drop-shadow, so this is probably a good candidate for JPEG format.

To save as JPEG, choose **Save As** from the File menu to see the dialog shown in the next screenshot. Type a name for the image in the usual way, and choose the **JPEG** option from the **Save as type** drop-down list, then click **Save**.

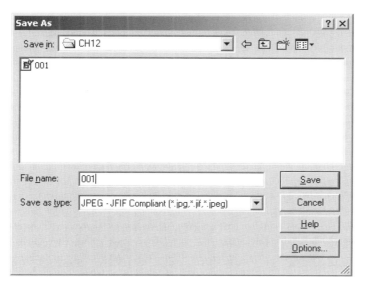

◀ Pick the image format to save, and click Options to choose settings specific to that format.

BY THE WAY

The progressive option

After selecting the type of file format you want to save, you can click the **Options** button in the Save dialog to make extra choices. For JPEG images, you can adjust the amount of compression used (but beware: higher compression = lower quality!). A more interesting option is to save using **progressive encoding**. Where a standard JPEG image appears in horizontal strips on the page as it downloads, a progressive JPEG appears first as a rather blurred poor-quality image which gradually sharpens as the file downloads. There's little to choose between the resulting file sizes, so pick whichever style you prefer.

For a 'belt-and-braces' approach, you may still want to save in GIF format and compare results. If so, you first need to reduce the colour depth of the image to 256 colours (skip back to *Dithering* (*Or Faking It*) in Chapter 11 for details), then choose **Save As** again, this time picking **CompuServe Graphics Interchange** from the **Save as type** list.

In fact, the feathered effect we used for the coloured blocks is the clincher. The GIF version of the image faithfully reproduces the antialiased text and drop-shadow, but the feathered shading has very obvious circular bands. Worse still, the GIF image is almost 4 Kb larger than the JPEG, so the decision about which to use in a web page will be an easy one. I've included both versions of the image in this chapter's folder on the CD-ROM to let you make your own comparison.

A Word About Layers

So far I've pretty much ignored **layers**, but they're a major feature of Paint Shop Pro and other good graphics programs, and it's well worth getting to know how they work. Put simply, layers are a stack of transparent pictures placed on top of your original to form a more complex image. As you build up your image, you can make adjustments to one layer without affecting anything on a different layer, delete a layer, make a copy of a layer, and so on.

Saving & flattening

A useful bonus in using layers is that you can save the finished image in Paint Shop Pro's own format ('Paint Shop Pro Image') which retains all the layer information. At any time, you can reopen the file and edit a layer or two to make a slightly different image. To save in any other format requires the layers to be **flattened** – squashed down to a single-layer image from the Layers/Merge menu. If you do use layers, consider whether you'll want to edit the image in future, or reuse a couple of layers in a different image, and if so, save as a PSP Image file too.

Taking the image we just created as an example, let's say we're thinking of adding an underline and overline to the text. Choose **New Raster Layer** from the Layers menu, choose a name such as 'Lines' for the layer to make it easy to recognize in future, and leave the other settings as they are. The original image (in fact the bottom layer) is still visible, but you'll see that the image's title bar now says **(Lines)** to indicate the transparent layer we're working on. Using the original as a guide, we can draw horizontal lines above and below the text, shown in the next screenshot.

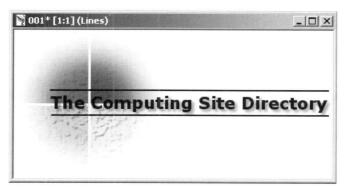

◀ An added layer named 'Lines' containing two horizontal lines.

If you make a mistake, you can select something on this new layer and delete it without affecting the layer beneath. You can also view this layer by itself by choosing **View, Current Only** from the Layers menu. And, of course, if you agree with me that the result isn't worth keeping, choose **Delete** from the Layers menu to banish it forever.

And Finally...

You can tell by looking at Paint Shop Pro's menus and Tool Options window that there are a lot more features available than we've covered above. Let's round off this chapter with a quick look at some of the most useful or unusual.

Dropper (or Colour Picker) The Dropper tool saves you endless forays into the colour dialog to choose a different colour. If you've used a particular colour in the image already, switch to the Dropper (called a Colour Picker in some other programs) and click an area that uses that colour. As when painting, use the left mouse button to set the foreground colour and the right mouse button to set the background. (If you're using the Paint Brush or Flood Fill tools, you can briefly switch to the Dropper by pressing the Ctrl key.)

Saving & Loading Selections After selecting an area of an image, you can save the selection coordinates as a separate file by choosing **Save To Disk** from the Selections menu. You can load this selection file into any image to automatically select the same coordinates. (The selection marquee can be moved using the **Mover** tool and the right mouse button.)

Painting Gradients & Textures Rather than filling an area with a solid colour, you can fill it with a gradient effect using the Flood Fill tool and choosing the appropriate Fill style from the Tool Options window. When you use the Paint Brush and Airbrush tools, switch to the middle tab of the Tool Options window and you can choose a Paper Texture effect to paint with.

Picture Tube The Picture Tube is a tool that drops preset small images onto the canvas, with offerings such as Clouds, Crawlers, Traffic Signs, Water Drops and Grass Blades.

▶ Fun with the Picture Tube tool!

Transparency One of the great benefits of the GIF image format is the ability to make a single colour transparent. When placed on a web page, the areas of the image using the transparent colour will be replaced by whatever is beneath them (usually your page's own background colour or tiled background image). We'll look at GIF transparency in more detail in the next chapter.

13

IMAGES IN ACTION

Once you're armed with your trusty graphics program and an arsenal of filters and effects, the world is your lobster – you're limited only by your imagination. The next step is deciding how and where to use your creations. In Chapter 6 we looked at the HTML required to put an *inline image* on the page using the <IMG> tag, and we've talked about background tiles a few times, but there are many more practical or effective ways to use images on your site. In this chapter we'll look at the most useful of those, along with a few neat tricks.

Side-Panel Background Tiles

The traditional type of background image is a square pattern which the browser tiles horizontally and vertically to fill the entire window – its role is purely stylistic. The 'side-panel' background has a different purpose: it splits the window into two vertical sections, as shown in the screenshot of the ScienceDaily Magazine site below, and it's often used by designers who prefer not to use frames to divide up their content. Splitting the window in this way adds some interest to the page as well as giving you an ideal place to put your navigation that will draw the visitor's eye.

▶ A side-panel background image in use at **www.sciencedaily. com**.

The panel is easy to create: it takes just one tiny image file that's a few pixels high (or perhaps just a single pixel) and extremely wide. Set the colour of the entire image to the colour you'd like to use for the main body of your page, and then create a rectangle of 150–200 pixels wide at the left of the image using a different colour.

There's a catch with this trick that you need to watch out for: when you decide on the width of the image, remember that some of your visitors may have larger screen resolutions than your own – up to 1600 × 1200. If your image is narrower than that, it won't just be tiled vertically, but *horizontally* too, giving the result shown in the next screenshot. It won't add much to your image's size to make it 1600 pixels wide, and it ensures that your design and content will appear as intended at any screen resolution.

BY THE WAY

Don't cross the line!

Make sure the panel is wide enough to display the navigational links without any text overlapping into the main body of the page. A good way to do this is to create a table containing the entire page content (see Chapter 7), with a single cell on the left containing the links. Set this cell to the same width as the panel section of the image, and the worst that can happen is that text will wrap onto the next line.

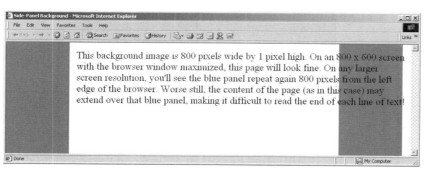

◀ The background will still be tiled horizontally if the browser is wider than the image, so don't skimp on the image width!

▶ *Two more popular tricks with background images are the non-scrolling background (see page 159) and the watermarked background (page 165).*

LOWSRC: **Poor Quality Pays Off!**

Attracting visitors to a site isn't easy, so you want to do all you can to keep them there when they do show up! Making your site load quickly (or *feel* as though it's loading quickly) will make visitors more inclined to explore. That's a good reason for establishing a single 'images' directory and reusing the same image files wherever possible, as I mentioned in Chapter 3. Here's another option you can use to give the impression that your images are loading quickly.

After creating and saving an image in the required format, edit it to make a *second* image file containing a low-quality copy and save it with a slightly different name so that you can tell which is which. Both images must have the same dimensions, but they needn't both be the same format – you might convert your highly coloured JPEG image to a 256-colour or 16-colour GIF, or create a greyscaled version. The result you want is the smallest possible file size of a bearable quality.

With the two images created, add this tag to your page:

```
<IMG SRC="image.jpg" WIDTH=58 HEIGHT=162 LOWSRC="imagelow.gif">
```

The LOWSRC attribute directs the browser to the low-quality image. As your page loads, the browser downloads and displays this image, allowing it to build the page more quickly. When the page is complete, the browser takes a second pass through the page to load the high-quality image. The result is that although more data is ultimately being downloaded, the visitor sees a complete page a lot sooner.

Slideshows & Thumbnail Galleries

If the purpose of your site is to display pictures (software screenshots, photographs, artwork and so on) using inline images on a single page is a definite no-no! Even using the LOWSRC attribute mentioned above, the page will take too long to load, scaring away even your most ardent visitor. The solution is to display the images as either a slideshow or as hyperlinked thumbnails.

The **slideshow** option simply involves creating a template page containing an image along with links to the next and previous pages. You can then copy this page as many times as you need, altering the <IMG SRC> to point to the correct image, and the Previous/Next links to point to the appropriate pages in the sequence. The slideshow method assumes that the visitor wants to see every image, and gives no option to pick and choose.

◀ A slideshow page containing links to the next and previous pages in the sequence.

A **thumbnail gallery** gives the visitor complete control. With this method, you create small versions of each image (known as 'thumbnails') using your graphics software's Resample or Resize options, save each with a different name from the original image, and display them on a single page. By wrapping an anchor tag around each of the <IMG> tags, as I've done in the code below, you can make each thumbnail act as a link to its full-size counterpart. The result is shown in the next screenshot and, of course, included in this chapter's folder on the CD-ROM. When the visitor clicks a thumbnail, the larger image is loaded. The visitor then has to use the browser's Back button to return to the gallery page, but you could easily combine this with the slideshow idea: create an attractive page containing each image and make the thumbnails link to pages.

```
<TABLE BORDER="0" CELLPADDING="20">
```

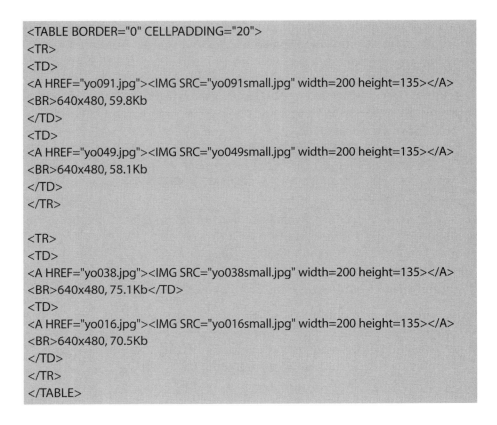

```
<TABLE BORDER="0" CELLPADDING="20">
<TR>
<TD>
<A HREF="yo091.jpg"><IMG SRC="yo091small.jpg" width=200 height=135></A>
<BR>640x480, 59.8Kb
</TD>
<TD>
<A HREF="yo049.jpg"><IMG SRC="yo049small.jpg" width=200 height=135></A>
<BR>640x480, 58.1Kb
</TD>
</TR>

<TR>
<TD>
<A HREF="yo038.jpg"><IMG SRC="yo038small.jpg" width=200 height=135></A>
<BR>640x480, 75.1Kb</TD>
<TD>
<A HREF="yo016.jpg"><IMG SRC="yo016small.jpg" width=200 height=135></A>
<BR>640x480, 70.5Kb
</TD>
</TR>
</TABLE>
```

▶ A thumbnail gallery: tiny versions of each image can be clicked to see the corresponding full-size versions.

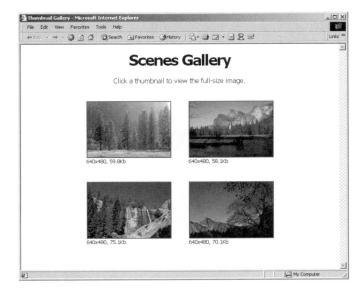

214

GOOD QUESTION!

Why not just use the <IMG> tag's width and height attributes to display thumbnail versions?

The benefit of using separate images is that they'll be small files. In the gallery example I've included the file sizes of the original images on the page, and they range from about 58 Kb upwards, but the thumbnails are no more than 11 Kb each. Forcing the browser to display the original images at a smaller size wouldn't change the fact that it first has to download each 58 Kb file!

Image Maps & Hotspots

We've talked about using images as links, but here's an option that's a little different. Instead of making the *whole* image act as a link to a single URL, you can create an **image map** that defines particular areas of an image, and each *area* will act as a separate link. In the screenshot below, for instance, each piece of text links to a different page, but clicking elsewhere in the image does nothing.

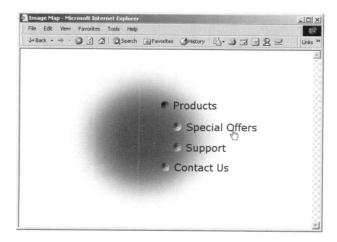

◀ A simple image map with four rectangular linking areas.

The first part of the job is straightforward enough – you have to create and save your image in the normal way. Second, you need to find out the coordinates of the areas that should act as links (known as the *hotspots*). You should be able to select an area using the Selection Tool, read its coordinates (Paint Shop Pro displays selection coordinates in the bottom-left corner of its window), and make a note of them.

Add the image to your web page using the <IMG> tag in the usual way, but include this new attribute: **USEMAP="#map1"**. This tells the browser that we're using the image as an image map, and directs it to a list (or **map**) of the coordinates to use for the hotspots. The # symbol means that the map is included in the current web page, which is the sensible place to put it. I've chosen the name 'map1' for simplicity, but you can pick something more imaginative. (If you use more than one image map in a page, each coordinate map will need a different name.)

Now we need to define the map itself, which introduces two new tags. The first is **<MAP>**, which takes a single attribute, **NAME**, the name we chose for this map. Contained between the <MAP> and </MAP> tags we create an **<AREA>** tag for each hotspot. The <AREA> tag needs three attributes:

▶ SHAPE. A choice of RECT (rectangle), CIRCLE or POLY (any irregular shape).

▶ HREF. The URL that this hotspot should link to.

▶ COORDS. A list of coordinates separated by commas. For a rectangular area, the coordinates will be *left, top, right, bottom* (which is the order in which Paint Shop Pro displays them).

The complete code for the image map in the example looks like this:

```
<MAP NAME="map1">
        <AREA SHAPE="RECT" HREF="products.htm" COORDS="224,93,316
        114">
        <AREA SHAPE="RECT" HREF="offers.htm" COORDS="249,139,401,162">
        <AREA SHAPE="RECT" HREF="support.htm" COORDS="249,183,336,
        206">
        <AREA SHAPE="RECT" HREF="contact.htm" COORDS="226,226,342,
        246">
</MAP>
```

If you want to define circular or irregular areas instead of rectangles, the COORDS attribute works a little differently. For circles, there will be three figures corresponding to *horizontal-centre, vertical-centre, radius*. For polygons, each point is entered as a pair of coordinates corresponding to *horizontal-position, vertical-position*; enter as many pairs of coordinates as the shape has points (so a triangular area would have three pairs of coordinates). You don't have to stick with a single shape in a map, so your image can contain differently shaped hotspots.

◀ To find the coordinates of an area in Paint Shop Pro, drag the Selection Tool and look at the figures in the bottom-left corner.

Light the blue touch-paper...

If you're using Fireworks to create your images, most of the tough stuff in image mapping is done for you automatically. Just choose the shape you want, select an area of the image and type a URL, and Fireworks will create all the HTML code required. You'll find similar options in version 7 of Paint Shop Pro.

BY THE WAY

Using GIF Transparency

If your page uses a background pattern and you add text banners and other non-rectangular graphics to the page, you'll see solid blocks of colour over your page background, similar to the screenshot below. There's no escaping the fact that images are rectangular – you can't save the irregular shaped graphic as an irregular shaped image file.

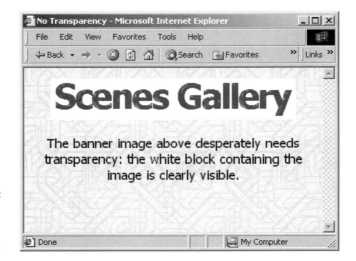

▶ A banner image asking for either transparency or public humiliation.

This is where the GIF format's option to set a single colour as transparent leaps to your rescue. When you've created the image, first reduce its colour depth to 256 colours or fewer (this is a requirement of the GIF format that we covered in Chapter 11). Next, select your graphics program's option to make one of those 256 colours transparent and pick the image's background colour. (In Paint Shop Pro you'll find this option on the **Colors** menu.)

▶ In Paint Shop Pro, you can set the transparency to your current background colour, or simply click the image to pick which colour should be transparent.

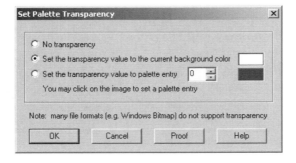

Finally, save the image choosing the CompuServe GIF format from the Save As Type box in the Save dialog, and add the image to your page in the usual way. As in the screenshot below, your irregular shaped graphic should sit neatly on your page's background pattern without a hint of the solid background.

Watch out for the halo effect!

BY THE WAY

If you plan to make part of an image transparent, be careful when using antialiasing to blur the jagged edges of text, or applying shadows and blurs. These will remove the clean join between one colour and the next, so when you make the background transparent you may get a kind of 'halo effect' caused by a scattering of oddly coloured pixels that no longer blend in with what's behind them. To minimize this, design your image using a background colour as similar as possible to that of your web page's background image.

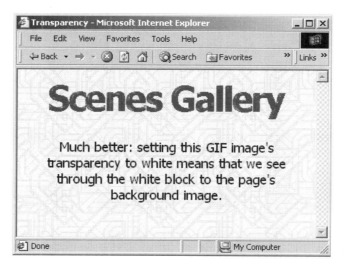

◀ With the white background now transparent, the banner sits cleanly on the page.

Your Personal Site Icon

If you use Internet Explorer for your browsing, you may have noticed that once in a while when you visit a site you see a different icon in the address bar. If you drag that icon to your desktop to make a shortcut or add the site to your Favorites, the same icon is used. It's a neat way to add a little extra personality to your site (although currently only Internet Explorer will take any notice of it), and it's easy to do.

▶ Several personalized site icons on Internet Explorer's Favorites menu.

First you need to get your hands on an icon editor (most graphics programs won't work with icons). You'll find a huge list to choose from at **http://www.davecentral.com/iconed.html** or, if you're a bit of an icon fan, visit **http://www.impactsoft.com** and grab a copy of Microangelo, the king of icon editors.

Using this program, create a 16-pixel-square icon and save it in your 'Site' directory (not in your 'images' directory) as **favicon.ico**. Then add the following tag to the head of your site's first page (usually named index.htm or index.html), which will also be in that 'Site' directory:

```
<LINK REL="SHORTCUT ICON" HREF="favicon.ico">
```

You won't see the result by looking at the hard disk copy of your website, but as long as the icon is uploaded to the server along with the rest of your site's files (see Chapter 23) you and your visitors will see it when the site is viewed online.

Optimize Your Graphics!

The two popular graphics formats, JPEG and GIF, include built-in compression, as I've already mentioned. This is how a 250 Kb bitmap image can be converted to a 10 Kb JPEG with no noticeable loss of quality. (The quality *is* reduced, but the compression techniques are clever enough to disguise that.) Although this is a huge reduction already, if your site is heavy on the graphical content you want to squeeze those file sizes down as far as they'll reasonably go – in other words, you want to do a spot of **image optimization**.

For this you need an image optimization program, and one of the best is Ulead SmartSaver Pro which I've included on the CD-ROM. It's a rather complicated looking program (it can help you with image maps and other tricks besides optimization) – if you find it daunting, Ulead have simpler programs to do the same job, as well as a huge range of other graphics tools, at **http://www.ulead.com** and **http://www.webutilities.com**. You may find similar features built into your graphics program too; in fact, both Fireworks and the latest version of Paint Shop Pro include optimization tools.

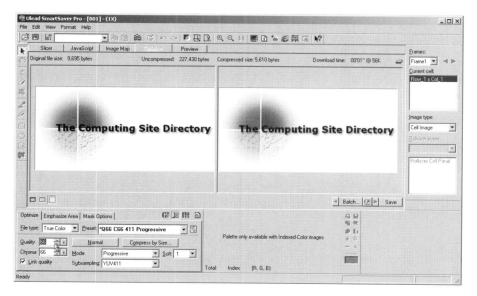

◀ Spot the difference... the original (**left**) and optimized images. The only obvious change is a 40% drop in file size!

SmartSaver Pro works with JPEG, GIF and the lesser used PNG (Portable Network Graphics) formats, and the controls you need are in its lower-left corner. Keeping an eye on the quality of the optimized image and its file size, decrease the **Quality** value. If you click the **Advanced** button you can use the **Soft** control to apply a measure of blurring, which helps disguise the effect of the quality reduction.

When you think you've tweaked things as far as they can safely be tweaked, choose **Save Optimized Image As** from the File menu and save the image with a different name from the original. This gives you a chance to check the result on the web page and make sure you haven't gone a tweak too far before you delete the original image.

ANIMATION WITH GIF & FLASH

Animation is one of the first ingredients you think of when you set out to design an all-singing, all-dancing multimedia website. Something that moves, after all, catches the eye far more quickly than something that doesn't, which is why most advertising banners are animated. But there's a balance to be struck here, as usual: a site that sings or dances *too much* is just annoying! Animated images can be used to good effect to draw the eye towards your logo or to create small animated bullets beside your links, but animations shouldn't be scattered over a wide area of the page.

In this chapter we'll look at how to create animated images and the software needed, then turn to the wider view with Flash animation, which can be used to produce anything from a linking button to a fully interactive multimedia presentation for your pages.

Easy Animation With DYNSRC

The most used type of animation is the animated GIF, which we'll look at in a moment, but here's a lesser used option you might like to play with: linking an AVI movie file to an <IMG> tag with the **DYNSRC** attribute. This creates an animation that can only be viewed in Internet Explorer; other browsers will show the static image referred to in the <IMG> tag's SRC attribute.

I've written a little program called AVIMaker to create the movie, which you'll find on the CD-ROM. It's very easy to use: just create a set of images which, when shown in rapid succession, would give a cartoon-like impression of movement, and save them all as Windows bitmap (.bmp) files, then save the first image in the sequence as a GIF or JPEG too. Load all the bitmaps into AVIMaker in the correct order, set the desired speed, and save the result into your images directory.

You need to keep the single GIF or JPEG image and the newly created AVI movie file, but you can delete the other bitmap files. Add the usual <IMG> tag to your page to display that single image, and add the two new attributes, DYNSRC and LOOP:

```
<IMG SRC="red.jpg" width=20 height=20 DYNSRC="square.avi" LOOP=Infinite>
```

The DYNSRC attribute gives the URL of the AVI movie, and LOOP can be set to a number (for a particular number of repetitions) if you don't want the animation to repeat endlessly. You can also include **START=MOUSEOVER**, which causes the animation to start only when the mouse moves over the static image. You'll find an example page using AVI animation in this chapter's folder on the CD-ROM.

Using GIF Animation

The methods of creating GIF animations are almost identical to the brief process I mentioned above for AVIs. The main differences are that you don't have to keep a separate copy of the first image in the sequence, and the end result can be viewed using any browser, making this the better format by far. If you want to create animated banner advertisements for display on other sites, they'll almost always have to be in GIF format.

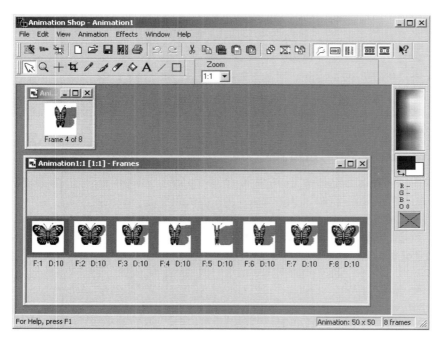

◀ Animation Shop displaying one of its sample animations and the eight separate images from which it was formed.

I can't offer you a homemade 'GIFMaker' program to handle the creation process, but I can point you towards some commercial applications:

▶ **Animation Shop**, an animation program included with Paint Shop Pro from **http://www.digitalworkshop.com**.

▶ **Ulead GIF Animator** from **http://www.ulead.com**.

▶ **Macromedia Fireworks**, one of the graphics programs I mentioned in Chapter 11, has built-in animation options. Visit **http://www.macromedia.com** for this one.

I'm going to plump for Animation Shop, but the methods and options will be very similar whatever program you decide to use yourself.

BY THE WAY

Animation, or a very fast slideshow?

It's not easy to judge how smooth the animated result will be while you're creating a set of still images. To keep the file size down, the number of **frames** (separate images) should be kept to a minimum, but the differences between each frame should be small enough to give smooth transitions from one to the next. After creating three or four images, load them into your animator and check the result before going any further – if the animation looks too jerky after adjusting the delay times of each frame, you'll have fewer images to edit!

Creating An Animated GIF

The first job, of course, is to create the sequence of separate images that will form the frames of the animation. Animation Shop can use images in most formats, but since the final movie file will be in GIF format, it's sensible to save each image as a GIF too, reducing the colour depth to 256 colours or fewer. To save headaches later, make sure the dimensions of each image are identical.

Fire up Animation Shop and choose **Animation Wizard** from the File menu. Follow the six steps to set the amount of time most (if not all) the images should be displayed, and choose a background colour or (if you created transparent GIFs) set the same transparent colour for the animation. At step 5, shown in the next screenshot, click the **Add Image** button to select all the separate images you created, and use the two **Move** buttons to assemble them into the correct order.

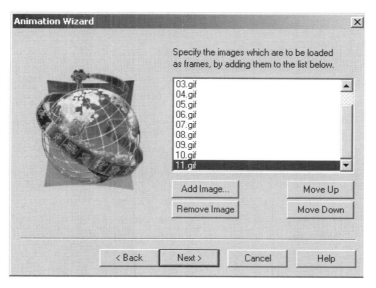

◀ Use the
Animation Wizard
to set the basic
options and
organize your
images into the
right order.

When you've completed the Wizard, the strip of frames will be shown, as in
the next screenshot, and you can make changes to any single frame. For
example, if a frame should be displayed for a different amount of time from
that set in the Wizard, right-click it, choose **Properties** and type a new delay
time. You can also drag frames to different locations or insert new frames.
You can preview the result at any time by choosing **Animation** from the
View menu.

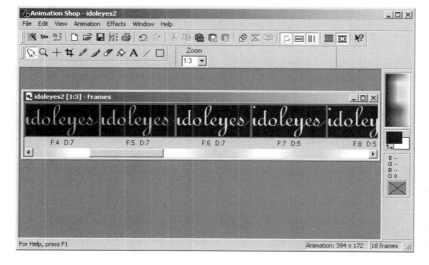

◀ Animation
Shop displays
each frame along
with its index
number in the
sequence and its
delay time.

Animation Shop includes a set of effects and transitions on its **Effects** menu that you can apply to an animation – in fact, you can create an entire animation by combining just a single image with one or more effects. Pick carefully though: these effects create extra frames in your animation and may make a huge difference to its size. The very tasty Stained Glass effect took my simple 25 Kb animation up to an unusable 636 Kb! Use the options in the **Define effect** section to choose how long the effect should last and how many frames it should cover.

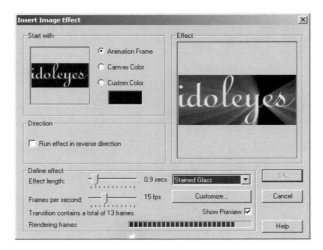

▶ Select a frame and choose a transition or effect to be inserted after it.

When you're happy with the result of previewing the animation, choose **Save As** from the File menu and save the result. Next, start the **Optimization Wizard** (also on the File menu) to experiment with reducing the size of the file. I do recommend saving *before* optimizing and holding onto that original animation. If you decide you've over-optimized and lost too much quality, you can reload the original animation and try again.

BY THE WAY

Easy animation editing

Another great benefit of animated GIFs is that they're easy to edit. You don't have to keep the original sequence of files, you can simply load the animated file into any GIF animator to view, edit or export individual frames, adjust timings and transparency, and so on.

The final step is to put the animation on your web page. There's nothing clever involved here at all: the file has a .gif extension and is added to the page using the <IMG> tag's SRC attribute, exactly as if it were a static image.

Flash: Animation With All The Trimmings

Flash is a proprietary animation format designed by Macromedia, Inc. (**http://www.macromedia.com**), although to refer to Flash files as 'animations' doesn't really do them justice: they're closer to the multimedia presentations produced by the likes of Microsoft PowerPoint than they are to the animated GIF. You can incorporate sound effects or complete soundtracks, for instance; items can be interactive, allowing new phases of animation to be started with a mouse click, or web links to be opened; a timeline lets you specify exactly when particular events should occur and how long they should last; and that's barely skimming the surface!

Common uses for Flash are to make a smart and stylish gateway page for a site (see Chapter 10), provide simple animations *à la* GIF, create navigational button bars, or build entire interactive pages and sites.

Describing Flash on paper is like nailing jelly to the ceiling. If you haven't come across Flash animation before, visit Macromedia's Flash Gallery at **http://www.shockwave.com/shockzone/edge/flash** to find out what you've been missing.

To Flash Or Not To Flash?

That, as Shakespeare said, is a bit of a poser. The benefits of Flash speak for themselves when you take a tour of the Flash Gallery site mentioned above, with the added advantage that the animation will be exactly the same in every browser.

There are two main disadvantages. First, the learning curve in getting to grips with Flash is a steep one. But the second drawback is more significant still. The reason why Flash animations are identical in every browser is that they require the visitor to your site to have the Flash Player plug-in installed, and it's this plug-in which actually displays the animation. On the bright side, it's not a huge download at a little over 200 Kb, it's free, and many web users already have it. The HTML code that places an animation on the page can automatically offer unequipped visitors the option of installing the plug-in (which involves a detour to Macromedia's website). On the darker side, visitors to your site that don't have the plug-in and don't want to wait while it's installed will see a blank rectangle on your page (if they stay around long enough!).

plug-in

A plug-in is a software program which works as a 'helper' for your web browser to handle a particular type of file for which the browser itself has no built-in support. When your browser encounters a Flash animation file, for example, it starts the Flash plug-in program. Instead of opening in its own separate window, the plug-in occupies a space on the page, just like an image.

If you do decide to use Flash, try to include a link to an HTML alternative so that users without the plug-in can still get at your content. Make sure gateway pages and presentations offer a 'Skip' button that the regular visitor can click to move past the animation. Gateway pages should also have an HTML link to the body of the site so that non-Flash users can still find a way in!

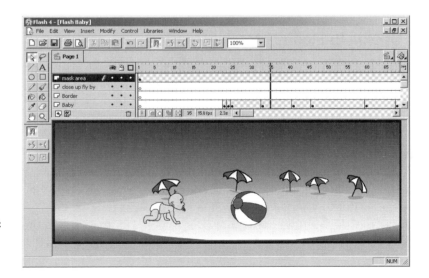

▶ Macromedia Flash, playing one of its sample animations.

Getting Flash

IT'S ON THE CD

Being a proprietary format, if you fancy giving Flash a whirl there are no difficult choices to make about software: you need Macromedia Flash, a commercial application from **http://www.macromedia.com/software/downloads.**

Although there's a lot to learn when you're starting out with Flash, it's not uphill all the way. If you open its Help menu, you'll find instant access to a set of eight lessons that take you through the basics in a very user-friendly, interactive way. There's also a set of over 20 sample files you can load and pull apart to find out how they work, and built-in libraries of buttons, graphics, sounds and movies you can include in your own creations.

Flash's own lessons and samples will get you off to a flying start without my help, so I'll leave you to it. When you've finished your own masterpiece, you'll save two files with the same name, but different extensions. The first has a .fla extension, and is your master file for use when you want to make changes to the animation in the future. The second, with a .swf extension, is the animation file you'll link to your web page. The animation is loaded using some tags we haven't yet encountered: **<OBJECT>** and **<EMBED>**. To make sure all browsers can understand the code, the two are used in combination, with the <EMBED> tag placed immediately before the closing </OBJECT> tag:

```
<OBJECT CLASSID="clsid:D27CDB6E-AE6D-11cf-96B8-444553540000"
WIDTH=100 HEIGHT=100
CODEBASE="http://active.macromedia.com/flash5/cabs">
<PARAM NAME=MOVIE VALUE="movie.swf">
<PARAM NAME=PLAY VALUE=true>
<PARAM NAME=LOOP VALUE=true>
<PARAM NAME=QUALITY VALUE=high>

<EMBED SRC="movie.swf" WIDTH=100 HEIGHT=100 PLAY=true LOOP=true
QUALITY=high
PLUGINSPAGE="http://www.macromedia.com/shockwave/download/index.cgi
P1_Prod_Version=ShockwaveFlash">
</EMBED>

</OBJECT>
```

The parts of the code that you'll need to change are shown in bold type – the name of the file and the dimensions of the animation. There are two other options you may want to change, each included twice: PLAY can be true or false according to whether the animation should start as soon as it's been loaded; LOOP has the same two options to determine whether the animation should play once or cycle repeatedly.

GOOD QUESTION!

What's that <PARAM> tag for?

The <OBJECT> tag is used to place various types of media content on the page, and alone it just specifies the type of content, its location and its dimensions. Other available settings have friendly names and a range of values to choose from, and the media object reads these from the <PARAM> tags using its two compulsory attributes: NAME and VALUE. We'll revisit the <PARAM> tag in the next chapter and in Part 3 when we deal with Java applets.

15

WEB MULTIMEDIA

Yup, it's showtime! Up to this point in the book, we've only dealt with text, images and animation which, although they obviously fall into the *multimedia* definition, don't really have the glitz conjured up by that magic word. In this chapter we'll take a look at some of the other forms of media you can add to your pages, from the obvious (audio and video) to the less obvious (live camera feeds and small interactive programs). Along the way I'll show you how to convert your music and video files to *streaming* media, removing that agonizing wait while a large file downloads.

How Does Web-Based Multimedia Work?

By itself, the web browser has built-in support for a very small range of media types – essentially just text and a few image formats. For other types of media it relies on extra software in the form of a **plug-in** or **viewer**, and uses a system called **MIME** (Multipurpose Internet Mail Extensions) to determine which of the user's installed plug-ins to use for a particular type of content.

Whenever content is sent from the web server to the user's browser, that content is accompanied by a **MIME type** such as **text/html, text/css, image/gif** or **video/mpeg**. If the browser recognizes the type as something it can handle unaided (as with the first three types) it gets on with it. If not, it looks at the user's system to see if any installed software has been set to handle the type. If it has, the software will appear on the page as a plug-in, or in its own window as a viewer, and take over the management of that particular piece of content from the browser.

JARGON BUSTER

viewer, plug-in

A viewer is an entirely separate program that you could run by itself if you wanted to. Most plug-ins can also be used as viewers, so if you were to install a plug-in that would handle a particular type of movie format found on a web page, it could probably be used to play any movies of the same type that you'd saved to your hard disk. A plug-in is a program that embeds itself into the web page, rather like an image.

So what happens if there's *no* compatible software installed? In some cases, the browser will offer to download the file containing the anonymous content so that the user can save it and play it later (after installing some suitable software). In other cases, the browser may simply ignore the content and place a little 'broken multimedia' icon on the page to indicate that the content can't be displayed, or it may offer to install the required plug-in. (A good example of this is the HTML code from Chapter 14 that places Flash content on a page: if no software is installed to handle the MIME type **application/x-shockwave-flash**, the browser prompts the user to install it, and whisks him off to the URL included in the code if he agrees.)

Linked vs. Embedded Media

When you decide to add multimedia content to a page, you have to make a choice: do you want to embed it into the page, or link it?

▶ **Embedded** media appears on the page like an image, and therefore has to be downloaded along with all the other items on the page.

▶ Using **Linked** media means adding a link to the file on your page, letting visitors choose whether to click-and-play or ignore it. The URL in the link may point directly at the media file, or it may point to a different page in which you've *embedded* the media.

As a general rule, if the media file is particularly large or the user is unlikely to have a compatible plug-in installed, use a link. That way, you can add a note to tell users the size of the file and where to download the plug-in before they continue.

Background Sounds (If You Must!)

It seems to me that however much you dislike the people that visit your site, forcing them to endure background music is just inhumane. At best, they'll be forced to mute their computer's audio output; at worst, they'll be gone so fast they leave skid-marks. Will anyone actually *enjoy* it? Perhaps, but only the first time they visit, and only if the music doesn't loop endlessly.

▶ An embedded audio file, with visible controls giving visitors a chance to turn it off!

If I haven't deterred you with that (and I hope I have!), here's the HTML code to embed a background audio file into the page:

```
<EMBED SRC="island.mid" LOOP=FALSE HIDDEN=FALSE>
```

The SRC attribute does the same job here that it does with the <IMG> tag, giving the URL of the audio file to be used. You can specify any type of sampled sound or MIDI file, but it's best to stick with common formats such as .wav, .mp3, .mid and .au.

The LOOP attribute can be true or false, but I strongly recommend using false, meaning that the file plays just once. The HIDDEN attribute offers the same two values to determine whether the control interface for the player plug-in will be visible (shown in the screenshot above). This gives your long-suffering visitors a chance to turn off the music, but the interface is rarely attractive. Fortunately it doesn't matter where you place the <EMBED> tag, so you can put it at the bottom of your page to avoid detracting from your other visible content.

What about the <BGSOUND> tag?

GOOD QUESTION!

You may have seen background sounds loaded into web pages using a different tag, <BGSOUND>. This tag is specific to Internet Explorer and uses the same SRC attribute to specify the sound file's URL. The LOOP attribute can be any number (1 is ideal!) or the word 'infinite'. Controls are never shown, so these two attributes are all you need.

Play-On-Demand Audio

Remember that your audio options aren't limited to embedded background sounds. You can create links to sound files using the audio equivalent of the picture gallery we looked at in Chapter 13, and let visitors choose which files to listen to. (The same applies to videos, animations and any other type of media you want to include, of course.)

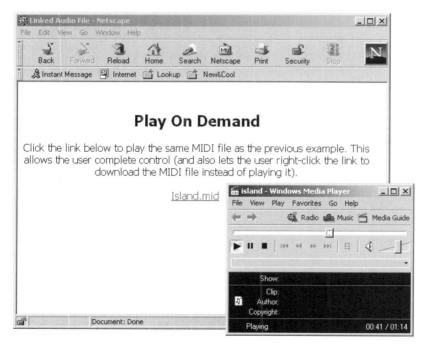

◀ Using links to media files (or to pages containing embedded media files) hands control back to the visitor.

If you fancy creating your own audio files, there's plenty of software around to help you do it. In fact, your operating system may already offer everything you need: most versions of Windows include the Sound Recorder utility, for instance, to create digital audio recordings. If you have musical talents, you can create your own MIDI files using software such as Cubase (**http://www.us.steinberg.net**), Cakewalk (**http://www.cakewalk.com**) or the simpler Band-In-A-Box (**http://www.pgmusic.com**). Or you can convert existing CD tracks and wave audio files to the popular MP3 format using Xing's AudioCatalyst or MP3 Encoder (**http://www.xingtech.com**). Most web users will have plug-ins that can handle the types of audio file I've mentioned so far. However, the MP3 format is a comparatively recent arrival, so you may want to point visitors in the direction of the free Winamp plug-in (**http://www.winamp.com**) if your site is going to include MP3s.

Movie Time: Adding Video

Video files are pretty rare things on the Web, chiefly used to show clips from feature films and home movies. They're also *big* files: 20 seconds of video can easily amount to over 1 megabyte, meaning that it takes a lot longer to download the movie than it does to watch it!

There are three video formats in use:

▶ **AVI** is the Windows video format I mentioned in Chapter 14, and it's best avoided for movies unless you also offer one of the following formats as an alternative.

▶ **QuickTime** is a movie format from Apple (**http://www.apple.com/quicktime**) which requires the QuickTime Viewer plug-in. An interesting alternative to the video file is QuickTime VR, an interactive virtual reality format. Click the **Developer** link on this site's button bar to learn more about the QuickTime Pro content creation program.

▶ **MPEG** (pronounced *emm-peg*) is the best-known video format. To create MPEG video files or convert from existing image and movie formats you need an MPEG encoder such as the Xing MPEG Video Encoder (**http://www.xingtech.com**).

As with the popular audio formats, most of your visitors will have an MPEG-compatible movie viewer (particularly since Windows 98 and later all include Microsoft's ActiveMovie or Media Player), but it won't necessarily be able to handle QuickTime videos. If you plump for the QuickTime video or VR formats, include the attribute **PLUGINSPAGE="http://www.apple.com/quicktime/download"** in your <EMBED> tag. The browser will then offer unequipped visitors the option of installing the QuickTime Viewer.

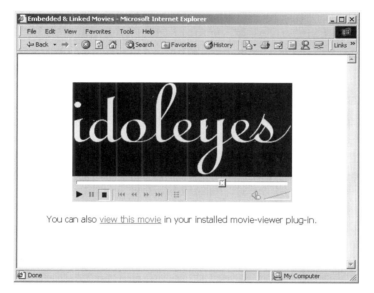

◀ An embedded movie file, shown using the Windows Media Player plug-in.

This is probably old news by now, but here's the tag you'll use to embed a video into your web page. Remember not to include the HIDDEN attribute for video embedding, or the movie won't be visible!

```
<EMBED SRC="mymovie.mpg" LOOP=FALSE>
```

Streaming Audio & Video

The big problem with audio files, and especially with videos, is that the visitor has to wait until the entire media file has been downloaded before he or she can view it. If you've done some of that waiting around yourself, you'll be very tempted to reduce the quality (and thus the size) of the files you add to your own site, or chop the movies down to a few seconds in length.

Fortunately there's an alternative: create **streaming** media files. With the right type of file and the right type of viewer, the audio or video clip is played *as it downloads*. Apart from a short pause while the viewer grabs enough of the file to stay a few jumps ahead of the stream (known as **buffering**), the visitor's thumb-twiddling time is cut to almost zero.

The number one plug-in for streaming audio and video is the free RealPlayer from **http://www.real.com/products/player**. The majority of visitors to your site will already have RealPlayer installed, but it's best to include an obvious link to that URL somewhere on your site for the few who haven't.

The content itself is known as RealAudio or RealVideo, and the program you need to create it is RealSystem Producer Plus from **http://www.realnetworks.com/products/producerplus**. This is a commercial program, but there's a free cut-down edition called RealProducer Basic which you can download from **http://www.realnetworks.com/products/producer**. This gives you everything you'll need to add streaming media to your site.

BY THE WAY

Have you really got a RealServer?

If the company providing your web space has RealServer installed (and will give you access to RealAudio streams) you can create enhanced content using Real's SureStream system. This system automatically adjusts the quality of the streaming content according to how busy the network is, ensuring that there are no breaks in transmission. Unless you're sure RealServer is available, always pick options marked for a standard web server.

Making It Stream

Creating the content and associated files can be a complicated business, and although RealProducer can do this for you, it does so by taking away some of your control, so here's a walk-through you can follow to create a single streaming audio or video file. (Following these steps, the RealPlayer window will be shown when a visitor clicks the link to the file. If you'd prefer to embed the player control, I do recommend that you use RealProducer's tools for creating and publishing the web page by selecting them from the Tools menu after completing step 5 below.)

1 Start RealProducer and choose **Record From File** in the Wizard dialog that pops up.

2 In the following steps of the Wizard, select an existing audio or video file to convert, enter your choice of Author and Copyright information, and choose the appropriate type of server (usually **Single rate for Web Servers**).

3 Choose the connection speed you expect the majority of your visitors to be using. Avoid choosing too high a setting: **56 K Modem** is usually suitable. In the next step(s), choose the type of audio and/or video that best describes your original file.

4 In the final step of the Wizard, choose where RealProducer should place the file it creates and click the **Finish** button. When the Wizard closes, you'll be returned to the main screen where you can check and change any details. If you're happy that everything is okay, click the **Start** button to create the output file.

5 After a few seconds of activity, you'll find a new file with an .rm extension in the folder you chose in step 4. This file is compressed, and should be a good deal smaller than the original.

6 This is the step where you take control! Using a text editor such as Windows Notepad, create a document containing a single line: the absolute URL of the .rm file's location on your website. This will be something like **http://www.mysite.com/audio/myfile.rm**. Save that file to the same folder as the .rm file and with the same name, but with a **.ram** extension (so you'd use **myfile.ram** for an audio file named myfile.rm).

7 Finally, add a link to your web page. All you need for this is a normal anchor tag, but make sure the link points to the .ram file you just created: <A HREF="myfile.ram">Listen to My File</A>.

When someone clicks the link, the RealPlayer will step in to read the URL inside the .ram file, connect to that URL and begin streaming the content. You can follow the steps above to create as many streaming audio and video files as you like.

GOOD QUESTION!

Can I listen to the file from my hard disk?

Yes you can. Open the .ram file in a text editor and replace the URL with the complete path to the file on your hard disk, prefixed with **file:///** (note the three slashes!). Click the link in your web page and listen. Don't forget to re-edit the .ram file when you're done!

The Live Cam Experience!

If you haven't come across live cam sites, the whole idea will probably seem a bit weird. You buy a little webcam for around £50, connect it to your computer, and set a few options in the software that accompanies it – how often it should take a picture, how to upload the result to your website, and so on – then point it at something interesting. If you'd like a sample, try the New Jersey Diner Cam at **http://www.nj.com/dinercam/live.html**.

◀ The wonders of
live cam at the
New Jersey Diner
Cam website.

The whole live cam thing is a gimmick, of course, but it does have practical values. Live cam sites are popular, and good sites (where the camera is actually switched on and something moves once in a while) are few and far between, so this really can attract visitors. You may be able to think of something useful to point the camera at, too; for instance, there are live cams showing up-to-the-minute snow conditions in ski resorts, and traffic conditions at busy intersections in major cities.

The catch with live cam is that a new picture has to be uploaded to your web server every minute or so at most: if there's too much waiting around involved, visitors won't bother. The software bundled with your camera can do all this for you, but if you have to pay call charges for your Internet connection it'll cost a small fortune! It's an option best suited to those with DSL, cable or some other form of 'always on' connection.

Java Applets: Action & Interactivity

In computer terms, an **applet** is a small application or utility that forms part of a bigger piece of software. On the Web, it's a small program written in a programming language called **Java** and slotted into the page like an image. Being a program rather than a single type of content, a Java applet can do quite a lot: it can be animated; it can display GIF or JPEG images; it can play sounds; it can provide hyperlinks; it can react to mouse movement and clicks in any way you wish, and a lot more.

BY THE WAY

Vested interest alert!

I won't ramble on about the life-enhancing qualities of Java applets. My own company designs Java applets, so of course I think they're pretty great. Nevertheless, they're just another option to consider, and you may feel they're not suitable for your own site.

In many ways, then, Java applets are similar to the Flash animation we met in Chapter 14. There are a lot of differences, of course – not least that it's much easier to design a Flash animation than it is to write an applet – but Java has an important advantage: most browsers from Netscape 3 and Internet Explorer 3 upwards will be able to display the applet without a plug-in. (Netscape 6 and Opera *do* use a plug-in, but this will usually be installed along with the browser.)

Although Java programming is more complicated than HTML (you can learn about it in Part 3), there are many free applets available on the Web, and for this section I'll assume that you've got your hands on one of those and just need to slot it into your page. I've included a simple applet in this chapter's folder on the CD-ROM, but here are a few places to find free Java online. Whatever applet you use, make sure it comes with documentation or an example web page.

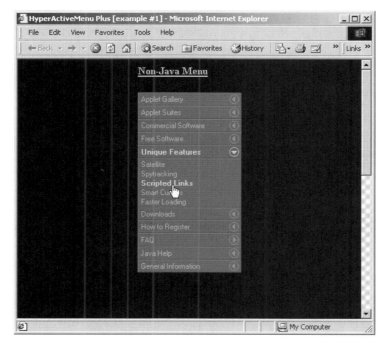

◀ An animated, interactive Java menu system in action, with an HTML link to an alternative non-Java page.

▶ **Cool Focus at http://www.coolfocus.com**, freeware and shareware applets from my own company (you knew I'd get that in somewhere, didn't you?)

▶ **JavaSoft at http://www.javasoft.com/applets**, free applets from Sun, the creators of Java.

▶ **JavaFile.com at http://www.javafile.com**, a collection of applets from a variety of companies and programmers.

A Java applet consists of one or more files with a .class extension, which together form the program itself. Along with the .class files, there may be image and sound files. You might have a file with a .jar extension: this is a zip-like compressed archive file that contains the .class files (and perhaps copies of those images and sounds). Modern browsers can find all the necessary files in the .jar archive, making the applet download and start running more quickly.

Java applets have their own tag for placement on a page, the **\<APPLET\>** tag. A very simple Java applet could be placed on the page like this:

```
<APPLET CODE="myapplet.class" WIDTH=100 HEIGHT=100>
</APPLET>
```

The three attributes, CODE, WIDTH and HEIGHT are all required. The CODE attribute is the important one: it gives the name of the .class file that the browser should load. (If your applet uses several .class files, check the documentation to find out which one should be used here.) Note that this isn't a URL, it must be just the *name* of the file.

To these attributes, you can add ALIGN, HSPACE and VSPACE, using the same alignment and spacing options as the <IMG> tag (see Chapter 6). If the applet came with a .jar file, add the attribute ARCHIVE="myapplet.jar", once again using just the name of the file, not its URL.

The CODEBASE Attribute: Find Those Files!

As yet, then, we haven't included any URLs at all in the <APPLET> tag, so the browser is going to assume that the applet files are in the same directory as the current web page. If you prefer to put all the files somewhere else, such as your 'images' directory or a new 'applets' directory, you need to tell the browser to look in the right place. Another attribute, **CODEBASE**, is used for the job.

The CODEBASE attribute is a URL, but it's the URL of a directory, not a file. The way to work it out is to take the URL of one of the applet files, strip the filename from the end, and put the remainder into the CODEBASE attribute. So if your web page is the root directory of your site (your 'site' directory) and the applet files are all in a subfolder called 'applets', the attribute would be CODEBASE="applets/". (The slash at the end is optional.)

Help – Class not found

If you load a page containing an applet and see a blank box on the page, with the words "Class … not found" shown in the browser's status bar, the browser can't find your .class file(s). Make sure you've got the correct name in the **CODE** attribute, and the path to the correct directory in **CODEBASE**. Also make sure that all the files are in the same directory, and that you really have been given every file you need!

Choosing Options With Parameters

Most Java applets have a range of options you can choose from to customize their appearance or behaviour, and these are specified using the **<PARAM>** tag we encountered briefly in the previous chapter. You can include as many <PARAM> tags as you need to, placed in any order between the <APPLET> and </APPLET> tags.

The <PARAM> tag has two compulsory attributes, NAME and VALUE, and this is where it's vital to have some documentation for the applet or an example web page – you need to know which parameter names you can use, and what the available values are for each. (Guesswork is no good here: applet designers make up their own names, and can choose anything they like!) Here's an example of a complete <APPLET> tag that includes three parameters:

```
<APPLET CODE="myapplet.class" WIDTH=100 HEIGHT=100
CODEBASE="../classes">
<PARAM NAME="BackgroundColour" VALUE="800000">
<PARAM NAME="Text" VALUE="Home Page">
<PARAM NAME="URL" VALUE="../index.htm">
</APPLET>
```

Adding Those User-Friendly Touches

When you use Java on your site, remember that a few users won't be able to see it. There's still a small percentage of web users out there whose browsers don't support Java, and others who've chosen to switch off their browsers' Java support. To keep your site friendly and usable for those non-Java surfers, it's a good idea to add two extra items to your HTML code.

First, add an ALT attribute to the <APPLET> tag containing a brief description of the applet, such as **ALT="Navigational Java menu applet"**. Users who've turned off their Java support will see this text in place of the applet. Second, add any ordinary HTML code you like before the final </APPLET> tag. For example, if your applet is a menu system that contains links to all your pages, you might choose to include ordinary anchor tags containing the same set of links. This HTML will be displayed in any browser that doesn't support Java.

If you're relying on the applet to provide your entire site navigation, it's best to take a belt-and-braces approach: create a separate web page containing HTML links to the pages, and include HTML links on both pages leading to the alternative page (as in the screenshot on page 245).

What Else?

In this chapter we've covered all the major types of web multimedia, but there are other 'less major' types – an example would be virtual reality (VRML), which was much hyped as the future of web design a couple of years ago, and has since pretty much vanished. The catch with VRML, as with many other forms of media, is that companies created their own extensions to the VRML language to add irresistible new features, all of which required the user to download a huge proprietary plug-in. A diehard VRML fan could arm himself with 20 megabytes of plug-ins and *still* find virtual reality scenes he couldn't view!

If you stick with Flash, Java, RealAudio/Video, and the common types of sound and movie format we've talked about, you can be sure that a large part of your audience will have the necessary software to enjoy them. If you're tempted towards a less common type of media, bear these final tips in mind:

▶ Include a clear link to the site from which the plug-in can be downloaded (don't just include it in the <EMBED> tag).

▶ If the plug-in is more than a few hundred kilobytes in size, you'll have to do a good selling job to explain why visitors should install it! Try to include links to other sites that use it.

▶ Avoid embedding unusual media types into pages and catching visitors by surprise. Let them read about the format, install the plug-in, and follow links to the media pages.

3

WEB SCRIPTING & PROGRAMMING

▶ **IN THIS PART**

16

THE BASICS OF JAVASCRIPT

Up to this point in the book, your pages are inert: they can't interact with the user, other than by fetching a document after a link is clicked, and they can't react when something happens, such as a mouse-movement or click. HTML was simply designed to *display* content in a clear and universal way, with no added bells and whistles. CSS arrived later, giving more control over the appearance of the content (see Chapter 9). And scripting introduced yet more flexibility, giving us the chance to make the content interactive and dynamic.

In this chapter and the three that follow you'll learn about **JavaScript**, the language that provides these extra features, and how to write your own scripts. That's if you want to, of course – if you'd rather skip the actual learning, you'll find plenty of examples to use in your own pages just by copying the code. Remember that you can try it all out for yourself using the example pages on the CD-ROM.

What Is JavaScript?

As a quick definition, JavaScript is a **scripting language**, a text-based language that extends the capabilities of an application by allowing the user to write his or her own features, shortcuts and macros. For our purposes, the 'application' we're talking about is the web browser and the documents it displays. Although JavaScript isn't technically a *programming* language (you can't write complete programs with it), it does have a lot of the same features – you could write a complete scientific calculator in JavaScript, for example.

GOOD QUESTION!

Is JavaScript the same as Java?

No, they're very different animals. For one thing, Java is a programming language. There are similarities in the way JavaScript and Java code is written, though, because both were based on an earlier language called C (yup, just 'C'). JavaScript was originally called 'LiveScript', and went through an impromptu change of name to benefit from the hype surrounding Java.

If you read about CSS in Chapter 9, the basic workings of JavaScript will be familiar. Like CSS, JavaScript is used in combination with HTML in a web page, and you can choose whether to place scripts in a block on the page, build them into HTML tags, or store them in a separate file linked to the page. And best of all, you can write your scripts in the same text editor you use to write your HTML and CSS pages!

Properties, Methods & Events

I'm not going drag you into a lot of technical detail, but these three items are the basis of any scripting or programming language, so it helps to know what they refer to. Here's a thumbnail description of each:

▶ **Properties** are the attributes of an item. JavaScript works with a web page, and the page has *properties* such as its background colour, its title and its URL.

▶ **Methods** are commands built into the JavaScript language that make something happen. JavaScript is known as an *object-oriented* language – it regards items such as the window and the web page as *objects*. One object can contain other objects (the window contains the web page, for example), and each object may have several methods that can be used with it. As an example, the browser window contains a **history** object that keeps a list of the pages previously visited, and the history object has a **back()** method that does the same as clicking the browser's Back button. (We'll meet the history.back() method again in a moment.)

▶ **Events** are things that happen within the browser, such as a link being clicked. You can write a script that watches for a particular event and, when it happens, takes a particular action.

Finally, before we get into the tastier stuff, a word about JavaScript versions. Like all applications and programming languages, JavaScript has passed through a few different versions, and at the time of writing it stands at v1.2. This version of the language can be used in browsers from Netscape 4 and Internet Explorer 4 upwards. Version 1.1 can be used in Netscape 3 upwards (IE arrived late at the JavaScript party and never provided support for JavaScript 1.1). Almost all the example code in this book uses v1.0 of the language and will therefore work in Netscape 3+ and Internet Explorer 4+.

In the next chapter we'll use some features that were added in JavaScript 1.2 and I'll show you how to make sure the browser is recent enough to understand it.

Note: Unlike HTML, JavaScript does take notice of line breaks! Splitting a line of code into two by pressing the Enter key may prevent the code from working. Unfortunately this book has a fixed width, unlike your text editor, so I've had to break apart long lines of code. In those cases, I've used this symbol ⌐ to indicate that the following line is a continuation of the current one.

Simple JavaScript Methods

The simplest way to use JavaScript is to include it in anchor (<A>) tags. Instead of putting the URL of a document in the HREF attribute, we can call a JavaScript method to make something happen when the visitor clicks the link. There are several very useful JavaScript methods you can use in this way and they make a painless introduction to the world of JavaScript.

Getting Historical: The back() Method

The *history list* is the list of previously visited pages maintained by the browser (or, in JavaScript terms, by the *window* object). Clicking the Back button loads the page one step back in the list – the last page viewed by the visitor.

For this example, I've created a pair of joke/punchline pages. Clicking the text of the joke leads to the page containing the punchline, and that second page includes a link to whatever page the visitor last viewed. In this case, of course, we know what page that was and we could have used a URL to link back to it. Here's a more practical use: your site may use a single glossary page explaining technical terms, with many pages linking to it. This method allows the visitor to check a glossary definition and return to the page he or she was reading.

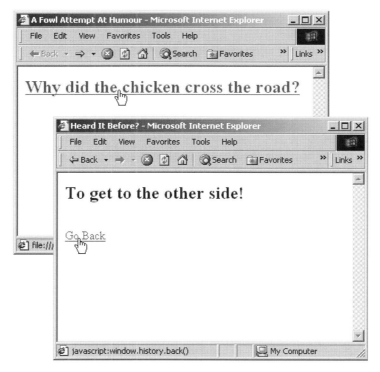

◀ Clicking the link in the first window opens a new page containing the punchline, along with a link that takes the visitor back one step in the history list.

Here's the code that makes the link, with the part that matters shown in bold type:

```
<A HREF="javascript:window.history.back()">Go Back</A>
```

Since that was our first JavaScript example, let's skip through some important points about it. First, JavaScript is case sensitive: if you type History.back() or history.Back(), the link won't work and the browser will let you know in some way that there's an error in the code. Second, the brackets after the word back are vital. All JavaScript method names are followed by an opening and closing bracket (sometimes with something between them, as we'll see in a moment).

Finally there's the format of the code itself. The word **javascript:** tells the browser that what follows is a piece of script, in the same way that using mailto: in a link says that what follows is an email address (see page 55). The dots separating each little chunk of code are also vital: they're the programming equivalent of the slashes we use in URLs and filenames.

257

BY THE WAY

Windows, windows everywhere...

The word **window** in the example code is actually not necessary. If we left it out, using just javascript:history.back(), the code would still work because in JavaScript everything stems from the **window** object so browsers usually take it for granted. I'm going to keep using it for clarity in the following examples, but feel free to leave it out of your own code (making sure you also remove the dot that follows it).

Going hand-in-hand with the back() method, although not as useful, you can use the **forward()** method to provide a link that does the equivalent of a click on the browser's Forward button: javascript:window.history.forward().

Closing The Window

Working in exactly the same way as the back() and forward() methods, there's the **close()** method which closes the browser window. As before, you can use it in an anchor tag like this:

```
<A HREF="javascript:window.close()">Close Window</A>
```

There's a tiny catch with the close() method in Internet Explorer: the user will be asked for permission to close the window, as in the next screenshot. This doesn't happen with windows that were opened using JavaScript methods such as the window.open() method covered later in this chapter, so you might open a small popup window to provide extra information and include this link to let the user close it again.

Getting Argumentative: The alert() Method

The methods we've looked at so far each do one straightforward job, and they don't need any extra information to do it. The **alert()** method is different: it displays any message you choose in a dialog box, so you need some way to specify the message.

This leads to a new term: **arguments**. An argument is a piece of information passed to a method inside its brackets. In general, an argument can be

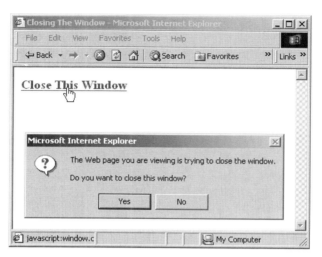

◀ Internet Explorer doesn't let you silently close a window with script unless you also **opened** it with script.

anything at all: text, a number, or any object or property, as long as the method knows what to do with it. Because the alert() method displays messages, it expects you to supply some text and wouldn't know what to do with anything else. Programming languages refer to text as a **string** (it's a *string* of characters), and strings are always enclosed in quote marks.

Using the anchor tag again, here's how to display a message when the user clicks the link, giving the result shown in the screenshot below:

```
<A HREF="javascript:window.alert('Hello!')">Say Hello!</A>
```

◀ The result of passing a string to the alert() method.

GOOD QUESTION!

Why use single-quotes instead of double-quotes?

Unlike HTML, JavaScript lets you use either single or double quote marks and treats both the same, so in some cases you can use whichever you prefer. In this case, though, we have to enclose the entire contents of the anchor tag's HREF attribute in double-quotes. If we also used double-quotes to pass the string argument in the **alert()** method, the browser would assume that the quote symbol before the word **Hello** marked the end of the HREF attribute rather than the beginning of the argument, and the whole thing would fail miserably.

Confirmations & Prompts

There are two other methods that use arguments in a similar way to alert(). One displays a message dialog to ask a question, offering a choice of Yes/No or OK/Cancel. The other asks a question and provides space for the user to type an answer. In both cases you use arguments to choose what question should be asked, but there's one big difference: this time we're not just telling the user something, we're asking for information. So the two following methods *return a value* to us that we can use for something later.

The first of the two new methods is **confirm(*question*)**. In the next screenshot, the code I've used is:

```
<A HREF="javascript:window.confirm('Are you sure you want to do that?')">Yes or No?</A>
```

Used by itself, of course, the question is meaningless: we'll incorporate it into something more useful later. What's interesting right now is the result – the value returned when a button is clicked. This value is called a **boolean**, and it can be either true or false. If the user clicks the OK button, we'll get a value of *true*; if the Cancel button is clicked we'll get *false*. (In fact, if you try this example yourself, you'll actually see a blank page containing the word 'true' or 'false'.)

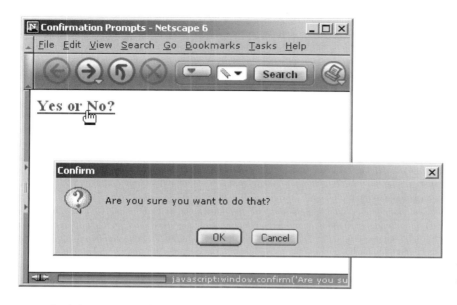

◀ Using the
confirm() method
to ask the user a
yes/no question.

The second of the new methods is **prompt(*question, default-answer*)**. For
this we pass two arguments: the question to be asked, and the answer to
return if the user doesn't type anything into the dialog box.

```
<A HREF="javascript:window.prompt('What is your name?', 'I have no
name!')">Tell Me...</A>
```

To pass more than one argument in a method, just separate them with a
comma and (if you want to make things more readable) a space. When the
user clicks the link, a dialog box will appear like the one in the next
screenshot, asking the question and displaying the default reply. The value
returned this time will be a string (a piece of text). If the user clicks the OK
button, we'll get whatever is in the text field of the dialog. If the user
presses the Cancel button, we'll get a **null** value.

Once again, if you try this example yourself you'll see a blank web page
containing the result (or the word 'null' if you click the Cancel button).

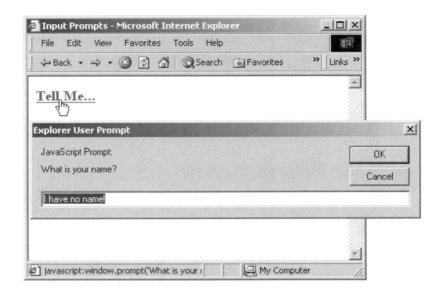

▶ The prompt()
method asks the
visitor for
information.

JARGON BUSTER

null

Strings are unusual types of data in that they can be **null**, or empty. It's rather an abstract idea, because it doesn't just mean that the string contains no characters (such as "") – it means that the string contains no value at all. If you tried to display a string containing no characters you'd just be displaying a blank piece of text. Trying to display a null string would result in an error. An important part of programming is second-guessing what the user might do and making sure you've got the result you expected before using it for anything.

The Void Keyword

Try this: type **javascript:'Hello!'** into your browser's address bar and press Enter. This command tells the browser to use JavaScript to display the string *Hello!*, and you'll see a blank page containing that word.

In the two examples above, when the dialog box closed we were immediately whisked to a new page displaying our answer. The reason for that is twofold: first, we were using the anchor tag which, after all, is supposed to lead *somewhere*; and second, both examples gave a return value, unlike the earlier example using the alert() method. The combination of the word **javascript:** and the value returned by the method gives **javascript:***return value*, so in the example using the prompt() method, if we'd chosen the default answer, the browser would have been left to deal with the equivalent of **<A HREF="javascript:'I have no name!'">**. That's a perfectly valid thing to put in an anchor tag (although it's not much use for anything) so the browser deals with it by displaying that string.

Although none of the examples has been particularly useful so far, there will certainly be times when you want to use a link to run a piece of JavaScript code without taking the user away from the current page. Fortunately there's an easy way to do just that. Include the word **void** and a space immediately after the word **javascript:** like this:

```
<A HREF="javascript:void window.prompt('What is your name?','I have no name!')">Tell Me...</A>
```

The word void is a special keyword that cancels the usual behaviour of the anchor tag, meaning that you can use the familiar look of the tag to indicate that something can be clicked without linking anywhere. You only need to use this when the JavaScript method returns a value, but it doesn't hurt to use it in all cases.

New Windows & Popups

Let's try something a little more useful! In Chapter 8 I explained how to open documents into new browser windows using the anchor tag's TARGET attribute. The catch with that method is that the user has to click the link to open the window. Once in a while you might want to open a new window automatically, perhaps to display news of a special offer as soon as your site loads, and that's a job for JavaScript. Here's the code that does it:

```
window.open('mypage.htm', 'mynewwindow')
```

The open() method has two arguments, both of which are strings so we enclose them in quotes: the first is the URL of the page to open, and the second is the name we want to assign to the new window. (You can also use HTML's built-in names _new and _blank here, explained on page 120.)

New or used?

BY THE WAY

The **open()** method isn't limited to opening new windows. If your second argument contains the name of an existing frame or window (or the HTML names _self, _parent or _top), the document will be opened into that.

That's how new browser windows are opened, but by itself it doesn't do what you're probably hoping for: a **popup**. Popups are windows that you can open with a particular size and location, and often without toolbars, menus and so on. To create a popup, we still use the open() method, but we add a third argument to it containing the features we need. The third argument is another string value containing a list of features each separated by a comma, like this:

```
window.open('mypage.htm', 'mynewwindow', 'width=200, height=100, top=250, ↵
left=250, location=no, toolbar=no, status=no, menubar=no, scrollbars=yes, ↵
resizable=yes')
```

Depending on the settings and features you want to specify, that third argument can get a bit unwieldy! If you leave out any of those individual settings, the browser will use its own default setting (or the preferences previously set by the user). If you're not concerned about the position of the window, for instance, you can remove the settings for top and left. If you use this method in response to a click on an anchor tag, you'll need to include the void keyword, because the open() method does return a value.

While we're on the subject, remember that most web users find popup windows irritating. Avoid using them unexpectedly: a user may be annoyed to find a popup window appearing as soon as he arrives at your site, but may be quite pleased to see a small window open containing the information he wanted when he clicks a link. Remember too that many

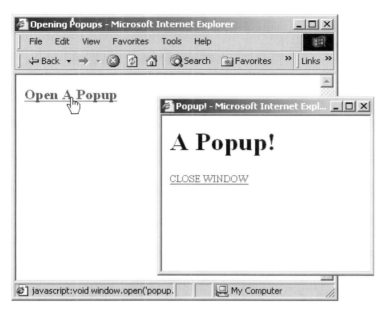

◀ Use the window.open() method to open a perfectly sized custom window anywhere you want it.

users close popups as a reflex action as soon as they appear, so an auto-opening popup isn't the place to put important information!

Writing Real Scripts

As a way of dipping your toe into the waters of JavaScript we've stuck to using *inline* script – calling built-in methods inside anchor tags. Now it's time to do some serious paddling: to make the most of JavaScript you need to write your own methods, which can be called in exactly the same way. These are longer than the examples we've looked at so far, and it isn't sensible (or possible) to squeeze them into HTML tags, so we gather them together into a **script block** on the page. A script block isn't any great departure from what you're used to; in fact, it's almost identical to the way we gathered style rules together in Chapter 9:

```
<SCRIPT LANGUAGE="JavaScript" TYPE="text/javascript">
<!--
...your script goes here...
// -->
</SCRIPT>
```

This code introduces a new HTML tag, **<SCRIPT>**, which contains all the script between its opening and closing tags. The two attributes of the tag simply tell the browser which scripting language we're using, and you'll rarely need to change these. As with style sheets (see page 143), we enclose all our script between HTML comment tags so that browsers that don't understand the <SCRIPT> tag won't treat our script as text to be displayed. There's one small addition to be made, though: we have to insert a double-slash before the closing comment tag. This is a JavaScript comment which forces the JavaScript interpreter to ignore the remainder of the line. Without this, the interpreter would try to make sense of that HTML comment tag, resulting in an error.

JARGON BUSTER

JavaScript interpreter

An **interpreter** is a small hidden program that reads the script we write as ordinary text and quickly converts it into complete gobbledegook that the computer can understand and work with.

Writing A Simple Function

The methods you write yourself are called **functions**, and the bare bones of a function look like this:

```
function functionName()
{
        do something useful...
}
```

A function starts with the word 'function' followed by the name you've chosen for the function, and the script carried out by the function is contained between curly brackets. The function's name shouldn't contain spaces or punctuation other than the underscore symbol (_).

In JavaScript and Java there are conventions that it's worth sticking to when choosing names: they don't make much difference to anything, but they do show other programmers that you know your onions! The convention in method and function naming is that the name begins with a lowercase letter and, if the name is formed by joining two or more words together, those words each start with an uppercase letter. A few conventional looking function names as illustrations are: go(), comeBack(), getUserName(). Notice that, like methods, your function names will also finish with a pair of brackets.

Let's write a simple function that displays a message box:

```
<SCRIPT LANGUAGE="JavaScript" TYPE="text/javascript">
<!--

function showMessage()
{
        alert('Here is a message.');
}

// -->
</SCRIPT>
```

The alert() method was used earlier in the chapter, so that should be familiar, and the body of the function currently contains just this one line. I've started that line with a tab indent which helps to make the code more readable; JavaScript ignores spaces, tabs and blank lines, so you can spread your code out in any way that suits you.

GOOD QUESTION!

Why does the line end with a semi-colon?

The semi-colon marks the end of a single self-contained statement: if you repeated the same piece of script immediately after this, the interpreter would know where the first statement ended and the second began. Although this isn't always necessary in JavaScript, it is required in Java and many other languages, so it's a good habit to get into.

267

After placing this code into our page (anywhere within the head or body of the page), we can now call this function from an anchor tag, as before:

```
<A HREF="javascript:showMessage()">Show me a message</A>
```

We're now calling our new function which, in turn, calls the alert() method to display the message. So far, so good. Now let's improve it by allowing different messages to be shown…

Passing Arguments To Functions

To vary the text displayed in the dialog box, we have to be able to pass string arguments to our function, which means making an alteration to the function itself:

```
function showMessage(message)
{
      alert(message);
}
```

I've made two changes in the script above: first I've inserted the word *message* between the brackets following the function name. Second, I've replaced the text of the message in the alert() method with the same word. That's it in literal terms, but in scripting terms I've used a **variable**. A variable is a named holding place for any kind of value, and you can choose almost any name you like as long as it's not a word that has a particular meaning in JavaScript (such as 'function' or 'window').

We can now create several anchor tags in the page that all call this function, but pass it different strings to display. In the function itself, any reference to the variable named *message* will be treated as a reference to the string that was passed to it.

```
<A HREF="javascript:showMessage('Number One')">First Message</A><BR>
<A HREF="javascript:showMessage('Number Two')">Second Message</A><BR>
<A HREF="javascript:showMessage('Number Three')">Third Message</A>
```

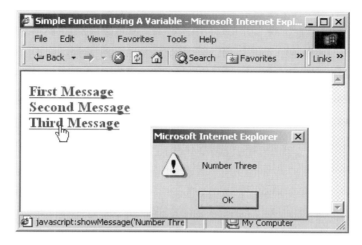

◀ The result of passing an argument into the function to be displayed.

Getting & Using Values

Now let's take things a step further by prompting the user for information, checking it for errors, and then displaying it in a dialog box. First, then, we're going to write two new functions. Take a deep breath!

```
function ask(question, defanswer)
{
        var answer = prompt(question, defanswer);

        if (isOkay(answer)) alert(answer);
        else alert('You clicked Cancel!');
}
function isOkay(input)
{
        if (input == null) return false;
        return true;
}
```

The functions are both short, but they introduce quite a lot that's new. Let's start with the first function: ask(question, defanswer). This uses two variable names so that we can pass two items to this method: the question to be asked and an answer to be used by default.

269

Next I've declared another variable called **answer** (I'll explain this use of variables later in the chapter). When the user closes the prompt window by clicking its OK or Cancel button, his response will be stored in the *answer* variable so that we can use it.

The last two lines of the first function introduce a construction that's used a lot in any language (including English): the **if ... else ...** construction. This is used to test whether a particular expression is true or false, and react accordingly. Here's an English example:

> if (you have no money) go to work;
> else stay home and vegetate;

The expression we want to test for trueness is enclosed within brackets, and it's followed by the action to take if the expression *is* true. We can leave it at that, or we can provide a course of action to take if the expression is false by adding the word *else* and that alternative action.

GOOD QUESTION!

Why do I need two functions for this?

In truth, you don't. I've done it this way to illustrate how two functions can be used together, but I could have scrapped the second function and changed the second and third lines of the first function to this:

```
if (answer == null) alert('You clicked Cancel!');
else alert(answer);
```

A side-effect of using two functions is that there's now a handy function in the page that can be used for checking whether a string is valid from any other function.

The expression we're testing here involves another function: we're sending the user's response (stored in the *answer* variable) to the isOkay() function to check that it's a valid string. If the user clicked the Cancel button, we want to know about that and display our own choice of message. So inside the brackets which always follow the *if*, we put isOkay(answer).

The is Okay method uses another *if* statement to test whether the string it was sent is null. The double equals sign means 'is the same as'. If the string *is* the same as null, we don't have a valid string, so this function sends back the response *false*. Otherwise it sends back *true*. From looking at the script, you might be expecting the function to send back a *true* straight after a *false* as well because I haven't used the word *else* before the words *return true*. The reason it doesn't is that when a function is told to return a particular value, it does so there and then, and ignores the remaining script in the function. So if the string isn't valid, the function returns a value of *false* and never gets to the next line.

GOOD QUESTION!

Why does the isOkay() function talk about input, not answer?

I could have chosen the name **answer** for this variable again, but because this is a separate function, I can use a different set of names. The **input** variable still holds whatever string value was passed into the function. Working on the principle that this function can be used to check any string passed from any number of other functions, it makes sense to pick an anonymous name like **input**.

Okay, you can breathe out now! The easy final step is to test this lot and see what happens, so we'll add a couple of anchor tags to the page. The composite screenshot overleaf shows the two dialog boxes that appear in succession when one of the Question links is clicked.

```
<A HREF="javascript:ask('What is your name?', 'I have no name!')">Question 1
</A><BR>
<A HREF="javascript:ask('What is your favourite colour?', 'red')">Question 2
</A><BR>
```

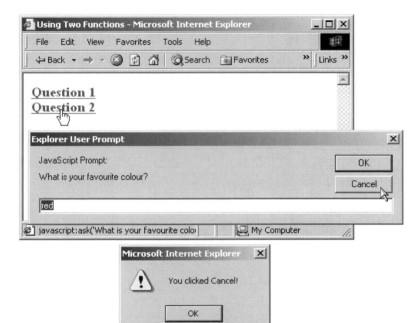

▶ When the
question has been
answered, the
answer is
displayed in a
second dialog,
unless the user
clicked the Cancel
button.

JavaScript Short Takes

Let's round off this chapter with a dash through some of the vital JavaScript bits and pieces you'll need to know when you write your own scripts. We'll be using these in the next few chapters, so you'll find plenty of examples over later pages if they don't make immediate sense.

Declaring & Using Variables

A **variable** is a named holding-place for a particular value, letting you work with the value without knowing precisely what it is. In the example above, for instance, the script asked the user for information, checked the result was valid, and displayed it, simply by referring to the response (whatever it turned out to be) as *answer*. We knew the answer would be a string value (text), but variables can hold numbers, boolean values, objects and property values.

A variable has to be *declared* – that is, you have to choose a name for a variable *before* you can give it a value. Variables are declared with the keyword **var**. Here are a few examples:

```
var username;
var num = 5;
var isloaded = false;
var myname = 'Rob Young';
var h = window.history;
var x, y, z;
```

The first line declares a variable named *username*, with no value assigned to it yet. Later in the code we could assign a value by saying username = 'Me' or username = getName().

The second line declares a variable named *num* and assigns a value of 5 to it (a number). Once a variable has had a particular type of value assigned to it, it must always use the *same* type of value. We can later say num = num + 2 (making num now equal 7), but we can't say num = 'Hello' because that would be trying to assign a string value to a numeric variable.

The third line declares a variable named *isloaded* and assigns the boolean value false. A boolean variable can hold a value that's either true or false.

The fourth line declares a variable named *myname* and assigns it a string value.

The fifth line illustrates how variables can hold objects, such as the window.history object we met earlier in the chapter. We could later use h.back() instead of window.history.back().

The final line declares three variables without assigning a value to any of them. These could all be different types of value, such as: x=5; y=false; z='Hello';.

JavaScript Comments

As in HTML, CSS and all other languages, it's useful to be able to add your own comments to your script to help you remember what does what (or to temporarily remove a chunk of script without actually deleting it). There are two ways to add comments to JavaScript:

```
x = 8 * 5; //x now equals 40
/* The bit below is where we get
 the background colour of the page */
var col = document.bgColor;
```

In the first line, the symbol // is used to comment out everything that comes after it on the same line. The symbols /* and */ cause everything between them to be treated as a comment; this could be anything from a small section of one line to a large multi-line block of script.

Using Reserved Characters In Strings

In Chapter 4 we covered *reserved characters* in HTML, characters such as < and " which have a special meaning to the HTML language. To display those characters on a page you have to use < and ". JavaScript has its own set of reserved characters that can be used in strings, formed by typing a backslash (\)followed by a particular character or symbol:

JavaScript	Meaning
\n	Inserts a line break, so the text that follows will appear on the next line: 'My first line.\nMy second line.'
\t	Inserts a tab indent.
\'	Inserts a single quote or apostrophe that will be displayed rather than marking the end of the string: 'I don\'t know.'
\"	Inserts a double quote in the same way.
\\	Because the backslash itself is a special character used in the items above, if you want to actually display a backslash, type two of them.

Comparing & Operating On Values

We've already seen a few ways to get your hands on values: prompting the user for information, or finding properties of objects such as document.bgColor, for example. Often you'll store these values in variables so that you can change them, check them or compare them. To do any of those things, you'll need a new set of symbols known as **operators**. These are **mathematical** and **logical** symbols, and you've probably seen most of them before.

Operator	Meaning
=	Assigns a value to a variable or property: x = 5 or **document.bgColor = FF0000**.
+, –, *, /	Standard mathematical operators for plus, minus, multiplied by, divided by, all used with numbers.
<	Less than.
>	Greater than.
<=	Less than or equal to.
>=	Greater than or equal to.
==	Is the same as. Used to compare two values and return a boolean (true or false) value.
!=	Is not the same as.
&&	Boolean And. Used when comparing two sets of values. If each set is true, the whole expression will be true; otherwise the expression will be false.
||	Boolean Or. Once again, used to compare two sets of values. If either set is true, the returned value will be true.

The last four operators in the list above are a bit weird, so here are a few examples to illustrate how they're used. Because they're all used for comparison tests, they'll almost always pop up in *if* statements.

```
var x = 5;
var y = 10;
var z = 15;
if (x+y == z) alert('True!');        //if x+y equals z (which is true)
if (x+y != z) alert('False!');       //if x+y is not equal to z (which is false)
if (x==5 && y==6) alert('True!');    //if x is 5 and y is 6 (which is false)
if (x==5 || y==6) alert('True');     //if x is 5 or y is 6 (which is true)
```

Although the + symbol is strictly a mathematical symbol, it can also be used to add one string value onto another like this:

```
var firstname = 'Rob';
var lastname = 'Young';
var fullname = firstname + ' ' + lastname; //fullname is now 'Rob Young'.
if (fullname == 'Rob Young') alert('True!');
```

Debugging JavaScript

When you've written your script you want to test it in your browser and make sure it works. Before publishing the page to your website, you should also test it in a range of target browsers: as a minimum, test in Netscape 4 and 6, and Internet Explorer 4 and/or 5.

One useful way to find or avoid **bugs** (mistakes in the script that prevent it working) is to use the alert() method to display the current value of a variable or property and make sure it's what you were expecting. As an example:

```
var x = 500;
alert(x);
var quitebig = (x > 100);
alert (quitebig);
```

First I've set the variable x to 500. The alert() method then shows the value of x so that I can check it. The result of testing whether x is greater than 100 is stored in the *quitebig* variable, and another alert() shows the result. If all goes well, the two dialog boxes will display '500' and 'true'. (You can see from this that although the variables store a number and a boolean respectively, the alert() method is happy to show both as a string.) If the code works, I can delete the two calls to alert().

▶ The exclamation icon in Internet Explorer's status bar indicates an error in the JavaScript. Double-clicking the icon displays a (sort of) explanation.

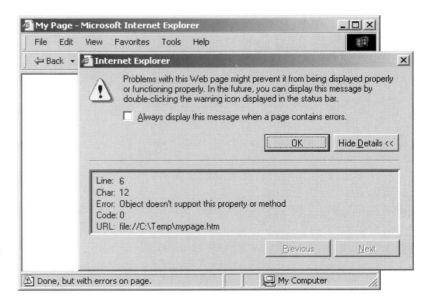

When you run scripts in Internet Explorer, keep watch for the exclamation icon in the status bar (shown in the previous screenshot) indicating that the script we've just tried to run contains an error. Double-clicking that icon opens a dialog box showing the number of the line containing the error to give you a clue to what went wrong.

In Netscape browsers, type **javascript:** into the address bar and press Enter to view a list of errors (if there were any). Netscape 6 also has a useful JavaScript Console you can open from its **Tasks** menu.

REAL-WORLD JAVASCRIPT

▶ **IN THIS CHAPTER**

Check users' browsers and load customized pages

Display your own text in the browser's status bar

Tell visitors when your page was last updated

Create mouse-sensitive 'rollover' image buttons

Make sure visitors always arrive at your front page

Once you're familiar with the basics of JavaScript that we covered in the last chapter, you can start to put that knowledge to good use. Although you may occasionally find a use for popup prompts and confirmation dialogs, in the real world of web design there are far more practical uses for JavaScript: reacting to mouse events to display messages in the browser status bar or creating 'rollover' button links; dynamically referring users of a particular browser to a different page; making sure visitors arrive at your 'front door' rather than a single out-of-context page from a frameset; and so on. In this chapter we'll look at the script needed to do these and other practical things.

Getting Browser Information

If you have a web page that will only display properly in a particular browser (such as Internet Explorer only) or in certain browser versions (such as v4 browsers and higher), it's useful to be able to send users of other browsers to different versions of the page automatically, without asking them to click a link. To do this, of course, you need to identify the browser, and JavaScript gives us a handy **navigator** object with two useful properties for this purpose: **appName** and **appVersion**. You can write a simple function to check those properties and display them back to you like this:

```
function checkBrowser()
{
alert(navigator.appName + '\n' + navigator.appVersion);
}
```

The composite screenshot below shows the result of displaying a page containing this script in a few different browsers. You can see that checking the *name* of the browser is easy enough, but there's some variation in the way browsers display their version numbers. Netscape 6 reports its version as 5, and Internet Explorer 5 reports the version as 4.

Let's assume you have a page that uses Internet Explorer-specific options (such as a <MARQUEE> tag), and you want to send non-IE users to an alternative page. Here's the script:

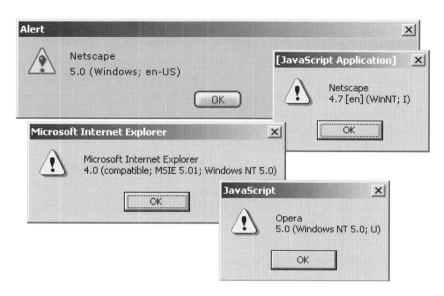

◀ The browser names and versions reported by Netscape 6 and 4.7, Internet Explorer 5.01 and Opera 5.0.

```
<SCRIPT LANGUAGE="JavaScript" TYPE="text/javascript">
<!--
if (navigator.appName !='Microsoft Internet Explorer') window.location =
'myotherpage.htm';
// -->
</SCRIPT>
```

There are two points to note about this script. First, it introduces a new property of the window object, **location**. By setting window.location to a different URL, the browser will load the document it refers to instead of the current one. Second, this isn't a JavaScript *function*, it's just a piece of script inside <SCRIPT> tags. We place this script in the head of the page, so that the browser reads and executes it before starting to load the body of the page.

GOOD QUESTION!

Why don't we write a function to do this?

A function can only run when called by name in response to an event (such as the visitor clicking a link) and we want to run this script automatically when the page starts to load. However, we could put this in a function and call that function when a visitor clicked a link to the browser-specific page.

Dealing with the browser version is a bit trickier; you need to know how different browsers represent their version numbers, and then extract the correct piece of information. The appVersion property is a string value, and JavaScript offers a number of built-in methods for working with strings. When you use these methods, it's vital to know that strings are *zero based* – that is, the first character of a string is regarded as character 0, not character 1. Two of the most useful methods are:

▶ **indexOf(*text*)**, which returns a number telling us the position of *text* in the string, or –1 if the string doesn't contain what we were looking for.

▶ **substring(*a, b*)**, which returns the chunk of text between the *a*th and *b*th characters of the string.

We can use the substring method to retrieve the first three characters of the reported version number (5.0, 4.7 or 4.0) like this:

```
var version = navigator.appVersion.substring(0, 3);
```

The substring method chops the string from just before the zero-th character to just before the third character and stores the result in the version variable. By combining the result with the appName we can accurately identify any browser version (remembering that Netscape 6 reports its version as 5.0) apart from Internet Explorer: is it *really* Internet Explorer 4, or is it 5? We can use the indexOf() method to find out:

```
var name = navigator.appName;
var version = navigator.appVersion.substring(0, 3);
if (name == 'Microsoft Internet Explorer' && version =='4.0')
 if (navigator.appVersion.indexOf('MSIE 5') > -1) version ='5.0';
```

The first two lines retrieve the name of the browser and its reported version, similar to the previous example. The first *if* statement tests whether we've found an Internet Explorer browser reporting its version as 4.0. If so, the second *if* statement looks for the position of the text 'MSIE 5' in the appVersion property. If the result is –1, that text doesn't appear in the property, so the version variable is left as it was. If the result is greater than –1, the text *does* appear in the property. We don't need to know exactly where it appears; the fact that it's there at all means we've found an Internet

Explorer 5. We can follow all this with more *if* statements to send particular browser/version combinations to different pages.

Browser Versions As Numbers

What if you wanted to send all Netscape versions below 4.7 to a different page? We've got the version stored in a string variable named version, but what we really need to do is convert it from a string to a number. Then we can write some script that effectively says: if the number is lower than 4.7, go somewhere else.

Just to complicate the issue, there are two types of number we can convert to in JavaScript. One is a *floating-point* number (or **float**), a number containing a decimal point such as 16.8. The other is an integer (or **int**), a whole number, such as 16. The two methods we can use to convert our string to either type of number are:

```
var vfloat = parseFloat(navigator.appVersion);
var vint = parseInt(navigator.appVersion);
```

If the browser had reported its version as '4.6', the vint variable would now be holding a value of 4, since parseInt ignores the decimal point and anything that follows it. The vfloat variable contains what we need, the number 4.6. So the code we use to direct Netscape versions lower than 4.7 to a different page looks like this:

```
var vfloat = parseFloat(navigator.appVersion);
if (navigator.appName == 'Netscape' && vfloat < 4.7) window.location =
'myotherpage.htm';
```

An Event! Custom Status Bar Text

When the visitor moves a mouse over a link, the URL that the link points to is shown in the browser's status bar. It's helpful and informative, but perhaps you'd rather display something different such as a quick description of the page? You can get at the status bar text using another of the window object's properties, **status**. Let's write a little function to do just that:

```
function setStatus(message)
{
        window.status = message;
}
```

That's a refreshingly simple piece of script! Because it's a function, it will only be called when we actually refer to it by name – the browser will never run it automatically while loading the page – so we can place it anywhere on the page, head or body, between the usual <SCRIPT> tags.

Sadly it isn't doing anything useful yet. We need to **trap an event** so that we know exactly when to call that function and tell it to display something. You may remember from the last chapter that an event is the general name for 'something happening': a mouse click or movement, for example. Most of the items on the page are firing events all the time as the mouse moves around the page, clicks and scrolls. Most of these events we ignore (in fact, we've ignored all of them so far!). If we want to respond when a particular event fires, we *trap* it. Here are some of the most useful events fired by items on the page, and the page itself:

Event	Meaning
onClick	The item has been clicked (a complete mouse down/mouse-up combination).
onMouseDown	A mouse button has been clicked down over the item.
onMouseUp	A mouse button has been released over the item.
onMouseMove	The mouse has moved over the item (every time the mouse moves by one pixel this event is fired, so there could be hundreds happening every second!).
onMouseOver	The mouse has moved onto the item.
onMouseOut	The mouse has moved out of the item.
onLoad	The item has been loaded (useful for the page itself and for images).
onUnload	The item has been removed (generally useful only for the page itself, when departing to another page).

We can build these events into almost any HTML tag that puts an item on the page or marks out an area, such as <IMG>, <P>, <DIV> and <HR>. Here's how:

```
<A HREF="doc.htm" onMouseOver="doSomething();return true">
```

We're now trapping the onMouseOver event in the <A> tag above and calling a function named doSomething() when that event occurs. It's a lot like the way we used JavaScript links in the same tag in the previous chapter, but with one essential difference: when trapping *events* in anchor tags, we must finish with a semi-colon and the words **return true**.

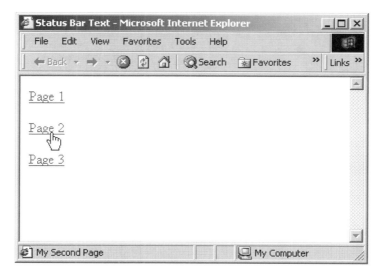

◀ Trapping onMouseOver and onMouseOut events to display custom text in the browser's status bar.

So, to return to our aim of showing custom text in the status bar, we need to trap two events: onMouseOver and onMouseOut. We'll use the first to display the text we want shown when the mouse moves over the link; the second will tell us when the mouse moves out of the link so that we can remove the status bar text:

```
<A HREF="page1.htm" onMouseOver="setStatus('My First Page');return true"
onMouseOut="setStatus('')">Page 1</A><P>
<A HREF="page2.htm" onMouseOver="setStatus('My Second Page');return true"
onMouseOut="setStatus('')">Page 2</A><P>
<A HREF="page3.htm" onMouseOver="setStatus('My Third Page');return true"
onMouseOut="setStatus('')">Page 3</A>
```

▶ *Events are the essence of Dynamic HTML, so we'll see more of them in Chapter 18. Don't rush away, though! Later in this chapter we'll use event trapping to create image rollovers.*

Page Modification Date

A good website is always changing – keeping your site fresh is one of the surest ways to keep your visitors returning. It's also helpful to tell visitors *when* a particular page was last updated, but it's not something you'll always remember to do. Still, why try to remember? Add some script to insert it automatically!

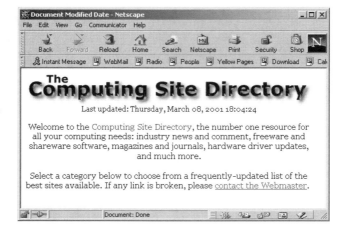

▶ Below the banner, a piece of JavaScript is inserting the page's modification date dynamically as the page loads.

Once again, this is a two-step affair. First we'll write a small function that puts together the text we want to display. Second, we'll add the script that actually places it on the page. The first step makes use of the window's **document** object, which refers to the current web page and has a handy property named **lastModified**. This is a string value containing the date and time the page was last saved. The function below simply creates a string containing the text we want to display on the page, with HTML tags to make it a little smaller than the other page text and place a paragraph break after it. When we call this function, it will return that string.

```
<SCRIPT LANGUAGE="JavaScript" TYPE="text/javascript">
<!--
function getModDate()
{
        var s ='<SMALL>Last updated:' + document.lastModified + ↵
        '</SMALL><P>';
        return s;
```

```
}
// -->
</SCRIPT>
```

We place this chunk of script into the head of the page, so that we can be sure it's been loaded before the browser starts putting together the body.

GOOD QUESTION!

Do I really need a variable in that function?

Good programming dictates that you aim for a balance between making your code readable and keeping it economic (since each variable requires some computer memory for storage). I've used the variable for clarity, but a better way would have been to use just a single line of code and no variable:

```
return '<SMALL>Last updated: ' + document.lastModified +'</SMALL><P>';
```

The second step introduces a method built into the **document** object, and an extremely useful one: **document.write(*string*)**. Between the brackets we put a string, or a reference to a string. If we place this somewhere on the page, the browser will display our chosen text at that point on the page.

The text we want will be supplied by the getModDate() function we just wrote, so we use the write() method like this: document.write(getModDate()). Here's an excerpt from the page shown in the previous screenshot showing how this all fits together. I've highlighted the relevant sections in bold type:

```
<HEAD>
<TITLE>Last Modified Date</TITLE>
<SCRIPT LANGUAGE="JavaScript" TYPE="text/javascript">
<!--
function getModDate()
{
var s = '<SMALL>Last updated: ' + document.lastModified + ↵
'</SMALL><P>';
return s;
```

```
}
// -->
</SCRIPT>
</HEAD>
<BODY BGCOLOR=#FFFFF0 TEXT=#000000>
<IMG SRC="banner.gif" WIDTH=503 HEIGHT=58 ALT="The Computing Site
Directory"><BR>

<SCRIPT LANGUAGE="JavaScript" TYPE="text/javascript">
<!--
document.write(getModDate());
// -->
</SCRIPT>

Welcome to the Computing Site Directory...

</BODY>
```

Putting It Together: Dynamic Page Contents

What we've just created is an example of a **dynamic** page. A dynamic page is a page that changes as it loads or while it's being used, and that's really the domain of Dynamic HTML, which we'll look at in the next chapter. But there are other things we can do with the document.write() method: some are useful, some are just playful, but they're all just as simple.

Although there's never any good reason for doing any of these things, I can't resist pointing them out. You can use the prompt() method from Chapter 16 to ask the visitor's name as the page loads, and then display **Hello** *Username* on the page using document.write(). You can display '**Your browser is** ' + **navigator.appName** or '**You came here from** ' + **document.referrer** (although both give the visitor the unnerving feeling of being watched!). The document.referrer property stores the URL of the document from which the visitor linked to this one, although in some browsers the property is empty when the pages are loaded from your hard disk.

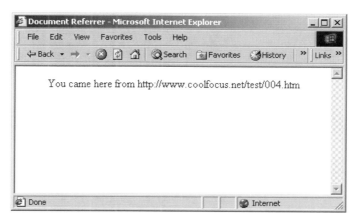

◄ Pointless, and perhaps slightly worrying for some users, but easy to do using document.write().

Here are two rather more sensible ways to use document.write(). If you have a page that definitely requires the use of a particular browser or version, you can use the code from the beginning of this chapter to determine whether visitors have the correct browser. If they do, your function will return an empty string (") to be displayed by document.write(). If they don't, the function can return a string containing a note that the browser is incompatible and providing a link to the Microsoft/Opera/Netscape website for download. Since you can build HTML tags into the string, it's possible to add links and even images dynamically like this.

The second situation is one I've encountered a lot when adding Java applets to a web page: the dimensions of the applet often need to be larger in non-Internet Explorer browsers. Rather than writing two pages and diverting non-IE users to the alternative, it's possible to build the appropriate part of the page dynamically. Starting with an HTML tag like this:

```
<APPLET CODE="MyApplet.class" WIDTH=100 HEIGHT=100>
<PARAM NAME="Colour" VALUE="Red">
</APPLET>
```

it's possible to swap between two versions of the <APPLET> tag containing different dimensions according to the user's browser:

```
<SCRIPT LANGUAGE="JavaScript" TYPE="text/javascript">
<!--
if (navigator.appName != 'Microsoft Internet Explorer') ↵
```

```
document.write('<APPLET CODE="MyApplet.class" WIDTH=80 HEIGHT=80>');
else document.write('<APPLET CODE="MyApplet.class" WIDTH=100 ⏎
HEIGHT=100>');
// -->
</SCRIPT>
<PARAM NAME="Colour" VALUE="Red">
</APPLET>
```

Checking JavaScript Versions

In Chapter 16 I mentioned the thorny issue of JavaScript versions, and once in a while you'll want to use a method or property that wasn't available in JavaScript 1.0. Examples are the Image object, which we'll be using for image rollovers in a moment, and the **Screen** object. The Screen object can be used to get the width, height and colour depth of the user's monitor screen by reading the properties Screen.width, Screen.height and Screen.colorDepth, each of which returns a number.

The Screen object was introduced in JavaScript v1.2, so it's available in v4 browsers and higher. If you include it in a page visited by someone with an older browser, they'll see an error message. The way around this is to ensure that incompatible browsers don't try to read a block of script containing JavaScript 1.2 references. You do that by specifying the minimum version in the <SCRIPT> tag:

```
<SCRIPT LANGUAGE="JavaScript1.2" TYPE="text/javascript">
<!--
        if (Screen.height < 600) alert('What a small screen!');
// -->
</SCRIPT>
```

If your script requires JavaScript 1.1 or 1.2, include that version number straight after the word 'JavaScript', as in the script above. Don't use 'JavaScript1.0' though: older browsers won't understand it.

Image Rollovers

Other than determining browser versions, the most popular use of
JavaScript is probably to create image rollovers – buttons that react when
the mouse moves over them by displaying an alternative image. This is
going to involve a number of issues we haven't covered before, but the
basics are simple enough. First we need to write two functions: one to load
the two sets of images, and one to handle the events fired by the mouse
moving over the images. Next we need to add the <IMG> tags to the page,
enclosed in anchor tags (since we'll be using these buttons as links),
trapping the onMouseOver and onMouseOut events as we did for the status
bar text earlier in the chapter.

◀ Interactive
image rollover
buttons using
JavaScript events.

The code below shows the bare bones of the <SCRIPT> tag containing the
two functions. We're going to use the JavaScript **Image** object, which is only
available in JavaScript 1.1 and higher, so we mark this block of script as
LANGUAGE='JavaScript1.1'.

Next I've declared a boolean variable, loaded, and set it to false so that we
can track whether the images have all loaded before we try to display them.
(While the page loads, the visitor might move the mouse over the part of
the page where the images will later be placed, firing the onMouseOver
event. The browser would try to display the alternative image which
doesn't yet exist, causing an error message to appear.) After we load the
images in the first function, we set loaded to true.

```
<SCRIPT LANGUAGE="JavaScript1.1" TYPE="text/javascript">
<!--
var loaded = false;

function loadImages()
{
        //load images here...
loaded = true;
}

function react(img, plain)
{

}
// -->
</SCRIPT>
```

GOOD QUESTION!

Why not declare the 'loaded' variable inside a function?

When variables are declared **inside** a function, they can only be used in that function. As far as other functions on the page are concerned, no variable with that name exists. Declaring a variable before the functions makes that variable available throughout the page: any function in this script block (and other script blocks that follow) can refer to it.

Now we'll add the code that loads the images, replacing that commented line in the first function. The script below loads one pair of images, and consists of two lines repeated. The first line creates an Image object with a width and height of 0, and names it img1plain. The second line specifies the URL of the image file (in exactly the same way as using the <IMG SRC="..."> tag) which causes the browser to load the image. We then do the same again, creating and loading an image we've named img1over.

```
img1plain = new Image(0,0);
img1plain.src = 'plain1.gif';
img1over = new Image(0,0);
img1over.src = 'over1.gif';
```

You can add as many pairs of images as you like, provided every image is given a unique name (for instance, replacing the '1' with '2', '3', and so on). In the example page in this chapter's folder on the CD-ROM, I've used three sets of images.

Now let's skip below the script block and write the HTML that displays the images and traps their events:

```
<A HREF="mypage.htm" onMouseOver="react('img1', false);return true"
onMouseOut="react('img1', true);return true"><IMG SRC="plain1.gif"
NAME="img1" WIDTH=150 HEIGHT=25 BORDER=0></A><BR>
```

This is simply an <IMG> tag enclosed between <A> tags to make the image act as a link. I've added a **NAME** attribute to the <IMG> tag, assigning it the name img1. By naming an image in this way, we can later refer to it by name in our script. The anchor tag traps the onMouseOver and onMouseOut events, calling our react() function and passing the name of the image along with a true or false boolean value. To add more images, simply copy the same chunk of HTML and change the 'img1' references to 'img2', 'img3', and so on.

Next we'll write the contents of the react() method which reacts to the mouse movements:

```
function react(img, plain)
{
        if (loaded)
                {
                if (plain) document[img].src = eval(img + "plain.src");
                else document[img].src = eval(img + "over.src");
                }
}
```

This function is passed two values from our anchor tags: img is the name of the image on the web page and plain is a boolean that specifies whether or not we want to display the plain image. First we want to be sure that the images are loaded, using the variable we declared earlier, so we start with if (loaded).

In previous uses of the *if* statement we've just used if (this is true) do that. Here we have to do it a bit differently because the 'do that' part consists of more than a single statement. Enclosing the next two statements in curly brackets means that both depend on the result of the if (loaded) test. If this test proves false, everything between the curly brackets will be skipped.

The two statements themselves form an *if...else* pair. If we passed true to the function as the second argument, we display the 'plain' image; if not, we display the 'over' image. A quick explanation of those two statements is needed:

▶ **document[img]** is a reference to an item on the web page with the same name as the one held in the img variable. So **document[img].src** is a reference to the URL of the image we passed into the function.

▶ **eval(img + "plain.src")** does two things. Inside the brackets we combine the name of the image held in the img variable with 'plain.src'. If we passed the name 'img1' into the function, we'd get 'img1plain.src', which we specified in the loadImages() function. But 'img1plain.src' is a string and we need it to be an object. Fortunately JavaScript has a built-in method, eval(), to convert a string to an object.

The combination of these two parts finds the image we moved the mouse over, finds an object containing the URL of the image we want to display instead, and switches the URL of the current image to the URL of the replacement.

Finally, we need to add the script that calls the loadImages() function to actually load the images. We do this by making use of another event: when the web page has finished loading it fires an onLoad event which we can intercept to load our images, as in the code below. Because this event isn't in an anchor tag, we don't need to include the words return true.

```
<BODY BGCOLOR="#FFFFFF" onLoad="loadImages()">
```

And that's pretty much all there is to it (ha ha). You'll find a complete example page using three images in this chapter's folder on the CD-ROM. But there's just one extra detail to add. Although we've specified the language of our script as JavaScript 1.1 to prevent errors from older browsers, we're calling the react() function in the anchor tags. As far as those older browsers are concerned, there isn't a react() function! To prevent errors, we need to add dummy functions for older browsers. Here's the script we'll add:

```
<SCRIPT LANGUAGE="JavaScript" TYPE="text/javascript">
<!--
function loadImages(){}
function react(img, plain){}
// -->
</SCRIPT>
```

We place this in the page *above* the real script. That way, browsers that are compatible with JavaScript 1.1 will replace their internal references to the two functions with the real functions that appear later in the page. In old browsers, when the loadImages() and react() functions are called, they'll use these dummy functions. We won't get image rollover effects in those browsers, of course, but now we won't get errors either!

Don't Lose Your Frameset!

If you've decided to base your site around frames (see Chapter 8), there's a danger that visitors might arrive at a single page from your frameset. For example, if your site uses two frames to display navigation in one and information in the other, a visitor may arrive at one of your informational pages and have no navigation frame! One frequent way this happens is when search engines index your site and include links to the individual pages they find (something we'll look at in more detail in Chapter 24).

Here's a piece of script that gets around that potential problem. Place this in the head of all your pages except the page that contains your <FRAMESET> and <FRAME> tags:

```
<SCRIPT LANGUAGE="JavaScript" TYPE="text/javascript">
<!--
if (self.location.href == top.location.href) self.location.href="url of index page";
// -->
</SCRIPT>
```

Replace the text in italics with the URL of your site's index page (the page that creates the frames). Here's what the script is doing:

▶ **self.location.href** is the URL of the current page.

▶ **top.location.href** is the URL of the topmost document in the browser. If your frames are loaded, this will be the URL of the page that created and loaded the frames. If the frames aren't loaded, this will be the same as self.location.href.

This chunk of script simply compares the two URLs. If they're the same, meaning that your frameset hasn't been loaded, it redirects to your index page.

Using External Scripts

All the example JavaScript we've written has been included in the web page itself, which means that if you wanted to use the same script in several pages you'd have to paste it into each page (and edit every page separately if you ever needed to alter the script!). To reuse a script block, it's best to put it in an external file and *link* it to the required pages, just as we did with style sheets in Chapter 9.

A script file is an ordinary text file, usually (but not necessarily) with the extension **.js**. Move your whole script block into this file, but without the opening and closing <SCRIPT> tags and without the comment tags (<!-- and // -->). To link this file to a web page, add an **SRC** attribute to the <SCRIPT> tag containing the URL of the file:

```
<SCRIPT LANGUAGE="JavaScript" TYPE="text/javascript"
SRC="myscript.js"></SCRIPT>
```

Don't forget the closing </SCRIPT> tag! You can link as many script files to a web page as you need to by repeating the line of code above for each file.

DYNAMIC HTML

Using scripting, style sheets (CSS), and something grandly called the Dynamic HTML Object Model, Dynamic HTML is a recent addition to the web designer's toolkit which gives us scriptable access to all the elements that make up a web page. And 'all' really is *all* – from small elements like a character or word, through images, paragraphs and divisions, right up to the web page itself. Using Dynamic HTML (or DHTML, as it's usually abbreviated) we can force elements to hide or show themselves, change size or colour, slide from one position to another, and much more. Although at times it can be actively useful, DHTML is predominantly used to add cool effects and interactivity to a website. In this chapter, I'll show you some of the ways you can use DHTML to add a little slice of cool to your own pages. But first...

There's A Catch!

Isn't there always? The catch with DHTML is that Microsoft and Netscape have designed their own formats. Although the two cross over in places, they're basically incompatible, and to support both Internet Explorer *and* Netscape with DHTML essentially requires two different scripts to be combined into one.

In this chapter I'm going to focus on Microsoft's DHTML, which is the more powerful, flexible and widely used of the two. Some of the following examples may produce the same result in browsers other than Internet Explorer. Most importantly, though, if you don't get the same result it's because the browser is gracefully ignoring the code rather than producing errors!

The Basics Of Dynamic HTML

In Dynamic HTML, everything on the web page is treated as an *object*: images, paragraphs, horizontal rules, chunks of text (in any way you want to define them), and the page itself. Every object has a set of *properties*, some of which we met in Chapter 9 when we talked about style sheets. For instance, an image's properties include its width and height, its position on the page, the width of the border around it, and its URL.

By giving any of these objects its own unique name, we can write scripts that refer to it by name and dynamically change its properties. In fact, we did a bit of that in the *Image Rollovers* topic of the previous chapter: by adding a NAME attribute to the <IMG> tag, we were able to identify which image the mouse was over and display a different image in its place. DHTML works in much the same way, but with one difference. The NAME attribute is peculiar to the <IMG> tag and a few others, so we need a similar attribute that we can use with *any* object on the page. The solution lies in the **ID** attribute, which was specifically added for the purpose of scripting.

Dynamic Styles

Here's a good way (if not exactly a useful one!) to illustrate how DHTML mixes styles with scripts. Every object on the page can have a CLASS attribute to specify a style, and in the same way it has a **className** property that we can access through scripting to switch from one style class to another.

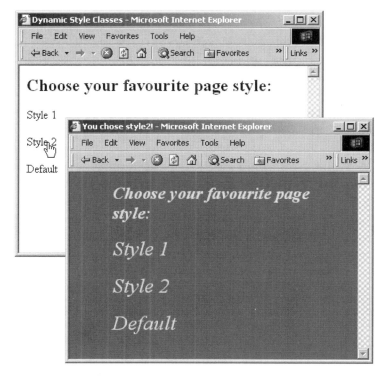

◀ Dynamic styles in action: clicking a style name applies the new style to the whole page.

We'll start by defining a few style classes and writing a script to switch between them. In the script below I've defined three styles. The page's <BODY> tag has been given the ID 'pagebody' so that we can refer to it by name, and initially uses the 'def' style. I've also included a line in the script that changes the document's title to show which style was chosen.

```
<STYLE TYPE="text/css">
<!--
.def {background: #FFFFFF; color: #000000; font-family: Times New Roman, serif}
.style1 {background: #FF0000; color: #FFFFFF; font-family: Arial,sans-serif; margin
left: 20px; margin-top: 80px; font-weight: bold}
.style2 {background:#C000C0; color: #FFFF00; font-size: 22pt; margin-left: 60px;
font-style: italic}
-->
</STYLE>

<SCRIPT LANGUAGE="JavaScript" TYPE="text/javascript">
<!--
function setStyle(s)
{
        pagebody.className=s;
        document.title='You chose' + s + '!';
}
// -->
</SCRIPT>
<BODY ID="pagebody" CLASS="def">
```

With all the mechanics in place, we need something the visitor can click to make the change. One option would be an anchor tag, which we've used a lot in previous chapters, but any text can be made to react to a click by trapping an onClick event in the same way we trapped onMouseOver events in Chapter 17. By wrapping <SPAN> tags around the text, we can set our own style and script handling for it:

```
<SPAN STYLE="cursor: hand" onClick="setStyle('style1')">Style 1</SPAN><P>

<SPAN STYLE ="cursor: hand" onClick="setStyle('style2')">Style 2</SPAN><P>

<SPAN STYLE ="cursor: hand" onClick="setStyle('def')">Default</SPAN><P>
```

The STYLE attribute makes a hand-cursor appear when the mouse moves over the text, letting the visitor know it can be clicked. By trapping the onClick event we pass the name of the style we want to use into the setStyle() function.

GOOD QUESTION!

What happens to the rest of the page when text gets larger or smaller?

One of the great wonders of Dynamic HTML is that the contents of the page are automatically adjusted to take account of objects resizing, appearing or disappearing. So if a heading suddenly triples in height, the content below it moves down to make space for it.

Changing Text & HTML

Here are two more properties you can use for unusual effects – **innerText** and **innerHTML**:

▶ **innerText** is the *text* between the current opening and closing tags containing the object. In the code <SPAN ID="text">My text</SPAN> the innerText is 'My text'.

▶ **innerHTML** is the *HTML* between the current opening and closing tags containing the object. In the code <SPAN ID="text">My <B>bold</B> text</SPAN> the innerHTML is '<B>bold</B>'.

And once we know how to get at it, of course, we can change it! In the example shown in the composite screenshot overleaf, I've used three functions to respond to onMouseOver, onClick and onMouseOut events by changing the text. As in the example above, I've combined that with changes of style (I won't bother showing you the style definitions, which are very straightforward).

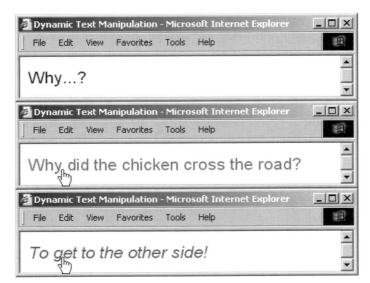

▶ Using the innerText property to change the original text (**top**) when the mouse enters (**middle**) and clicks (**bottom**).

First, here's the tag we place on the page. It's a <SPAN> tag that assigns the ID 'QandA' to the object it contains, and traps the three events we want to react to. When it first appears on the page, it will use a style class named 'basic'.

```
<SPAN style="cursor: hand" ID="QandA" CLASS="basic"
onMouseOver="question()" onClick="answer()"
onMouseOut="why()">Why...?</SPAN>
```

And here's the script block that goes into the head of the page to handle those events. Because we named that tiny piece of text 'QandA', we can now refer to its properties using its name followed by a dot and the property name.

```
<SCRIPT LANGUAGE="JavaScript" TYPE="text/javascript">
<!--
function question()
{
        QandA.innerText='Why did the chicken cross the road?';
        QandA.className='qstyle';
}
function answer()
```

```
{
        QandA.innerText='To get to the other side!';
        QandA.className='astyle';
}
function why()
{
        QandA.innerText='Why...?';
        QandA.className='basic';
}
// -->
</SCRIPT>
```

A DHTML Clock

If you think that last example was a bit too tricksy to be useful, I have to agree. But there *are* more practical ways to work with the innerText property, and a good example is a digital clock. Adding the following tag to the page, combined with a bit of JavaScript, gives the result shown in the next screenshot. I've used a <DIV> tag here to separate this block of text from any text above or below it, but you could replace DIV with SPAN to include the clock in a paragraph of otherwise static text.

```
<DIV ID="clock" STYLE="color: #0000C0; font-family: Arial; font-size:
36pt"> </DIV>
```

We want the clock to start as soon as the page loads, so in the body tag we trap the onLoad event (see Chapter 17) to call the runClock() function we're about to write: <BODY BGCOLOR="#FFFFFF" onLoad="runClock()">.

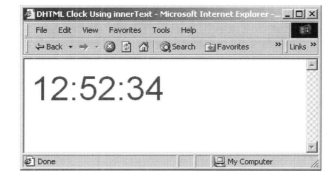

◀ A Dynamic HTML digital clock (it **is** running, trust me!)

That was the easy bit, of course, but the code that creates the text to display isn't too complicated thanks to a built-in JavaScript object called **Date()**. This gives us access to the current date and time by calling its built-in methods, such as **getHours()**. To prevent errors, the code begins with a browser test (see Chapter 17) and immediately stops if the visitor isn't using Internet Explorer.

Next we declare some variables. We make a copy of the current date and time in a variable imaginatively named 'date', define three string variables to hold the hours, minutes and seconds, and then use the built-in Date() method to get the hours, minutes and seconds as numbers. In the three if ... else statements, we check whether any of the numbers is less than 10, insert a '0' before it if necessary, and assign the numbers to our string variables. Finally we set the innerText property of the division we named 'clock' to display the result.

If we left it at that, we'd just get a static display of the time *when the page loaded* rather than a clock, so we need some way to make this function automatically repeat itself every second. The answer lies in the window.setTimeout() method: this takes two arguments, the name of a function to run, and the delay before running it in one-hundredths of a second, so the final line of the function simply calls the function again after a one-second delay. Here's the whole script:

```
<SCRIPT LANGUAGE="JavaScript" TYPE="text/javascript">
<!--
function runClock()
{
if (navigator.appName != 'Microsoft Internet Explorer') return;
var date = new Date();
var hours=", minutes=", seconds=";
var numhours = date.getHours();
var numminutes = date.getMinutes();
var numseconds = date.getSeconds();

if (numhours < 10) hours = '0' + numhours;
else hours = numhours;
if (numminutes < 10) minutes = '0' + numminutes;
```

```
else minutes = numminutes;
if (numseconds < 10) seconds ='0' + numseconds;
else seconds = numseconds;

clock.innerText = hours+':'+minutes+':'+seconds;

window.setTimeout("runClock()", 100);
}
// -->
</SCRIPT>
```

Hiding & Showing Page Elements

Here's another practical use of Dynamic HTML: it responds to mouse clicks on one page element to hide or show another element. The two elements can be anything you like: you could click a question to reveal its answer in a FAQ (Frequently Asked Questions) list; click an image to reveal its caption; or click a word to reveal a definition hidden in brackets beside it.

BY THE WAY

But why no answers...?

Like the examples above, this only works for Internet Explorer. If the hidden text is important (for instance, if it contains the answers in a FAQ) you'll have to redirect non-IE users to an alternative version of the page that displays the full content without any trickery. Turn to Chapter 17 to find out how to redirect particular browsers.

Let's start with the HTML tags to be placed on the page. In the next screenshot I've used three questions each with its own answer, but the tags for each will be almost identical to the code below; just change the 'hideshow1' references to 'hideshow2', 'hideshow3' and so on.

```
<DIV onClick="toggle('hideshow1')" CLASS="hideshow">Why did the chicken
cross the road?</DIV>
```

305

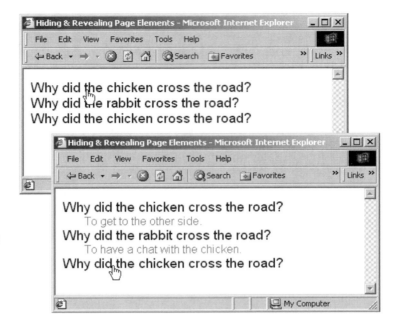

▶ Clicking the questions displays or hides the answers concealed below them.

```
<DIV ID="hideshow1" CLASS="hiddentext" STYLE="display: none">To get to the other side.</DIV>
```

The first division only exists so that we can trap an onClick event when the question is clicked. It passes the ID of the hidden division below it to a function called toggle() that we're about to write. It uses a style class called 'hideshow' which sets the cursor to 'hand' and applies some text formatting.

The second division also uses a style class, but that just sets some formatting so we'll ignore it. The important parts are the STYLE attribute, which hides the contents of the division, and the ID attribute which gives it a name.

Now for the script itself, a function I've called toggle() which receives a string containing the name of the element we want to hide or show. A *string* is no good to us, since we need to tell the browser about an *object* on the page, so we convert the string to an object using the eval() method we met in Chapter 17. The document.all. reference is a property containing a list of all the objects in the document, so by evaluating the string 'document.all.hideshow1' we'll get the object with the same name as 'element' into our variable 'e'.

```
<SCRIPT LANGUAGE="JavaScript" TYPE="text/javascript">
<!--
function toggle(element)
{
        var e = eval("document.all." + element);
        if (e.style.display == 'none') e.style.display = '';
        else e.style.display = 'none';


}
// -->
</SCRIPT>
```

In the last two lines, we check the display style of the element. If its display style is currently 'none' that means it's invisible, so we show it by setting its display style to an empty string. Otherwise, of course, it's visible, so we hide it by setting its display style back to 'none'.

Adding Page Transition Effects

How about something that doesn't need any scripting at all? Internet Explorer's Dynamic HTML includes a built-in method that can create any of 23 different transition effects as visitors move from page to page, and it's a doddle to add to your page. Just place the following line somewhere in the page's head section:

```
<META HTTP-EQUIV="Page-Enter" CONTENT="revealTrans(duration=1.500,
transition=23)">
```

When the page loads, the built-in revealTrans() method is called with two arguments: the length of time the transition should last (in seconds), and the number of the transition effect to use. You can adjust the two values after the equals signs to your own taste, using the effect numbers in the table overleaf.

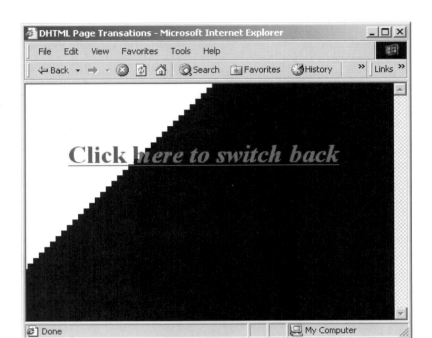

▶ Easy transition effects between web pages, courtesy of DHTML.

Index	Description	Index	Description
0	Box In	12	Random Dissolve
1	Box Out	13	Split Vertical In
2	Circle In	14	Split Vertical Out
3	Circle Out	15	Split Horizontal In
4	Wipe Up	16	Split Horizontal Out
5	Wipe Down	17	Strips Left Down
6	Wipe Right	18	Strips Left Up
7	Wipe Left	19	Strips Right Down
8	Vertical Blinds	20	Strips Right Up
9	Horizontal Blinds	21	Random Bars Horizontal
10	Checkerboard Across	22	Random Bars Vertical
11	Checkboard Down	23	Random (any effect)

Protect Your Source Code!

If you're of an inquisitive nature, you've probably tried right-clicking other people's pages to sneak a peek at their HTML source code or download an image. If so, maybe you found that instead of the usual popup menu, you got a message dialog telling you that right-clicks weren't allowed. Here's how you can810 protect your own source code from casual snooping in the same way – just add the code below to the head of the page:

```
<SCRIPT LANGUAGE="JavaScript" TYPE="text/javascript">
<!--
function doClick(e)
{
var message = 'Sorry, right-clicks are not allowed!';
if (document.all)  //for Internet Explorer
        {
        if (event.button==2) {alert(message); return false;}
        }
if (document.layers) //for Netscape
        {
        if (e.which == 3) {alert(message); return false;}
        }
}

if (document.layers) document.captureEvents(Event.MOUSEDOWN);
document.onmousedown=doClick;
// -->
</SCRIPT>
```

BY THE WAY

Privacy not guaranteed!

Getting around this is easy, of course: visitors can choose View Source from the browser's menu (unless you create a custom window containing no menu bar). If your site uses frames, visitors can view the source of the framesetting page, determine the URL of the framed page they're interested in, and open it in a separate window to repeat the manoeuvre. But it should discourage visitors who don't know all that, and make life a bit more difficult for those who do.

This script works for both Internet Explorer and Netscape (with the exception of Netscape 6). Below the function, there are two lines which capture mouse-down events anywhere in the document in either browser. In the function itself, we first find out which browser the visitor is using. Internet Explorer's document object has an **all** property (which we met earlier in this chapter); Netscape's uses a property named **layers** instead, so by testing whether either property exists we can identify these two browsers and exclude all others.

Next we check whether the button click event used the right mouse button and, if so, display a message. The function always returns false to override the default behaviour of the click.

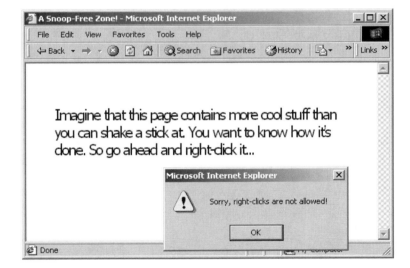

▶ Prevent amateur surfers from peeking at your source code (perhaps!)

What Else?

There's much more to Dynamic HTML than I could possibly go into here – entire books have been written about it. In a nutshell, though, once an item is placed on the page with HTML, you can change it, move it, animate it, apply filters and transitions to it, almost anything you can imagine. Knowing how to write your own DHTML effects is far more rewarding than trudging around the Web looking for free scripts, but if you prefer the sound of that second option, here are a few sites to save you some trudging:

▶ **Dynamic Drive** at **http://www.dynamicdrive.com**

▶ **DHTML Lab** at **http://www.webreference.com/dhtml**

▶ **MSDN Online Voices** at **http://msdn.microsoft.com/voices/dude.asp**

19

WEB FORMS

If you've ever used a search engine, subscribed to a mailing list, signed a website's guestbook, or bought something from an online store, you've used a form. The thing all those actions have in common is that they prompt you to enter information and then carry out particular actions based on your input. In that way, web forms are a unique area of HTML that let your audience interact with your site, and in this chapter you'll meet the various controls that make up a form and find out how they work.

But if forms are part of HTML, why is this chapter in the part of the book dealing with scripting? Simple – a form can only *take* your audience's input and pass it on somewhere for processing. That processing can either take place on the **client side** (in the visitor's own browser using JavaScript) or on the **server side** (by a program running on the web server). The server side solution is the more flexible and we'll take a look at it at the end of the chapter. The client side solution has two benefits: first, it's easier to use, simpler to test, and faster; and second, you *know* something about JavaScript already!

Forms & Form Controls

A form is really just a collection of input controls gathered between **<FORM>** and **</FORM>** tags to mark where the form starts and ends (similar to the way the <BODY> tags are used). There are four useful attributes to the <FORM> tag, all of which are optional:

Attribute	Meaning
NAME	Assigns a unique name to the form, so that you can refer to it (and the controls it contains) via scripting.
TARGET	When the form is submitted, a page is usually displayed giving the result of the form processing. Use this attribute to set the name of the frame or window in which to open the result page. The default is to use the current frame.
ACTION	Specifies the URL of a web page (or a program running on the server) that will receive the data entered into the form's controls.
METHOD	A choice of **POST** or **GET** to determine how the form data is sent to the URL given in **ACTION**. The **POST** method is preferred, and used when sending

Attribute	Meaning
	data to the server to be processed. The **GET** method limits the total length of the form data and will chop off any data beyond that limit, but you may need to use **GET** when doing client side processing rather than sending (posting) the data to a server program. Although **GET** is the default method, it's always wise to include the **METHOD** attribute if the form requires any sort of processing.

So the bare bones of a basic web form would look something like this:

```
<FORM NAME="MyForm" ACTION="result.htm" METHOD="GET">
        <!--form controls here -->
</FORM>
```

Now let's add some controls to the form to create something that looks like the example shown in the next screenshot. There are three basic types of control, each with its own tag: **<INPUT>**, **<TEXTAREA>** and **<SELECT>**.

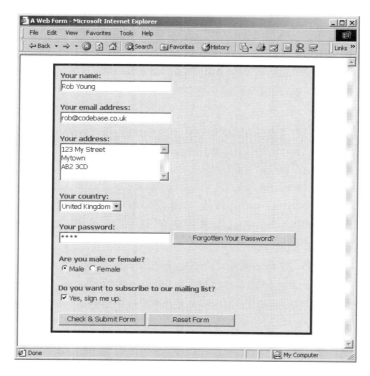

◀ A web form using all the useful types of input field.

The <INPUT> Controls

The <INPUT> tag is the big one: using this tag you can access eight useful types of input control by including the **TYPE** attribute to specify which of the eight you want. Each control will also have **NAME** and **VALUE** attributes. The NAME attribute gives the control its own unique name (so that the list of values you receive from the form can be related to something!). The use of the VALUE attribute is explained for each control below.

▶ **<INPUT TYPE=TEXT>** creates a single-line text field, like the first two controls shown in the screenshot. The VALUE attribute can be used to specify text shown in the control when the page first appears (or if the form is reset), or can be excluded to leave the field blank. If you use the <INPUT> tag without a TYPE attribute, this is the control you'll get by default.

▶ **<INPUT TYPE=PASSWORD>** also creates a single-line text field, but the text typed by the user is *masked* with asterisks so that anyone watching the user's screen won't be able to read what was entered. The fifth field in the screenshot is a password field. The VALUE attribute is used in the same way as for the TEXT field.

▶ **<INPUT TYPE=BUTTON>** creates a simple button which fires an event when clicked. The button beside the password field in the screenshot displays a message box (with some help from a JavaScript function!). The VALUE attribute specifies the text to be shown on the button.

▶ **<INPUT TYPE=RADIO>** creates one radio button (like the 'male' button in the screenshot). Radio buttons work in groups, and only one button in a group can be selected at a time: clicking another in the same group deselects the first. A group of radio buttons is formed by giving each button the same NAME, and each will have a different VALUE. In the screenshot, the two radio buttons are named 'Sex', one with VALUE=Male, the other with VALUE=Female.

▶ **<INPUT TYPE=CHECKBOX>** creates one checkbox, the 'Sign me up' control in the screenshot, used to provide yes/no choices. The VALUE attribute can be ignored; this control sends the value on if checked or off if not.

▶ **<INPUT TYPE=SUBMIT>** creates a button which, when clicked, will submit the form data to be processed. This needs no NAME attribute, but the VALUE attribute can be used to specify the text that is shown on the button (by default this is usually just the word 'Submit').

▶ **<INPUT TYPE=RESET>** creates a button which resets the form's controls to their initial state, letting the user start again. Once again, NAME can be ignored and VALUE can be used to change the text on the button from the default 'Reset'.

▶ **<INPUT TYPE=HIDDEN>** creates an invisible field that can hold a NAME and VALUE to be submitted along with the rest of the form's data.

Along with the NAME and VALUE attributes, there are three other attributes that can be used with one or more of the <INPUT> controls:

▶ **MAXLENGTH=** specifies the maximum number of characters that the user is allowed to enter in a TEXT or PASSWORD field.

▶ **SIZE=** specifies the width of the TEXT or PASSWORD control, in characters (although this tends to be a bit approximate). This doesn't limit the number of characters that can be typed, though.

▶ **CHECKED** is an empty attribute used with the RADIO and CHECKBOX controls to specify that the control should be initially shown as selected. (In a group of radio buttons, only one button in the group can be checked.)

The <TEXTAREA> Control

This creates a multi-line text field suitable for entering addresses or general comments. It works differently from the <INPUT> tag, needing a closing </TEXTAREA> tag. Between these two tags you can optionally type some text (but not HTML) that should be shown when the page is first shown:

```
<TEXTAREA ROWS=3 COLS=20 NAME="text">Some text here?</TEXTAREA>
```

Along with the usual NAME attribute, this tag can take three optional attributes:

▶ **ROWS=** specifies the number of lines of text that can be visible in the control without scrolling. It doesn't limit the number of lines that can actually be typed.

▶ **COLS=** specifies the width of the control in characters, in the same way as the SIZE attribute of the TEXT input control.

▶ **WRAP=** offers a choice of OFF, PHYSICAL or VIRTUAL to specify how a long line of text should wrap to the next line in the control. OFF means that text won't be wrapped; PHYSICAL means that text will be wrapped and carriage returns will be added at the end of each line; VIRTUAL (the preferable, and default, setting) means that text will be wrapped, but the text will be sent to the server as a single long string without carriage returns.

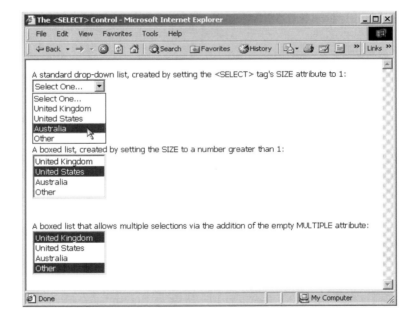

▶ The <SELECT> control can be used as a drop-down list, a standard list, or a multiple selection list.

The <SELECT> Control

The <SELECT> control lets the visitor choose one or more items from a list. As shown in the screenshot above, the list itself can be either a drop-down or a box. Along with the NAME attribute, there are two attributes you can add to the tag:

- ▶ **SIZE=** sets the number of items visible in the list at once. If set to 1, the result will be a drop-down list; set to a higher number, the list will change to a box shape of the right height to display the chosen number of items.

- ▶ **MULTIPLE** is an empty attribute which, if included, allows the user to select more than one item by holding the Ctrl or Command key while clicking the items.

So far, then, we've got a list but no items! List items are added using another tag, **<OPTION>**, like this:

```
<SELECT SIZE=1 NAME="Country">
<OPTION SELECTED>United Kingdom
<OPTION>United States
<OPTION>Australia
<OPTION>Other
</SELECT>
```

Like the <TEXTAREA> control, the <SELECT> control needs a closing tag, and the items are placed between the two, each following an <OPTION> tag. One of the <OPTION> tags can have the empty SELECTED attribute, indicating that it should be the selected item when the page appears. You'd usually pre-select the first item in the list, but there's no law against selecting a different one.

Putting It All Together

Although the controls of a form are all contained between opening and closing <FORM> tags, you're not restricted to using form controls alone: you can include any other HTML or text you like. Let's create a simple form to see how all this works together. The result is shown in the next screenshot.

```
<FORM NAME=MyForm METHOD=GET ACTION="result.htm">
Your name:<BR>
<INPUT TYPE=TEXT NAME=Name SIZE=40><P>

Your address:<BR>
<TEXTAREA ROWS=4 COLS=40 NAME=Address></TEXTAREA><P>
```

```
Your age:<BR>
<INPUT TYPE=RADIO NAME=Age VALUE="Young" CHECKED>Still young
<INPUT TYPE=RADIO NAME=Age VALUE="NotOld">Not old
<INPUT TYPE=RADIO NAME=Age VALUE="KeepingMum">Not saying<P>
<INPUT TYPE=CHECKBOX NAME=Designer CHECKED>I designed this form
myself<P>

<INPUT TYPE=SUBMIT VALUE="Go For It!">
<INPUT TYPE=RESET VALUE="Start Again">
</FORM>
```

▶ A simple (if unattractive) web form.

GOOD QUESTION!

Why does the form clear when I submit it?

When you click the Submit button we've labelled 'Go For It!', this tells the form to carry out its action – to send the form's data to the URL contained in the <FORM> tag's **ACTION** attribute. As we haven't included that attribute, it uses the URL of the current page, and in reloading the page it clears the form. If you look in your browser's address bar, you'll see the form's data tagged onto the end of the URL. (We'll look at that again in a moment.)

320

There are two problems with the result. The first is that the page looks dreadful; the second is that to select a radio button or checkbox you have to click the control itself, not its label. Let's fix those two defects.

Clickable Labelling

The text that appears alongside the radio buttons and checkboxes is just ordinary HTML text which, of course, isn't supposed to do anything when you click it. But in this case, it would be nice for a click on the label to toggle the control's selection on and off. Fortunately, Internet Explorer makes this fairly easy to achieve.

First we add an ID attribute to each button to give it a unique name. For simplicity I use the button's value as its ID:

```
<INPUT TYPE=RADIO NAME=Age VALUE="NotOld" ID="NotOld">Not old
```

Next we enclose the caption text between **<LABEL>** and **</LABEL>** tags. This tag needs one attribute, **FOR**, which specifies the ID of the control it applies to:

```
<INPUT TYPE=RADIO NAME=Age VALUE="NotOld" ID="NotOld"><LABEL
FOR="NotOld">Not old</LABEL>
```

Lo and behold, when the caption is clicked, Internet Explorer treats it as a click on the button itself!

Form Restyling

With that taken care of, the form is crying out for a makeover. Forms are one area in which use of style sheets is pretty much mandatory: the controls use fixed-width fonts and the colours are chosen for you by the browser. By adding a few style rules to the head of the page, we can add some elegance and interest to the page.

BY THE WAY

Everything's an input!

When you create style rules for forms, remember that any rules for the <INPUT> tag will be applied to all eight input types. Most of the time that's fine – you probably **want** a uniform look – but at times you may need to override the effect of the style rule by adding a STYLE= attribute to one or more <INPUT> tags directly.

Here are the style rules I've added to the head of the page, giving the result shown in the next screenshot. Notice that by setting a particular font for the 'input' and 'textarea' elements (both of which we set to 40 characters wide) they're now both the same width.

```
<STYLE TYPE="text/css">
<!--
body {background: FFFFFF}
form {background: FFFFF0; font-family: Tahoma,Arial,sans-serif; font-size: 11pt;
font-weight: bold; color: CC0000; border-width: 2pt; border-style: ridge; padding:
10pt}
label {color: 000000; font-weight: normal; font-size: 10pt}
input, textarea {font-family: Tahoma,Arial,sans-serif; font-size: 9pt}
-->
</STYLE>
```

Along with these style rules, I've made two other changes. In the SUBMIT and RESET buttons' tags I've added STYLE="font-weight: bold; width: 110" to fix both at the same width and override the font set in the style rule for 'input'. And in the text and textarea fields' tags I've included STYLE="background: FFFFF0" to set the field background to match the form's own background. Doing this in the style rule for 'input' would cause the two buttons to become this colour too.

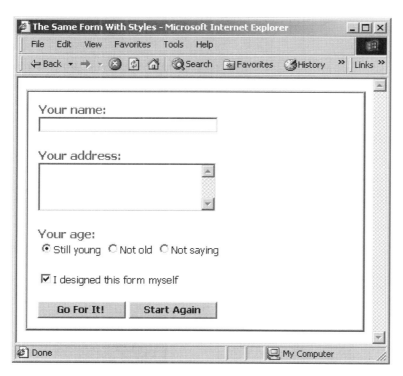

◀ Adding a few style rules can transform a dull looking form.

BY THE WAY

When is a form not a form?

Although we tend to think of a form as a collection of these controls grouped together, it could be just a single button that you use (along with some JavaScript) to link to a page or start a download. Although the HTML specification says that form controls can be used without enclosing them between <FORM>...</FORM> tags, in practice some browsers won't display them. Treat the <FORM> tags as obligatory when using any of these controls, although you can leave out its attributes if the form will never actually be submitted.

Two Practical Uses Of Form Controls

Quite apart from submitting form data to a server, which we'll look at in a moment, there are other useful things you can do with form controls. For instance, if you want visitors to agree to certain licence conditions before visiting a certain page, you could create an entry page containing a TEXTAREA and a SUBMIT button. In the <TEXTAREA> tag, add the empty attribute **READONLY**, which prevents the visitor from changing its content, and then place your licence conditions before the closing </TEXTAREA> tag. Set the <FORM> tag's ACTION attribute to the URL of the sensitive page, and set the submit button's VALUE attribute to 'I Agree'. When the visitor indicates agreement by clicking the button, the new page will open.

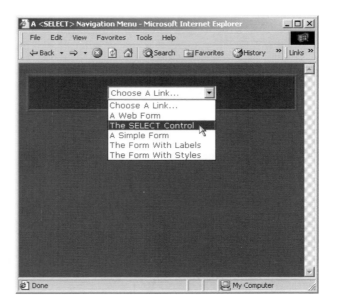

▶ A compact and effective drop-down menu of links, using the <SELECT> control.

Here's another suggestion, shown in the screenshot above: you can use the <SELECT> control to create a list of links to your pages (or to other websites). This needs a little bit of JavaScript to help it along, but nothing too complicated. First, here's the HTML code to create the menu itself:

```
<FORM NAME=MyForm METHOD=GET>
<SELECT NAME=menu ALIGN=CENTER onChange="handleChange()">
<OPTION SELECTED>Choose A Link...
```

```
<OPTION VALUE="001.htm">A Web Form
<OPTION VALUE="002.htm">The SELECT Control
<OPTION VALUE="003.htm">A Simple Form
<OPTION VALUE="004.htm">The Form With Labels
<OPTION VALUE="005.htm">The Form With Styles
</SELECT>
</FORM>
```

Like all form controls, <OPTION> can have a VALUE attribute, and we set
these to the URLs each item should open if selected. (The first item is a
dummy, allowing the visitor to open the menu and close it again without
linking anywhere.) In the <SELECT> tag, we need to catch this control's only
event, onChange, and send it to the JavaScript function below:

```
function handleChange()
{
        var index = document.MyForm.menu.selectedIndex;
        if (index == 0) return;
        var url = document.MyForm.menu.options[index].value;
        location.href = url;
}
```

The 'index' variable retrieves the index number of the selected item and, if
it's the first item (the dummy, numbered 0) the function stops. Next the
function reads the VALUE attribute of the selected option and stores it in a
variable named 'url'. Finally, we send the browser to this new location.

GOOD QUESTION!

How can I make this work in a frame-based site?

Using the **location.href** property would replace your whole frameset with the
new page, which you probably don't want. If you've placed the menu in a
small frame and want to open the new page into a 'main' frame, replace that
line of code with this:

```
window.open(url,"framename");
```

325

Handling Form Submission

When you submit a web form, the browser wraps up all the names and values into one long string and adds them onto the end of the URL given in the form's ACTION attribute following a question-mark symbol. Each name/value pair is separated by an ampersand (&). Here's an example of what the browser would add to the ACTION URL if we completed and submitted the form we created a few pages back:

?Name=Rob+Young&Address=123+Mystreet&Age=NotOld&Designer=on

Because the browser sends this as an extension of the URL, it has to make some changes to what we actually entered on the form – it replaces spaces with + signs, for instance, because spaces can't be used in URLs.

GOOD QUESTION!

Can I have the form's contents sent to me by email?

Yes you can, although it isn't a very slick system. By changing the form's **ACTION** attribute to a **mailto:** URL containing your email address and adding the attribute **ENCTYPE="text/plain"**, the message will be placed in the visitor's email Outbox ready for sending. A prompt will alert the visitor that the form is being submitted by email, revealing his or her email address, and offer a chance to cancel. Form-to-email is best handled using a program on the server to handle the job silently and without forcing visitors to reveal their email address.

Let's go back to the form in the screenshot on page 315, which you'll find in this chapter's folder on the CD-ROM. When the 'Check & Submit Form' button is clicked, a JavaScript function checks the form to make sure the visitor has entered a valid looking email address and selected a country. (It would be easy to add extra script that checks the Name and Address fields too – I'll leave that as a project for you!) If the form contents have been completed to our satisfaction, they're tagged onto the ACTION URL, a page named 'result.htm'. That page can then read the form content using the property **window.location.search**.

The screenshot below shows the result.htm page on the CD-ROM. This is a mostly blank page apart from a set of JavaScript routines that split up the received name/value pairs, display them, and allow them to be searched. I won't explain it all here: if you look at these pages in your own browser you'll find plenty of comments explaining what's happening, and you can copy the routines to adapt and use in your own pages.

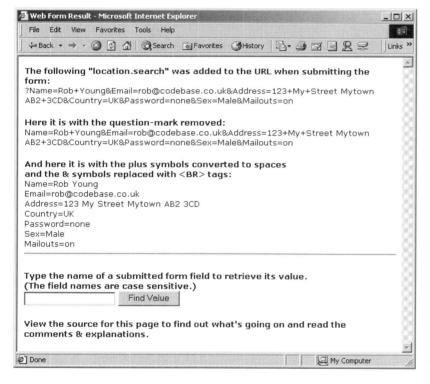

◀ A blank web page that uses JavaScript to evaluate the submitted form contents and display them using document.write(), along with a routine to extract any form value.

Submitting Forms To The Server

The most common use for forms is to gather information that's then sent to a program running on the web server. These programs are known as **CGI** programs (short for Common Gateway Interface). CGI isn't a programming language, but a system that allows conversations between the visitor's browser and the server to take place; the programs themselves can be written in any programming or scripting language supported by the server (the most common being a scripting language called Perl). These programs will be placed in a special directory on your web server, usually called **cgi-bin**. If you're paying for your web space, your web hosting company will probably include a cgi-bin directory in the charge. Free web hosts very rarely give you your own cgi-bin directory, but they may have a few stock CGI programs that they know and trust which you can access.

JARGON BUSTER

cgi-bin

A normal directory on your server just exists to hold files and send them to the browser when requested. The cgi-bin is different: when the URL of a program in the cgi-bin is sent to the server, the program doesn't start to download, it starts running. The cgi-bin usually allows a program to read the contents of files and add to them: for example, a CGI guestbook program can read the file containing all the guestbook entries, send them back to be displayed by the browser, and store any new entries sent via a web form.

Since every CGI program is different, it's important to read the documentation provided with it. You'll usually have to pick particular names for your form fields so that the program understands the data it receives, and you may have to include some script that validates the form before it's sent to ensure that any essential fields have been completed (some CGI programs will prompt the user when essential information is missing; others will expect you to handle that yourself).

▶ *Turn to Chapter 24 for more about CGI programs, or head for Appendix F to find a list of sites offering free CGI scripts you can use.*

GETTING STARTED WITH JAVA

▶ **IN THIS CHAPTER**

What you need for Java programming (almost nothing!)

Say Hello! Write & compile your first applet

Choose your own colours & fonts

Get interactive – make your applet react to the mouse

How to stop your applet flickering

If you didn't know this before, you're probably beginning to realize that the world of web design is a multilingual one (and becoming ever more so). Apart from HTML, we can use 'languages' such as CSS, JavaScript and Dynamic HTML, and link web forms to CGI programs on the web server. Because those all relate directly to a web page, they've got quite a lot in common. Over the next few chapters we're going to delve into a different language, and this really is a language: Java can be used to write complete programs such as word processors and web browsers. As a result, it's a bit of a departure from the others we've covered. What it has in common is that its main use is in designing small programs called **applets** for use in web pages.

The good news is that the construction of Java code is very similar to that of JavaScript, so if you've read the last few chapters (and I'm going to assume you have) you're off to a great start already! And there's more good news: you can design your own Java applets without buying any extra software at all, and your applets can be used in all the popular browsers.

Needless to say, there's a lot more to Java than I can fit into the available space, so I'm going to keep technical explanations to a minimum. As you follow the examples to build a tiny applet into something bigger and better, you'll soon understand the effect each new piece of code is having, and I'll show you how to adapt it to your own needs.

Getting Equipped For Java

Java is the trademarked name of a programming language developed by Sun Microsystems, Inc. **(http://java.sun.com)**, and one of its main uses is in creating small programs called applets that can be placed on a web page (see Chapter 15). To design your own applets, you need two things:

▶ A text editor such as the Windows Notepad accessory. I've included a few good editors on the accompanying CD-ROM.

▶ The Java Development Kit (JDK), a free but fairly large download from the Sun website. This contains a set of programs, the most important of which is one called **javac** that converts the code you write into a format that can be used in a browser. After installing the JDK, you'll have to restart your computer so that your system knows where to find these files.

Java Versions & Compatibility

Like everything in computing, the Java language has passed through a few different versions. The ones that matter are 1.0, 1.1 and 2.0. If we were writing Java *applications*, we'd obviously want to use the newest version and make the most of the latest and greatest features, but as we're only interested in *applet* programming we need to think a bit differently. We're going to be limited by how much support for Java is provided by particular browsers, shown in the table below:

Java version	Lowest compatible browser version (Windows)
1.0	Internet Explorer 2, Netscape 2, Opera 4
1.1	Internet Explorer 4, Netscape Navigator 4.06*, Netscape Communicator 4.5*, Opera 4
2.0	Opera 4, Netscape 6

* 1.1 support is incomplete in Netscape 4 browsers, but these are the earliest versions to approximate it.

We can ignore Java 2.0 for obvious reasons. That leaves a tough choice between 1.0 and 1.1: the language changed quite significantly between these versions. I've decided to cover Java 1.0 in these chapters so that the vast majority of your audience will be able to use the applets you design.

BY THE WAY

Windows wins!

For simplicity, I'm also going to assume that you're using a Windows operating system such as 98, ME, XP or 2000 in these chapters. Nevertheless, you can develop Java applets on almost any system: the Sun website (**http://java.sun.com**) will point you towards the correct JDK for your system, and tell you how to install and use it. The Java code you write yourself will be identical whatever system you're using.

From Blank Page To Applet

Before you embark on your first voyage into Java programming, it helps to have an idea of what lies ahead. Creating an applet is a three-step process (although the first involves quite a lot of little steps!). Here they are:

1   Write the program source code. The code is written as plain text, just like HTML and JavaScript, but in a file with the extension **.java**.

2   Compile the source code. This is where the JDK's javac program comes into play, using your .java file to make a new file with the same name and a **.class** extension.

3   Write the HTML code to place the applet on your web page, as we did in Chapter 15.

An Applet Template File

Every Java applet you create will start life as a text file containing your program code, and the bare bones of that file will always look the same. So let's kick off by making a template file that you can copy and use as the basis for every applet.

Start Notepad (or any text editor you prefer to use) and type the following:

```
import java.awt.*;
import java.applet.*;

public class template extends Applet
{


}
```

Take care not to use uppercase letters for anything I've written as lowercase: Java is a *case-sensitive* language, so the word 'Import' is different from 'import' and would result in an error message when you tried to compile the finished result.

Save this template with the name **template.java** to any folder you like. You might like to create a new folder called Applets on your hard disk, and then create a folder inside that for each new applet you create.

So what does that code actually mean? The first two lines tell the browser that our applet needs access to two parts of the Java language named awt and applet. These are packages of files that between them ensure that our applet behaves like an applet (not like an application), and give us access to a set of painting and colouring tools so that we can make the applet display something. (There are other packages we can import if we need to do other things, but those are the two we're always going to need.)

The next line means that we want to create a **class** called 'template' in this file. A 'class' is a collection of objects and functions that form one new object. Most of the classes you write will be based on an existing class built into the Java language, and you'll just add new features or change the way it behaves. And that's what we're doing when we create an applet. Java includes a class called Applet which doesn't do anything by itself; we write code that's based on the Applet class but adds more to it, so our class **extends Applet**.

Following that line there's a pair of curly brackets; all the applet code we write will go between those brackets, indicating that it's part of the 'template' class. One final important point before we get to the interesting stuff: the name of the class that appears in the 'extends Applet' line must exactly match the name of your source code file (minus its .java extension), and the resulting .class file will also be given that name.

A First Applet: Say Hello!

It's a tradition in programming that your first creation in a new language should simply print the words *Hello World* on the screen. This might not qualify as the most useful applet of your programming career, but it should be gratifying to see *something* appear. So let's start by building this little applet which, along the way, will show you the basic moves that take your applet from text editor to browser. Over the course of this chapter, we'll build on this small start to produce a button that reacts to mouse movement.

Make a copy of the template file you just created, change its name to **HelloWorld.java**, and open it in your text editor. As we've changed the name of the file, the first thing we need to do is to change the name of the class in the 'extends Applet' line to match. Next we add the code that displays the magic message:

```
import java.awt.*;
import java.applet.*;

public class HelloWorld extends Applet
{
        public void paint(Graphics g)
        {
                g.drawString ("Hello World!", 20, 35);
        }
}
```

You probably recognize the added code as being a lot like the functions we wrote in JavaScript, except that in Java we call them *methods*. What we've added is a method built into Java called **public void paint()**, and most of the applets you write will use this method. When an applet starts to run, it reads the paint() method and displays whatever we've told it to display.

The paint() method passes us a Graphics object called **g** which you could think of as an artist's canvas: when we draw something on 'g' we're actually drawing on the surface of our applet. This Graphics object has a number of built-in methods of its own for drawing shapes and images, among other things, but what we want to do right now is draw text which we do using its **drawString()** method. This method needs to know three things: the text to be displayed (always written using double-quote symbols), distance from the left edge of the applet in pixels, and the distance from the top edge of the applet in pixels, with each value separated by a comma (and, if you like, one or more spaces).

After adding this new code, save the HelloWorld.java file.

Compiling The Applet

Now we want to compile the applet to create a .class file, which we have to do from an MS-DOS Prompt (or Command Prompt) window. You can open this from the Start menu or by typing either **command** or **cmd** (depending on your version of Windows) into the Run dialog. With the prompt window open, follow these steps:

1 Use the **cd** (Change Directory) command to switch to the folder containing your HelloWorld.java file. You can do this by typing 'cd' and a space, then dropping the folder's icon into the prompt window and pressing Enter.

2 Type **javac HelloWorld.java** into the prompt window and press Enter. If all goes well, a file named HelloWorld.class should appear in the same folder as the source file.

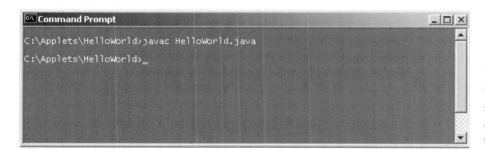

◀ Compiling the HelloWorld.java source to create an applet (.class) file.

GOOD QUESTION!

I didn't get the .class file! What went wrong?

If there are any errors in your code, the compiler won't be able to create the .class file, and you'll see the error(s) displayed in the prompt window. Each error message shows the line number containing the error in your text editor (make sure you've switched off the editor's word-wrap feature if it has one, or the line numbers won't match!). Check that line for spelling mistakes and make sure you've used uppercase letters only where they're supposed to be. Also make sure you haven't skipped any brackets, dots or commas. After you've found the mistake and corrected it, save the file and try to compile it again. It's worth noting that one small mistake (such as a missing bracket) can sometimes result in half-a-dozen different error messages, so you haven't always done as badly as you think!

▶ Java error messages tell you the line number, explain the mistake and show you the piece of code that's wrong. Here I've missed the 'w' out of 'drawString'.

```
Command Prompt                                                    _ □ x

C:\Applets\HelloWorld>javac HelloWorld.java
HelloWorld.java:8: Method draString(java.lang.String, int, int) not found in cla
ss java.awt.Graphics.
                g.draString ("Hello World!", 20, 35);
                       ^
1 error

C:\Applets\HelloWorld>_
```

Viewing The Applet

To view the applet, create a new web page in the same folder as the applet file (named anything you like) and add the following HTML code to it:

```
<APPLET CODE="HelloWorld.class" WIDTH=200 HEIGHT=200>
</APPLET>
```

Save the page and open it in a browser, and you should see something like the screenshot below. You can also test the page in Sun's own viewer, **appletviewer**, provided with the JDK. To do that, switch back to your prompt window and type **appletviewer** *mypage.htm* and press Enter. (The appletviewer utility can be useful if an applet is giving errors when it runs, or refusing to run at all: although the major browsers can help a little in tracking down bugs in your code, appletviewer's error messages are usually more helpful.)

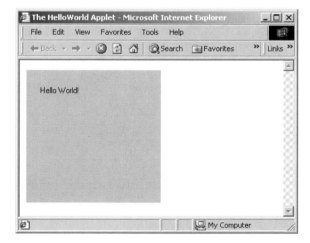

▶ The HelloWorld applet in all its, uh, glory.

Colouring The Text & Background

So far, so good. Well, okay, perhaps not exactly *good*! The text is black and the background is either white or grey (depending on which browser or viewer you're using). Let's start by colouring the text white by adding one line to our paint() method:

```
public void paint(Graphics g)
{
        g.setColor(Color.white);
        g.drawString ("Hello World!", 20, 35);
}
```

The added method, **setColor()**, is another method built into the Graphics object 'g'. When we set 'g' to a particular colour, it uses that colour to draw text, shapes and anything else specified in the code that follows, until we set it to something different. We do this by using another of Java's built-in objects, **Color**, which gives us access to 13 different colours by name. If you don't fancy white text, replace Color.white with one of these:

Color.lightGray	Color.orange
Color.gray	Color.yellow
Color.darkGray	Color.green
Color.black	Color.magenta
Color.red	Color.cyan
Color.pink	Color.blue

Save the source file, compile it again (which automatically replaces the current HelloWorld.class with a new one) and view the applet again – you should see that the text has been changed to the colour you chose.

GOOD QUESTION!

The applet hasn't changed. Why not?

If you're viewing the applet in a browser, simply pressing the Refresh or Reload button may not actually load the new version of the .class file. To force the browser to reload the page **and** load the latest versions of all applets and images, hold Ctrl when you click the Refresh button in Internet Explorer, or hold Shift while clicking the Reload button in Netscape.

Now let's change the colour of the background. This raises an important point about Java applets: they can't be transparent in the way that images can. Any part of the applet we don't paint over will remain that dull grey or white, so we want to fill the whole area with a more appropriate colour before drawing the text over the top. To do this, we'll insert two more lines at the beginning of the paint() method:

```
public void paint(Graphics g)
{
        g.setColor(Color.black);
        g.fillRect(0, 0, size().width, size().height);
        g.setColor(Color.white);
        g.drawString ("Hello World!", 20, 35);
}
```

You'll recognize the first line – it sets the current colour to black. Next I've used another new method, **fillRect()**. This fills a rectangle with the current colour, and needs four arguments to set the top-left corner of the rectangle (horizontal position followed by vertical position) and its width and height. The **size()** method gives us access to the width and height of the applet.

If you compile and view the new applet, you should now see that the applet's entire area on the page is coloured black, with the text displayed in white as before.

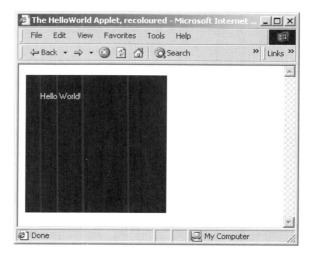

◀ The HelloWorld applet, with black background and white text.

GOOD QUESTION!

Why did the compiler give a note about a 'deprecated API'?

After adding the new code, the compiler may give a warning that 'HelloWorld.java uses a deprecated API.' It sounds like a medical emergency, but it's nothing to worry about, and won't prevent the applet from compiling. It means that your file contains code no longer used in Java 2.0 (in this case it's the **size**() method that's out of date). Since we're intentionally writing the code in Java 1.0, we'll continue to see (and ignore!) this warning.

Choosing A Font (From A Very Short List!)

We're currently stuck with the default font, text size and style set by the browser, so let's change that too. This is a good opportunity to introduce **variables** in Java. A variable is a named holding place for an object (a colour, a string, a number, or in this case, a font) as you'll remember from our discussion of JavaScript in Chapter 16, but they work slightly differently from JavaScript variables. When we create a variable (known as *declaring a variable*), we have to say what type of object the variable is to hold. We're going to

339

create a variable that will hold a font object, which Java very sensibly calls a **Font**. Here are the two lines we're going to add to the paint() method:

```
Font f = new Font("Helvetica", 3, 28);
g.setFont(f);
```

In the first line, we create a variable called 'f' that will hold a Font object. In the same line we also determine the font it should hold: the keyword new is used to create **new** objects, and we're creating a new Font object by specifying the name, style and size of the font.

▶ The **name** of the font has to be chosen from a tiny list of fonts built into the Java language: Dialog, Helvetica, Courier, TimesRoman and Symbol. (Symbol simply displays tiny pictures, like Windows' WingDings font, so you won't need to use that very often.)

▶ The **style** of the font can be 0 (for a plain font), 1 (bold), 2 (italic) or 3 (bold and italic).

▶ The **size** of the font can be any number you like, but on some systems the Dialog font will never be displayed at a size smaller than 12: if you want to use smaller text, use one of the other font names.

With the variable 'f' now holding the Font we've created, another Graphics method, **setFont(*font*)** is used to set the current font in the same way that we used setColor(*color*) earlier. As the font is only used when we draw text, this new code can be placed anywhere in the paint() method as long as it occurs before the line of code containing the drawString() method. For future editing, though, it's practical to keep it close to the code that it will actually be applied to, so insert it before or after the line g.setColor(Color.white);. Once again, compile the updated applet and take a look at the result.

GOOD QUESTION!

Why so few fonts?

Java is a **cross-platform** language: Java applets and applications should be able to run on any computer using any operating system. As a result, it can't work with the same font types as your own operating system (such as TrueType or PostScript) and has to include its own which are guaranteed to be available on any system that supports Java. It's a small set, but they do cover the bare essentials between them.

◀ The same applet looking better with our own choice of font.

Resizing The Applet

The size of the applet is determined by the WIDTH and HEIGHT attributes of the <APPLET> tag, rather than the applet's own source code, and it's a lot larger than we need. Change the dimensions to 210 by 50, as I have in the screenshot above, so that the applet uses a smaller space on the page.

Whenever you use an applet that displays text, always check the page in all the major browsers. Netscape and Opera apply more space to text than Internet Explorer, so what appears to be a perfectly sized applet in IE may be too small to display its entire content in others.

Drawing A Rectangle

Since we're aiming to produce a button, resizing the applet has helped, but let's give it a coloured border by drawing a rectangle. We can do this in almost exactly the same way we filled the applet with colour, but rather than using the fillRect() method we use **drawRect()** to draw only the outline. We'll make this rectangle a different colour, too.

```
g.setColor(Color.yellow);
g.drawRect(0, 0, size().width-1, size().height-1);
```

The only difference between this and the fillRect() method we used earlier is that we've subtracted 1 from the width and height of the rectangle. If the applet's size were 200 pixels square, Java would refer to those pixels as 0 to

199, so this time we need to specify the 199th pixel. If we didn't, the bottom and right-hand lines of the rectangle would always be drawn one pixel outside the applet where we'd never see them!

What we'll get is a 1-pixel-wide border around the inside edge of the applet, and that's pretty narrow, so let's add a second rectangle drawn inside that one to thicken it:

```
g.drawRect(1, 1, size().width-3, size().height-3);
```

In the same way, you could add similar lines to draw more rectangles and make the border fatter still: add 1 to the first two figures each time, and increase the amount being subtracted by 2.

We can put these new lines of code almost anywhere in the paint() method, but we need to watch out for one thing: the line of code containing fillRect() is painting the entire applet black, so the new code has to be placed somewhere after that line. We'll put it straight after that line, so that our whole paint() method looks like the code block below. Blank lines are ignored by the compiler, so I've separated the background and border code from the text setting code to make particular parts of the code easier to find when needed.

```
public void paint (Graphics g)
{
        g.setColor(Color.black);
        g.fillRect(0, 0, size().width, size().height);
        g.setColor(Color.yellow);
        g.drawRect(0, 0, size().width-1, size().height-1);
        g.drawRect(1, 1, size().width-3, size().height-3);

        g.setColor(Color.white);
        Font f = new Font("Helvetica", 3, 28);
        g.setFont(f);
        g.drawString ("Hello World!", 20, 35);

}
```

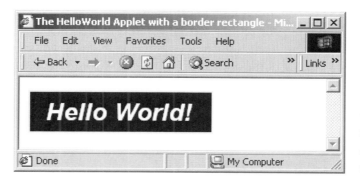

◀ Adding a 2-pixel-wide border using the drawRect() method.

Let's Get Interactive!

It's a button, Captain, but not as we know it! Although we'd like to call our applet a button, it doesn't actually do anything yet. Let's start by making the text change colour when the mouse moves over the applet. To do this, we need to declare another variable, a boolean (true/false) value that we'll call 'over'. When the mouse enters the applet we'll set it to true; when it exits we'll set it to false. Each time, we'll tell the applet to paint itself again, but with a change of text colour. Let's split all this into three steps.

Step 1: Catching The Mouse

First, let's catch those mouse movements. Along with the paint() method we've been using, the Applet class has methods for trapping mouse events, and we need to use two of those. Here's the code we're about to add:

```
public boolean mouseEnter(Event e, int x, int y)
{
        over = true;
        repaint();
        return true;
}

public boolean mouseExit(Event e, int x, int y)
{
        over = false;
        repaint();
        return true;
}
```

The two methods are almost identical, so I've highlighted the differences in bold type. The mouseEnter() method contains code that's run whenever the mouse enters the applet; the code in mouseExit() will be run when the mouse moves out of the applet. In both methods, we start by setting the 'over' variable to true or false. Next we have repaint(), which tells the applet to paint itself again. Both methods must finish with return true;. This is very similar to the way we returned values in JavaScript, but here the *type* of value we return is determined by the name of the function. The names of these two functions indicate that we have to return a boolean value; if we don't return anything (or we return something different, such as a number or a string) the compiler will display an error message. In all the mouse-related methods, you'll nearly always return a value of true.

GOOD QUESTION!

Why didn't we return a value in the paint() method?

Where the mouseEnter() and mouseExit() methods have the keyword **boolean**, the paint() method has the keyword **void**. A 'void' method is one that doesn't return any value – it just does its job and finishes.

Slot the code above into your source file. You can put it above or below the paint() method that's there already (the order in which methods appear in the file doesn't matter), but make sure you don't put it *inside* the paint() method!

Step 2: Declaring A Global Variable

Although we've used the 'over' variable in the two mouse methods, we haven't yet *declared* it – in other words, we haven't told the applet what that word 'over' actually means. When variables are declared in Java, there are two possible places you can put that declaration:

▶ **Inside a method.** We declared a Font variable called 'f' inside our paint() method earlier in this chapter. That variable is only accessible in the paint() method itself, and only in the lines of code that follow it. If we tried to refer to 'f' in either of the mouse methods, we'd get a compiler error. This type of variable is called a **local** variable.

▶ **Outside the methods.** This is called a **global** variable. If you declare a variable anywhere outside the applet's methods, you can use it in any method. Global variables are usually gathered together in a list straight after the first curly bracket of the class.

We need to make 'over' a global variable because we're using it in two methods already (and later we'll use it in the paint() method too). Here's what the beginning of the applet source will contain:

```
import java.awt.*;
import java.applet.*;

public class HelloWorld extends Applet
{
boolean over = false;
```

This added line simply tells the applet that 'over' will store a boolean (true/false) value, and that it should be set to false when the applet first appears on the web page.

Step 3: Reacting To The Mouse

So far, then, we're catching mouse movements, setting the 'over' variable to the appropriate value, and telling the applet to repaint itself. Until we change the paint() method, of course, the applet isn't actually going to *look* any different when it repaints. What we need to do is change the text colour according to the value of 'over'.

Find the line in the source code that sets the colour just before the text is drawn (unless you chose a different colour, the line is g.setColor(Color.white);), and replace it with this:

```
if (over) g.setColor(Color.green);
else g.setColor(Color.white);
```

We've added an *if ... else* clause, which is used in exactly the same as it was in JavaScript (see Chapter 16). If 'over' has been set to true by the mouse entering the applet, the colour will be set to green; otherwise it will be white. Go ahead and compile the applet to test it out for yourself.

▶ A bit of simple mouse reactivity: changing the text colour when the mouse enters.

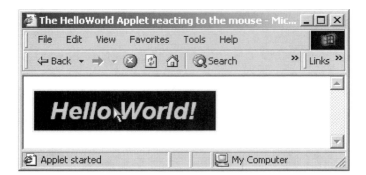

Getting Rid Of The Flicker

On some operating systems, particularly the Windows 95/98/ME series, you'll notice a distinct flicker each time the mouse enters or exits and the applet repaints. (If you're *not* using one of those systems, it's well worth testing your creations in one of them to make sure it's flicker-free.) This is happening because of the way an applet deals with our calls to repaint() in the mouse methods. Behind the scenes, this is actually calling two methods, a method called **update()** which clears the applet, and then the paint() method. In effect, this means the applet is being painted twice in quick succession, causing a flicker. To prevent this happening (as you'll want to do in any applet that has to repaint itself) we create our own update() method to override the one built into the Applet class, like this:

```
public void update(Graphics g)
{
        paint(g);
}
```

Now, whenever we call repaint(), our own update() method will be used which skips straight to the paint() method without stopping to clear the screen first.

▶ *If you're still plagued by flicker, you probably need to use double buffering. It's a lot easier than it sounds – skip ahead to Chapter 22 to find out how to do it.*

What Next?

In the next chapter we'll build on the same applet to create a *real* button you can use as a reactive link to a web page. In the meantime, though, why not experiment with the paint() method to add other reactions? By adding curly brackets to enclose the result of the *if* and *else* tests (as in JavaScript on page 294) you can change the colour of the rectangular border, the size of the font, the background colour, and more. Here's an example that changes the font style from bold-italic to bold:

```
public void paint (Graphics g)
{
        g.setColor(Color.black);
        g.fillRect(0, 0, size().width, size().height);
        g.setColor(Color.yellow);
        g.drawRect(0, 0, size().width-1, size().height-1);
        g.drawRect(1, 1, size().width-3, size().height-3);
        if (over)
            {
            g.setColor(Color.green);
            Font f = new Font("Helvetica", 1, 28);
            g.setFont(f);
            }
        else
            {
            g.setColor(Color.white);
            Font f = new Font("Helvetica", 3, 28);
            g.setFont(f);
            }
        g.drawString ("Hello World!", 20, 35);
}
```

BUILDING A BUTTON

The Hello World applet we wrote in Chapter 20 *looks* vaguely button-like, but you probably wouldn't call it a button just yet. It's too big to use on a web page, it doesn't do anything when clicked, and most importantly, its colours, fonts and text can only be changed by editing the source code and compiling again. In this chapter, we'll set about turning this little chap into a *real* button that reads your settings from the web page and links somewhere when clicked.

You probably don't want to call your button 'HelloWorld.java', so start by making a copy of your source code file and giving it a better name. I'm going to call it 'Button.java', but feel free to pick something more imaginative for your own. (To be sure we're starting from the same basic source code, you might like to copy my own Button.java from this chapter's folder on the CD-ROM.) Open Button.java in your text editor and change the name of the class to match the name of the source file.

Using init() To Set Variables

In Chapter 20 I mentioned that when an applet starts to run it reads and executes the paint() method. Before it does that, though, it does two other things. First, it reads the list of global variables that appear straight after the class's first curly bracket: we're currently declaring just one global variable, the 'over' variable. Second, it executes a method called **public void init()** (short for initialize). Because this is the *first method* an applet executes, it's the ideal place to set up all the display and behaviour preferences for the applet, so you'll probably use the init() method in all the applets you write. As usual, you can put it anywhere in the page, but it seems logical to make it the first method that appears in the source code too, so let's put it there:

```
public class Button extends Applet
{
boolean over = false;

        public void init()
        {

        }
```

Now let's use that init() method for something! At the moment we're using a local Font variable in the paint() method to set a particular font for the text, but later on we want to set a custom font by reading parameters in the web page, and we don't want to do that in the paint() method. We'll make the font a *global* variable (so that we can refer to it in any method) which involves two small steps: first, declare the Font variable; second, move the line of code that initializes it from the paint() method to the init() method:

```
public class Button extends Applet
{
boolean over = false;
Font f;

        public void init()
        {
                f = new Font("Helvetica", 3, 28);
        }
```

GOOD QUESTION!

Why not read the font parameters in the paint() method?

It will take a few lines of code to read the parameters and set up the font, but we only need to do that once. If we put these lines in the **paint()** method, they'll be executed every time that method is called (i.e. every time the mouse enters or exits the applet). The result will still work, but it adds a lot of unnecessary processing to our applet, and might have the effect of making each repaint take longer to finish.

There are two things to notice about the code added above. First, we've declared the variable using Font f;. With this, we're simply saying that we want to create a Font object called 'f'; unlike the boolean variable above it, we're not assigning a value to it yet. Second, the word Font has been removed from the line of code now moved to the init() method. As we've already declared that 'f' is a Font object, we mustn't do so again.

The result now is that when the paint() method is first called, the only reference to the font is in g.setFont(f). Because 'f' is now a global variable, and we've already *initialized* it (specified the settings for the font), we'll get exactly the same result as before.

Adding Colour & Text Variables

We made the font a global variable so that eventually we can set it up in the init() method by reading parameters in the web page and still be able to use it in paint(). Later on, we want to read the colours and text from the web page as well, so let's do a similar thing for each of those. First we need to declare four Color variables and give each a recognizable name, plus a String variable for the text:

```
Boolean over = false;
Font f;
Color background, button, text, textover;
String caption;
```

Next we initialize those new variables in the init() method:

```
public void init()
{
        f = new Font("Helvetica", 3, 28);
        background = Color.black;
        button = Color.yellow;
        text = Color.white;
        textover = Color.green;
        caption = "Hello World!";
}
```

Finally, we replace the colour and string values we've used in the paint() method with those variables. For instance, anywhere we want to use yellow, we replace Color.yellow with button.

```
public void paint (Graphics g)
{
        g.setColor(background);
        g.fillRect(0, 0, size().width, size().height);
```

```
        g.setColor(button);
        g.drawRect(0, 0, size().width-1, size().height-1);
        g.drawRect(1, 1, size().width-3, size().height-3);


        if (over) g.setColor(textover);
        else g.setColor(text);
        g.setFont(f);
        g.drawString (caption, 20, 35);
}
```

Creating A 3D Border

One of the problems with the button is that it has a plain border – surely a button should be 3-dimensional? Fortunately Java's Graphics object has two built-in methods like the fillRect() and drawRect() methods we used in Chapter 20: **fill3DRect()** and **draw3DRect()**. These two new methods need the same four arguments to set the position and size of the rectangle, plus one extra argument: a boolean (true/false) value to specify whether the rectangle should be raised or lowered.

Without further ado, go to your paint() method, and replace the two g.drawRect lines with this chunk of code:

```
if (over)
        {
        g.fill3DRect(1, 1, size().width-3, size().height-3, true);
        g.fill3DRect(2, 2, size().width-5, size().height-5, true);
        }
else
        {
        g.fillRect(1, 1, size().width-3, size().height-3);
        g.fillRect(2, 2, size().width-5, size().height-5);
        }
```

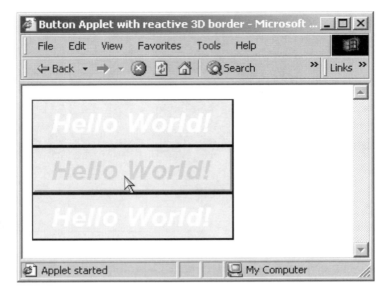

▶ Three Button applets on the page: a 3D border appears as you move over each button.

What we've done here is initially to display a flat rectangle, and make it 3-dimensional when the mouse enters, as the screenshot above shows. The rectangle is one pixel smaller than the applet now, to leave a small gap between each button when we use several of them on a page. You can also see why I chose the name 'button' for the colour variable instead of something like 'border' – we're now using that colour to create the button itself rather than just a border around its edge.

Reading Web Page Parameters

This is the bit you've probably been itching to get to! Right now, our colours, fonts and button caption are built into the applet itself – if you wanted several different buttons on a page you'd have to compile several slightly different versions of the applet!

We can get around that by reading *parameters* from a web page, as I mentioned in Chapter 15. The Applet class has a built-in method for that, **getParameter()**, which returns a string value. All we have to do is specify the name of the parameter we want to read.

Getting Text Parameters

Let's start by reading the button's caption from a parameter which we'll call 'Caption'. At the moment our init() method contains the line caption = "Hello World!"; so we need to replace that line with this:

```
caption = getParameter("Caption");
```

GOOD QUESTION!

Does it matter what I call a parameter?

You can choose any name for a parameter, including spaces if you wish. In theory, parameter names are case sensitive, so they should appear exactly the same way in your web page as they do in the Java source code, although most browsers are forgiving in this department.

The 'caption' variable now holds whatever we've specified in the Caption parameter on the web page. Compile the applet and then change your web page to look like this:

```
<APPLET CODE="Button.class" WIDTH=210 HEIGHT=50>
<PARAM NAME="Caption" VALUE="Home">
</APPLET><BR>
```

You can copy this HTML code a few more times to create a column of buttons as in the screenshot overleaf, changing the value of the parameter to the text you want to display. (If you do that, it's best to view the page in a browser. The appletviewer will open a separate viewer window for each applet, which rather spoils the effect!)

Building A Font From Parameters

To build a font we need to read three parameters – one each for the font's name, style and size. The code we use to read those parameters will be placed before the line starting f = new Font, and later we'll change that line so that it creates the font we set in the parameters.

355

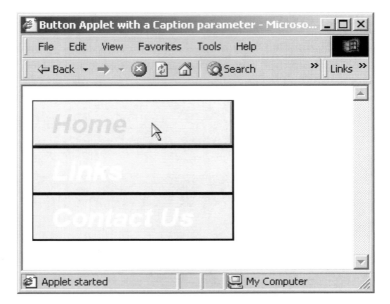

▶ With the applet now reading its button caption from a parameter, you can control it from the web page.

Getting the font's name is easy: the font's name is a string, just like the button caption, so we can declare a local String variable to hold the font name:

```
String fontname = getParameter("FontName");
```

Now we hit a snag. Whenever we read a parameter we're given a string, but the style and size of the font must be numbers (or, in Java terms, **integers**). So after reading the values of the style and size parameters we need to convert them from strings to integers. Here's how we do it:

```
String temp = getParameter("FontSize");
int fontsize = Integer.parseInt(temp);
temp = getParameter("FontStyle");
int fontstyle = Integer.parseInt(temp);
```

We've created a local variable called 'temp' to hold the first parameter. Next, the built-in method **Integer.parseInt(*string*)** converts a string to an integer. The integer is stored in another local variable called 'fontsize'. (Integer variables are initialized as **int**, always with a lowercase 'i'). Finally we do the same thing again to read and convert the style, but this time we don't need to declare 'temp' as a string – to do so would give a compiler error, because the compiler already *knows* it's a string.

Why use 'temp' instead of creating another variable?

Every variable we create uses a little memory. Even a local variable will exist until the **init**() method has completed, so if we created **another** string variable we'd be using two chunks of memory during this time. Once we've used 'temp' to get the font size as an integer in the second line, we don't need the value it contains any more, so we can use it to hold the value of the next parameter.

Finally we can slot those values into the line of code that actually creates the font, replacing the fixed values we were using originally:

```
f = new Font(fontname, fontstyle, fontsize);
```

After compiling the applet, add these parameters to your page.

```
<PARAM NAME="FontName" VALUE="TimesRoman">
<PARAM NAME="FontStyle" VALUE="3">
<PARAM NAME="FontSize" VALUE="36">
```

I wanna hold your hand...

The applet should really have some error-checking code to give a bit of hand-holding, but at the moment it relies on your web page to give the type of parameter it expects. If a parameter is missing, for example, the applet won't run. If the style and size parameters don't contain a value that can be converted to a whole number, it's another no-show, and the same will apply when we add the colour parameters, below. We'll look at error checking in the next chapter.

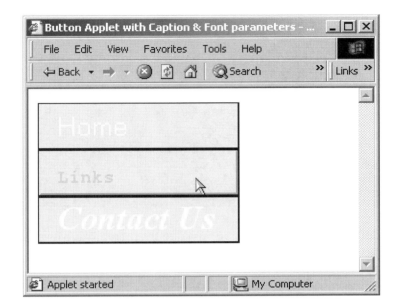

▶ By adding font parameters, each button can use a completely different font (if that's what you want!).

Setting Colours From Parameters

Finally, we want to be able to choose our own colours for the applet via parameters. That's not an easy job, and it's made more difficult because we don't really want to be restricted to the 13 colours Java recognizes by name – we want to use any hex colour just as we do in the web page itself, such as FF0000.

To accomplish this, I've written a new method that you can copy into your source code. I won't explain it all, but here are the basics. This method has the keyword 'Color' rather than the 'void' or 'boolean' we've seen in other methods, and this indicates that it returns a Color object. When we use it, we pass it two arguments: the name of the parameter we want to read, and a default colour to use if the parameter isn't included in the web page.

```
private Color getColorParam(String param, Color defCol)
{
String temp = getParameter(param);
if (temp != null)
    {
    Integer col = Integer.valueOf(temp, 16);
```

```
        return new Color(col.intValue());
        }
return new Color(defCol.getRGB());
}
```

With the new method added to your page, we can turn to the init() method
and replace the lines of code that set up the colours with these:

```
background = getColorParam("BgColor", Color.black);
button = getColorParam("ButtonColor", Color.yellow);
text = getColorParam("CaptionColor", Color.white);
textover = getColorParam("CaptionOverColor", Color.green);
```

Now you can experiment with complete colour schemes for the applet
by adding the colour parameters to your page. Here's one parameter as
an example:

```
<PARAM NAME="ButtonColor" VALUE="00CCCC">
```

◀ Each copy of
the applet on the
page can now
have its own
colours, font
and text.

BY THE WAY

Getting the best from 3D buttons

When you use the **draw3DRect()** or **fill3DRect()** methods, Java takes the current colour and creates lighter and darker shades to create the 3-dimensional edges. For best results, set your ButtonColor parameter to a mid-range colour. If you choose white or bright red, for instance, no lighter colour can be created, so the two bright borders won't look any different from the rest of the button. The same applies (in reverse) to very dark colours such as black.

FontMetrics: Centring The Caption

Now that we've added font parameters, you've probably tried setting the font size to something more reasonable, such as 12, and perhaps making the applet smaller. If so, you've already spotted the problem we're about to deal with: the button caption is drawn at a fixed position 20 pixels from the left edge and 35 pixels from the top. If we want our font options to be flexible, we need some way to work out the width and height of the caption and then centre it on the button.

We've met a few of Java's built-in classes already – Applet, Font, Color and Graphics – and here's another: **FontMetrics**. The FontMetrics class gives us access to information about a particular font using methods that include the following:

This method...	...does this
getAscent()	Gets the height of the font from its baseline to its top (characters such as 'a' sit on the baseline; 'p' drops below it).
getDescent()	Gets the height of the font from the baseline to the bottom (the lowest part of a 'p' or 'g').
getLeading()	Gets the line spacing for the font (the distance between the bottom of the descent of one line and the top of the ascent of the line below it).
getHeight()	Gets the total height of a font by adding its ascent, descent and leading.
stringWidth(*string*)	Gets the width of a particular string using the current font.

We'll start by declaring two more global variables to hold the left and top positions of the text. As these will both be integers (whole numbers) we declare them with the keyword int:

```
int textleft, texttop;
```

Now we'll turn our attentions to the init() method, where we'll set the values for those variables. The first job is to create a local FontMetrics variable that will hold the FontMetrics information about our font:

```
FontMetrics fm = getFontMetrics(f);
```

This has to be placed somewhere *after* the line of code beginning f = new Font. Before that point, 'f' didn't actually hold a font to get any information about! It must also come after the line caption = getParameter("Caption"), because we can't determine the width of a string until we know what the string contains.

Getting the horizontal starting point for the button-caption just involves getting its width and doing some simple arithmetic:

```
textleft = (size().width – fm.stringWidth(caption)) /2;
```

The first part of the equation, size().width – fm.stringWidth(caption), is placed in brackets because we want to treat the result as a single number to be divided by two, rather than dividing the string width by two and then subtracting it from the applet's width.

Centring text vertically takes a bit more thought about the way FontMetrics works. The aim is to find the amount of blank space above and below the font's baseline and divide it by two, like this:

```
texttop = fm.getAscent() + (size().height – fm.getHeight()) /2;
```

With the variables added and these three lines of code placed in your init() method, there's just one thing left to do before compiling and checking the result – change the fixed coordinates in the paint() method to the variables we've just defined:

```
g.drawString (caption, textleft, texttop);
```

Where's the top of the font?

BY THE WAY

When you tell an applet to draw some text at y pixels from the top of the applet, it treats y as the **baseline** of the text, not as its top. As an example, if you use the method **drawstring("Hello", 0, 0)** the text will be against the left of the applet, but the tops of the letters will be chopped off. Instead you need to get the FontMetrics of the font and change the method to **drawstring("Hello", 0, fm.getAscent())**.

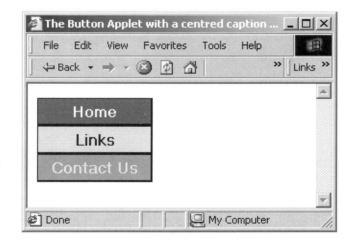

▶ Perfectly centred captions, regardless of font choices or the length of the caption.

Clickability: Reacting To Mouse Clicks

We're two steps away from a complete linking button. At the moment the applet is reacting to mouseEnter() and mouseExit() events, and we need it to respond to two more, **mouseDown()** and **mouseUp()**, in exactly the same way to make the button clickable. And as we did before, we're going to declare another global variable, 'up', to keep track of whether or not a mouse button is down. If I tell you that the two new mouse methods are identical to the other two we used in everything but name, you can probably work out what we're adding to the code:

```
boolean up = true;

// ... other methods here

public boolean mouseDown(Event e, int x, int y)
{
        up = false;
        repaint();
        return true;
}

public boolean mouseUp(Event e, int x, int y)
{
        up = true;
        repaint();
        return true;
}
```

The new variable goes into your list of global variables, and the added mouse methods can be placed anywhere after the variables as usual (though it's sensible to keep them near the other mouse methods to make them easy to find when you want to edit them).

To finish the job, we need to make the button *look* as though it's been clicked when 'up' has been set to false: we want the 3-dimensional border to be drawn lowered rather than raised. In the two lines beginning g.fill3DRect we specified true as the final argument to determine the style of the border, making it appear raised. All we need to do is replace the word 'true' with 'up'. Each time the applet is painted, the button will have a raised border if 'up' is true, and a lowered border if it's false.

There's just one more thing to do which will improve the *feel* of the click: we'll make the caption drop downward by one pixel when 'up' is false by altering the part of the paint() method where the text is drawn:

```
int addon = 1;
if (up) addon = 0;
g.drawString(caption, textleft, texttop+addon);
```

If the button is in the 'up' state, we'll add zero to the caption's vertical position, but when it's clicked the top position of the caption will increase by 1.

▶ Using the fill3DRect() method to lower the button border when the mouse is clicked.

A Link! Getting & Using A URL

Finally, let's make the button link to a URL when it's clicked. As a first step, we'll add two new parameters to the web page which will supply the URL and the name of the frame or window in which to open it:

```
<PARAM NAME="URL" VALUE="mypage.htm">
<PARAM NAME="Target" VALUE="_self">
```

Now we'll add some code to the mouseUp() method which will read the URL and Target parameters and (if they exist) handle the link. This code will come *after* the call to repaint() so that the button will be shown in its raised state again before the link code is executed.

Before we write that code, though, we need to add another Java package to the list at the very top of the source code. Currently we're importing two packages, java.awt and java.applet, but Java's support for networking and the Internet is in another package, **java.net**. We need to *import* that package into our applet so that we can use the classes it provides, so add the following line to the top of the page where the other two appear (their order doesn't matter):

```
import java.net.*;
```

Now let's edit the mouseUp() method. First we'll read the two new parameters into a pair of local variables:

```
String u = getParameter("URL");
String t = getParameter("Target");
```

Next we have to create a new variable, a URL object built into the java.net package we imported. The URL object is created using two arguments. The first is the location of the document containing the web page, which we can get using another built-in method, **getDocumentBase()**. This argument is used to derive an *absolute* URL if our parameter contained just a *relative* URL; the applet ignores this argument if we did use an absolute URL in the parameter. The second argument is the parameter itself.

With the *URL* object created and stored in a variable imaginatively named 'url', we can then use a couple more built-in methods in combination to open URL: **getAppletContext().showDocument(*URL, String*)**. Here's the resulting code:

```
URL url = new URL(getDocumentBase(), u);
getAppletContext().showDocument(url, t);
```

We're not quite done, though. Networking is a bit of a minefield, and all sorts of things could go wrong, so when we use networking methods Java insists that we watch out for errors (or, in Java language, **catch exceptions**). We do this by surrounding these two lines with something called a **try ... catch** statement. In English it works like this:

```
try {try to do something risky;}
catch (Exception ex) {optionally do something else if there was a problem}
```

The second line will only be executed if there was a problem executing the first. We'll look at that in a bit more detail in the next chapter, but for now we'll simply slot our two lines of networking code into the *try* statement, and we won't take any alternative action if the link fails.

```
try
{
URL url = new URL(getDocumentBase(), u);
getAppletContext().showDocument(url, t);
}
catch (Exception ex) {}
```

And that's it! You've written a linking button applet that can be included in any website without any modifications – everything you need to change is available through <PARAM> tags on the web page itself. Better still, you know *how* you did it! If you want to make changes to the way it looks or behaves, you can just delve into the code and do it.

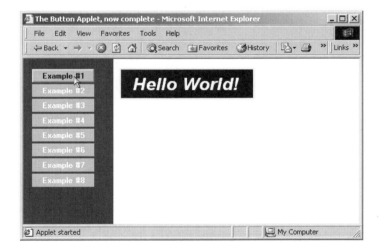

▶ The complete linking button, ready for use on any website, and adding only 3 Kb to your page weight!

GOOD QUESTION!

Is it okay to use several applets on one page?

If they're all instances of the same applet, the .class file will only download once, so your page weight remains the same whether you use it once or six times. But using it multiple times on a page does use more system resources, and some older browsers (v3 and earlier) were unable to take the strain of heavy use of Java. Small applets like this button won't cause any problems unless you're trying to use a few dozen of them, though.

JAVA PROGRAMMING TIPS

Over the last couple of chapters we've covered all the basic moves involved in creating a graphical applet – colours, fonts, font metrics, mouse events, and the all-important init() and paint() methods. If you've emerged from those chapters itching to design bigger and better applets for your pages (and I hope you have!) you'll be using everything we covered, and in much the same way.

There's a lot more to Java, of course, and although our button applet is finished and it works, there are still things we should do, could do, or might want to do. In this chapter I'll run through some extra programming tips and options, relating them to the button applet wherever possible. As usual, you'll find the complete source code for all the separate routines in this chapter's folder on the CD-ROM, along with example web pages to let you test the result.

Checking For Errors

Although we skipped it when coding the button applet, the issue of error checking is an important one, and as soon as we start reading parameters from a web page the chances of an error occurring increase enormously. It's possible that when the applet tries to read a parameter it can't find it – perhaps because the name is spelt wrongly in the web page, or because the parameter just hasn't been included. The resulting string will be **null** (see Chapter 16), and if we try to process a null string in any way at all (convert it to a colour or number, display it, and so on) we'll get an error: But this is the worst kind of error: rather than a compiler error that you can fix by finding the mistake in your source code, it's a **runtime** error – it happens when the applet is used on a web page and trying to run.

The simple rule is: anywhere you read a parameter, check that you didn't get a null string. If you then convert that to something else (such as an integer), check that it really *was* possible to convert it. Let's take a couple of examples.

In the button applet's init() method, we read the 'Caption' parameter and, later on, we find its width and display it on the button. If there's no Caption parameter in the web page, we're in trouble several times over, so we'll check the result and supply a default string if necessary:

```
caption = getParameter("Caption");
if (caption == null) caption = "No Caption";
```

Another example: in the init() method, we read the 'FontSize' parameter and convert it to an integer. As before, if the parameter doesn't exist, we've got a problem. But what if the parameter says something like <PARAM NAME=FontSize VALUE="Hello">? The word 'Hello' can't be converted to an integer, so it's Trouble City again. Here's the solution:

```
String temp = getParameter("FontSize");
if (temp == null) temp = "12";
int fontsize;
try {fontsize = Integer.parseInt(temp);}
catch (Exception ex) {fontsize = 12;}
```

After the first line, lifted straight from the Button.java code, we test for a null string in line 2 and, if necessary, replace it with a valid string that can be converted to an integer. In line 3 we declare 'fontsize' as a local variable, and the last two lines use a try ... catch statement, covered in Chapter 21. In other words, we *try* to convert 'temp' to an integer and store it in 'fontsize'; if we fail for any reason, we set 'fontsize' to 12.

GOOD QUESTION!

Why do we have to declare 'fontsize' before converting the string? We didn't do that before!

In the original code we used **int fontsize = Integer.parseInt(temp);** which was fine before we added error checking. In a nutshell, whenever you declare a variable inside a pair of curly brackets, it can only be used by other code inside the **same** pair of curly brackets. If we declare 'fontsize' between the **init()** method's brackets, we can use it anywhere in the **init()** method. But if we declare it inside the **try** statement's brackets, it ceases to exist when the code in the brackets has been executed. So when we referred to 'fontsize' a little later to create the new font, we'd get a compiler error.

We should do exactly the same checking for the value of the 'FontStyle' parameter. Later, in the mouseUp() method, we should check for valid values in the 'URL' and 'Target' parameters. If the URL is null we can skip the rest of the code in that method by returning a value of true. If the target is null, we should supply a default target name. In this chapter's source code folder on the CD-ROM, you'll find a file named Extra01.java which contains an error-checked revision of the button applet.

Better Still: Using Default Values

If your applet has to gather a dozen or more parameters, error checking them all this way means adding a dozen or more lines of code to your page which all do the same job. A better solution is to write your own method which retrieves a parameter and returns a default value if the parameter turns out to be null. (In fact, it's an unwritten rule of programming that you should try to avoid repeating code that already appears elsewhere in the source file: it's usually possible to write a method or function that can be called to do the job when needed.) Here's a method that does just that:

```java
public String getStringParam(String param, String defvalue)
{
        String s = getParameter(param);
        if (s == null) s = defvalue;
        return s;
}
```

With this method included in your source, you can replace all your pairs of param-getter/param-checker lines with something like this:

```java
caption = getStringParam("Caption", "No Caption");
```

This way, your source code becomes much easier to read, you're guaranteed a valid result, and your .class file becomes a tiny bit smaller too! How about a similar method to read a parameter and convert it to a number?

```java
public int getIntParam(String param, int defvalue)
{
```

```
        int result = 0;
        String s = getParameter(param);
        if (s != null)
                {
                try {result = Integer.parseInt(s);}
                catch (Exception ex) {result = defvalue;}
                }
        else result = defvalue;
        return result;
}
```

After adding this method, you can retrieve parameters as integers in one line of code like this:

```
int fontsize = getIntParam("FontSize", 12);
```

The source file Extra02.java on the CD-ROM rewrites our error-checked applet to use the two methods above. You'll see immediately how much shorter and simpler the init() method now looks.

Displaying Status Bar Messages

In Java it's easy to display messages in the browser's status bar – simpler than it is in JavaScript, in fact. It just takes one method call, **showStatus(*string*)**. Taking our button applet as an example, let's display a message in the status bar when the mouse enters, and clear it again when the mouse exits. I'm sure you can write the code without my help, so I'll just point out the basic steps.

1   Add a global String variable called 'message' (or something similar).

2   In the init() method, read the parameter containing the message into that 'message' variable. If the result is null, reset it to an empty string (message = "").

3   After repainting the applet in mouseEnter(), add the magic code: showStatus(message); (replacing the word 'message' with whatever you called your variable).

4   Add showStatus("") in the same part of the mouseExit() method.

Why should the status bar message be handled after repainting?

Actually, you can do it wherever you like. But the applet's interface should react to whatever the user does as fast as possible, to give a feeling of responsiveness, so it's wise to repaint it as soon as possible. If the status bar text changes a tiny bit later, that's much less noticeable.

▶ The button returns, now showing a custom status bar message when the mouse enters.

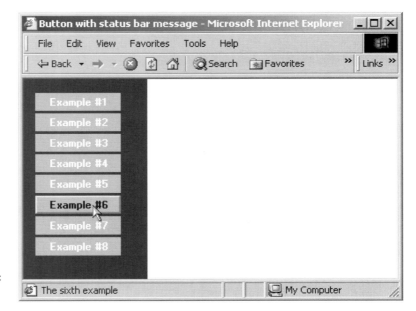

More Mouse Handling: It's A Drag!

There's something very messy about our button applet: if you click a button and then drag the mouse out of it, the button stays 'pressed'. The reason most users will drag out of the button is because they've belatedly changed their minds about linking anywhere for the moment, so they're not going to like what happens next: the link is handled when they release the mouse button, *wherever* the mouse happens to be!

That's all very sloppy design, and we need to sort it out. We can do that using another of the Applet class's mouse methods, **mouseDrag()**. Since the code we put into that method will only be executed when the user drags the mouse inside the button area, we can test to find out if the mouse leaves. (No, mouseExit() doesn't cover that: the mouseExit() method only fires if no mouse button is down when the mouse exits.)

You've probably noticed that in all the mouse methods we've used, we're passed some arguments. These include two integers named x and y which hold the current position of the mouse: x is the horizontal location, y is the vertical. We can use these to test whether that position is inside the applet. If it isn't, we'll reset the 'up' and 'over' variables, repaint the applet, and clear the status bar message.

```
public boolean mouseDrag(Event e, int x, int y)
{
        if (x < 0 || y < 0 || x >= size().width || y >= size().height)
                {
                up = true;
                over = false;
                repaint();
                showStatus("");
                }
        return true;
}
```

Most of that code should be self-explanatory. In the first line, we're testing whether x or y is less than zero or greater-than-or-equal-to the applet's width or height. The double-pipe symbol | | means 'or' – if any one of these is true, the mouse has exited and we want to execute the code in the curly brackets. If *all* the tests had to be true before the code was executed we'd use a double-ampersand &&, meaning 'and'. These are known as **logical operators**; Java uses exactly the same logical and mathematical operators as JavaScript, listed on page 275.

If you were to compile and test the result, you'd find that although the *visual* behaviour of the applet is perfect now, it still processes the link when we eventually release the mouse button. Because the mouseDown event happened within the applet, it still receives the mouseUp event, and there's nothing conditional happening in our mouseUp() method – the link will *always* be processed. Fortunately that's easily fixed. When the mouse was dragged out of the applet we set the 'up' variable to true. So we'll add the following line right at the start of the mouseUp() method to check that 'up' is false. If it isn't, the method returns without going any further:

```
if (up) return true;
```

BY THE WAY

The dangers of moving & dragging...

There's another method similar to the **mouseDrag()** method we used above: **mouseMove()**. The mouseMove() method catches movements in the applet when no button is pressed. The thing these methods have in common is that they're fired every time the mouse moves by a single pixel, giving the coordinates of the new location. If you were to use **mouseMove()** to test whether the mouse is **inside** the applet, and repaint if it is, you'll get a repaint occurring many times a second, making the whole thing flicker something rotten! Once in a while you may need to use **mouseMove()** to check whether the mouse is in a particular **area** of the applet and repaint if it is: when you do, always use a boolean variable to test that the mouse wasn't in that area of the applet last time; if it was, you don't need to repaint again.

Where's The Bug?

When you compile an applet and the compiler tells you there's an error, it helpfully gives you a line number and other information to track it down. But sometimes you'll find that an applet compiles without any problem and then promptly fails to do what you were expecting when you run it, leaving you asking questions like *Why didn't it change colour?* or *Why is that text halfway out of the applet?*

When the unexpected happens, the cause may be a *runtime* error in the applet – the result of not checking that a certain value is valid before using it. When runtime errors occur, they're automatically printed out to the Java console window which, if you're using appletviewer to view an applet, means the MS-DOS command prompt window. If you're using a browser, though, you won't automatically see the console window. Here's where you'll find it:

▶ In **Internet Explorer**, choose View, Java Console. If you can't see that entry on the View menu, go to Tools, Internet Options, Advanced, scroll down to the Microsoft VM section and check the box labelled **Java console enabled**. Click OK, then close and reopen the browser.

▶ In **Netscape**, go to Tasks, Tools, Java Console (v6), Communicator, Tools, Java Console or Window, Java Console (v4), or Options, Show Java Console (v3).

▶ In **Opera**, go to Window, Special, Java Console.

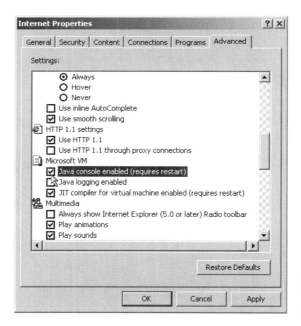

◄ Enabling the Java Console window in Internet Explorer.

The details shown in a browser's console aren't quite as helpful as those provided by appletviewer, but they'll still point you towards the method containing the error if not the precise line number.

But the real benefit of the console is that you can build your own progress messages into an applet which will be shown as they're executed. This is done using the method **System.out.println(*string*);** (note the capital 'S' of 'System'). This gives you a great way to find the setting of a variable at a particular point in the code, or to find out which line was the last to be completed before an error occurred. Here's some example code that illustrates the second of those:

```java
public void init()
{
        String s1 = "Hello";
        System.out.println("1");
        String s2 = "World";
        System.out.println("2");
        String s3 = s1 + " " + s2;
        System.out.println("3");
        int daftThingToDo = Integer.parseInt(s3);
        System.out.println("4");
}
```

Between each line of code I'm printing out a simple numerical marker. To find out where the error occurs, I can just look at the console to see which marker was the last to be printed before the error message appeared, which tells me that whatever appeared in the source code between that marker and the next must contain the error.

▶ The console output for the code above shows that after printing the third marker the applet ran into the code containing the error.

BY THE WAY

Printing non-String values to the console

The **System.out.println()** method works a lot like JavaScript's **alert()** method, but with one small difference: if the value you're trying to print out isn't actually a string, you'll get a compiler error. Fortunately you can convert almost anything to a string – integers, fonts, colours, font metrics, you name it. Java contains a built-in **toString()** method for this (such as **myfont.toString()** to get a string representation of a font), but for console purposes there's a much simpler way: **System.out.println("" + myfont)** is accepted as a valid String value and does exactly what you want.

Get A Better Colour!

In Chapter 21 I showed you how to read a parameter containing a hex string and convert it to a colour, but if you want to use a colour that *isn't* read from a parameter you're still stuck with Java's 13 colour names. Although you can't directly use the hex system in Java, you *can* use the RGB colour model used by most graphics programs (see Chapter 5) to create a colour using **new Color(r, g, b)**. Here's a simple example resulting in bright red:

```
Color backgroundcol = new Color(255, 0, 0);
```

Of course, you can combine this with the getColorParam() method we wrote in the previous chapter to provide one of 16 million default colours rather than just one of 13:

```
button = getColorParam("ButtonColor", new Color(0, 192, 255));
```

Double Buffering For Flicker-Free Painting

At the end of Chapter 20, we added a tiny piece of code to override the Applet class's update() method and reduce the flicker that can occur during repainting. That's enough to keep things smooth in an applet that doesn't have much to paint, but an applet with a slightly more complex paint() method will still flicker. The reason for this is that every time we draw something using a line beginning **g.** we're drawing straight onto the applet. In our button, for example, we use g.fillRect() three times (or g.fill3DRect() if the mouse is over the button) followed by g.drawString(). These four separate items are drawn in quick succession onto the applet every time we call repaint(), which of course means four successive changes to the appearance of the applet. The flicker isn't too bad in the button, but imagine what it would look like if we were drawing 50 separate lines of text or a few dozen small rectangles!

The solution is to use a technique known as **double buffering** (or, sometimes, off-screen graphics, which is a bit more descriptive). In a nutshell, this means creating a blank image the same size as the applet, painting each item onto that image, and then painting that completed image onto the applet. All those dozens of tiny changes occur in this hidden image, leaving just one big change to be made to the applet itself afterwards. The result looks identical, but the flicker is reduced to almost nothing! Let's convert our button applet to use double buffering.

To begin with, we need to declare two global variables: a Graphics object and an Image object. I call these 'offG' and 'offI', short for off-screen graphics and off-screen image to remind me that they're hidden, but you can choose any names you like, of course:

```
Graphics offG;
Image offI;
```

In the init() method, we set the new image's dimensions to match those of the applet, and load a copy of the image's canvas into 'offG' so that we can draw on it (in the same way we draw on the applet's canvas using 'g'):

```
offI = createImage(size().width, size().height);
offG = offI.getGraphics();
```

Finally, we need to make two changes to the existing paint() method. The first is to replace every instance of g. with offG. so that all the font setting, colour setting and painting we're doing onto the applet's canvas is now done onto the image's canvas instead. Second, right at the end of the paint() method, we paint the image onto the applet at its top-left corner by adding this line:

```
g.drawImage(offl, 0, 0, this);
```

And that's all there is to it! The only thing you have to remember is that added line at the end of paint(). If you forget that, your applet will always be blank!

GOOD QUESTION!

What does the word 'this' mean in the drawImage() method?

Whenever we draw an image onto a canvas, the final argument will be an object called an **ImageProducer** which notifies the applet when the image painting has been completed. It sounds complicated, but luckily the applet itself can act as the ImageProducer, and we refer to the applet using the keyword 'this'.

Displaying Images

As we've already worked with the Image object in the double-buffering routines above, let's use it to display a *real* GIF or JPEG image on the button when the mouse enters. There are a few steps involved in this: first we'll load the image into a variable; next we'll find its width and move the button's caption to a position just to the right of where the image will appear; finally we'll draw the image itself.

The first job is to declare a global variable for the new Image object called 'img', as you did in the double-buffering routine. Next, we turn to the init() method and load the image file. We need to use a URL for that, which means that we must import the java.net package and enclose the code in a *try ... catch* statement, just as we did at the end of Chapter 21. Here's how we load the image:

```
try
    {
        img = getImage(getDocumentBase(),"arrow.gif");
        MediaTracker tracker = new MediaTracker(this);
```

```
        tracker.addImage(img, 0);
        tracker.waitForID(0);
        }
catch (Exception ex) {img = null;}
if (img != null) imgwidth = img.getWidth(this);
else imgwidth = 6;
```

In the first line, I've used a fixed filename, 'arrow.gif', but you could easily read the URL from a parameter. The second line creates a **MediaTracker** object, which tracks the loading status of images, and the third adds our image to its list of tracked images giving it the ID number 0. The final line tells the tracker to start loading all images that have the ID 0. You can assign the same ID number to as many images as you like. If any of that code causes an exception, we'll assume the image wasn't loaded and set 'img' to null. Finally we get the width of an image into another global variable, an integer named 'imgwidth'. If the image wasn't loaded, we set 'imgwidth' to 6 (which is the width of the image we're trying to load in this example).

Next we'll go to the paint() method and draw the image on the button when the mouse enters by adding this line in the if (over){} section:

```
if (img != null) offG.drawImage(img, 5, (size().height – img.getHeight(this)) /2,
this);
```

It's vital to check that we don't have a null image first. We'll draw the image five pixels from the left edge of the button, and vertically centred. Finally we'll change the drawString() method to display the caption four pixels to the right of the image. This means adding together the five pixels to the left of the image, the four to its right, and the width of the image:

```
offG.drawString(caption, 9+imgwidth, texttop+addon);
```

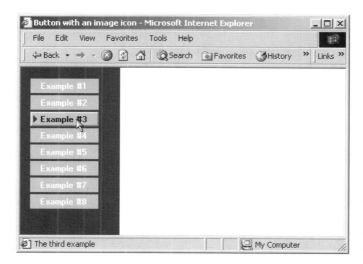

◀ The infamous button applet, now sporting a small image when the mouse enters.

Adding Sound To Applets

If an applet can display images, why not get it to play sound effects too? It's easy to do, and it adds a little extra user feedback to a button. The only catch is that Java uses Sun/NeXT format audio files (files with an .au extension) which aren't easy to come by unless you have audio-processing software, but I've included a couple on the CD-ROM which we'll use for this example.

In Java, a sound is an **AudioClip** object, so we need to create two global variables of this type:

```
AudioClip downsound, upsound;
```

Because these are files, we need to load them using URLs, remembering to include the line import.java.net.*; at the beginning of the source. Here's how we load the sound files into the variables:

```
try {downsound = getAudioClip(getDocumentBase(),"buttondown.au");}
catch (Exception ex) {downsound = null;}
try {upsound = getAudioClip(getDocumentBase(),"buttonup.au");}
catch (Exception ex) {upsound = null;}
```

GOOD QUESTION!

Why not do the whole thing in just one try...catch statement?

That's an option, and not a bad one. By using two separate statements, as in the example, if one sound can't be loaded we might still successfully get the second. If we combined this code in a single try...catch statement, we'd have to set both sounds to null in the event of an exception. You may prefer that, since the result would be either complete audio support or nothing.

With the sounds loaded, we can insert the code to play the sounds in the mouseDown() and mouseUp() methods by adding the lines below to the appropriate method just after the call to repaint():

```
//in mouseDown()
if (downsound != null) downsound.play();

//in mouseUp
if (upsound != null) upsound.play();
```

4

WEBSITE PUBLISHING & PROMOTION

▶ **IN THIS PART**

FROM HARD DISK TO WEB

▶ **IN THIS CHAPTER**

How to find and choose a web hosting company

Register your own snappy domain name

Keep it cheap: free hosting and web redirection services

Get your site online using FTP

Testing times – checking and troubleshooting your new site

Designing a website should be fun, whether it's a commercial or promotional site for a business, or a more personal site providing information or entertainment. But this is where the fun stops – you've finished! You're about to publish the site and then embark on the never-ending job of maintaining it, promoting it, and tweaking it to make it do what you were hoping it would.

Perhaps you won't enjoy these new tasks quite as much as the design and construction, but this should be an exciting time, and if all goes well, a satisfying one too. You've built a complete website and made it accessible to millions of net users all over the world! Will they like it? Will they visit it? Will they even know it's there? And how will *you* know what's happening? In the following chapters we'll delve into the nitty-gritty of running a website, attracting visitors and learning what they want, and building your site into something bigger and better. First, though, let's get that site onto the Web!

The Perfect Host

Publishing your site means copying all the files in the 'Site' directory on your hard disk to a similar directory on a web server. That directory will have its own URL, formed from the name of the server and the directory's name, and that's the URL you'll give out to anyone who'll listen when you promote the site. It may not be a very good URL (too long, hard to remember, difficult to type, and so on) so you might want to pick your own snappy *domain name* – we'll look into that later in the chapter.

The first job is to find a **hosting company** that will give you space on their web server. There are hundreds of hosting companies in the UK, and thousands more around the world, and all they ask in return for this service is money. I've included a list of UK hosting companies in Appendix E, and you can find many more by searching for 'web hosting' at any search engine or by picking up a computing or Internet magazine.

So how do you cut these long lists down to a few suitable companies? To a certain extent, that depends on what services you need. If your site has specific requirements, you can simply rule out companies that don't fit the bill and sift through what's left. At this stage, though, unless you've got a clear idea about how your site will develop in future, you're probably more concerned about the price.

It's All About The Money...

If you look into web hosting charges, you'll find they vary enormously and there's little apparent sense to them. For instance, some companies will charge you £10 per megabyte of disk space while others charge 30p. So the first step is to decide on a budget: £50 a year, £500 a year, it's up to you. With this in mind, you can visit a few websites or pick up the phone and find out what you can get for that price. Try to check any of the features or services in the list below that you feel are important, or may be needed in the future. If they're not included at the price you're willing to spend, find out whether you can add them later and, if so, how much they'll cost.

I Know What I Want...

There are a number of services that you might insist upon having. Here are some of the most common:

▶ **Domain name transfer.** If you register your own domain name, your hosting company will be happy to transfer it to your web space so that when someone types that snappy address they'll arrive at your site. Any company will do this for you, but charges vary from zero to about £150.

▶ **Domain name registration.** Any hosting company will register your chosen domain name for you, if it's available. Again they'll charge between zero and about £300. You can do this yourself very easily, and for next to nothing, as you'll learn later in this chapter.

▶ **CGI applications.** If you want to use CGI scripts and applications, you'll need a cgi-bin (see Chapter 19). In itself that's unlikely to be a problem – any good web host that charges you money will provide one – but be sure to specify it and tell the host exactly what you want to use. The majority of web servers run a UNIX operating system, which is fine for Perl scripts but Windows CGI programs can't be used. If you want to use Java servlets (similar programs written in Java) make sure the company offers that feature.

▶ **Microsoft FrontPage Extensions.** If you design your site in FrontPage and include certain items from the Insert/Component menu, you'll need a host that supports these Extensions, preferably on a Windows rather than UNIX server.

▶ **Secure server**. If you plan to sell products or services online using credit card transactions, or receive other types of sensitive information from visitors, you'll usually need a host that provides SSL (Secure Sockets Layer). This may be an extra-cost option. We'll look at this option in more detail in Chapter 25.

▶ **Technical support.** A final, fundamental point: is any technical support available? If so, when is it available, and is it handled by phone or email? Email support isn't always a bad option, provided the company does actually answer its email, but it's often easier to be able to discuss a technical problem on the phone.

It's worth noting that some hosting companies just host your website, while others will also act as your ISP (Internet service provider), giving you a dial-up connection to the Internet, one or more email accounts, and other services. If you don't yet have an ISP, or you're stuck with one of the less reliable free ISPs, this could be a valuable bonus.

Pros & Cons Of Free Hosting

If you do have an ISP, as you probably do, then you almost certainly have some web space already. When you take an account with an ISP, a certain amount of web space is usually included in the deal, even if you use a free ISP such as Virgin Net or Freeserve. It won't give you the greatest sounding URL (http://freespace.virgin.net/~myname, for instance) but it could get you off to a flying start.

Even if you don't have any free web space with your ISP account, it's easy to come by. Believe it or not, there are companies out there that provide web space completely free of charge. Here are a few to try:

▶ **GeoCities** at **http://uk.geocities.yahoo.com**

▶ **EasySpace** at **http://www.easyspace.com**

▶ **Tripod** at **http://www.tripod.com**

▶ **FortuneCity** at **http://www.fortunecity.com**

◀ Free web space and a stack of useful tools at FortuneCity.

Nothing good comes easy, as they say, and free web hosting does tend to be suspiciously easy. You may find that your pages and graphics are unusually slow to load; you might be required to display the hosting company's choice of banner ads or logo on your pages (or the company may insert these automatically at the server); in some cases, a popup advertising window will open whenever a link is clicked. Be sure to look at a few sites belonging to other users of the service before committing yourself.

Apart from the points above, there are other considerations. For instance, you have no **service-level agreement** with the company – they don't guarantee that your site will be available for a certain percentage of the time, or offer to compensate you if they don't meet that target. You also won't be able to use CGI, FrontPage Extensions, SSL or any of the other twiddly bits mentioned earlier.

It's not your space!

Whether you opt for free or pay-for hosting, remember that the space isn't actually yours. The hosting company shares legal responsibility for its content with you, and they decide the terms and conditions. Some free hosts will disallow certain types of file, or delete them from your site, and most hosts will remove content they regard as illegal or immoral.

The Name Game

Whether you buy web space, use web space provided by your ISP, or go to one of the free space providers, you'll be given a username for the account and a directory with the same name on their server (perhaps prefixed with a ~ symbol) such as www.mywebhost.com/~myname, and that will be the URL of your website. It's long, it isn't easy to remember (particularly if it contains numbers as well as letters), and it gives a poor first impression of your site. Fortunately you have several options available to replace this with something shorter and snappier.

If content is king, who cares about the URL?

The reason I say content is king is that however well you handle everything else, if your content doesn't live up to it your site will be a 'one hit wonder' – no-one will come back. The 'everything else' package is a big one, but it comes down to two things: what first impression you give, and **how you deliver** the content. Most potential visitors get a first impression before they even visit your site, judging your promotion, your reputation and your domain name (or lack of one).

Option 1: Register & Transfer A Domain Name

Although your web host may be willing (eager, in fact) to register a domain name for you and charge a handsome fee for doing so, it's something you can do yourself in minutes. There are hundreds of companies in the UK selling domain names on the Web, and you can simply choose the name you want, pay for it, and then decide how you want to use it. The price you pay gives you ownership of the domain name for two years, with an option to renew it annually when the two-year period is up. There are some variations in pricing depending upon the type of **top-level domain** you choose (a .co.uk domain can be bought for under £10 if you shop around, whereas a .com or .net domain will usually cost £30 or more).

It's important to buy your domain name from a reputable company, partly so that you can be sure you really have got the rights to it, and partly because if the company goes out of business it's just possible that you won't get a renewal reminder and your domain name could go back into the pool to be bought by someone else. Here are some well established companies to consider:

▶ **NetNames at http://www.netnames.co.uk**

▶ **DomainsNet at http://www.domainsnet.com**

▶ **UK Reg at http://www.ukreg.com**

Each of these sites gives plenty of straightforward information about the process and the services available. In a nutshell, you start by choosing a name (such as 'dodgygoods'), then pick one or more top-level domains (such as .com), and then check to see whether the chosen combination is available. (Don't include a 'www.' prefix: that's only used in the address of your website, it's not a part of the domain name.) If it hasn't been snapped up by someone else, you can slap your money on the table and register it.

JARGON BUSTER

top-level domain

A domain name comes in two parts: the unique name ('dodgygoods') and a suffix (.com, .net, .org, .co.uk and so on). This suffix is called the **top-level domain** (TLD). The four I just mentioned are the well established TLDs for UK users, but from June 2001 it should be possible to register domains for seven more TLDs: .aero, .biz, .coop, .info, .museum, .name and .pro. The .eu TLD should also be available soon. Bear in mind that some TLDs are restricted to limited companies, governments and so on. If you run a company that trades in other countries, you may want to register the same name using those countries' TLDs too, such as dodgygoods.de for Germany, or dodgygoods.se for Sweden, though the rules on foreign ownership of national domains vary from one country to another.

Once you've got your domain name, just contact your hosting company and ask them to transfer it to your web space. You may need to provide some information about the registration company you used, and this will vary according to your choice of TLD and how the various companies choose to operate, but it won't be too complicated.

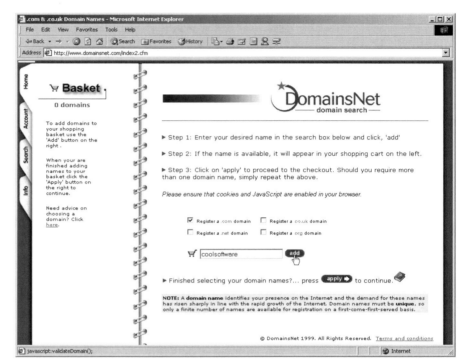

▶ At DomainsNet, just type a name, pick a TLD, and click Add to add it to the shopping basket. If it's not available, a message will tell you.

Option 2: Use Web & Email Forwarding

This option is almost identical to the first, in that you register and pay for a domain name. The difference is that you don't transfer it to your web host, you use the registration company's **forwarding** service. Most registration companies offer this service, and few charge for it.

The way this works is that after registering the name, you fill in a form that gives your current, horrible web URL and your preferred email address. You tell everyone your snappy new URL (www.dodgygoods.com) and email address (me@dodgygoods.com), and the registration company's servers automatically *forward* visitors to your website and redirect email messages to the email address you gave.

The benefits of using web forwarding services are twofold. First, it's quick and easy, and it saves you money if your host charges for domain transfers. Second, if you decide to switch to a different hosting company later on, you can simply visit the registration company's site and change the forwarding details.

Option 3: Get A Free Redirect URL

Finally a cheap'n'cheerful option that works in a similar way to web forwarding. If you visit **http://www.v3.com**, you can choose a URL along the lines of come.to/dodgygoods or surf.to/dodgygoods, and enter the real URL of your website. Although this fails the 'first impressions' test before it's even started, it's free, and it is at least short and snappy!

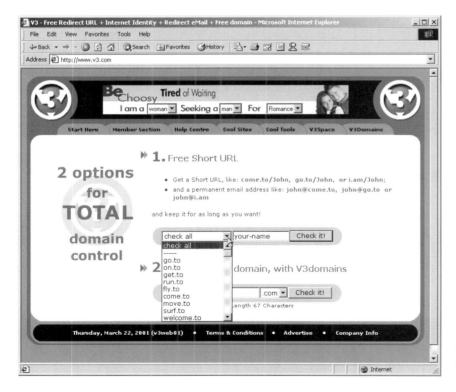

◀ Surf to V3 and choose a free short URL like surf.to/mysite.

Tools Of The Trade

Before you publish your site, load its index page into your browser and check every page one by one. Test all your internal links (links to other pages from your own site) by clicking them, and make sure all your images and other content are displayed. Test the site in every browser you can get your hands on, particularly the current versions of Internet Explorer, Opera and Netscape. Internet Explorer is far more forgiving of errors in HTML code than other browsers, so if you used IE as your main browser during the design stages this is an especially important step.

Every file used by your site should be in your 'Site' directory or one of its subdirectories, so if the site works for this offline test, it should still work when you upload the contents of the 'Site' directory to the server. You probably used a spellchecker on each page as you finished it, but if you didn't you should do that now.

Testing a site is a vital step, not only when you first upload a site, but whenever you add or alter pages – you can make a whole page of content disappear just by missing out a closing script, style or comment tag, forgetting a closing quote, or deleting a > symbol! Fortunately there's any number of useful tools and services available that will help you spot flaws in your pages and fix them. Here are a few of the best, but it's well worth taking a look around Tucows (**http://tucows.mirror.ac.uk**) to find hundreds more.

▶ **CSE HTML Validator** from **http://www.htmlvalidator.com** checks web pages for errors in the HTML code and potential problems in certain browsers.

▶ **LinkGuard Classic** at **http://www.linkguard.com** is the free version of a commercial service that will check your online site for broken links.

▶ **CyberSpyder Link Test** from **http://www.cyberspyder.com** is a program (rather than an online service) that tests links and includes other handy monitoring tools.

▶ **HTML Search & Replace** from **http://www.serpik.com** makes it easy to find and replace text in a batch of web pages all in one go.

▶ **Web Site Garage** at **http://websitegarage.netscape.com**
offers several free 'tune up' and site analysis tools.

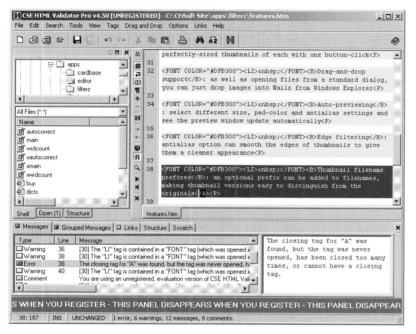

◀ Run your pages
through HTML
Validator to find
and fix mistakes in
the code.

Uploading Your Site

When you're ready to put your site on the Web, you'll use a system called
FTP (File Transfer Protocol). FTP is one of the two major systems used to
transfer files around the Internet, along with HTTP. The HTTP system is
used for the Web, but it can only be used for *downloading* files (sending web
pages to your browser, for instance, which is why web URLs begin http://).
FTP can be used to download files, but it can also *upload* them – send them
to a remote server – which is what you need to do.

This is one of the few tricks your browser can't easily do, so you need to get
your hands on an FTP program. Here are a few of the best:

▶ **FTP Explorer** from **http://www.ftpx.com**

▶ **CuteFTP** from **http://www.cuteftp.com**

▶ **WS_FTP Professional** from **http://www.ipswitch.com**

I'm going to assume you're using FTP Explorer, but most FTP programs look and work in much the same way. When you install FTP Explorer, it will offer to create a set of *Profiles* for you. These are links to FTP sites you can visit, a lot like browsers' Favorites and Bookmarks lists, so it's worth saying yes to this offer. You'll be prompted to enter your email address the first time you use the program, but you shouldn't need to change anything else.

Creating A Profile

When you signed up for web space, the hosting company should have given you all the details you need to log into it – a username, a password and an FTP host address. The first job is to create a 'profile' for the site so that you can log in with a couple of clicks anytime you want to make changes, so follow these steps:

1   Start FTP Explorer and, if you don't see the Connect dialog shown in the next screenshot, choose **Connect** from the Tools menu. Click the **Add** button to create a new blank profile.

2   In the **Profile Name** box, type any friendly name that you'll recognize as being your own site.

3   Type the FTP host address you were given into the **Host Address** box. If the address includes a path (forward slashes and directory names) only use the host name itself – the part before the first forward slash.

4   As this isn't a public FTP site that you log into anonymously, remove the checkmark from the **Anonymous** box then type your username and password in the **Login** and **Password** boxes.

5   If you had to leave out path details from the address in step 3, type that path into the **Initial Path** box, starting with the first forward slash. This is the directory that FTP Explorer should open when it connects to the host.

6   Click the **Save** button, and you'll see the new profile appear in the list to the left.

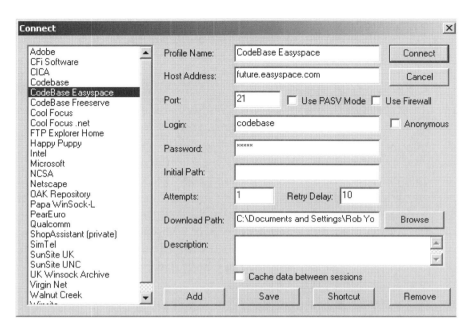

◀ Creating a new profile for your web space in FTP Explorer.

JARGON BUSTER

anonymous FTP

An FTP site is a collection of directories and files on a server, and an FTP program displays these in the same way your own computer displays the contents of your hard disk. Some of these sites are **private**, and can only be accessed by someone with the correct username and password (your own web space is an example of a private site – you wouldn't want anyone else editing or deleting your files!). Others are public (such as the sample profiles created by FTP Explorer) and you can log into these anonymously by entering your email address as the password and the word 'anonymous' as the username.

You're Ready To Upload!

With your FTP profile created (or the equivalent in your chosen FTP program), you're ready to publish your site to the Web. Select this profile in the Connect dialog's list and click the **Connect** button. In a few seconds you should be logged into your web space and you'll see a two-pane view that should be familiar to Windows users: directories are shown in the left pane, with the contents of the current directory shown on the right. At the moment, of course, you won't see much there at all!

Find the 'Site' directory on your hard disk containing all the files belonging to your website and open it so that you can see the files and directories it contains. Select its entire contents and drag-and-drop them into FTP Explorer's window. This is the simplest way to upload – it saves you having to remember which files you've uploaded and which you haven't. FTP Explorer will copy all the files to your web space one by one, creating new directories as needed, and you can just sit back and watch. (Some FTP programs don't allow drag-and-drop, or won't let you drop directories, so you might have to click a button to create a directory with the same name as one in your 'Site' directory, and then upload the files it contains.)

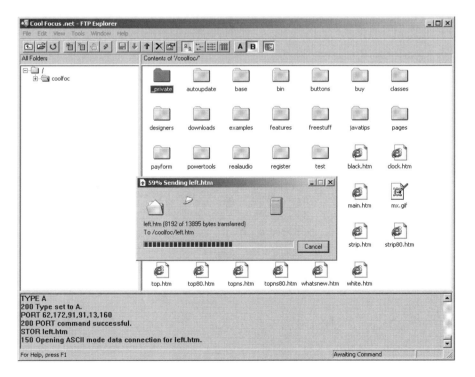

▶ Drop your site's files and directories into FTP Explorer, then make coffee while it all happens for you!

If you need to create a new folder manually in FTP Explorer, just right-click on a blank area in the main window, choose **New** and **Folder**, and type a name. You can then just double-click this new folder to open it and start copying files into it.

GOOD QUESTION!

Which transfer mode should I use?

Most FTP programs give you a choice between two transfer modes, **ASCII** and **Binary** (FTP Explorer has buttons labelled A and B on its toolbar for this). ASCII mode can only be used to transfer plain text files, and will do so a tiny bit faster than Binary mode, which has to be used for any other type of file (zip files, images, programs, Java applets and so on). Since text files tend to be small anyway, the time saved by using ASCII mode is negligible, and you'd probably spend more time choosing and switching modes than you could ever save! It's simplest to stick with Binary mode for everything.

And Now...Test!

This is the big one! Fire up your browser, type the URL of your website into its address bar and press Enter, and you should see its index page. If you don't, take a look at the troubleshooting tips later in this chapter. If you do, congratulations!

Now you need to calm down, get a grip, and do a thorough test of every page, every link and every item of content. It's not unusual to find that odd things have 'broken' in the transfer from hard disk to web, and you may need to do some fixing. Along with testing all your internal links (and 'hidden' links such as external style sheets and script files), you can now check links to other sites. At long last you'll be able to judge the speed of your site too.

Shooting Your Troubles

If everything goes right first time, your site will work just as well online as it worked on your hard disk. Just in case you hit a snag, though, here are a few troubleshooting tips to help you sort it out. If you need to make changes to a page, remember to change the copy on your hard disk. You can then upload that to the same online directory to replace the original version. Similarly, if you rename an online file using your FTP program, rename the copy on your hard disk too – keeping both copies of the site identical will help your future maintenance no end!

'I can't see my site!' First, make sure you've typed your URL correctly and you really are online. Next, check that the HTML file that should form the front page of your site can be found – try including it in the URL like this: http://www.mysite.com/index.htm. If the page loads, that means that your web server uses a different default filename, such as default.htm, which your hosting company can tell you. If so, rename the file on your hard disk and use your FTP program to rename the online copy.

'My links don't work!' Make sure none of the files you're linking to has a space in its name. If you find a space, rename the local and online copies of the files to remove the space, and edit any pages linking to it. Next, check that you haven't used any uppercase letters in links that don't appear in the filenames (or vice versa). On the majority of web servers, filenames are case sensitive. Finally, of course, make sure you really have uploaded the files you're linking to, and that they're in the same relative location online as they are on your hard disk.

'Everything takes ages to download!' That may be a problem of page weight: using the hard disk copy of your site, look at the size of the HTML file and any images, applets, scripts and other content that it links to, and add up the sizes. If the page loads a frameset, remember that it's actually loading two or more pages and all their content. Try experimenting with the images to see if you can reduce their size, or cut down the amount of content by splitting a large single page into two smaller linked pages. Of course, the problem may be that your host's server is slow (either temporarily or chronically), a common problem with free hosting especially.

'Part of the page has disappeared!' This is more likely to be something you spotted during the offline testing, but it usually has an easy answer: a closing tag has gone missing! Check the offending page for <SCRIPT>, <STYLE>, <APPLET> and other content-related tags and make sure that each has a matching closing tag (such as </SCRIPT>). If the page uses tables, make sure you have a closing </TABLE> tag and that every <TD> and <TR> tag is closed before the next cell or row begins.

'The links open in a new window instead of a frame!' This is something else that you'd pick up in local testing. It means that the TARGET attribute of the <A> or <BASE> tag is set to a frame name that doesn't exist. Compare the name in that attribute with the names in the <FRAME> tags of your frame setting page: you've probably spelt the name wrongly in one or the other, or used an uppercase letter that should be lowercase.

'My CGI scripts don't work!' You need a cgi-bin directory among your other online folders, and this isn't just an ordinary directory *named* 'cgi-bin'. If your host has provided this, upload the scripts or programs to that directory. If the host server is running Windows, that should be enough, so talk to your hosting company if you still have problems – it may be that the cgi-bin hasn't been properly set up, or that the server doesn't have Perl script support installed. If the server runs UNIX (as the majority do), you'll need to use your FTP program to change the attributes of the script file after it's been uploaded. This means setting the file to behave as 'executable', using the command CHMOD 755 to set its attributes to 'rw-rw-rw-'.

'My Java applet doesn't load!' The probable reason is that the browser can't find the applet's .class file. Make sure the CODE attribute of the <APPLET> tag contains only the *name* of the primary .class file; if the files aren't in the same directory as the web page, the CODEBASE attribute should give the absolute or relative location of their directory (without a filename on the end). Check the browser's Java Console (see Chapter 22) for clues to the problem if all the files seem to be in the right places.

HIT HUNTING: PROMOTING YOUR SITE

▶ **IN THIS CHAPTER**

Get listed with the major (and not so major) search engines

Swap links with sites that complement your own

Use free banner exchanges or buy advertising space

Start a mailing list or use newsgroups to publicize your site

Counters & statistics – how to chart your site's popularity

There are millions upon millions of websites out there you've never heard of, and behind most of them there's someone just like you wondering how to get more hits. You'd probably visit some of those sites – perhaps you'd even go back regularly – but you'll *never* hear about them. In the same way, your own website is a tiny drop in the Web's ocean, and unless it's remarkable enough to build a respectable number of hits by word of mouth, you'll need to actively promote it.

There are lots of ways to promote a website; some are easy, quick and cheap; others are complicated, long term and expensive; some are vital; some are optional; and some won't be suitable for your particular site. In this chapter we'll look at the main promotional tools you can use, and how to get the best out of them.

No Excuses!

Here's a simple rule before we start: *If it's not ready, don't promote it!* No-one will be impressed by a site that promises lots of features it doesn't deliver, so you could easily find yourself attracting visitors who'll never bother coming back. Wait until you're completely happy with the look, feel and content of the site, get family and friends to give you a no-holds-barred appraisal, and *then* turn your attentions to promotion.

On a similar subject, don't fall into the trap of adding excuses to your site, such as 'This site is under construction'. A good website is always under construction as it evolves and adapts. If you need to change a page, check it carefully offline and only upload the new version when it's ready and working. If you add a new section to the site, upload it to a new directory and test it yourself before linking it to your existing pages.

Know Your Competition

Whatever your site offers, it undoubtedly has competition. Before you start promoting it, spend some time getting to know your competitors' sites and comparing them to your own. Ideally you want to find your own niche – some aspect of your site that's bigger, better or unique to you. If your site sells a product or service, you'll want to compare the products as well for the same reason. Maybe your site targets a different type of user? Perhaps you give better value, or include free products and services that others charge for? Or maybe you have a unique approach to the topic of the site?

BY THE WAY

Well, it's just a lot nicer...

Remember that whatever you decide to use as a hook to catch prospective visitors must be fact rather than opinion. If your site really **is** cooler or easier to navigate than the competition, for instance, that makes for a good visitor experience, but no-one's going to believe it just because your promotion says it's so. Tell them you offer free delivery, or a question-and-answer forum, and it's a whole different ballgame.

This is the essence of the 'big idea' we talked about in Chapter 2, and hopefully you already know exactly why someone would visit you rather than your competition. You probably designed the site with this in mind, making sure that the big idea is fairly apparent. Whether you did or not, you'll need to be flexible from here on in, as you begin to learn which parts of your site work best, which don't work at all, and what visitors would like to see added and changed.

Getting Listed With Search Engines

Search engines are an important part of website promotion: if someone's looking for a site like yours, a search engine like Yahoo!, Google or AltaVista is one of the first places they'll go. If you can get a good **ranking** with the major search engines, you should certainly see some hits as a result. The 'ranking' is the position in which your site appears when someone searches for sites like your own, and you should obviously aim to appear on the first page of results.

This is very much a black art – there are specialist companies that will happily charge you large amounts of money to establish and maintain a high search engine ranking for you – but it's well worth having a crack at it yourself.

There are thousands of search engines on the web, although only a dozen or so that really qualify as 'major'; many of the others are speciality engines covering, for example, medical sites or entertainment sites. Along with the most popular search engines, try to find suitable speciality engines (perhaps by searching for **search engine +***keyword*, replacing *keyword* with the topic of your site). Although you can probably find hundreds of engines, it pays to remember that the vast majority of search-engine-introduced hits come from the five big players: Yahoo!, Google, Excite, AltaVista and Lycos.

GOOD QUESTION!

How important is a high search engine ranking?

If your site doesn't appear in the first two or three pages of search results, it probably won't do you much good. But search engines don't have quite the clout you'd expect: the majority of surfers discover a website by word of mouth, and the second biggest draw is a link on a different website. Search engines are only third in the chart of site introductions.

Search engines can essentially be split into two groups (although there's some overlap between them) – those that take direct submissions from Webmasters, and those that don't. For the first group, you can simply visit the search site and submit the details of your site. The second group builds its indexes of websites using a 'robot', a software program that constantly trawls the Web, reading pages, extracting details, and following links. To include search engines in your promotion strategy, you need to take care of both groups of engines.

Choosing Your Keywords

The first job is to think about what keywords people are likely to type into a search engine, and in what combination. New web users will often type just one word, or perhaps two, whereas a skilled surfer will construct a precise search query involving several key words and short phrases to find only very specific types of site. You want to think of as many of those possible words and phrases as you can, and sort them into order of their likely use. If you're not sure which keywords are good candidates, visit

http://inventory.goto.com/inventory/Search_Suggestion.jhtml, a handy site that can tell you how many searches were carried out for a particular term at the GoTo search engine, and help you refine your list of words.

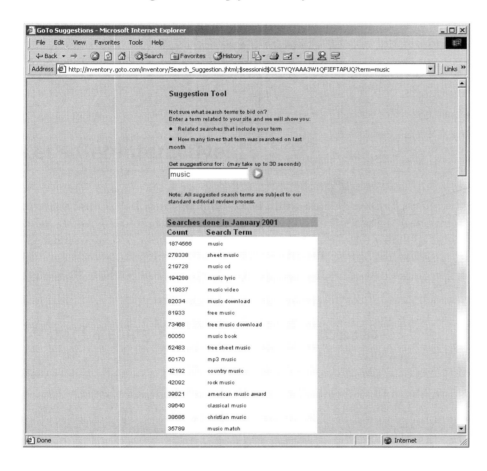

◀ The GoTo Suggestion Tool can help you choose and evaluate likely keywords.

Once you've put together a list of a couple of dozen keywords, you can test them out by visiting any search engine and see how many matches a search yields for each in turn. If you get a large number of matches for a particular word, you can remove that word from your list – you're unlikely to get a place in the first couple of pages of a 100-page list! At the end of this process, you should have a shorter list of words that combine relevance and accuracy with a good chance of a high ranking.

Cheating the system

We all know that certain keywords appear a lot in web searches: 'sex' is one, 'mp3' is another. It stands to reason that if you use the most popular keywords to describe your site you'll get a lot of hits, doesn't it? Actually it doesn't. Search engines are smart enough to spot keywords that have nothing to do with the content of the site. In some cases they'll ignore those words, but in the majority they'll just ignore your whole site! Your ranking will also suffer if you endlessly repeat the same keyword (relevant or not) or try to 'hide' keywords in a text colour that matches the background. Play it straight, and you should at least get some kind of ranking.

Working With Robots

Different search engines' robots work in different ways, but there are certain things that they all have in common. First, they'll read the titles of your pages, the text between the <TITLE> and </TITLE> tags. Second, they'll read your meta tags (which I'll explain in a moment). Third, they'll examine the content of the page itself, including heading tags, ALT attributes in images, the clickable text in hyperlinks, and the first few lines of 'ordinary' text. Each of these areas of your pages should be as distinctive, descriptive and tempting as possible since they could all affect your position in the rankings of search engines, and they should make use of at least one of your tried and tested keywords if you can slot them in without making the text difficult to read.

Adjusting the titles of your pages is easy, of course, and keywords tend to have greater impact on your ranking when used in the title than anywhere else, so make the most of the opportunity. Don't resort to lists of keywords in titles, though – a title should still be readable, and should act as a brief description of a page's content. Follow the same approach with headings (<H1>...</H1> tags, etc.) and the other page elements mentioned above, still balancing readability with the inclusion of one or more keywords.

Keep it legal!

BY THE WAY

It's worth looking at your competitors' meta tags for ideas, but **never** copy meta tags lock, stock and barrel from another site – it's illegal, and several court cases have established that beyond doubt. For the same reason, you can't get away with using your competitors' trademarks in your meta tags.

The final step is to create your **meta tags**. These are a pair of tags placed in the head of the page, and they list your keywords and a description of your site. The description should also include several of your most important keywords. The two tags could look something like this:

```
<META NAME="keywords" CONTENT="keyword1, keyword2, keyword3,
keyword4">
<META NAME="description" CONTENT="A description of my page, including a
few keywords, that could be shown in the search results">
```

Keywords and short phrases should all be entered in lowercase, separated by commas, and each keyword should only appear once, organized into order of importance. If you have a particular product or trading name that's likely to be searched for with an initial capital, you can include it a second time to give it the capital letter it deserves. As a rough guide, stick to about 10–20 keywords and keep the length of the description below about 100 words.

Submitting To Search Engines

After you've made your pages more search engine friendly following the steps above, it's time to submit your site to the search engines. This can be a long, slow process, but it's a worthwhile one, so stick with it! Visit every search site you can think of (you'll find a few dozen listed in Appendix F), and look for a button or link labelled something like **Submit A Site**, usually a small link at the foot of the page.

In some cases (such as Excite, HotBot and AltaVista) you'll just enter your site's URL, and the robot will visit your site to extract the information it needs from your pages. At other sites (such as Yahoo! and Starting Point) you'll fill in a form giving all your site details including keywords and description.

GOOD QUESTION!

Why does it cost money to submit my site?

When you click the Submit A Site link at some of the major search engines these days, you'll get the impression that it's going to cost you money. In a few cases there's no other choice, but at most sites a bit of perseverance will lead to a link for free submission. The pay-for option is usually a 'fast-track' service that will have your site listed within a couple of days (if it's accepted).

Make sure you read the instructions carefully at each site – different search engines have their own rules for submission, and a simple mistake could get your submission ignored! One of the most desirable search sites to be listed on, Yahoo!, is also the trickiest, as the index is hand built by humans who personally visit your site and judge its suitability. If you pick an unsuitable category for your site, or dress up your keywords and description to suggest your site is something it isn't, the submission will fail. If you submit the same site several times using different keywords, descriptions or domain names, you're likely to be blacklisted. In fact, only about one in five submissions to Yahoo! is actually accepted, so make sure you read the submission rules and tips to maximize your chances!

Automatic Site Submission

If you don't have the time or patience to visit dozens of different search sites, read their rules and fill in their forms, there are services available that can do the legwork for you. You just fill in a single form, then follow a step-by-step process to submit to a bundle of sites. Along the way you'll be prompted for extra information needed by a particular site (such as picking a subject category) without repeatedly entering the same information. Here are three free services to start you off:

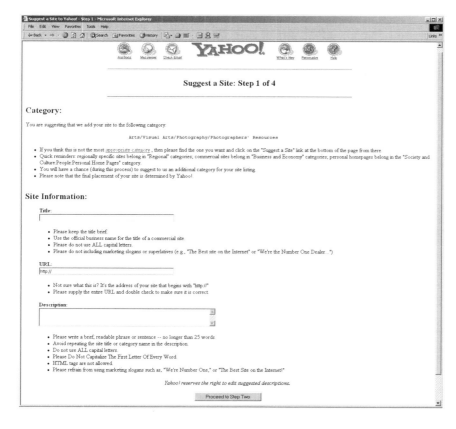

◀ Submitting your site to Yahoo! – an important step that takes care and attention.

▶ **AddMe** at **http://www.addme.com** submits your site to 25 search engines.

▶ **CNET Search.com** at **http://www.search.com** submits to up to 15 engines.

▶ **Submit Express** at **http://www.submitexpress.com** will submit to 40 search sites.

Before you plump for one of these services, it's worth knowing that some search engines always give a lower ranking to sites that were 'auto-submitted', preferring webmasters to submit by actually clicking their own Submit link. It's worth submitting to the half-dozen or so major search engines by hand, and using auto-submission services just for the lesser known engines.

▶CNET
Search.com can
submit your site
to 15 search
engines quickly
and painlessly.

These are *just* submission services, of course – they won't help you improve
your rankings, resubmit regularly to help you keep your position, or
optimize your pages and meta tags. These extras qualify as valuable
marketing tools, so they're something you'll have to pay for if you want
them. If you're willing to cross palms with silver to improve your site's
chances, try one of these:

▶ **Submit It!** at **http://www.submit-it.com**, an online service
that submits to over 400 search engines.

▶ **WebPosition Gold**, shareware software from
http://www.webposition com.

▶ **SignPoster**, shareware software from
http://www.signposter.com.

Be Friendly: Link Exchanges

Here's a nice easy way to gain a few hits. Contact the webmasters of sites covering similar or complementary subjects to your own and ask if they'd like to exchange links – you add links to their sites in return for links to yours. You might arrange to do this on a general 'Useful Links' page, or agree to trade banner ads or buttons in particular positions on your sites. Striking up a relationship with sites similar to your own could pay dividends in all sorts of unexpected ways in the future.

Using Banner Advertising

We've all got used to seeing banner ads on web pages, and quite a lot of experienced web users move from page to page without even noticing they're there, but they're still one of the most effective promotion tools available on the Internet. Some of the major Internet-based companies such as MSN and Amazon spend millions each year on online advertising.

Unless your website has something to sell, you're probably not enthusiastic about spending millions (or even hundreds), but you don't need to. A handy free service called Banner Exchange operates in a similar way to the link exchange suggestion above: in return for displaying other members' advertising banners on your own site, your ads will be displayed on theirs. The more pages you're willing to include a banner on, the more your own banners will be shown. If you fancy using this method, visit one of the sites below, fill in the online forms, add the HTML code generated by the service to your pages, and then upload your own banners.

▶ **Banner Exchange** at **http://bannerexchange.mycomputer.com**.

▶ **UK Banners** at **http://www.ukbanners.com**.

▶ **Link Exchange** at **http://store.bcentral.com/le/index.html**.

So how do you actually design a banner ad? To begin with, you need to get the dimensions right: the standard dimensions for banner ads are 486 × 60 pixels, which is the only size accepted by Banner Exchange. If you plan to

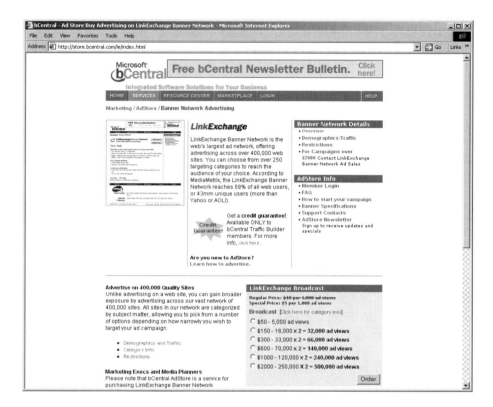

▶ Visit Microsoft bCentral to trade advertising space with other members.

advertise elsewhere, there are other sizes in popular use which could achieve better results by being a bit unusual – you can find more information about them at the Internet Advertising Bureau **(http://www.iab.net)**. Most sites that accept advertising will insist on a maximum file size of about 15 Kb and will want the banners to be in JPEG or GIF format. You can usually use GIF animation, and this gives you a far better chance of catching the visitor's eye than a static image. Don't use transparency, or parts of your banner will change colour at every site they appear on!

Beyond these basics, most sites and agencies have their own rules for banner design (some will allow the use of 'rich media' banners created using Flash, for example) so read the rules carefully before firing up your graphics program.

The catch with Banner Exchange and similar services is that you're not getting *targeted* advertising – your banners will appear on sites covering

Don't forget the 'call to action'!

The most successful banner ads tend to be those that include the words 'Click Here' somewhere clearly visible. This is known as the **call to action** – telling a potential visitor that your ad can be clicked often makes a big difference to the ad's click-through rate.

every subject under the sun, and visitors to those sites may not be remotely interested in what you have to offer. Targeting your ads to the right audience will usually cost money (unless you can arrange to do a bit of mutual banner swapping with some suitable sites). To find out *how much* money, visit the sites you think your target audience is visiting and look for information about how to advertise, or visit Ad Store at **http://store.bcentral.com** for a useful overview. This is a good time to introduce a couple of pieces of banner-ad jargon:

▶ **Page impressions.** Most sites that sell advertising space will base the cost on the number of 'page impressions' – the number of times your banner is actually shown. Each page impression costs you money, whether the ad is clicked or not.

▶ **Click-throughs.** A 'click-through' is a single click on your banner. If the price you pay is based on click-throughs (which isn't an offer you'll find very often) you pay only when someone actually clicks the ad.

Most sites will sell you a block of page impressions at a particular price, and it's up to you to make your banner as enticing as you can to maximize the chances of a click-through. As you look around, be ready for a vast difference in pricing policies. As you'd expect, sites that get a large number of hits can be expensive (£15 to £40 per thousand impressions, and more still if you want your ad to appear in a particular part of the site). Since the holy grail of advertising is getting your product under the noses of the people who'll be most interested in it, sites that attract an audience with specific interests will often charge a lot: here it's the *quality* of the page impressions rather than the quantity that's valuable, and you should expect to get a larger ratio of click-throughs to page impressions.

Watch, learn and react!

Most sites that buy advertising space talk about **advertising campaigns**, and treat the campaign as an ongoing occupation. Keep an eye on which sites are giving you the most click-throughs, and which of your banners is the most successful. Experiment with small alterations, different sized banners and so on, to find a combination that produces the best results.

Announce It!

Since word of mouth plays an important part in attracting new visitors to a site, an important part of your promotion is to make your site a regular port of call for your existing users. I've already mentioned the value of having a *What's New?* page listing the latest additions and changes to the site along with dates and links, but there are other methods you can use to actively *announce* the changes:

▶ **Start a mailing list.** Invite visitors to join a mailing list by sending you their name and email address. You can manage this from your own email program and address book, or buy dedicated list management software (take a look at **http://tucows.mirror.ac.uk/mail95.html** for a selection). If you use your email program to send these messages, always address the message to yourself and put the list of recipients in the BCC (Blind Carbon Copy) field. This keeps the size of the message to a minimum by not including every subscriber's details in the message itself, and protects their privacy.

▶ **Announce to newsgroups.** If you can track down newsgroups related to your site's subject, you could send a short message announcing the new additions to your site. Your newsreader program should help you find groups whose names contain a particular keyword, or you can search at **http://www.deja.com**. Tempting as it is to send to every group you can find, make sure you stick to the very few that really should be interested in what you're offering.

◄ Newsreader programs like Outlook Express let you filter the list of newsgroups with keywords to find related groups.

▶ **Issue press releases.** If there are magazines and journals covering the same topic as your site, why not issue press releases when you make a major change or addition to the site? If the release is published, this gives you widespread advertising on paper or online for nothing! Visit **http://www.ereleases.com** for a release writing service (which you'll have to pay for) and some useful tips (which you won't).

BY THE WAY

Do's and don'ts of mailing lists

If you decide to operate a mailing list, your site should include an easy to find privacy policy explaining how you'll use the information provided – whether you'll sell the list or give anyone else access to it, for example. You may also have to register under the UK's Data Protection Act (**http://www.hmso.gov.uk/acts/acts1998/19980029.htm**) – see Chapter 25. It's wise to tell potential subscribers roughly how often you're planning to email them too – many users will be happy to sign up for a weekly or monthly message, but may not want a daily one.

Getting Sticky: Adding Extra Value

Making your website *sticky* is a great way to improve your word of mouth score. It sounds messy, but a 'sticky' site is one that users can't tear themselves away from, and one that they'll want to keep returning to. In an ideal world, your content itself will have all the stickiness that's needed as long as you update it regularly, but your site may cover a subject that rarely or never changes, denying you the chance to get sticky that way. Luckily there are all sorts of value-added features and services you can include to increase your stickiness quotient. Here's a tiny collection of suggestions:

▶ Spice up your site with games written in Java, Flash or Dynamic HTML. A quick trawl with a search engine should lead to dozens of free online games.

▶ Add a discussion area or chat room where visitors can leave messages, ask questions and read responses. Once again, a search engine will lead to dozens of freely available discussion boards and chat rooms, but try visiting **http://www.freeforums.com**, **http://www.ezboard.com** and **http://www.quickchat.org** for some of the best.

▶ Add a regularly changed *poll* – a question with several choices of answer – allowing users to state their preference or opinion and (hopefully) come back to see the final result. You'll find a free poll among the mass of other content at MyComputer **(http://www.mycomputer.com)** and another at **http://www.pollit.com**.

▶ Include reference and conversion tools such as currency converters, dictionaries (particularly those that specialize in your site's own topic) and thesauruses. You can also find 'ticker' utilities that display constantly updating news headlines, weather, travel information, entertainment gossip, TV highlights and so on.

▶ Look for search engines that specialize in the same subject as your site, and find out whether you can include the engine on your own pages. You'll find a huge list of specialized search engines at **http://www.searchability.com**.

If you're stuck for ideas, visit ZapZone at **http://www.zzn.com** to find a vast range of free content and services you can add to your site. If you don't have access to a cgi-bin, check carefully whether you have to host the scripts and applications on your own site and discount any that say you do. A visit to the CGI Resource Index's Remotely Hosted list (**http://cgi.resourceindex.com/Remotely_Hosted**) can point you towards scripts hosted on other servers.

Remember that one of the surest ways to attract visitors is to give something of value for free, and the way to keep them coming back is to regularly change *what* you're giving away!

So... Has It Worked?

With your promotion under way you obviously need some way of knowing how many people are actually visiting your site – at the very least you need a hit counter. But why settle for a simple tally of the number of visitors to a particular page when you can get a complete statistical analysis? As you've probably come to expect, this is something you can get your hands on for free.

BY THE WAY

Ask your hosting company about statistics and logs

If you're paying for web hosting, the hosting company may offer its own counters and stats services as part of the deal. These will be more reliable than an outside service as a result of running from the same server as your site. Your web host should also be able to give you access to your site logs which could also be very informative. Log files tend to be tough to understand, though, so take a look at **http://tucows.mirror.ac.uk/log95.html** for a wide choice of utilities that can help you get to grips with them.

Two of the best site stats services are at **http://www.webstat.com** and **http://www.thecounter.com**. At either of these, sign up for a free account, entering your site's URL and your email address, and you'll receive a small chunk of HTML code in return. Place this code at the bottom of your site's index page, and every visitor's details will be logged by the service. At any time you can log into your account and check how many hits you're getting, where they're coming from, which browsers they're using, and lots more. Even if it's not all actually *useful*, you'll find it fascinating.

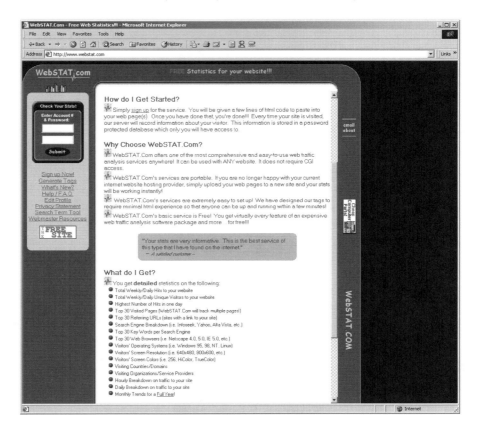

▶ WebSTAT.com can tell you everything you want to know about who's visiting your site, when, and how.

TINY ACORNS, MIGHTY OAKS

▶ **IN THIS CHAPTER**

Encourage feedback with guestbooks and email links

Create a password-protected members-only zone

How to keep the customer satisfied (and amazed!)

E-commerce: sell your products and services online

Website law: copyright, trademarks, links and privacy

A good website should be constantly evolving and adapting as you learn more about your audience or think of new ways to improve and expand. There are thousands of websites out there (my own included) that started life as an enjoyable hobby and grew into a successful business venture. It can happen in lots of ways: the obvious one is that you offer a product or service and realize that people are willing to pay for it (or an enhanced version of it), but equally you might find that your informational or entertainment site becomes successful enough to attract paid advertising or sponsorship. Who knows – two years down the line you may even be able to sell the site and retire on the proceeds!

From tiny acorns, as they say, mighty oaks grow. In this final chapter, we'll look at some of the extras you can add to your site, and the issues and options you may want to explore as your site evolves. Along the way, I'll point out a few tips on running your site with a businesslike approach to help you keep your own oak tree a bit leafier than that of your competition!

What Do *You* Think?

As a webmaster, your number one resource is your audience – if they like what you've got, you're onto a winner, if they don't, you lose. So an important part of running a website is to encourage visitors to give you feedback. You want to know what they liked or found useful, of course, but crucially you want to know about any *negative* opinions: What didn't they like? Which areas should be expanded? Did they have trouble navigating or finding particular sections? How do they rate your site against your competitors? What's missing from the site?

There are two good ways to encourage feedback. The first is to make sure you've made email links easily accessible (see Chapter 4), either by placing them on every page or by adding a Contact Us link to your site's main navigation. Along with the links, add a few lines to make it clear that you really do encourage feedback and you're not just fishing for compliments!

The second method is to add a **guestbook** to the site. Visitors can visit the guestbook page to read the comments left by others and add their own, and

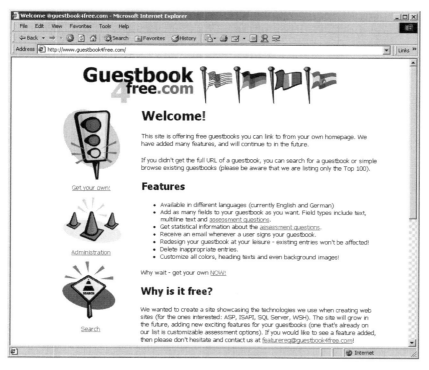

◀ Sign up for a free, flexible guestbook at guestbook4free. com.

this option has a few benefits over relying on email feedback alone. To begin with, visitors are likely to be interested in reading what other people are saying, which could spur them into leaving their own comment. They're also more likely to do this than to write an email message. In addition, the fact that you're willing to have a few negative comments shown on your site indicates a measure of confidence and commitment (particularly if you add your own replies and notes of action taken).

As with so much in web life, guestbooks are something you can find for free. Two services worth a look are Guestbook4free.com at **http://www.guestbook4free.com** and TheGuestbook at **http://www.theguestbook.com**, but a search for 'guestbook +free' at any search engine should turn up a mass of links to others.

BY THE WAY

Beware of offsite content!

There are any number of guestbooks, counters, chat rooms and discussion boards you can add to your site for free. These are all CGI applications, but because the CGI programs themselves are running on the service's own servers, you don't need a cgi-bin directory of your own. The trouble is, some of these services can be abysmally slow, you have no control over how they work (or whether they work at all), and you may not be able to customize them to suit your site's own style. If you pay for web hosting, make the most of your cgi-bin by downloading CGI applications from sites like **http://www.webresource.net/cgi/scripts** and installing them on your own server instead of using offsite services.

Creating A Members-Only Area

If your site deals in information or in 'downloadable' products such as graphics, you may decide to split your site into two distinct sections: a general use area offering previews, free samples and teasers, and a members-only section accessible only to visitors with a valid username and password.

There are two ways to do this, and as usual you'll get the best result if you're paying for web hosting. The simple way is to download a JavaScript from the Security section at Cut-N-Paste JavaScript **(http://www.infohiway.com/javascript)**. Although scripts like this are claimed to be crack-proof, they don't actually provide much security. As soon as a visitor has successfully reached the 'protected' page once, he can bookmark it or link to it from his own site: the page that prompts for a password before allowing entry can be neatly sidestepped.

For *real* security, this section of your site has to be protected at the server. You can do this using a CGI script such as Account Manager Lite from **http://www.webresource.net/cgi/scripts/security**, but a better way is to ask your hosting company to set up a password-protected directory for you. Most will do this without charge, and it really is secure: it doesn't matter who knows the URLs of the protected pages, no-one can get in without entering the correct password.

Customer Service? It's Easy!

There's no such thing as an 'Internet business' – a business is a business the world over, and if yours does the majority of its trading via its website, that's just a marketing detail. It does have an impact, though. As well as knowing how to run a business, you also need to know what net users expect when they deal with a business *online*. The answer, increasingly, is: not much.

So the fact that your business is largely based on the Internet can give you a massive advantage over your rivals, if you choose to make the most of it. Many large companies have tried to exploit the Internet revolution by opening an online storefront, but without making an effort to understand the Internet, its users and their expectations. In recent years, millions of brand new businesses have started up on the Web, long on ideas and funding, but short on business sense.

The key to building a business is to aim to keep every customer satisfied, and with all the technology at your disposal that's easy to do. When you receive an email request for information or support, just reply to it the same day! If a customer leaves a telephone message, pick up the phone and call them back. If you make a mistake, or have to break a promise made to a customer, apologize immediately and try to offer something extra to compensate.

BY THE WAY

You can be huge!

On the Web, no-one can tell how small you are! You have the same presence and opportunities as your largest rival, and your site can give the impression that your business is larger than it really is (without actually lying, of course). For example, just giving different email addresses for different 'departments' implies a certain size, even if you receive and read every message yourself!

The suggestions above may sound obvious, but if you actually follow them you'll be among a tiny percentage of online businesses that do, and that's your foot in the door. Although online consumers *should* expect a fast and efficient service, a prompt response usually comes as an unexpected surprise, and one that they'll remember.

Phone Me: Real Time Contact

If you agree that the tips above sound like a sensible approach to customer service, maybe you'd like to go a step further? If you're willing to spend a little money, you can add a 'Phone Me' link to your website, and if visitors have a query they can simply click the button and speak to you on the phone. You'll pay the call charges yourself, and of course you'll have to be sure there's someone available to actually take the calls! Here are a couple to sites to visit that offer this type of service:

▶ **PhoneMe** at **http://www.phoneme.co.uk**

▶ **NetCall800** at **http://www.netcall800.co.uk**

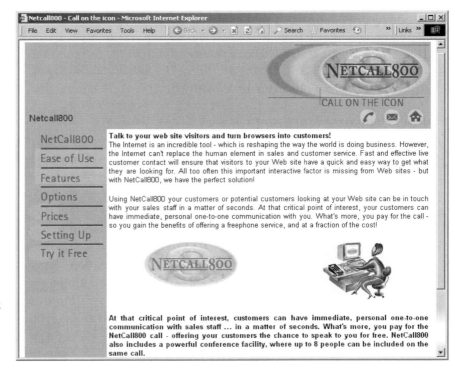

▶ With a NetCall800 link on your site, customers can talk to you instantly just by clicking a button.

If you like the approach but you're not as enthusiastic about the cost, there are other ways to offer real-time customer service. Instant messaging programs such as ICQ **(http://www.icq.com)** let you place an icon on your site that indicates whether or not you're online: using this type of system, users can click this link to 'talk' to you via text or voice over the Internet. If you add a CGI-based chat room to your site, you could make sure you're logged in and ready to answer questions at specified times every day.

Getting Equipped For E-Commerce

If you have a website and a product or service to sell, the logical next step is to convert your site from a shop window to a store, where visitors can select products, pay for them using a credit card, and either arrange delivery or download them immediately. That's **e-commerce**, one of the major buzzwords of the last couple of years: it'll mean that you're running an *e-business* and people will probably refer to you as an *SME* (Small to Medium-sized Enterprise). In fact, you'll be *e-tailing* – retailing by electronic means. Embarrassing, isn't it? Nevertheless, it's something that's becoming cheaper and easier to do, so don't let the silly names put you off.

To start selling from your website, you'll need to buy or arrange two or three things:

1 **Shopping cart/online catalogue software.** There are literally hundreds of systems available that can add a 'shopping cart' to your site that tracks the items a visitor wants to buy. Systems cover a broad spectrum from fairly cheap, easy to use packages to heavyweight, database-driven applications. Some require access to a cgi-bin while others use JavaScript or Java to remain self-contained in the browser. A few products to look at are Click and Build **(http://www.clickandbuild.com)**, Actinic Catalog **(http://www.actinic.com)** and Shop@ssistant **(http://www.shopassistant.net)**.

2 **A Payment Service Provider (PSP).** The PSP is the company that processes the credit card information entered by your buyer and handles the transaction for you. They'll take a few percent of each transaction and pass the rest onto you. Since the information is passed to the PSP by your shopping cart system, you'll need to check which PSPs your chosen

▶ An example
e-commerce
site using Click
and Build.

shopping cart supports. Popular PSPs include WorldPay
(http://www.worldpay.com), SecurePay **(http://www.securepay.com)** and
NetBanx **(http://www.netbanx.com)**.

3 **Secure web space using SSL.** When sensitive data such as credit card
numbers are passed between the visitor's web browser and your web
server (as they may be when the visitor submits the order), a secure
connection is needed which encrypts the data. Depending upon how
your shopping cart and PSP operate, you may not need this: in the case
of NetBanx, for instance, the visitor's credit card details are typed into
a form that resides on the NetBanx server, which itself is secure, so the
sensitive data never touches your own site's server. If you do need
SSL (Secure Sockets Layer), your hosting company should be able to
provide it.

The precise details from this point onward will vary according to the
choices of product and service you make, which in turn depend on the type

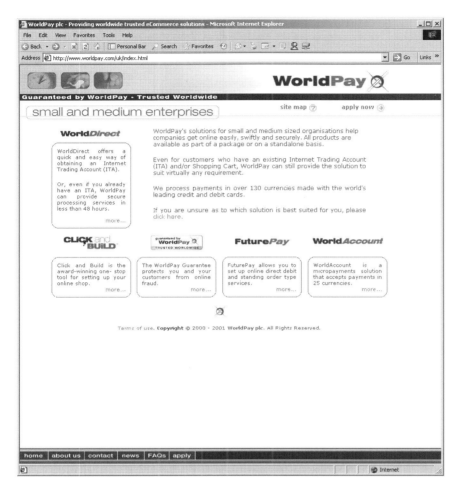

◀ WorldPay is one of many PSPs who can handle credit card transactions when your customers want to buy from your site.

and quantity of products you want to sell. The most important choice is the first one: a simple shopping cart system might seem like a good idea at the start, but it may lack the flexibility you need – introducing special offers, offering discounts and 'three for two' deals, or handling VAT, for instance. Try to pay attention to what you're likely to need in future, as well as what you need right now.

Although PSPs tend to be the easy, convenient solution which can tie in neatly with your shopping cart system, they're not always the best route to take. Since their role is essentially that of a middleman, they have little power to protect you against **chargebacks** (see below), and they introduce

Do I have to do all this to sell online?

If you'd rather not have the palaver of setting up your own e-commerce site, there are plenty of online services that specialize in handling this for you. You simply register with the service to create a payment page for your product, and then direct visitors to that page when they want to buy. A few services worth a look are DigiBuy (**http://www.digibuy.com**), RegSoft (**http://www.regsoft.com**) and Element 5 (**http://www.element5.com**).

another set of software on another server into the equation, making another link in the chain that can go wrong.

Before you commit yourself to either a cart system or a PSP, have a word with your bank to see whether they can provide a solution. Barclays and NatWest (among others) provide their own *merchant services* accounts, and their systems are likely to be considerably faster and more reliable, as well as being cheaper. The big banks are a lot warier than PSPs about who to take on, though, so you may find that you have to build up a track record using a PSP account for a year or two before a bank will talk turkey.

Although e-commerce is becoming ever more accepted, some net users are still unwilling to use their credit cards for online purchases, and for others (particularly companies and organizations) it involves so much red tape that they'd prefer not to. To cover all bases, remember to offer alternative payment methods such as cheque and bank transfer, and include related information such as your mailing address and bank details.

Chargebacks & CNP Transactions

When you take payments by credit card, either online or by phone or fax, these are known as 'cardholder not present' (CNP) transactions. Unlike face-to-face purchases, you have no signature and no proof that the purchaser really is entitled to use the card. As a result, you're likely to receive occasional *chargebacks*, meaning that the cardholder has disputed the payment and is asking for a refund. This can be due to a misunderstanding (perhaps the cardholder didn't recognize the name on the credit card statement), a disagreement (the goods didn't arrive or they weren't what the customer expected), or the card may have been stolen. In some cases, it can also be that the customer received the goods and simply decided it would be nice to have them for free.

Although you may be asked to supply evidence that the payment was authorized, the amount was confirmed and the products were delivered, you'll usually find that your arguments carry little weight and you'll have to refund the full cost of the transaction (losing the commission you paid to your PSP in the process). This is a particular problem for businesses selling 'soft' products delivered online – graphics, music, information and software, for example – which can't be returned to you, and it's worth asking a prospective PSP what suggestions they have for minimizing the chances of chargebacks occurring. Unfortunately, banks and PSPs have little incentive to stick up for the merchant since their risk of losing any money themselves is minimal.

BY THE WAY

Online payments are a done deal!

When a transaction takes place successfully online and you receive a notification of an order from your PSP, you're already liable for the PSP's commission charge. If the order seems suspicious and you decide to cancel rather than supply the goods, or you refund the payment at a later stage, you're unlikely to get that commission back.

I certainly don't mean to put you off e-commerce – the above is simply intended to explain the risks involved and whose risks they are. You can minimize them by getting as much information from the customer as possible (including an address, telephone number and email address), insisting on a street address rather than an anonymous PO box, and being wary of first-time customers who buy a large number of products or seem unconcerned about the total price. Above all, regularly ask your PSP or bank what new services they can offer to protect you or to help you verify that transactions are legitimate.

Keep It Legal!

Whether you're running your site as an online business or not, your content is being published to the world at large, and it's subject to the same laws as other published works. To round off this chapter, let's run through a few of the issues that may crop up, and what you can do to avoid potential pitfalls. As you read this section, remember that I'm not a lawyer – don't treat this as a substitute for real legal advice!

Copyright: Theirs & Yours!

Everything you write, design and create for your website belongs to you – in other words, you hold the legal copyright. Under UK law (and that of many other countries), copyright is automatic and you don't have to register with anyone. To be safe, however, you should still make your ownership clear by adding a line like the following to each page and, if necessary, alongside any graphics or other content you value: Copyright © 2001 Your Name.

The same goes for content you find on other people's sites, of course, whether or not they display a copyright message. Unless content is clearly marked as being free to take and use on your own site, treat it as copyright material and contact the webmaster to ask for permission before you use it. ('Using it' includes linking to it as well, as mentioned in *Deep Linking*, below: linking an image from someone else's site into your own page is no different from copying the image to your own server to use.)

Claiming Trademarks

There are two different types of trademark, the *registered* and *unregistered* (or common-law) trademark. These are denoted by two symbols, ® and ™ respectively. The registered trademark symbol can only be used after a trademark has been registered with the Patent Office (not just applied for), which gives you legal and enforceable ownership of the mark if you're successful. Visit the UK Patent Office's website at **http://www.patent.gov.uk** to find out more about the process.

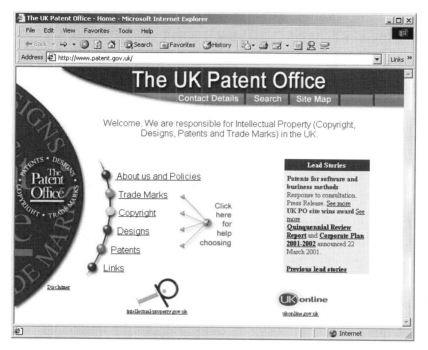

◀ The Patent
Office site
contains a mine of
useful information
about copyright
and trademarks.

You can place the ™ symbol beside any trading name or image you want to claim as a trademark, but you should check first that the mark isn't already being used by someone else using a few search engines along with a search at the UK Patent Office. If it is, find out whether it's being applied to a type of service or product similar to your own: you could probably still use the mark yourself if, for example, you want to trademark the name of a software product and they're using it for a brand of cheese. Whether the other user has registered the mark or not makes a big difference: if they're claiming it as a ™ mark too, neither of you has any automatic legal right to it (although the first to use a mark usually has the strongest case).

Deep Linking

The term 'deep linking' means adding links to your site that point to pages buried deeply in another, rather than linking to the site's front page. As a general rule, you can do this if you're opening the page into a new browser window or into the current window over the top of your own site (meaning that the visitor is effectively leaving your site), but opening someone else's page into one frame of your frame-based site is a definite no-no, and it's likely to be deemed illegal. It's yet to be proven in the courts, but only because the offending parties in every case so far have caved in and settled without a fight. In one recent case, for example, an online newspaper used deep linking to display news stories from one of its rivals in its own frameset.

The issue is one of 'passing off' – presenting someone else's content in a manner that suggests it's your own. You may feel that you can get around this by being clear about where the content is coming from, but the best policy is always to ask permission first. The same thing applies (only more so) if you're linking to someone else's images, scripts, applets and so on.

Privacy & Data Protection

If you gather and keep information about visitors to your site that can be used to identify and contact them (such as email addresses, credit card numbers, addresses or phone numbers) you need to do two things, whether you're operating the site as a business or not. The first is a legal requirement: you need to register under the UK's Data Protection Act 1998, which you can do online at **http://www.dpr.gov.uk** in a process known as *notifying*.

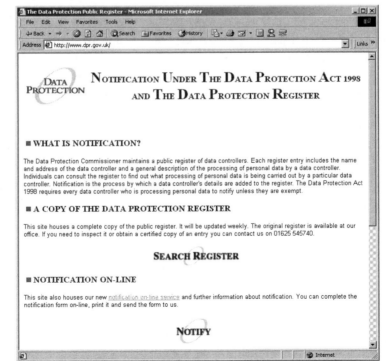

▶ If you keep personal information about your site's visitors or customers, visit the Data Protection Register site to find out how to comply with the Act and notify.

The second step is to write a privacy policy page and link it to the main page of your site. In general terms, a privacy policy tells visitors to your site who you are, how to contact you, what information you're gathering about them, who will have access to it, and how it will be used. This needn't be written in obscure legalese, it just needs to be clear and concise (perhaps as half a dozen short bullet points).

In particular, you should tell users whether you intend to use their details for marketing purposes (such as sending out mailshots), and to whom, if anyone, you'll give or sell the information. If the information will be used for any form of direct marketing, the Data Protection Act requires that you give users a chance to opt out of this.

APPENDICES

▶ **IN THESE APPENDICES...**

HTML TAG REFERENCE

The following is an alphabetical quick reference guide to the most useful HTML tags and their attributes, cross-referenced to chapters containing examples where applicable. The emphasis is very much on *useful* here: I haven't included every tag and attribute available in the HTML specification, or majored on any particular browser. Instead I've stuck to the tags and attributes you're most likely to want to use.

The list is set out as follows:

▶ For HTML elements that must have a closing tag, both the opening and closing tags are included, separated with an ellipsis (...) which is where your own text or other HTML will go.

▶ Italic text indicates that you'll enter your own value here, such as a frame name, URL or style definition. The word *string* means that you'll enter a text string; *n* indicates a number.

▶ Where a choice of attribute values is available, these have been separated with a pipe symbol, such as **left|right|center**, indicating that you can choose any of those values.

<!-- ... -->

Specifies that the enclosed text or code is a comment that shouldn't be displayed by the web browser. See Chapters 4 and 10.

<A> ... </A>

Creates a hypertext link using the HREF attribute, or a named anchor in a document using the NAME attribute. See Chapters 4 and 10.

ACCESSKEY=*character*	A shortcut key accessed by pressing ALT+*character*.
CLASS=*classname*	Applies a style sheet class.
HREF=*url* | *#name*	A hypertext link to the URL or a link to the anchor named *name* (or a combination of the two).
ID=*string*	Assigns a name, enabling the tag to be accessed through scripting.

NAME=*string*	Defines a named anchor in a document.
STYLE=*string*	Applies inline style settings.
TARGET=*window*|_self|_top| _new | _parent|_blank	Specifies the frame or window to open the link into.
TITLE=*string*	Informational tooltip text.
OnEvent=*script*	An inline event-handling script, such as OnClick="alert('Hello')".

<ACRONYM> ... </ACRONYM>

Specifies that the enclosed text is an acronym, such as 'JPEG'.

CLASS=*classname*	Applies a style sheet class.
ID=*string*	Assigns a name, enabling the tag to be accessed through scripting.
STYLE=*string*	Applies inline style settings.
TITLE=*string*	Informational tooltip text.
OnEvent=*script*	An inline event-handling script, such as OnClick="alert('Hello')".

<ADDRESS> ... </ADDRESS>

Specifies that the enclosed text is an address, usually shown as a separate
paragraph formatted in italics.

CLASS=*classname*	Applies a style sheet class.
ID=*string*	Assigns a name, enabling the tag to be accessed through scripting.
STYLE=*string*	Applies inline style settings.
TITLE=*string*	Informational tooltip text.
OnEvent=*script*	An inline event-handling script, such as OnClick="alert('Hello')".

<APPLET> ... </APPLET>

Places a Java applet on the page. The CODE, WIDTH and HEIGHT attributes are
required. Often used in conjunction with the <PARAM> tag. See Chapter 15.

ALIGN=TEXTTOP|TOP|MIDDLE| BOTTOM|BASELINE|LEFT|RIGHT| ABSMIDDLE|ABSBOTTOM	Sets the alignment of the applet.
ALT=*string*	Alternative text for browsers with Java support switched off.
ARCHIVE=*jarname*	Name of a compressed .zip or .jar file containing the applet classes.
CLASS=*classname*	Applies a style sheet class.
CODE=*classname*	The name of the applet .class file.
CODEBASE=*URL*	The URL of the directory containing the applet's class and/or .jar files.
HEIGHT=*n*	Height of the applet in pixels.
HSPACE=*n*	Horizontal spacing in pixels.
ID=*string*	Assigns a name, enabling the tag to be accessed through scripting.
MAYSCRIPT	Allows applet/JavaScript communication if included.
NAME=*string*	Applies a unique name to this instance of an applet on the page.
STYLE=*string*	Applies inline style settings.
VSPACE=*n*	Vertical spacing in pixels.
WIDTH=*n*	Width of the applet in pixels.

<AREA>

Defines the shape and coordinates of a hotspot in an image map, in conjunction with the <MAP> tag. The COORDS attribute is required. See Chapter 13.

CLASS=*classname*	Applies a style sheet class.
COORDS=*coordinates*	Sets the coordinates of the hotspot.
HREF=*url*	The URL to which the hotspot links.
ID=*string*	Assigns a name, enabling the tag to be accessed through scripting.
SHAPE=RECT|CIRCLE|POLY	Defines the shape of the hotspot.
STYLE=*string*	Applies inline style settings.
TARGET=*window*|_self|_top| _new|_parent|_blank	Specifies the frame or window to open the link into.

TITLE=*string*	Informational tooltip text.
OnEvent=*script*	An inline event-handling script, such as OnClick="alert('Hello')".

\<B\> ... \</B\>

Displays the enclosed text using a bold typeface. See Chapter 3.

CLASS=*classname*	Applies a style sheet class.
ID=*string*	Assigns a name, enabling the tag to be accessed through scripting.
STYLE=*string*	Applies inline style settings.
TITLE=*string*	Informational tooltip text.
OnEvent=*script*	An inline event-handling script, such as OnClick="alert('Hello')".

\<BASE\>

Sets the base URL from which all relative links should be resolved, and/or the frame or window name to target for all \<A\> tags in the page that have no TARGET attribute. See Chapter 8.

HREF=*url*	The URL to use as the base.
TARGET=*window|_self|_top|_new|_parent|_blank*	The frame or window to use by default.

\<BASEFONT\>

Sets the default font face, size and colour for the page (although only the SIZE attribute is supported by Netscape 4). See Chapter 5.

CLASS=*classname*	Applies a style sheet class.
COLOR=*colour*	The default text colour.
FACE=*font1,font2,font3...*	The default font for the document.
ID=*string*	Assigns a name, enabling the tag to be accessed through scripting.
SIZE=*n*	The default size of body text in the document.

\<BGSOUND>

Plays a background sound (in Internet Explorer only). Use \<EMBED> for cross-browser support – see Chapter 15. The SRC attribute is required.

BALANCE=*n*	Sets stereo balance using a value between –10000 and 10000 (where 0 is centre).
CLASS=*classname*	Applies a style sheet class.
ID=*string*	Assigns a name, enabling the tag to be accessed through scripting.
LOOP=*n*|INFINITE	Sets the number of times the clip will play, or allows 'infinite' looping.
SRC=*url*	The URL of the audio file to play.
TITLE=*string*	Informational tooltip text.
VOLUME=*n*	Sets the volume of the clip using a value between –10000 and 0, where 0 is equal to the user's current volume setting. (The clip can't be played louder than the user's own setting.)

\<BIG> ... \</BIG>

Displays the enclosed text at a slightly larger font size. See Chapter 5.

CLASS=*classname*	Applies a style sheet class.
ID=*string*	Assigns a name, enabling the tag to be accessed through scripting.
STYLE=*string*	Applies inline style settings.
TITLE=*string*	Informational tooltip text.
OnEvent=*script*	An inline event-handling script, such as OnClick="alert('Hello')".

\<BLOCKQUOTE> ... \</BLOCKQUOTE>

Signifies that the enclosed text is a quotation, usually by placing it in a new paragraph evenly indented at the left and right. See Chapter 3.

CLASS=*classname*	Applies a style sheet class.
ID=*string*	Assigns a name, enabling the tag to be accessed through scripting.

STYLE=*string*	Applies inline style settings.
TITLE=*string*	Informational tooltip text.
OnEvent=*script*	An inline event-handling script, such as OnClick="alert('Hello')".

<BODY> ... </BODY>

Specifies the beginning and end of the body of the page, containing all content to be displayed. See Chapters 3, 5 and 10 (among others!).

ALINK=*colour*	The colour of an active link.
BACKGROUND=*url*	The URL of an image to use as the page's background.
BGCOLOR=*colour*	The colour of the page background.
BGPROPERTIES=FIXED	In IE only, prevents a background image from scrolling with the page content.
BOTTOMMARGIN=*n*	In IE, the height of the bottom page margin.
CLASS=*classname*	Applies a style sheet class.
ID=*string*	Assigns a name, enabling the tag to be accessed through scripting.
LEFTMARGIN=*n*	In IE, the width of the left page margin.
LINK=*colour*	The colour of hypertext links.
MARGINHEIGHT=*n*	In Netscape, the height of top and bottom page margins.
MARGINWIDTH=*n*	In Netscape, the width of left and right page margins.
RIGHTMARGIN=*n*	In IE, the width of the right page margin.
STYLE=*string*	Applies inline style settings.
TEXT=*colour*	The default colour of the page's body text.
TITLE=*string*	Informational tooltip text.
TOPMARGIN=*n*	In IE, the height of the top page margin.
VLINK=*colour*	The colour of visited links.
OnEvent=*script*	An inline event-handling script, such as OnClick="alert('Hello')".

Inserts a line break, with text that follows appearing on a new line. See Chapters 3 and 6.

CLASS=*classname*	Applies a style sheet class.
CLEAR=ALL|LEFT|RIGHT	Forces the next line to begin at the first point on the page where there is a clear margin at the left, right or both.
ID=*string*	Assigns a name, enabling the tag to be accessed through scripting.
STYLE=*string*	Applies inline style settings.
TITLE=*string*	Informational tooltip text.

<CAPTION> ... </CAPTION>

Creates a caption to be displayed beside or above a table, used in conjunction with the <TABLE> tag. See Chapter 7.

ALIGN=TOP|RIGHT|BOTTOM|LEFT	Sets the alignment of the caption.
CLASS=*classname*	Applies a style sheet class.
ID=*string*	Assigns a name, enabling the tag to be accessed through scripting.
STYLE=*string*	Applies inline style settings.
TITLE=*string*	Informational tooltip text.
VALIGN=TOP|BOTTOM	Sets the vertical alignment of the caption.
OnEvent=script	An inline event-handling script, such as OnClick="alert('Hello')".

<CENTER> ... </CENTER>

Centres all content enclosed between these tags on the page (or within a table cell, etc.). See Chapter 3.

CLASS=*classname*	Applies a style sheet class.
ID=*string*	Assigns a name, enabling the tag to be accessed through scripting.
STYLE=*string*	Applies inline style settings.
TITLE=*string*	Informational tooltip text.

<CODE> ... </CODE>

Specifies that the enclosed text is code (such as a programming or scripting language), usually by displaying it using a fixed-width font.

CLASS=*classname*   Applies a style sheet class.
ID=*string*   Assigns a name, enabling the tag to be
                           accessed through scripting.
STYLE=*string*   Applies inline style settings.
TITLE=*string*   Informational tooltip text.
OnEvent=*script*   An inline event-handling script, such as
                           OnClick="alert('Hello')".

<DD>

Specifies that the following text is the definition of a term in a definition list, used in conjunction with <DL> and <DT>. See Chapter 4.

CLASS=*classname*   Applies a style sheet class.
ID=*string*   Assigns a name, enabling the tag to be
                           accessed through scripting.
STYLE=*string*   Applies inline style settings.
TITLE=*string*   Informational tooltip text.
OnEvent=*script*   An inline event-handling script, such as
                           OnClick="alert('Hello')".

<DIV> ... </DIV>

Defines a 'division', a section of a web page that can contain other content. See Chapters 3 and 9.

ALIGN=CENTER|LEFT|RIGHT   Sets the alignment of the division's content.
CLASS=*classname*   Applies a style sheet class.
ID=*string*   Assigns a name, enabling the tag to be
                           accessed through scripting.
STYLE=*string*   Applies inline style settings.
TITLE=*string*   Informational tooltip text.
OnEvent=*script*   An inline event-handling script, such as
                           OnClick="alert('Hello')".

447

<DL> ... </DL>

Creates a definition list by the inclusion of <DT> and <DL> tags to specify the terms and their definitions. See Chapter 4.

CLASS=*classname*	Applies a style sheet class.
COMPACT	Formats the list in a more compact style if included.
ID=*string*	Assigns a name, enabling the tag to be accessed through scripting.
STYLE=*string*	Applies inline style settings.
TITLE=*string*	Informational tooltip text.
OnEvent=*script*	An inline event-handling script, such as OnClick="alert('Hello')".

<DT>

Specifies that the following text is a term in a definition list, used in conjunction with <DL> and <DD>. See Chapter 4.

CLASS=*classname*	Applies a style sheet class.
ID=*string*	Assigns a name, enabling the tag to be accessed through scripting.
STYLE=*string*	Applies inline style settings.
TITLE=*string*	Informational tooltip text.
OnEvent=*script*	An inline event-handling script, such as OnClick="alert('Hello')".

<EM> ... </EM>

Emphasizes the enclosed text, usually by displaying it in italics as with the <I> tag.

CLASS=*classname*	Applies a style sheet class.
ID=*string*	Assigns a name, enabling the tag to be accessed through scripting.
STYLE=*string*	Applies inline style settings.
TITLE=*string*	Informational tooltip text.
OnEvent=*script*	An inline event-handling script, such as OnClick="alert('Hello')".

<EMBED> ... </EMBED>

Embeds media objects such as sounds and animations into the page to be played or displayed using a plug-in. The SRC attribute is required. See Chapters 14 and 15.

ALIGN=TEXTTOP|TOP|MIDDLE| BOTTOM|BASELINE|LEFT|RIGHT| ABSMIDDLE|ABSBOTTOM	Sets the alignment of the embedded content.
ALT=*string*	Alternative text for display by browser unable to display the embedded content.
BORDER=*n*	Creates a border around the content.
CLASS=*classname*	Applies a style sheet class.
HEIGHT=*n*	The height of the content.
HIDDEN=TRUE|FALSE	Specifies whether the plug-in's user interface should be shown.
HSPACE=*n*	The horizontal space around the content.
ID=*string*	Assigns a name, enabling the tag to be accessed through scripting.
NAME=*string*	Assigns a name to the tag, as with the ID attribute.
PLUGINSPACE=*url*	Directs the user to a URL where the required plug-in can be downloaded if it isn't installed.
SRC=*url*	The URL of the content to be embedded.
STYLE=*string*	Applies inline style settings.
TITLE=*string*	Informational tooltip text.
TYPE=*mime-type*	Describes the MIME type of the embedded content, enabling the browser to determine which plug-in to use.
VSPACE=*n*	The vertical space around the content.
WIDTH=*n*	The width of the content.
OnEvent=script	An inline event-handling script, such as OnClick="alert('Hello')".

<FONT> ... </FONT>

Applies a particular font face, size and/or colour to the textual content enclosed by the tag pair. See Chapter 5.

CLASS=*classname*	Applies a style sheet class.
COLOR=*colour*	Sets the colour of the font.
FACE=*font1,font2,font3…*	Specifies the name or family of the font to use. The first available font listed will be applied.
ID=*string*	Assigns a name, enabling the tag to be accessed through scripting.
SIZE=1|2|3|4|5|6|7	Sets the size of the font.
STYLE=*string*	Applies inline style settings.
TITLE=*string*	Informational tooltip text.
OnEvent=*script*	An inline event-handling script, such as OnClick="alert('Hello')".

<FORM> ... </FORM>

Specifies that the enclosed content is a web form. Controls are added using <INPUT>, <TEXTAREA>, <SELECT> and <OPTION> tags. See Chapter 19.

ACTION=*url*	The URL to which the name/value data of the completed form are to be sent when the form is submitted.
CLASS=*classname*	Applies a style sheet class.
ENCTYPE=*mime-type*	The MIME type that should be used to encode the form data for submission.
ID=*string*	Assigns a name, enabling the tag to be accessed through scripting.
METHOD=POST|GET	Specifies the method used by the browser to access the URL given in the ACTION attribute.
NAME=*string*	As with ID, assigns a name to the form for access by scripting.
STYLE=*string*	Applies inline style settings.
TARGET=*window*|_self|_top|_new|_parent|_blank	Specifies the frame or window to use when displaying the results of the form submission (if any).
TITLE=*string*	Informational tooltip text.
OnEvent=*script*	An inline event-handling script, such as OnClick="alert('Hello')".

<FRAME>

Used within <FRAMESET> tags to define a single frame in a browser and load a web page into it. See Chapter 8.

BORDERCOLOR=*colour*	Sets the colour of the frame's borders.
CLASS=*classname*	Applies a style sheet class.
FRAMEBORDER=0|1	In IE, specifies whether the frame will have a visible border ('1') or not ('0').
FRAMESPACING=*n*	In IE, creates space around frames to give an effect similar to the <IFRAME> tag.
ID=*string*	Assigns a name, enabling the tag to be accessed through scripting.
MARGINHEIGHT=*n*	Sets the height of the frame's top and bottom margins.
MARGINWIDTH=*n*	Sets the width of the frame's left and right margins.
NAME=*string*	Assigns a name to the frame to allow it to be targeted using the TARGET attribute of <A>, <FORM> and other tags.
NORESIZE	Prevents a frame from being resized if included.
SCROLLING=AUTO|YES|NO	Specifies whether scrollbars should be visible to allow the user to scroll through the frame's content. The default is AUTO.
SRC=*url*	The URL of a document to be loaded into the frame.
STYLE=*string*	Applies inline style settings.
TITLE=*string*	Informational tooltip text.

<FRAMESET> ... </FRAMESET>

A container for frames (defined using the <FRAME> tag) and optionally for more framesets within those frames. See Chapter 8.

BORDER=*n*	In Netscape, the width of the borders of frames within the frameset.
BORDERCOLOR=*colour*	Sets the colour of the frameset's borders.
CLASS=*classname*	Applies a style sheet class.

COLS=*string*	A comma separated list of column widths corresponding to the number of frames required in the frameset.
FRAMEBORDER=0|1	In IE, specifies whether the frame will have a visible border ('1') or not ('0').
FRAMESPACING=*n*	In IE, creates space around frames to give an effect similar to the <IFRAME> tag.
ID=*string*	Assigns a name, enabling the tag to be accessed through scripting.
ROWS=*string*	A comma-separated list of row heights corresponding to the number of frames required in the frameset.
STYLE=*string*	Applies inline style settings.
TITLE=*string*	Informational tooltip text.
OnEvent=*script*	An inline event-handling script, such as OnClick="alert('Hello')".

<HEAD> ... </HEAD>

A collection of tags containing information (in any order) about the document and how it's to be displayed. Common tags used within the <HEAD> section are <TITLE>, <META>, <SCRIPT> and <STYLE>.

CLASS=*classname*	Applies a style sheet class.
ID=*string*	Assigns a name, enabling the tag to be accessed through scripting.
STYLE=*string*	Applies inline style settings.
TITLE=*string*	Informational tooltip text.

<H*n*> ... </H*n*>

A set of six tag pairs that format the enclosed text as a heading, where *n* is a figure from 1 to 6. See Chapter 3.

ALIGN=LEFT|RIGHT|CENTER	Sets the alignment of the heading.
CLASS=*classname*	Applies a style sheet class.
ID=*string*	Assigns a name, enabling the tag to be accessed through scripting.

STYLE=*string*	Applies inline style settings.
TITLE=*string*	Informational tooltip text.
OnEvent=script	An inline event-handling script, such as OnClick="alert('Hello')".

<HR>

Places a 'horizontal rule' on the page – a dividing line to break up the page's content. See Chapter 5.

ALIGN=LEFT|RIGHT|CENTER	Sets the alignment of the rule.
CLASS=*classname*	Applies a style sheet class.
COLOR=*colour*	In IE, sets the colour of the rule.
ID=*string*	Assigns a name, enabling the tag to be accessed through scripting.
NOSHADE	Turns off shading to create a solid rather than a 3-dimensional rule.
SIZE=*n*	Sets the height of the rule.
SRC=*url*	In IE, allows an image to be used as a rule by specifying its URL. (This is more reliably done using the <IMG> tag.)
STYLE=*string*	Applies inline style settings.
TITLE=*string*	Informational tooltip text.
WIDTH=*n*	Sets the width of the rule, either in pixels or as a percentage of the page width.
OnEvent=script	An inline event-handling script, such as OnClick="alert('Hello')".

<HTML> ... </HTML>

Identifies the document as an HTML page. This pair of tags encloses the entire document, making them the first and last tags on the page.

| TITLE=*string* | Informational tooltip text. |

<I> ... </I>

Displays the enclosed text using an italic typeface. See Chapter 3.

CLASS=*classname*	Applies a style sheet class.
ID=*string*	Assigns a name, enabling the tag to be accessed through scripting.
STYLE=string	Applies inline style settings.
TITLE=*string*	Informational tooltip text.
OnEvent=*script*	An inline event-handling script, such as OnClick="alert('Hello')".

<IFRAME> ... </IFRAME>

Creates an inline (or 'floating') frame within a page that can contain other pages and can be targeted by <A> links. Supported by IE and Netscape 6 only. See Chapter 8.

ALIGN=TEXTTOP|TOP|MIDDLE| BOTTOM|BASELINE|LEFT|RIGHT| ABSMIDDLE|ABSBOTTOM	Sets the alignment of the frame.
BORDER=*n*	Sets the width of the frame's border.
BORDERCOLOR=*colour*	Sets the colour of the frame's border.
CLASS=*classname*	Applies a style sheet class.
FRAMEBORDER=0|1	In IE, specifies whether the frame will have a visible border ('1') or not ('0').
FRAMESPACING=*n*	In IE, creates space around frames to give an effect similar to the <IFRAME> tag.
HEIGHT=*n*	The height of the frame.
HSPACE=*n*	The horizontal space around the frame.
ID=*string*	Assigns a name, enabling the tag to be accessed through scripting.
MARGINHEIGHT=*n*	Sets the height of the frame's top and bottom margins.
MARGINWIDTH=*n*	Sets the width of the frame's left and right margins.
NAME=*string*	Assigns a name to the frame to allow it to be targeted using the TARGET attribute of <A>, <FORM> and other tags.

NORESIZE	Prevents a frame from being resized if included.
SCROLLING=AUTO|YES|NO	Specifies whether scrollbars should be visible to allow the user to scroll through the frame's content. The default is AUTO.
SRC=*url*	The URL of a document to be loaded into the frame.
STYLE=*string*	Applies inline style settings.
TITLE=*string*	Informational tooltip text.
VSPACE=*n*	The vertical space around the frame.
WIDTH=*n*	The width of the frame.
OnEvent=*script*	An inline event-handling script, such as OnClick="alert('Hello')".

\<IMG\>

Places an inline GIF or JPEG image on the page. The SRC attribute is required. See Chapter 6.

ALIGN=TEXTTOP|TOP|MIDDLE|BOTTOM|BASELINE|LEFT|RIGHT|ABSMIDDLE|ABSBOTTOM	Sets the alignment of the image.
ALT=*string*	Alternative text to display if image display options have been switched off.
BORDER=*n*	The width of the border displayed around the image.
CLASS=*classname*	Applies a style sheet class.
CONTROLS	In conjunction with DYNSRC, specifies that movie-player controls are visible, if included.
DYNSRC=*url*	In IE, the URL of an AVI video clip to display in place of the image.
HEIGHT=*n*	The height of the image.
HSPACE=*n*	The horizontal space around the image.
ID=*string*	Assigns a name, enabling the tag to be accessed through scripting.
LOOP=*n*|INFINITE	In conjunction with DYNSRC, sets how many times the movie is repeated.

LOWSRC=*url*   The URL of a lower quality (but faster
                         loading) image to display while the
                         remaining page contents are loading.

NAME=*string*   Assigns a name to the image, as with ID,
                         allowing it to be accessed in scripts.

SRC=*url*   The URL of the image to display.

START=MOUSEOVER   In conjunction with DYNSRC, specifies that
                         the movie plays only when the mouse
                         moves over the static image.

STYLE=*string*   Applies inline style settings.

TITLE=*string*   Informational tooltip text.

USEMAP=*url#mapname*   The URL (if necessary) and name of a
                         coordinate map created with the <MAP> tag,
                         used when the current image is an image
                         map.

VSPACE=*n*   The vertical space around the image.

WIDTH=*n*   The width of the image.

OnEvent=*script*   An inline event-handling script, such as
                         OnClick="alert('Hello')".

<INPUT>

Places a form input field such as a checkbox, text field or button on the
page. Used in conjunction with the <FORM> tag. See Chapter 19.

CHECKED   If included, specifies that the checkbox or
                         radio button control is marked as 'selected'.

CLASS=*classname*   Applies a style sheet class.

DISABLED   If included, prevents the input field from
                         being selected or its contents changed by
                         the user.

ID=*string*   Assigns a name, enabling the tag to be
                         accessed through scripting.

MAXLENGTH=*n*   When the input type is 'text', specifies the
                         maximum number of characters that may be
                         entered.

NAME=*string*   The name of the field, to be returned (along
                         with its value) when the form is submitted.

READONLY	If included, the user can select this field but can't modify its contents.
SIZE=*n*	Specifies the width of a text field (the number of characters that may be seen at once, rather than the number that can be entered).
SRC=*url*	When the input type is an image, specifies the URL of the image to display.
STYLE=*string*	Applies inline style settings.
TITLE=*string*	Informational tooltip text.
TYPE=BUTTON|CHECKBOX| HIDDEN|IMAGE|PASSWORD| RADIO|RESET|SUBMIT|TEXT	The type of input field to create.
VALUE=*string*	Specifies the initial value of the input field (such as the text shown in a text field), or the button label if the input type is a button, or the value to be returned from a checkbox or radio button if selected.
OnEvent=*script*	An inline event-handling script, such as OnClick="alert('Hello')".

<LABEL> ... </LABEL>

Creates a text label for a form input control such as a checkbox or radio button, allowing the control to be checked or unchecked by clicking the label. The FOR attribute is required. Supported by IE only. See Chapter 19.

CLASS=*classname*	Applies a style sheet class.
FOR=*input-ID*	Specifies which form control on the page this label will activate, using the name given in the control's ID attribute.
ID=*string*	Assigns a name, enabling the tag to be accessed through scripting.
STYLE=*string*	Applies inline style settings.
TITLE=*string*	Informational tooltip text.
OnEvent=*script*	An inline event-handling script, such as OnClick="alert('Hello')".

<LI>

Creates a list item in an ordered or unordered list, in conjunction with the <OL> or <UL> tags. See Chapter 4.

CLASS=*classname*	Applies a style sheet class.
ID=*string*	Assigns a name, enabling the tag to be accessed through scripting.
STYLE=*string*	Applies inline style settings.
TITLE=*string*	Informational tooltip text.
TYPE=1|a|A|i|I|DISC|CIRCLE|SQUARE	Resets the type of bullet or numbering system used for this and subsequent items.
VALUE=*n*	In an ordered list, resets the number-count to the chosen value from this item onwards.
OnEvent=script	An inline event-handling script, such as OnClick="alert('Hello')".

<LINK>

Used to define relationships between documents, although few browsers now support this concept. The primary use is in linking an external style sheet to a document. See Chapter 9.

CLASS=*classname*	Applies a style sheet class.
DISABLED	If included, indicates that the link is to be ignored in this document (for instance, the style sheet's rules won't be applied).
HREF=*url*	The URL of the related document.
ID=*string*	Assigns a name, enabling the tag to be accessed through scripting.
REL=*relationship*	The relationship being defined, such as STYLESHEET.
STYLE=*string*	Applies inline style settings.
TITLE=*string*	Informational tooltip text.
OnEvent=script	An inline event-handling script, such as OnClick="alert('Hello')".

<MAP> ... </MAP>

Defines the shapes and coordinates of the hotspots used in a client side image map, in conjunction with the <AREA> tag. The NAME attribute is required. See Chapter 13.

CLASS=*classname*	Applies a style sheet class.
ID=*string*	Assigns a name, enabling the tag to be accessed through scripting.
NAME=*string*	Assigns a name to the map, allowing it to be linked to an image via the <IMG> tag's USEMAP attribute.
STYLE=*string*	Applies inline style settings.
TITLE=*string*	Informational tooltip text.
OnEvent=*script*	An inline event-handling script, such as OnClick="alert('Hello')".

<MARQUEE> ... </MARQUEE>

In Internet Explorer only, scrolls the enclosed text in an animated fashion across the screen. See Chapter 5.

ALIGN=LEFT|RIGHT|TOP|MIDDLE|BOTTOM	Sets the alignment of the marquee.
BEHAVIOR=SCROLL|SLIDE|ALTERNATE	The animation behaviour of the marquee.
BGCOLOR=*colour*	The background colour of the marquee.
CLASS=*classname*	Applies a style sheet class.
DIRECTION=LEFT|RIGHT	Sets the direction in which the marquee should move.
HEIGHT=*n*	The height of the marquee in pixels, or as a percentage of page height.
HSPACE=*n*	The horizontal space around the marquee.
ID=*string*	Assigns a name, enabling the tag to be accessed through scripting.
LOOP=*n*|INFINITE	How many times the animation should be looped, or 'infinite' looping.
SCROLLAMOUNT=*n*	Sets the number of pixels the text should move between each repaint.

459

SCROLLDELAY=*n*	Sets the number of milliseconds to pause between each repaint of the scrolled text.
STYLE=*string*	Applies inline style settings.
TITLE=*string*	Informational tooltip text.
VSPACE=*n*	The vertical space around the marquee.
WIDTH=*n*	The width of the marquee in pixels, or as a percentage of page width.
OnEvent=*script*	An inline event-handling script, such as OnClick="alert('Hello')".

\<META\>

Used in the head of the page to include document-specific information. The CONTENT attribute is required, along with one or both of the other attributes. See Chapters 10, 18 and 24.

CONTENT=*string*	The value, setting or information to be associated with the given meta name or HTTP response header.
HTTP-EQUIV=*reponse-header*	Specifies an HTTP response header (read by the server when providing the document) to which the information relates.
NAME=*string*	The name of the meta information to be created.

\<NOBR\> ... \</NOBR\>

Prevents the enclosed text from wrapping to a new line. If the window size would normally cause a line break to occur somewhere between these tags, the enclosed text will be moved to the next line intact. Can be used in conjunction with \<WBR\>.

CLASS=*classname*	Applies a style sheet class.
ID=*string*	Assigns a name, enabling the tag to be accessed through scripting.
STYLE=*string*	Applies inline style settings.
TITLE=*string*	Informational tooltip text.

<NOFRAMES> ... </NOFRAMES>

Used in a document that defines a frameset and frames (using the
<FRAMESET> and <FRAME> tags) to provide alternative HTML content for
browsers without frame support. See Chapter 8.

CLASS=*classname*	Applies a style sheet class.
ID=*string*	Assigns a name, enabling the tag to be accessed through scripting.
STYLE=*string*	Applies inline style settings.
TITLE=*string*	Informational tooltip text.

<OBJECT> ... </OBJECT>

Allows media objects such as ActiveX controls to be inserted into a web
page. Often used in conjunction with the <PARAM> tag. Currently supported
by IE only. See Chapter 14.

ALIGN=TEXTTOP|TOP|MIDDLE|BOTTOM|BASELINE|LEFT|RIGHT|ABSMIDDLE|ABSBOTTOM	Sets the alignment of the image.
BORDER=*n*	The width of the border displayed around the object.
CLASS=*classname*	Applies a style sheet class.
CLASSID=*string*	A unique identifier specifying a particular installed object.
CODEBASE=*url*	Directs the user to a URL where the required object can be downloaded if it isn't installed.
HEIGHT=*n*	The height of the object in pixels, or as a percentage of page height.
HSPACE=*n*	The horizontal space around the object.
ID=*string*	Assigns a name, enabling the tag to be accessed through scripting.
NAME=*string*	Assigns a name to the object, as with ID, allowing it to be accessed in scripts.
STANDBY=*string*	Like the ALT attribute in other tags, displays alternative text while the object is being downloaded.
STYLE=*string*	Applies inline style settings.

TITLE=*string*	Informational tooltip text.
VSPACE=*n*	The vertical space around the object.
WIDTH=*n*	The width of the object in pixels, or as a percentage of page width.
OnEvent=script	An inline event-handling script, such as OnClick="alert('Hello')".

<OL> ... </OL>

Creates an ordered (numbered) list, using the <LI> tag to create list items. See Chapter 4.

CLASS=*classname*	Applies a style sheet class.
COMPACT	Formats the list in a more compact style if included.
ID=*string*	Assigns a name, enabling the tag to be accessed through scripting.
START=*n*	Allows the list to begin at a number other than 1.
STYLE=*string*	Applies inline style settings.
TITLE=*string*	Informational tooltip text.
TYPE=1|a|A|i|I	The type of numbering system to be used.
OnEvent=script	An inline event-handling script, such as OnClick="alert('Hello')".

<OPTION>

Adds an item to a <SELECT> form field. See Chapter 19.

CLASS=*classname*	Applies a style sheet class.
ID=*string*	Assigns a name, enabling the tag to be accessed through scripting.
SELECTED	Sets this option as selected when the control appears.
STYLE=*string*	Applies inline style settings.
TITLE=*string*	Informational tooltip text.
VALUE=*string*	The value to be returned if this option is selected when the form is submitted.
OnEvent=script	An inline event-handling script, such as OnClick="alert('Hello')".

<P> [... </P>]

Specifies a new paragraph of text. The closing tag is required only when one or more attributes are added to the opening tag. See Chapter 3.

ALIGN=LEFT|RIGHT|CENTER   Sets the alignment of the paragraph.
CLASS=*classname*   Applies a style sheet class.
ID=*string*   Assigns a name, enabling the tag to be accessed through scripting.
STYLE=*string*   Applies inline style settings.
TITLE=*string*   Informational tooltip text.
OnEvent=script   An inline event-handling script, such as OnClick="alert('Hello')".

<PARAM>

Provides optional settings for an embedded object or Java applet, and used in conjunction with the <APPLET> or <OBJECT> tags. The NAME and VALUE attributes are required. See Chapters 14, 15 and 21.

ID=*string*   Assigns a name, enabling the tag to be accessed through scripting.
NAME=*string*   The name of the parameter to which the value should be applied.
VALUE=*string*   The value to apply to the named parameter.

<PRE> ... </PRE>

Treats the enclosed text as 'pre-formatted' and displays it as is, using a fixed-width font and observing use of spaces and carriage returns.

CLASS=*classname*   Applies a style sheet class.
ID=*string*   Assigns a name, enabling the tag to be accessed through scripting.
STYLE=*string*   Applies inline style settings.
TITLE=*string*   Informational tooltip text.
OnEvent=script   An inline event-handling script, such as OnClick="alert('Hello')".

<SCRIPT> ... </SCRIPT>

Embeds a block of script into a web page. See Chapters 16–19.

ARCHIVE=*url*	The URL of a .zip or .jar file containing one or more external script files.
CLASS=*classname*	Applies a style sheet class.
EVENT=*event-name*	In conjunction with the FOR attribute, specifies an event for the element which would cause this script to be executed. IE only.
FOR=*id*	Specifies the ID of an element on the page to which the script should apply. IE only.
ID=*string*	Assigns a name, enabling the tag to be accessed through scripting.
LANGUAGE=JAVASCRIPT| JSCRIPT|VBSCRIPT	The language in which the script is written.
SRC=*url*	The URL of an external file containing a script to be used with the current document.
STYLE=*string*	Applies inline style settings.
TITLE=*string*	Informational tooltip text.

<SELECT> ... </SELECT>

Adds a selection list to a form, either in box or drop-down style, in conjunction with the <OPTION> tag. See Chapter 19.

ALIGN=TOP|MIDDLE|BOTTOM| LEFT|RIGHT|TEXTTOP|BASELINE| ABSBOTTOM|ABSMIDDLE	The alignment of the list.
CLASS=*classname*	Applies a style sheet class.
DISABLED	If included, specifies that the user cannot select or alter the control.
ID=*string*	Assigns a name, enabling the tag to be accessed through scripting.
MULTIPLE	If included, specifies that more than one item can be selected in the list.
NAME=*string*	The name to be associated with this control's value when the form is submitted.

SIZE=*n*	The number of items visible at one time. Use '1' for a drop-down list, or any higher number for a box.
STYLE=*string*	Applies inline style settings.
TITLE=*string*	Informational tooltip text.
OnEvent=*script*	An inline event-handling script, such as OnClick="alert('Hello')".

<SMALL> ... </SMALL>

Displays the enclosed text at a slightly smaller font size. See Chapter 5.

CLASS=*classname*	Applies a style sheet class.
ID=*string*	Assigns a name, enabling the tag to be accessed through scripting.
STYLE=*string*	Applies inline style settings.
TITLE=*string*	Informational tooltip text.
OnEvent=*script*	An inline event-handling script, such as OnClick="alert('Hello')".

<SPAN> ... </SPAN>

Specifies inline CSS styles for the enclosed text when no other tag (such as <B>, <P> or <IMG>) is available or wanted. See Chapter 9.

CLASS=*classname*	Applies a style sheet class.
ID=*string*	Assigns a name, enabling the tag to be accessed through scripting.
STYLE=*string*	Applies inline style settings.
TITLE=*string*	Informational tooltip text.
OnEvent=*script*	An inline event-handling script, such as OnClick="alert('Hello')".

<STRIKE> ... </STRIKE>

Displays the enclosed text as strikethrough ('crossed out') type. See Chapter 3.

CLASS=*classname*	Applies a style sheet class.
ID=*string*	Assigns a name, enabling the tag to be accessed through scripting.
STYLE=*string*	Applies inline style settings.
TITLE=*string*	Informational tooltip text.
OnEvent=*script*	An inline event-handling script, such as OnClick="alert('Hello')".

<STRONG> ... </STRONG>

Displays the enclosed text with strong emphasis, usually by making it bold.

CLASS=*classname*	Applies a style sheet class.
ID=*string*	Assigns a name, enabling the tag to be accessed through scripting.
STYLE=*string*	Applies inline style settings.
TITLE=*string*	Informational tooltip text.
OnEvent=*script*	An inline event-handling script, such as OnClick="alert('Hello')".

<STYLE> ... </STYLE>

Defines a style sheet (a set of CSS style rules) that will be available for the current document. See Chapters 9 and 18.

DISABLED	If included, indicates that the style rules are to be ignored. IE only.
ID=*string*	Assigns a name, enabling the tag to be accessed through scripting.
SRC=*url*	The URL of an external file containing style information to be imported. Netscape 4 only.
TITLE=*string*	Informational tooltip text.

_{...}

Displays the enclosed text as subscript, using a smaller font. See Chapter 3.

CLASS=*classname*	Applies a style sheet class.
ID=*string*	Assigns a name, enabling the tag to be accessed through scripting.
STYLE=*string*	Applies inline style settings.
TITLE=*string*	Informational tooltip text.
OnEvent=*script*	An inline event-handling script, such as OnClick="alert('Hello')".

^{...}

Displays the enclosed text as superscript, using a smaller font. See Chapter 3.

CLASS=*classname*	Applies a style sheet class.
ID=*string*	Assigns a name, enabling the tag to be accessed through scripting.
STYLE=*string*	Applies inline style settings.
TITLE=*string*	Informational tooltip text.
OnEvent=*script*	An inline event-handling script, such as OnClick="alert('Hello')".

<TABLE> ... </TABLE>

Creates a table on the page in conjunction with the <TR> and <TD> tags. See Chapter 7.

ALIGN=LEFT|RIGHT|CENTER	Sets the alignment of the table.
BACKGROUND=*url*	The URL of a background image to be tiled behind the table's cells.
BGCOLOR=*colour*	The background colour of the table.
BORDER=*n*	The thickness of the table border, or 0 to remove the border and the space held in reserve for it.
BORDERCOLOR=*colour*	The colour of the table's border.
BORDERCOLORDARK=*colour*	The colour of the two darker edges of a 3-dimensional border.

BORDERCOLORLIGHT=*colour*	The colour of the two lighter edges of a 3-dimensional border.
CELLPADDING=*n*	The number of blank pixels between the inner edge of a table cell and the cell's content.
CELLSPACING=*n*	The number of blank pixels placed between each of the table's cells.
CLASS=*classname*	Applies a style sheet class.
FRAME=VOID|ABOVE|BELOW| HSIDES|VSIDES|LHS|RHS|BOX	In conjunction with the BORDER attribute, specifies which external borders of the table are to be shown.
HEIGHT=*n*	The height of the table in pixels or as a percentage of page height.
ID=*string*	Assigns a name, enabling the tag to be accessed through scripting.
RULES=NONE|BASIC|ROWS| COLUMNS|ALL	In conjunction with the BORDER attribute, specifies which internal borders of the table are to be shown.
STYLE=*string*	Applies inline style settings.
TITLE=*string*	Informational tooltip text.
VALIGN=TOP|MIDDLE|BOTTOM	The vertical alignment of text in a table's cells.
WIDTH=*n*	The width of the table in pixels or as a percentage of page width.
OnEvent=*script*	An inline event-handling script, such as OnClick="alert('Hello')".

\<TD\> ... \</TD\>

Adds a cell to a row in a table, in conjunction with the \<TABLE\> and \<TR\> tags. See Chapter 7.

ALIGN=LEFT|RIGHT|CENTER| JUSTIFY	Sets the alignment of the cell's content.
BACKGROUND=*url*	The URL of a background image to be tiled behind this cell.
BGCOLOR=*colour*	The background colour of the cell.
BORDERCOLOR=*colour*	The colour of the cell's border.

BORDERCOLORDARK=*colour*	The colour of the two darker edges of a 3-dimensional border.
BORDERCOLORLIGHT=*colour*	The colour of the two lighter edges of a 3-dimensional border.
CLASS=*classname*	Applies a style sheet class.
COLSPAN=*n*	The number of table columns this cell should span.
HEIGHT=*n*	The height of the cell in pixels or as a percentage of table height.
ID=*string*	Assigns a name, enabling the tag to be accessed through scripting.
NOWRAP	If included, prevents lines of text in the cell from being wrapped.
ROWSPAN=*n*	The number of table rows that this cell should span.
STYLE=*string*	Applies inline style settings.
TITLE=*string*	Informational tooltip text.
VALIGN=TOP|MIDDLE|BASELINE|BOTTOM	The vertical alignment of the cell's content.
WIDTH=*n*	The width of the cell in pixels or as a percentage of table width.
OnEvent=script	An inline event-handling script, such as OnClick="alert('Hello')".

<TEXTAREA> ... </TEXTAREA>

Adds a multi-line text control to a form. Default text can be shown in the control by enclosing it between the opening and closing tags. See Chapter 19.

ALIGN=TOP|MIDDLE|BOTTOM|LEFT|RIGHT|TEXTTOP|BASELINE|ABSBOTTOM|ABSMIDDLE	The alignment of the list.
CLASS=*classname*	Applies a style sheet class.
COLS=*n*	The width of the control, as a number of fixed-width characters.
DISABLED	If included, specifies that the user cannot select the control or change its content.
ID=*string*	Assigns a name, enabling the tag to be accessed through scripting.

NAME=*string*	The name to be associated with this control's value when the form is submitted.
READONLY	If included, the text in the control can be read and selected by the user, but not altered.
ROWS=*n*	The number of lines of text that the control should be able to display at one time.
STYLE=*string*	Applies inline style settings.
TITLE=*string*	Informational tooltip text.
WRAP=VIRTUAL|PHYSICAL|OFF	Determines whether and how multiple lines of text are wrapped within the control, and how they're formatted for form submission.
OnEvent=*script*	An inline event-handling script, such as OnClick="alert('Hello')".

\<TITLE> ... \</TITLE>

Specifies the title of the current document, usually displayed in a browser's title bar. See Chapters 3 and 24.

| ID=*string* | Assigns a name, enabling the tag to be accessed through scripting. |
| TITLE=*string* | Informational tooltip text. |

\<TR> ... \</TR>

Adds a row to a table, in conjunction with the \<TABLE> tag. See Chapter 7.

ALIGN=LEFT|RIGHT|CENTER|JUSTIFY	Sets the alignment of the cell's content.
BACKGROUND=*url*	The URL of a background image to be tiled behind this cell.
BGCOLOR=*colour*	The background colour of the cells in this row.
BORDERCOLOR=*colour*	The colour of this row's cell borders.
BORDERCOLORDARK=*colour*	The colour of the two darker edges of a 3-dimensional border.
BORDERCOLORLIGHT=*colour*	The colour of the two lighter edges of a 3-dimensional border.

CLASS=*classname*	Applies a style sheet class.
ID=*string*	Assigns a name, enabling the tag to be accessed through scripting.
NOWRAP	If included, prevents lines of text in the cells from being wrapped.
STYLE=*string*	Applies inline style settings.
TITLE=*string*	Informational tooltip text.
VALIGN=TOP|MIDDLE|BASELINE|BOTTOM	The vertical alignment of this row's cell content.
OnEvent=*script*	An inline event-handling script, such as OnClick="alert('Hello')".

\<TT> ... \</TT>

Displays the enclosed text in a fixed-width typewriter-style font. See Chapter 3.

CLASS=*classname*	Applies a style sheet class.
ID=*string*	Assigns a name, enabling the tag to be accessed through scripting.
STYLE=*string*	Applies inline style settings.
TITLE=*string*	Informational tooltip text.
OnEvent=*script*	An inline event-handling script, such as OnClick="alert('Hello')".

\<U> ... \</U>

Displays the enclosed text as underlined. See Chapter 3.

CLASS=*classname*	Applies a style sheet class.
ID=*string*	Assigns a name, enabling the tag to be accessed through scripting.
STYLE=*string*	Applies inline style settings.
TITLE=*string*	Informational tooltip text.
OnEvent=*script*	An inline event-handling script, such as OnClick="alert('Hello')".

\<UL\> ... \</UL\>

Creates an unordered (bulleted) list, using the \<LI\> tag to create list items. See Chapter 4.

CLASS=*classname*	Applies a style sheet class.
COMPACT	Formats the list in a more compact style if included.
ID=*string*	Assigns a name, enabling the tag to be accessed through scripting.
STYLE=*string*	Applies inline style settings.
TITLE=*string*	Informational tooltip text.
TYPE=DISC|CIRCLE|SQUARE	The style of bullet to be used.
OnEvent=*script*	An inline event-handling script, such as OnClick="alert('Hello')".

\<WBR\>

When a line of text is enclosed between \<NOBR\> ... \</NOBR\> tags to prevent line breaks occurring, the \<WBR\> tag can be used to insert a 'soft' break that tells the browser where the text can be broken if necessary.

CLASS=*classname*	Applies a style sheet class.
ID=*string*	Assigns a name, enabling the tag to be accessed through scripting.
STYLE=*string*	Applies inline style settings.
TITLE=*string*	Informational tooltip text.

HTML COLOUR NAMES

Colours in HTML come in two flavours: *named colours and hex numbers representing colours*. The hex system explained on page 69 is the more flexible by far, giving access to 16.7 million different colours, but if you have trouble getting to grips with it you can use any of the 140 colour names listed below. The corresponding hex numbers are given here too, and you can enter either into your HTML documents – the tag <FONT COLOR=FF0000> means just the same as <FONT COLOR=RED>. For want of a better system, the colours are simply presented in alphabetical order by name.

Name	Hex	Name	Hex
AliceBlue	F0F8FF	DarkMagenta	8B008B
AntiqueWhite	FAEBD7	DarkOliveGreen	556B2F
Aqua	00FFFF	DarkOrange	FF8C00
Aquamarine	7FFFD4	DarkOrchid	9932CC
Azure	F0FFFF	DarkRed	8B0000
Beige	F5F5DC	DarkSalmon	E9967A
Bisque	FFE4C4	DarkSeaGreen	8FBC8F
Black	000000	DarkSlateBlue	483D8B
BlanchedAlmond	FFEBCD	DarkSlateGray	2F4F4F
Blue	0000FF	DarkTurquoise	00CED1
BlueViolet	8A2BE2	DarkViolet	9400D3
Brown	A52A2A	DeepPink	FF1493
Burlywood	DEB887	DeepSkyBlue	00BFBF
CadetBlue	5F9EA0	DimGray	696969
Chartreuse	7FFF00	DodgerBlue	1E90FF
Chocolate	D2691E	Firebrick	B22222
Coral	FF7F50	FloralWhite	FFFAF0
CornflowerBlue	6495ED	ForestGreen	228B22
Cornsilk	FFF8DC	Fuchsia	FF00FF
Crimson	DC143C	Gainsboro	DCDCDC
Cyan	00FFFF	GhostWhite	F8F8FF
DarkBlue	00008B	Gold	FFD700
DarkCyan	008B8B	Goldenrod	DAA520
DarkGoldenrod	B8860B	Gray	808080
DarkGray	A9A9A9	Green	008000
DarkGreen	006400	GreenYellow	ADFF2F
DarkKhaki	BDB76B	Honeydew	F0FFF0

Name	Hex	Name	Hex
HotPink	FF69B4	MidnightBlue	191970
IndianRed	CD5C5C	MintCream	F5FFFA
Indigo	4B0082	MistyRose	FFE4E1
Ivory	FFFFF0	Moccasin	FFE4B5
Khaki	F0E68C	NavajoWhite	FFDEAD
Lavender	E6E6FA	Navy	000080
LavenderBlush	FFF0F5	OldLace	FDF5E6
LawnGreen	7CFC00	Olive	808000
LemonChiffon	FFFACD	OliveDrab	6B8E23
LightBlue	ADD8E6	Orange	FFA500
LightCoral	F08080	OrangeRed	FF4500
LightCyan	E0FFFF	Orchid	DA70D6
LightGoldenrodYellow	FAFAD2	PaleGoldenrod	EEE8AA
LightGreen	90EE90	PaleGreen	98FB98
LightGray	D3D3D3	PaleTurquoise	AFEEEE
LightPink	FFB6C1	PaleVioletRed	DB7093
LightSalmon	FFA07A	PapayaWhip	FFEFD5
LightSeaGreen	20B2AA	PeachPuff	FFDAB9
LightSkyBlue	87CEFA	Peru	CD853F
LightSlateGray	778899	Pink	FFC0CB
LightSteelBlue	B0C4DE	Plum	DDA0DD
LightYellow	FFFFE0	PowderBlue	B0E0E6
Lime	00FF00	Purple	800080
LimeGreen	32CD32	Red	FF0000
Linen	FAF0E6	RosyBrown	BC8F8F
Magenta	FF00FF	RoyalBlue	4169E1
Maroon	800000	SaddleBrown	8B4513
MediumAquamarine	66CDAA	Salmon	FA8072
MediumBlue	0000CD	SandyBrown	F4A460
MediumOrchid	BA55D3	SeaGreen	2E8B57
MediumPurple	9370DB	Seashell	FFF5EE
MediumSeaGreen	3CB371	Sienna	A0522D
MediumSlateBlue	7B68EE	Silver	C0C0C0
MediumSpringGreen	00FA9A	SkyBlue	87CEEB
MediumTurquoise	48D1CC	SlateBlue	6A5ACD
MediumVioletRed	C71585	SlateGray	708090

Name	Hex	Name	Hex
Snow	FFFAFA	Turquoise	40E0D0
SpringGreen	00FF7F	Violet	EE82EE
SteelBlue	4682B4	Wheat	F5DEB3
Tan	D2B48C	White	FFFFFF
Teal	008080	WhiteSmoke	F5F5F5
Thistle	D8BFD8	Yellow	FFFF00
Tomato	FF6347	YellowGreen	9ACD32

SPECIAL CHARACTERS IN HTML

There are certain characters that can't be displayed correctly in a web page just by typing them into your HTML source. Obvious examples are the opening and closing tag symbols < and >, which the browser will always interpret as being part of an HTML tag, but there are others such as the ampersand and double-quote symbols, along with foreign and mathematical symbols.

Fortunately there are other ways to display these, as explained in Chapter 4. Wherever one of the characters in the table below should appear in your page, just replace it with the corresponding HTML code or decimal code. It doesn't matter which you choose (although the decimal code is the more likely to work in all browsers) and you can use both formats interchangeably.

Character Name	Character	HTML Code	Decimal Code
Less than	<	&lt;	&#60;
Greater than	>	&gt;	&#62;
Ampersand	&	&amp;	&#38;
Double-quotes	"	&quot;	&#34;
Left angle quote	«	&laquo;	&#171;
Right angle quote	»	&raquo;	&#187;
Non-breaking space			
Copyright	©	&copy;	&#169;
Registered trademark	®	&reg;	&#174;
Trademark	™	&trade;	&#153;
One quarter	$\frac{1}{4}$	&frac14;	&#188;
One half	$\frac{1}{2}$	&frac12;	&#189;
Three quarters	$\frac{3}{4}$	&frac34;	&#190;
Cents	¢	&cent;	&#162;
Pounds	£	&pound;	&#163;
General currency	¤	&curren;	&#164;
Yen	¥	&yen;	&#165;
Middle dot	·	&middot;	&#183;
Soft hyphen		&shy;	&#173;
Broken vertical bar	¦	&brvbar;	&#166;
Paragraph	¶	&para;	&#182;

Character Name	Character	HTML Code	Decimal Code
Section	§	&sect;	&#167;
Superscript 1	¹	&sup1;	&#185;
Superscript 2	²	&sup2;	&#178;
Superscript 3	³	&sup3;	&#179;
Micro	µ	&micro;	&#181;
Not	¬	&not;	&#172;
Feminine ordinal	ª	&ordf;	&#170;
Masculine ordinal	º	&ordm;	&#186;
Degrees	°	&deg;	&#176;
Plus or minus	±	&plusmn;	&#177;
Multiply	×	&times;	&#215;
Divide	÷	&divide;	&#247;
Inverted exclamation	¡	&iexcl;	&#161;
Inverted question mark	¿	&iquest;	&#191;
Umlaut (dieresis)	¨	&uml;	&#168;
Macron accent	¯	&macr;	&#175;
Acute accent	´	&acute;	&#180;
Cedilla	¸	&cedil;	&#184;
A grave	À	&Agrave;	&#192;
a grave	à	&agrave;	&#224;
A acute	Á	&Aacute;	&#193;
a acute	á	&aacute;	&#225;
A circumflex	Â	&Acirc;	&#194;
a circumflex	â	&acirc;	&#226;
A tilde	Ã	&Atilde;	&#195;
a tilde	ã	&atilde;	&#227;
A umlaut	Ä	&Auml;	&#196;
a umlaut	ä	&auml;	&#228;
A ring	Å	&Aring;	&#197;
a ring	å	&aring;	&#229;
AE dipthong	Æ	&AElig;	&#198;
ae dipthong	æ	&aelig;	&#230;
C cedilla	Ç	&Ccedil;	&#199;
c cedilla	ç	&ccedil;	&#231;

Character Name	Character	HTML Code	Decimal Code
E grave	È	&Egrave;	&#200;
e grave	è	&egrave;	&#232;
E acute	É	&Eacute;	&#201;
e acute	é	&eacute;	&#233;
E circumflex	Ê	&Ecirc;	&#202;
e circumflex	ê	&ecirc;	&#234;
E umlaut	Ë	&Euml;	&#203;
e umlaut	ë	&euml;	&#235;
I grave	Ì	&Igrave;	&#204;
i grave	ì	&igrave;	&#236;
I acute	Í	&Iacute;	&#205;
i acute	í	&iacute;	&#237;
I circumflex	Î	&Icirc;	&#206;
i circumflex	î	&icirc;	&#238;
I umlaut	Ï	&Iuml;	&#207;
i umlaut	ï	&iuml;	&#239;
Eth (Icelandic)	Ð	&ETH;	&#208;
eth (Icelandic)	ð	&eth;	&#240;
N tilde	Ñ	&Ntilde;	&#209;
n tilde	ñ	&ntilde;	&#241;
O grave	Ò	&Ograve;	&#210;
o grave	ò	&ograve;	&#242;
O acute	Ó	&Oacute;	&#211;
o acute	ó	&oacute;	&#243;
O circumflex	Ô	&Ocirc;	&#212;
o circumflex	ô	&ocirc;	&#244;
O tilde	Õ	&Otilde;	&#213;
o tilde	õ	&otilde;	&#245;
O umlaut	Ö	&Ouml;	&#214;
o umlaut	ö	&ouml;	&#246;
O slash	Ø	&Oslash;	&#216;
o slash	ø	&oslash;	&#248;
U grave	Ù	&Ugrave;	&#217;
u grave	ù	&ugrave;	&#249;
U acute	Ú	&Uacute;	&#218;
u acute	ú	&uacute;	&#250;

Character Name	Character	HTML Code	Decimal Code
U circumflex	Û	&Ucirc;	&#219;
u circumflex	û	&ucirc;	&#251;
U umlaut	Ü	&Uuml;	&#220;
u umlaut	ü	&uuml;	&#252;
Y acute	Ý	&Yacute;	&#221;
y acute	ý	&yacute;	&#253;
y umlaut	ÿ	&yuml;	&#255;
THORN (Icelandic)	Þ	&THORN;	&#222;
thorn (Icelandic)	þ	&thorn;	&#254;
sharp s (German)	ß	&szlig;	&#223;

CSS STYLE PROPERTIES

The following is a list of properties included in the CSS and CSS 2 specifications, along with their available values. Remember that some properties can't be usefully applied to particular elements (for example, specifying a 'font-family' in a rule for the <IMG> tag is pointless), and certain values won't be valid in some situations. Added to that, some browsers don't yet support all the possible properties and values; Netscape 4, in particular, has quite a long list of unsupported CSS properties.

When unsupported or illogical properties or values are specified in a style rule (rather than in a Dynamic HTML script) they will be gracefully ignored rather than causing errors. Where numeric values are required, these are entered using the measurement units listed on page 147. Colours are specified using a hex value such as **#FF0080**, or an RGB triplet such as **RGB(255,0,128)**. Where a default value exists, this is shown in italic type.

As a general rule (which doesn't work in all cases), to refer to style properties in a Dynamic HTML script, remove the hyphen and capitalize the first letter of the property name's second word. For example, to refer to the 'font-family' property in a DHTML script, you'd call it 'fontFamily'. Single-word property names are usually used unaltered.

Fonts

Property: font-family
Description: One or more font face names or generic names separated by commas.
Values: Generic names available are: cursive, fantasy, monospace, sans-serif, serif.

Property: font-size
Description: The size of the font as a numeric unit or a keyword.
Values: xx-small, x-small, small, *medium*, large, x-large, xx-large, or a numeric unit such as 12pt.

Property: font-weight
Description: The weight of the font, where Normal=400 and Bold=700.
Values: lighter, *normal*, bold, bolder, 100, 200, 300, 400, 500, 600, 700, 800, 900.

Property: font-style
Description: The style of the font.
Values: *normal*, italic, oblique.

Property: font-variant
Description: An optional small-capitals variant of the selected font face.
Values: *normal*, small-caps.

Property: font-stretch
Description: Sets the horizontal expansion or condensation of the font.
Values: *normal*, ultra-condensed, extra-condensed, condensed, semi-condensed, semi-expanded, expanded, extra-expanded, ultra-expanded.

Property: font-size-adjust
Description: Specifies the aspect ratio of the font size to the font's *x*-height.
Values: *none*, numeric unit.

Property: color
Description: The colour of the font.
Values: Any colour as a hex value (e.g. **#FF0080**) or an RGB triplet such as **RGB(255,0,128)**.

Property: font
Description: Defines a complete font, accepting values for font family, style, size, weight, variant and line height separated by spaces.
Values: Space-separated values for each of the six sub-properties.

Text Formatting

Property: text-decoration
Description: A choice of styles to apply to the text.
Values: *none*, underline, overline, line-through.

Property: text-align
Description: Aligns text to the left, right, or centre, or justifies it.
Values: *left*, right, center, justify.

Property: text-indent
Description: Sets the horizontal indent of text elements.
Values: Any valid numeric unit.

Property: text-transform
Description: Changes the case of text elements.
Values: *none*, capitalize, lowercase, uppercase.

Property: text-shadow
Description: One or more comma-separated values giving text-shadowing effects (colour, *x*-offset, *y*-offset, blur radius).

Values: A colour and three numeric units to specify the colour, offset and radius of shadowing.

Property: text-underline-position
Description: When text-decoration is set to 'underline', determines the position of the underlining.
Values: *below*, above.

Property: vertical-align
Description: Aligns surrounding elements with the baseline of the text.
Values: top, text-top, middle, bottom, text-bottom, baseline, sub, super, or a numeric unit.

Property: line-height
Description: Sets the height of a line of text.
Values: *normal*, or a numeric unit.

Property: word-spacing
Description: Sets the horizontal spacing between words.
Values: *normal*, or a numeric unit.

Property: letter-spacing
Description: Sets the horizontal spacing between letters (*kerning*).
Values: *normal*, or a numeric unit.

Property: word-wrap
Description: Specifies whether a line of text breaks if wider than its bounding box.
Values: *normal*, break-word.

Property: white-space
Description: Specifies how white space within the element is to be treated.
Values: *normal*, pre, nowrap.

Backgrounds

Property: background-color
Description: Sets the background colour of the element.
Values: *transparent*, or a colour.

Property: background-image
Description: Specifies an image to use as the element's background.
Values: The URL of an image to use.

Property: background-repeat
Description: Specifies how (or whether) the background image will be repeated or tiled.
Values: *repeat*, no-repeat, repeat-x, repeat-y.

Property: background-attachment
Description: Specifies whether or not the image will scroll with the page.
Values: *scroll*, fixed.

Property: background-position
Description: Sets the position of the background image.
Values: Two of the following keywords to give the *x* and *y* positions of the image: top, center, bottom, left, right, or a numeric unit.

Property: background
Description: Combines all background attributes into a single space-separated rule.
Values: Five values giving colour or image URL (specified as **url(*image-url*)**), repeat, attachment, x-position, y-position.

Borders & Outlines

Property: border
Description: A width, style and colour to be applied to all borders.
Values: Three values for border-width, border-style and border-color properties separated by spaces.

Property: border-top, border-right, border-bottom, border-left
Description: A width, style and colour to be applied to a particular border.
Values: Three values for border-width, border-style and border-color properties separated by spaces.

Property: border-color
Description: Sets the colour of all borders.
Values: Any colour value.

Property: border-style
Description: Sets the style of all borders.
Values: *none*, solid, double, dotted, dashed, groove, ridge, inset, outset.

Property: border-width
Description: Sets the thickness of all borders.
Values: thin, *medium*, thick, or a numeric value.

Property: border-top-width, border-right-width, border-bottom-width, border-left-width
Description: Sets the thickness of a particular border.
Values: A numeric value.

Property: outline
Description: Sets a width, style and colour for the element's outline, separated by spaces.
Values: Three values for width, style and colour.

Property: outline-color
Description: Sets the colour of the element's outline.
Values: invert, or any colour value.

Property: outline-style
Description: Sets the style of the element's outline.
Values: *none*, solid, double, dotted, dashed, groove, ridge, inset, outset.

Property: outline-width
Description: Sets the width of the element's outline.
Values: thin, *medium*, thick, or a numeric value.

Margins & Padding

Property: margins
Description: Sets the size of the margin on all four sides.
Values: A numeric value.

Property: margin-top, margin-right, margin-bottom, margin-left
Description: Sets the size of the margin on a particular side.
Values: A numeric value.

Property: padding
Description: Sets the amount of padding between an element and its border or margin on all four sides.
Values: A numeric value.

Property: padding-top, padding-right, padding-bottom, padding-left
Description: Sets the amount of padding between an element and its border or margin on a particular side.
Values: A numeric value.

Lists

Property: list-style
Description: Sets the type, image and position of items in the list.
Values: Space-separated attributes for the list-style-type, list-style-image and list-style-position attributes. Image is specified by **url**(*image-url*).

Property: list-style-type
Description: Sets the style of numbering or bullets (as appropriate to the type of list) to be used.
Values: disc, circle, square, decimal, decimal-leading-zero, lower-roman, upper-roman, lower-alpha, upper-alpha, lower-greek, lower-latin, upper-latin, armenian, georgian, hebrew, none.

Property: list-style-image
Description: Specifies an image to use as the list-item bullet.
Values: The URL of an image to be used.

Property: list-style-position
Description: The position of the list-items' bullets or numbering.
Values: inside, outside.

Property: marker-offset
Description: The amount of offset between the bullet or numbering and the list-item.
Values: *auto*, or a numeric value.

Dimensions

Property: top
Description: The distance between an element and the top of its parent element.
Values: A numeric value.

Property: left
Description: The distance of an element from the left of its parent element.
Values: A numeric value.

Property: width
Description: The width of an element.
Values: A numeric value.

Property: height
Description: The height of an element.
Values: A numeric value.

Property: min-width, min-height
Description: The minimum width/height of an element.
Values: A numeric value.

Property: max-width, max-height
Description: The maximum width/height of an element.
Values: *none*, or a numeric value.

Layout & Positioning

Property: position
Description: Sets the type of positioning used when placing an item in its parent.
Values: static, absolute, relative, fixed.

Property: z-index
Description: Sets the 'front-to-back' overlapping of elements on a page, defining which appears on top. Elements with higher z-indexes appear above those with lower values. Positive values appear above 'normal' text on the page; negative values force elements below the normal text.
Values: A positive or negative number.

Property: float
Description: Forces elements that follow this one to be wrapped to one side rather than being placed below it.
Values: *none*, left, right.

Property: clear
Description: Forces elements that follow this one be placed below it at the next point a particular margin is clear.
Values: *none*, left, right, both.

Property: display
Description: Specifies how (and whether) the element is to be displayed.
Values: inline, block, marker, list-item, compact, run-in, none.

Property: visibility
Description: Specifies whether or not the element is visible.
Values: *inherit*, visible, hidden, collapse, hide, show.

Property: overflow
Description: Specifies how excess data is handled in an element with fixed dimensions.
Values: *none*, clip, scroll.

Property: clip
Description: Optionally defines four coordinates creating a rectangular area when overflow = clip.
Values: *auto*, rect(top, right, bottom, left).

Tables

Property: border-collapse
Description: Specifies whether adjacent cells share borders or have separate borders.
Values: collapse, separate.

Property: border-spacing
Description: When border-collapse is 'separate', sets the spacing between adjacent cells.
Values: A numeric value.

Property: caption-side
Description: Sets the position of CSS or HTML table captions.
Values: top, right, bottom, left.

Property: empty-cells
Description: When border-collapse is 'separate', specifies whether to draw borders around empty cells.
Values: show, hide.

Other

Property: cursor
Description: Specifies a cursor to use when the pointer moves over the element.
Values: *auto*, default, n-resize, ne-resize, e-resize, se-resize, s-resize, sw-resize, w-resize, nw-resize, crosshair, pointer, move, text, wait, help, hand.

Property: zoom
Description: Sets the magnification level of the element.
Values: *normal*, or a numeric value.

Property: scrollbar-3d-light-color, scrollbar-arrow-color, scrollbar-base-color, scrollbar-dark-shadow-color, scrollbar-face-color, scrollbar-highlight-color, scrollbar-shadow-color

Description: Used with the BODY element to set the colours of particular parts of the page scrollbars.

Values: For each property, any colour value.

UK WEB HOSTING
COMPANIES

Finding the right hosting company for your website isn't an exact science. To a large extent, it depends what you're willing to pay. Along with the budget, you need to consider what you need. For instance: How much space will you need? Do you need to use CGI scripts and applications? Do you need Microsoft FrontPage Extensions? Do you need to transfer a domain name? Will you need *secure* space for e-commerce? Do you also want a dial-up and email account?

Most companies offer a range of preset packages at particular prices (although they can usually add extra services from other packages at an extra cost if required), and these packages are constantly changing in features and price. Rather than giving a snapshot of what companies are offering at the time this book was written, the list below points you to the websites of a selection of UK hosting companies, where you can check the details and make a shortlist of the companies offering what you need.

Company	Website
Abel Internet	www.abelgratis.com
AdeptWeb	www.adeptweb.net
altohiway	www.altohiway.com
btclick for business	www.btclickforbusiness.com
BT Internet	www.btinternet.com
Cerbernet	www.cerbernet.net
City NetGates	www.netgates.co.uk
CIX	www.cix.co.uk
Claranet	www.clara.net
Cybase	www.cybase.co.uk
Demon Internet	www.demon.net
Easynet	www.uk.easynet.net
Enterprise	www.enterprise.net
Freeserve	www.freeserve.net
Griffin Internet	www.griffin.net.uk
Hiway Communications	www.hiway.co.uk
Hosting UK	www.hostinguk.net
Internet Central	www.netcentral.co.uk
Internet For Business	www.ifb.net
Internet UK	www.ukinternet.net

Company	Website
IntoNet	www.intonet.co.uk
London Web Communications	www.londonweb.net
Mistral Internet	www.mistral.co.uk
NetBenefit	www.netbenefit.com
Netlink Solutions	www.nslnet.net
NicNames	www.nicnames.co.uk
Nildram	www.nildram.net
Onyx Internet	www.onyxnet.co.uk
OrbitalNet	www.orbital.net
Pipex	www.pipex.net
Rednet	www.red.net
Sonnet Internet	www.sonnet.co.uk
Total Connectivity Providers	www.tcp.net.uk
Totalserve	www.totalserve.net
UK Hosting	www.ukhosting.co.uk
U-NET	www.u-net.net
Virtual Internet	www.vi.net
Wave Rider Internet	www.waverider.co.uk
Web Fusion	www.webfusion.co.uk
Zetnet Services	www.zetnet.co.uk

F

USEFUL WEBSITES

HTML & General Reference

Website	URL
Bare Bones Guide to HTML	webach.com/barebones
BrowserWatch	browserwatch.internet.com
Cnet.com – Web Building	www.cnet.com/webbuilding
Facts & Stats	www.dotcom.com/facts/quickstats.html
Freesite UK	www.freesiteuk.com
HTML Code Help	www.netmechanic.com
HTML Goodies	www.htmlgoodies.com
The HTML Writers Guild	www.hwg.org
ISP Review	www.ispreview.co.uk
Searchterms.com – The Top 10	www.searchterms.com
SiteExperts.com	www.siteexperts.com
StatMarket	www.statmarket.com
W3C – World Wide Web Consortium	www.w3.org
WebDeveloper.com	www.webdeveloper.com
Web Developer's Virtual Library	www.wdvl.com
WebMonkey	hotwired.lycos.com/webmonkey
WebReference	www.webreference.com
webresource.net: HTML Center	www.webresource.net/html
WebSiteGoodies	www.websitegoodies.com
Web Site Garage	www.websitegarage.com
yesWebmaster.com	www.yeswebmaster.com

Graphics

Website	URL
Absolutely Free Backgrounds	www.free-backgrounds.com
Abstract Dimensions PSP Filters	psptips.com/filters
Andrew's GraphXKingdom	www.graphxkingdom.com
ArtToday.com	www.arttoday.com
bannerblast.com	www.bannerblast.com
Clipart.com	www.clipart.com
ClipArtConnection.com	www.clipartconnection.com

Website	URL
CoolText.com	www.cooltext.com
Corbis	www.corbis.com
Filter Factory Plug-ins	showcase.netins.net/web/wolf359/ plugins.htm
Free Graphics	www.freegraphics.com
Free Images	www.freeimages.co.uk
HitBox Image Search	hitbox.gograph.com
IconBazaar	www.iconbazaar.com
Jeffrey Zeldman Presents	www.zeldman.com
MediaBuilder	www.mediabuilder.com
PhotoDisc	www.photodisc.com
ScreamDesign	www.screamdesign.com
Textureland	www.textureland.com
webresource.net: Graphics Center	www.webresource.net/graphics
yesWebMaster.com Graphics	www.yeswebmaster.com/graphics

Flash

Website	URL
ExtremeFlash	www.extremeflash.com
Flahoo	www.flahoo.com
Flash Kit	www.flashkit.com
Flash Planet	www.flashplanet.com
Macromedia	www.macromedia.com
ShockFusion	www.shockfusion.com
shockwave.com	www.shockwave.com

JavaScript

Website	URL
Cut-N-Paste JavaScript	www.infohiway.com/javascript/indexf.htm
Dynamic Drive	www.dynamicdrive.com
JavaScript.com	www.javascript.com
JavaScript City	www.javascriptcity.com
JavaScript Search	www.javascriptsearch.com
JavaScript Source	javascript.internet.com
JavaScript Tip of the Week	www.webreference.com/javascript
JavaScript World	www.jsworld.com
WebCoder.com	www.webcoder.com
webresource.net: JavaScript Center	www.webresource.net/javascript

Dynamic HTML

Website	URL
Comet Cursor	www.cometcursors.com
DHTML Lab	www.webreference.com/dhtml
Dynamic Drive	www.dynamicdrive.com
Dynamic HTML Developer Zone	www.projectcool.com/developer/dynamic
Dynamic HTML Resource	www.htmlguru.com
Dynamic HTML Zone	www.dhtmlzone.com
Experience DHTML!	www.bratta.com/dhtml
MSDN Online Voices	msdn.microsoft.com/voices/dude.asp
WebCoder.com	www.webcoder.com

Java

Website	URL
Cool Focus	www.coolfocus.com
Gamelan	softwaredev.earthweb.com/java
JARS	www.jars.com
JavaSoft (Sun)	www.javasoft.com
The Java Boutique	javaboutique.internet.com
webresource.net: Java Center	www.webresource.net/java

CGI

Website	URL
The CGI Directory	cgidir.com/Scripts
CGI Resource Index	cgi.resourceindex.com
CGI Resource Index – Remotely Hosted	cgi.resourceindex.com/Remotely_Hosted
Matt's Script Archive	www.worldwidemart.com/scripts
The Perl Archive	www.perlarchive.com
ScriptSearch.com	scriptsearch.internet.com
webresource.net: CGI Center	www.webresource.net/cgi/scripts
YourCGI.com	www.yourcgi.com

Guestbooks, Counters & Statistics

Website	URL
1-2-3 WebTools	www.freeguestbooks.com
Beseen Free Web Tools	www.beseen.com
theCounter.com	www.thecounter.com
theGuestBook.com	www.theguestbook.com
Guestbook4free.com	www.guestbook4free.com
GuestBooks.net	www.glacierweb.com/home
HitBox.com	www.hitbox.com
I-Count	www.icount.com

Website	URL
MyComputer.com	guestbook.mycomputer.com
RealTracker Free	www.showstat.com
WebTracker	www.fxweb.holowww.com/tracker
XOOMCounter	www2.pagecount.com
ZapZone	www.zzn.com

Forums, Chat & Other Content

Website	URL
Ballot-Box.net	www.ballot-box.net
BeSeen Bulletin Board	www.beseen.com/board
BeSeen Chat	www.beseen.com/chat
BeSeen Enhance: Quizlet	www.beseen.com/quiz
BoardHost	www.boardhost.com
EZBoard	www.ezboard.com
EZPolls	ezpolls.mycomputer.com
Free Forums	www.freeforums.com
Free Site Search Engine	www.freefind.com
Free Tools	www.freetools.com
liveuniverse.com	liveuniverse.com
Mister Poll	www.misterpoll.com
Multicity.com	www.multicity.com
NetVotes	www.netvotes.com
ParaChat	www.parachat.com
PollIt	www.pollit.com
QuickChat	www.quickchat.org
Web BBS	awsd.com/scripts/webbbs
ZapZone	www.zzn.com

Domain Name Registration

Website	URL
DomainBook.com	www.domainbook.com
Domains365	www.domains365.co.uk
DomainsNet	www.domainsnet.co.uk
interNIC	www.internic.net
NetNames	www.netnames.co.uk
Simply Names	www.simplynames.co.uk
UK Reg	www.ukreg.com

Website Promotion, Marketing & Advertising

Website	URL
AddMe	www.addme.com
AdValue	www.advalue.co.uk
BannerExchange	bannerexchange.mycomputer.com
Bpath	www.bpath.com
DoubleClick	www.doubleclick.com
EReleases	www.ereleases.com
GoTo Search Suggestions	inventory.goto.com/inventory/Search_Suggestion.jhtml
Internet Advertising Bureau	www.iab.net
Internet PR Guide	www.internetprguide.com
JimTools	www.jimtools.com
Microsoft bCentral	www.bcentral.com
Refer-It.com	www.refer-it.com
SearchAbility	www.searchability.com
Search Engine Watch	www.searchenginewatch.com
Submit Corner	www.submitcorner.com
Submit Express	www.submitexpress.com
Submit It!	www.submit-it.com
SubmitWizard	submitwizard.mycomputer.com
TopWebSite	www.topwebsite.co.uk
ukaffiliates.com	www.ukaffiliates.com

Website	URL
UK Banners	www.ukbanners.com
ValueClick	www.valueclick.com/uk
WebPromote	www.webpromote.com
WEBpromotion.co.uk	www.webpromotion.co.uk
Web Site Garage	register-it.netscape.com

Cool Site Collections & Awards

Website	URL
Cool Central	www.coolcentral.com
Cybersmith's Hot Site of the Day	www.cybersmith.com/hotsites
Dr Webster's Site of the Day	www.drwebster.com
Family Site of the Day	www.worldvillage.com/famsite.htm
Hot 100 Websites	www.web21.com
Too Cool!	www.toocool.com
Webby Awards	www.webbyawards.com
Web Pages That Suck	www.webpagesthatsuck.com
World Best Websites	www.worldbestwebsites.com
Xplore's Site of the Day	www.xplore.com

E-commerce & Business

Website	URL
Actinic Catalog	www.actinic.com
Barclays Merchant Services	www.barclaysmerchantservices.co.uk
BizBlast.com	www.bizblast.com
Clearlybusiness	www.clearlybusiness.com
DataCash	www.datacash.com
DigiBuy	www.digibuy.com
Electronic Commerce Guide	ecommerce.internet.com
element 5	www.element5.com
Moreover	www.moreover.com
NetBanx	www.netbanx.com

Website	URL
RegSoft.com	www.regsoft.com
SecurePay	www.securepay.com
Shop@ssistant	www.shopassistant.net
TheBiz	www.thebiz.co.uk
Virgin biz.net	www.virginbiz.net
WorldPay	www.worldpay.com

Shareware Directories

Website	URL
32bit.com	www.32bit.com/software
DaveCentral	www.davecentral.com
Jumbo	www.jumbo.com
KeyScreen	www.keyscsreen.com
MacShare.com	www.macshare.com
NoNags	www.nonags.com
Shareware.com	www.shareware.com
Thingamabobs	www.thingamabobs.com
Tucows	tucows.mirror.ac.uk
WinSite	www.winsite.com
ZDNet Downloads	www.zdnet.com/downloads

Search Engines

Website	URL
All The Web	www.alltheweb.com
AltaVista	www.altavista.com
AOL Search	search.aol.com
Ask Jeeves	www.ask.com
Canada.com	www.canada.com
CNET Search.com	www.search.com
Direct Hit	www.directhit.com
Dogpile	www.dogpile.com

Website	URL
Excite	www.excite.com
Galaxy	www.galaxy.com
GO.com	www.go.com
Go2Net	www.gotonet.com
Google	www.google.com
GoTo.com	www.goto.com
HotBot	www.hotbot.com
ICQ Search	www.icqit.com
InfoSpace	www.infospace.com
LookSmart	www.looksmart.com
Lycos	www.lycos.com
Mamma.com	www.mamma.com
MetaCrawler	www.metacrawler.com
Mirago	www.mirago.co.uk
MSN	search.msn.com
NationalDirectory	www.nationaldirectory.com
NBCi	www.nbci.com
Netscape Search	search.netscape.com
Northern Light	www.northernlight.com
OneSeek	www.oneseek.com
Open Directory Project	www.dmoz.org
ProFusion	www.profusion.com
Scrub The Web	www.scrubtheweb.com
Search Engine Colossus	www.searchenginecolossus.com
Search UK	uk.searchengine.com
Starting Point	www.stpt.com
UK Plus	www.ukplus.co.uk
WebCrawler	www.webcrawler.com
WebTop.com	www.webtop.com
WebZone	www.infohiway.com
whatUseek	www.whatuseek.com
Yahoo!	www.yahoo.com

INDEX

Licensing Agreement

This book comes with a CD-ROM software package. By opening this package you are agreeing to be bound by the following.

The software contained on this CD-ROM is, in many cases, copyrighted, and all rights are reserved by the individual licensing agreements associated with each piece of software contained in the CD-ROM. THIS SOFTWARE IS PROVIDED FREE OF CHARGE, AS IS, AND WITHOUT WARRANTY OF ANY KIND, EITHER EXPRESSED OR IMPLIED, INCLUDING, BUT NOT LIMITED TO, THE IMPLIED WARRANTIES OF MERCHANTABILITY AND FITNESS FOR A PARTICULAR PURPOSE. Neither the book publisher, authors nor its dealers and its distributors assumes any liability for any alleged or actual damage arising from the use of this software.